C0-ARE-121

Mission from the Margins

Mission from the Margins

Selected writings
from the life and ministry
of **David A. Shank**

James R. Krabill, editor

Published by Institute of Mennonite Studies

Copublished with Herald Press

Library of Congress Cataloging-in-Publication Data
Shank, David A.
Mission from the margins : selected writings from the life and ministry of David A. Shank / James R. Krabill, editor.
p. cm.
"Bibliography of the writings of David A. Shank": P.
Includes bibliographical references.
ISBN 978-0-936273-44-0 (alk. paper)
1. Missions—Theory. 2. Mennonites—Missions. 3. Christianity and culture—Africa, Sub-Saharan. 4. Mennonites—Missions—Africa, Sub-Saharan. I. Krabill, James R. II. Title.

BV2063.S485 2010
266'.97—dc22

2010037821

Unless otherwise indicated, Scripture readings are from the New Revised Standard Version Bible, Copyright © 1989, by the Division of Christian Education of the National Council of the Churches of Christ in the USA, and are used by permission.

Mission from the Margins: Selected Writings from the Life and Ministry of David A. Shank

Copyright © 2010 by Institute of Mennonite Studies, Associated Mennonite Biblical Seminary, Elkhart, IN 46517. All rights reserved
Copublished with Herald Press, Scottdale, PA 15683 and Waterloo, ON N2L 6H7
Published in collaboration with Mennonite Mission Network
Library of Congress Catalog Card Number: 2010037821
International Standard Book Number: 978-0-936273-44-0
Printed by Evangel Press, Nappanee, IN
Book design by Mary E. Klassen
15 14 13 12 11 10   10 9 8 7 6 5 4 3 2 1

To order or request information, please call 1-800-245-7894, or visit www.heraldpress.com.

Contents

Ackowledgments

Primary acknowledgements for the content of this volume go to David A. Shank, who for more than half a century has worked diligently and creatively to share the good news of Jesus, the Messiah, in the various contexts where God has placed him.

Other Shank family members have also contributed time to making this collection of writings a reality through photo selection, editorial suggestions, sharing family memories, and general support and counsel throughout the process. These include Wilma Shank (David's wife and ministry companion of many years) and the four Shank children: Michael H. Shank, Stephen Shank, Crissie Judith Buckwalter, and Rachel A. Shenk. Several of David and Wilma's grandchildren have also provided suggestions or assistance along the way.

Special gratitude also goes to Wilbert R. Shenk for his insightful introductory chapter on David's contribution to missiological thinking; to Karen Hallis Ritchie, for many hours of copyediting; to Hatoko Inoue, for scanning the original publications of the articles appearing here; to Marcella Hershberger, who obtained permissions for previously published pieces; and to Mary Klassen of Associated Mennonite Biblical Seminary, for book design.

Gratitude is also owed to Herald Press and to Institute of Mennonite Studies at AMBS for their support for this project. Thanks especially to tireless IMS volunteer James Nelson Gingerich, for devoting many hours to formatting the text and attending to many details, and to IMS managing editor Barbara Nelson Gingerich for overseeing the project.

J. R. K.

Section I Reflecting on David Shank's contribution

David and Wilma Shank at Home of Hope in Ohain, Belgium (1953)

On reading David Shank

Wilbert R. Shenk

Rereading his writings spanning more than fifty years confirms what I have come to expect from David Shank: thoughtful engagement with context through identifying and probing the pressing issues that define the present situation, in the light of history, philosophy, biblical faith, and missiological purpose. There is no better place to begin than with his programmatic essay, "A Missionary Approach to a Dechristianized Society."[1]

Commissioned by Mennonite Board of Missions for missionary service in Europe, the Shank family arrived in Belgium in 1950. During the 1952 post-Easter season, a group of young American Mennonites working and studying in Europe met in Amsterdam as the Concern Group. A second meeting took place a year later in Zurich. In the face of the disillusionment that pervaded European culture following two world wars, these young Mennonites were burdened by the "deep inadequacies in the spiritual resources within our brotherhood." They discerned that the world was in the grip of a spiritual crisis and that the stakes were high. American Mennonites had suddenly been thrust onto this stage but were unable "to define or communicate the message that seemed implicit in our professed position."[2] While the "decline of the West" was writ large, the "partial sterility of our efforts at home and abroad" was not reassuring. Studies of the sixteenth-century Anabaptists confirmed that renewal of the church would take the form of covenanted

---

Wilbert R. Shenk directed overseas ministries of Mennonite Board of Missions (1965–90) and then taught at Associated Mennonite Biblical Seminary (1990–95) and Fuller Theological Seminary (1995–2005). He has written and edited many articles and books on mission history, missiology, and church renewal.

[1] David A. Shank, "A Missionary Approach to a Dechristianized Society," *Mennonite Quarterly Review* 28, no. 1 (January 1954): 39–55. Reprinted as chapter 8 in the present volume.

[2] Both quotations are from the introduction to Concern No. 1 (June 1954), 3.

local congregations. But observed trends in the church in North America suggested that Mennonites were uncritically hurrying to join the cultural mainstream, hardly a positive prospect.

David began the piece with an ironic observation: a North American Mennonite church—a small rural group descended from the left wing of the Reformation—has sent him as a missionary motivated by "a compulsion to be an agent of [Jesus Christ's] reconciliation" to Europe to work out an effective expression of this compelling motivation. At the time of writing, David had been in Belgium eighteen months. He was dividing his time between "religious and social work with all levels of European society," language study, and preparation for ministry. He observes that during this time he had "met dechristianization at its grass roots." In order to introduce contemporary Europeans to Jesus Christ, it was essential to understand what a dechristianized society was and why it had evolved in that direction.

Materials for studying the European situation in 1950 were abundant, and David immersed himself in study and reflection. For a generation, philosophers, historians, sociologists, and novelists had attempted to interpret the new Europe—now largely cut off from its Christian roots. Philosophers Martin Heidegger and Jean-Paul Sartre advocated atheistic existentialism, while novelist Albert Camus promoted a pagan and "pre-Christian" vision.[3] Still other Europeans wanted to reclaim their Christian heritage. The French writer François Mauriac argued that "there must be a politically neutral, yet spiritually dynamic, and life-giving message in the midst of this dechristianized society."[4] Thoughtful people recognized that this reclaiming would not be easy. Reflecting on David's 1952 article assessing the European scene, Harold S. Bender noted that "in his search for the right answer, Shank reaches out into difficult areas of criticism of Western Christianity, with a sharp alertness to the present challenge from the Communist side." He added perceptively, "The overtones of this critical analysis carry implications far beyond the local situation in Western Europe."[5]

What then constitutes a viable missionary approach to this unprecedented kind of mission field—a culture long regarded as Christian that

---

[3] Twenty years later, W. A. Visser 't Hooft called for the evangelization of "neo-pagan Europe." See "Evangelism in the Neo-Pagan Situation," *International Review of Mission* 63 (1974): 81–86; and "Evangelism among Europe's Neo-Pagans," *International Review of Mission* 66 (1977): 349–60.

[4] Quoted in Shank, "A Missionary Approach to a Dechristianized Society," 48.

[5] Editorial, *Mennonite Quarterly Review* 28, no. 1 (January 1954): 2.

is now patently dechristianized, even anti-Christian? David proposed a message that moves between two poles: conservative and creative. The gospel is a conservative force inasmuch as it does not change over time. What God has done in Jesus Christ remains the point of our encounter with God's self-revelation. But the gospel is also a creative power. God's redemptive love engages us wherever we are, bringing about a fundamental reorientation, that is, reconciliation of the self to God. Life is now viewed against the eschatological horizon of God's promised new heaven and new earth.

This proposal led naturally to the question of the means by which such a witness can be carried out. The classical professional missionary was unacceptable in Europe. What were the alternatives? A variety of groups, including Roman Catholics, were searching for an effective witness to post–World War II Europe. To the consternation of the Vatican, Henri Godin, a French Catholic priest associated with the worker-priest movement, published a book asking this provocative question: *France, a Mission Field?* Brother Roger Schutz established the ecumenical Taizé Community in Eastern France in the 1940s. Francis Schaeffer founded L'Abri in Switzerland in 1948. Both Taizé and L'Abri focused on reaching young people. The writings of Dietrich Bonhoeffer, especially his call to costly discipleship and a renewed church, resonated with many. Traditional forms of church life no longer engaged the vast majority of Europeans. Impressed by experiments such as the Catholic worker-priest movement, David suggested that the most promising approach was the "lay apostolate"—men and women trained to witness in their workaday relationships. Such equipping would take place not in the conventional parish church but in a study center, a place devoted to study, worship, and testimony.

A reliable indicator of missionary effectiveness is the way the missionary is affected, changed, and engaged by the host context over time. One of the most important potential assets a missionary has is outsider status. But being an outsider holds both positive and negative possibilities. The evidence is that David was both stimulated by and offered stimulation to each context in which he served. His challenging article, "The Shape of Mission Strategy,"[6] grew out of more than two decades of creative and sustained effort to find an effective missionary approach to a dechristianized society. The missionary posture should be defined christologically with (1) self-denial, as the prerequi-

---

[6] David A. Shank, "The Shape of Mission Strategy," *Mission Focus* 1, no. 3 (1973): 1–7. Reprinted as chapter 7 in the present volume.

site; (2) servanthood, the stance; (3) identification, the risk; (4) humble obedience, the contradiction; and (5) the cross, the consequence. Here, strategy and spirituality merge. Sound missiology draws on both biblical and contextual resources. This article remains a constructive and pioneering critique of the notion of mission strategy.[7]

Belgium was a fascinating laboratory of political, social, and economic experimentation in the post–World War II period. The European Economic Community and North Atlantic Treaty Organization were headquartered in Brussels. As a former colonial power, many Africans were coming to Belgium as students, political refugees, and immigrants. By the mid-1960s, David and Wilma were in contact with a variety of African Christians, including the Kimbanguists, an indigenous church in Congo that professed commitment to the way of nonviolence. In 1971, the head of the Kimbanguist Church invited David to attend the fiftieth anniversary of their founding. This development opened a door into a dynamic and (for them) strange new world. Increasingly, Africa would beckon David and Wilma Shank.

Aware of work being done by Mennonite colleagues in Nigeria who were relating to the same phenomenon, David began studying African-initiated movements such as the Kimbanguists elsewhere in Africa. The existing literature showed that most missionaries and scholars regarded these movements as nativistic or syncretistic. They held indigenous movements at arm's length. Such groups were not allowed to join Christian councils or send students to theological schools. But if one listened carefully to leaders of these groups, a different story emerged. They were asking to be taken seriously and wanted access to Bible study and theological training. And many of these movements traced their founding to prophets who had had visions or revelations in which God spoke directly to them. Could it be that at least some of these movements were authentic prophetic or messianic movements? Might attention to this dynamic furnish a conceptual and theological bridge between these indigenous movements and biblical faith?

Interacting with the work of other scholars, including Henri Desroche, John Howard Yoder, and Gottfried Oosterwal, David developed through his teaching and writing an analytical framework within

---

[7] The only other discussion of the basis for mission strategy that I am aware of is C. Peter Wagner, *Frontiers in Missionary Strategy* (Chicago: Moody Press, 1971). It is useful to read the Shank article in the context of a fine historical study of American missionary work in France following World War II; see Allen V. Koop, *American Evangelical Missionaries in France, 1945-1975* (Lanham, MD: University Press of America, 1986).

which to follow the narrative of the *missio Dei,* the mission of God. Such movements arise in situations where people have lost hope because of oppression and injustice. Announcement of the coming reign of God awakens hope that a new order is possible. Typically, there are those who hear the gospel primarily as a spiritual call and hive off to establish a new ecclesial community. Others hear the gospel as a summons to establish a new sociopolitical order and proceed to work this out. Both of these are incomplete and lopsided responses to the messianic invitation, with the result that over time the messianic dimension disappears. Eventually, the same process will be repeated when the gospel of the kingdom is once more proclaimed with cogency and power. Evidence on the ground suggested that this yearning for liberation and a new beginning, so manifestly present during the earthly ministry of Jesus the Messiah, has never ceased to stir the hopes of peoples the world over. Sensitivity to this dynamic would enable the missionary to connect with individuals and groups that are searching for the Messiah.

This way of understanding brings the biblical narrative to bear on the historical experiences of people across the world. In the scriptures, the messianic dynamic is expressed supremely in the ministry of Jesus Christ. We can also trace the irrepressible Spirit-inspired messianic dynamic breaking forth in the formation of monastic communities, renewal movements, including the sixteenth-century Reformation, and missionary witness across the centuries. Each has been inspired by a fresh vision of Jesus the Messiah. David lectured on this topic for two decades in Europe, North America, and Africa. Finally, he gathered the fruit of his reflections in a second programmatic essay, "Jesus the Messiah: Messianic Foundation of Mission."[8]

In 1976, David and Wilma went to Aberdeen University to do advanced studies in preparation for their new assignment relating to the Harrist Church in Côte d'Ivoire. David wrote a comprehensive three-volume study of the Prophet Harris. Subsequently, Dr. Jocelyn Murray edited this dissertation into a one-volume book, *Prophet Harris, the "Black Elijah" of West Africa.*[9]

One of the important resources to Mennonite Board of Missions during these years was Dr. Harold W. Turner, a New Zealander who be-

---

[8] David A. Shank, "Jesus the Messiah: Messianic Foundation of Mission," in *The Transfiguration of Mission,* ed. Wilbert R. Shenk (Scottdale, PA: Herald Press, 1993), 37–82. Reprinted as chapter 5 in the present volume.

[9] David A. Shank, *Prophet Harris, the "Black Elijah" of West Africa,* abridged by Jocelyn Murray (Leiden: E. J. Brill, 1994).

gan teaching Old Testament at Fourah Bay College, Freetown, Sierra Leone, in 1956 and stumbled onto indigenous African Christianity in 1957. The study of these movements quickly became Turner's main preoccupation for the rest of his life. Turner made the acquaintance of Mennonite missionaries in Nigeria in the early 1960s after he joined the faculty at the new University of Nsukka. In the conclusion to a major survey of "Religious Movements in Primal (or Tribal) Societies" in 1981, Turner observed: "Mennonites in particular have a special vocation, already well exhibited, for relationships with these new religious movements. This derives from their own history as a minority with experiences of rejection and persecution, from their rural background and simple lifestyle, and from a form of Christianity that is strongly biblical but noncredal."[10] Turner constantly counseled and encouraged Mennonite ministry among African Indigenous Churches.

In an essay in honor of Dr. Turner that built on his work, David Shank explored the concept of religious itinerary.[11] He showed the varied paths people take as they journey from a traditional worldview toward biblical faith. David also wrote several pieces about what Western Christians can learn from African-initiated churches.[12]

David Shank's half-century missionary pilgrimage has not followed the conventional path of the modern mission movement. The pattern that has characterized missions for more than two centuries has meant sending missionaries from the "Christian" West to other continents to found churches and institutions that would build up a Christian community where there had been none. The first half of David's missionary sojourn was in a dechristianized Western culture. The second half was spent among indigenous Christian movements in Africa. This, indeed, has been a remarkable itinerary.

---

[10] Harold W. Turner, "Religious Movements in Primal (or Tribal) Societies," *Mission Focus* 9, no. 3 (September 1981): 45–55.

[11] "African Christian Religious Itinerary: Toward an Understanding of the Religious Itinerary from the Faith of African Traditional Religion(s) to that of the New Testament," in *Exploring New Religious Movements: Essays in Honour of Harold W. Turner,* ed. Andrew F. Walls and Wilbert R. Shenk (Elkhart, IN: Mission Focus Publications, 1990), 143–62. Reprinted as chapter 13 in the present volume.

[12] "What African Indigenous Churches Can Teach Western Churches," *Mission Focus* 13, no. 1 (March 1985): 5–8; *What Western Christians Can Learn from African-Initiated Churches,* Mission Insight series, no. 10, ed. James R. Krabill (Elkhart, IN: Mennonite Board of Missions, 2000); and "Reflections on Relating Long Term to Messianic Communities," in *Evangelical, Ecumenical, and Anabaptist Missiologies in Conversation,* ed. James R. Krabill, Walter Sawatsky, and Charles E. Van Engen (Maryknoll, NY: Orbis Books, 2005), 149–57 (reprinted as chapter 15 in the present volume).

2

A view from the dining room table

The children of David and Wilma Shank

Stephen Shank

I am struck, as I read the texts included in this collection of writings, by how little I know about David Shank's work—he who wrote, thought, taught, and did what he did professionally so well.

I self-consciously choose the word *professionally* rather than *vocationally,* in light of Dad's perennial use of the word *calling* and its central place in his own life. I also choose *professionally* because thinking, teaching, writing, and speaking were after all his profession, simply the way he earned his living as the breadwinner for our family of six.

Finally, I say *professionally*, because the word *vocation* or *calling* bestows a usurped quality on someone's life, installs a halo over a task that is really no different from the task of the cobbler who repairs shoes in order to put food on the table and pay the rent, as the baker bakes bread, or the builder builds houses. I need to eat: I am a sociologist, historian, anthropologist, preacher, teacher, counselor, missionary, writer—this is how I put food on the table. "I've been called," on the other hand, treads stormy waters. It sometimes translates "I didn't choose," when in the Anabaptist tradition, choice is of the essence and lies at the core of our heartbeat—baptism *by choice,* following *by choice,* confronting *by choice,* dissenting *by choice.* And these are all at the very center of Dad's life.

Stephen Shank lives in Brussels, Belgium. Crissie Judith Buckwalter has lived on four continents, in five countries and more than a dozen cities. She and her husband, Tim, have recently made another move, to Hyattsville, Maryland. Rachel A. Shenk bakes and writes in Goshen, Indiana. She and her husband, Jim, frequently cross the ocean to Europe. Michael H. Shank teaches the history of science at the University of Wisconsin-Madison.

So this collection of writings bears witness to the fruit of David Shank's profession. And yet as I work on it, I find it almost impossible to read Dad's writing, not because I am not interested, but because I have found more meaning in Dostoevsky, Pascal Mercier, or Jeanette Winterson than in what appears, to my theologically untrained eye, like Chinese, as I sift through the terminology, the Canaan jargon, and the richness of ideas, arguments, postulates and assumptions. Don't get me wrong, if I had a son who spoke and wrote in Chinese, I would love him just as much as one who had limited his work to French.

On the other hand, I would be the first to say that Dad's approach to mission and theology cannot *not* be interesting, challenging, curiosity arousing, stimulating, and profound for those concerned. And this is the case because as people, Mom and Dad are interesting, determined, and on the edge of uncompromise; challenging, curiosity arousing, stimulating, and profound; and I cannot imagine that what they were as people did not shine through in their work and pour forth from Dad's writing.

Probably more than anything else, it is these—the curiosity, the challenge, the interest, the determination, sometimes the lack of compromise, the stimulation—all profound and focused on making sense of our place in our times—that shaped us children and gave us a legacy not of material wealth but of a rather heavy sense of responsibility in this world.

Many of Dad's correspondents or coworkers shared meals at our table and spent the night in our home. Dad always kept his office *à domicile* ("in the home"). As children, we were warmed, no doubt sometimes burned, by the cauldron of his work. "Double, double toil and trouble." "Fair is foul and foul is fair." We could not quite be sure what would come out of Dad's pot—a recorded version of the first chapters of Genesis with sound effects? A sermon in which he would throw the family television from the pulpit? Or one in which, standing on a ladder at the front of the church, he would call on Adam to come forth? Would he walk out to tell us somberly that President Kennedy was shot? Would we find him on all fours on the floor, cutting out illustrations of Giotto's Scrovegni Chapel? Or, as we walked by his office, would we hear him practicing out loud for a radio program, or hear him laughing until he choked and coughed as he and mother "went over the accounts"?

Would he appear with a new painting framed for the dining room? Would he be uninterruptible for two or three hours, because he was attempting over the phone to resolve a conflict with another church leader, while the local telephone operator listened in? Or was he preparing one of three sermons for the following Sunday, one in French, one in English, and one to be translated into Spanish? Or was he organizing another ecumenical Bible study with the local Benedictine nuns or giving shape to a debate between free thinkers, Catholics, and Protestants on issues of sexuality or the sociocultural shake-up of May 1968?

When interrupted by a knock on the door and a "Dad, I don't have anything left to read," he would immediately search through his library, tipping out book after book from the shelves that covered the four walls of the room, and pull out, this time Gide, next time Wright, or Bonhoeffer, or perhaps Irving Stone's *Lust for Life* novel on Van Gogh, or the correspondence of Vincent and Theo.

Dad's suggestions inevitably did lead to double the toil and double the trouble. The reading was strong and always challenging, and it raised more questions and more thirst to know, to find out. It was the kind of toil and trouble I liked.

We were to knock before entering his office, and not to disturb him lightly. I learned to read his responses. If he didn't answer, I would assume he was on the phone. If he said a firm "yes," I knew he would be totally available. If I got an "uh-huh," I knew I would get half of his attention. He always had writing paper ready for us, scrap paper in the top right-hand drawer of his desk, virgin sheets in a cupboard to the left of the desk that had two sides facing each other, one for mother, and one for him. The only differences between their spaces was that his faced the door and mother's was not heaped high in apparent chaos; the order on his side only he appreciated.

He worked late into the night, and I remember waking up with asthma in a dark house, but finding the light seeping out from under the door of his office. If he fell asleep on the living room couch after an evening meal, mother would put a finger to her lips, indicating that we were to let him sleep, which we did. His work did come first. Perhaps therein lies the difference between profession and vocation—profession has a timetable, a scheduled rhythm of hours; vocation, on the other hand, gives license to work with no limits, no constraints, no order—me, my work, and my call.

I believe that one of Dad's qualities is a strong balance of reason and affection. These traits would at times come in conflict with each other, but most of the time they worked well together. He was first and foremost a people person. He also had a powerful sense of vision. When his feelings got in conflict with the principles he held, he would not rest from dialogical debate until he was told to shut up and leave.

Dad was above all process oriented. And of course in the American educated upper middle class, which tends to be *product* oriented, anyone intent on *process* and perceived as slowing down product achievement is considered a gadfly or a grouch. Neither of these describes Dad, yet I did hear both terms used on occasion by his detractors. On issues where he and I had differences, we never gave up on each other and always came to a tender, caring, and continuously growing relationship.

Dad always said one should "talk to the king the same way one talks to the maid." Our parents insisted we should never shove with our elbows, never impose ourselves. To take center stage was considered vulgar. They *did* teach us to love justice and speak out against injustice, whatever the cost.

Our dinner table was an open table and always seemed to have more than six—often ten, sometimes twice that. I even remember eighty.

I grew up in a family where there was no normative cultural standard that would have made a qualitative comparative judgment between Richard Wright and Émile Zola; James Baldwin and Victor Hugo; Martin Luther King, Gandhi, Chinua Achebe and Molière; Leopold Senghor and Dostoevsky; Langston Hughes and Voltaire; Madeleine L'Engle and Marguerite Yourcenar; La Fontaine and Charles Schultz; Buddha, Wadé Harris, Simon Kimbangu, and Francis of Assisi.

Mother took us to the theater, and we discovered together the world premieres of Béjart and the 20th Century Ballet, the Living Theater. And the voice of my father, a charismatic speaker, still rings in my ears, be it at a conference, from the pulpit, or from the head of our dinner table. There are sections of his sermon that I imagine all four of us children could deliver, down to the pauses, voice inflections, and intonations.

Mother rhythmed our days with Mahalia Jackson and Harry Belafonte, all the while singing Bach and Handel or playing Mozart and Czerny. We played thumb piano while listening to Bizet, Tchaikowsky, Brahms, Gesualdo, Mahler, and Barber. We watched in fascination the films that Dad brought back from The American Cultural Center in Brussels—Kussevitsky at Tanglewood, Charlie Chaplin, and—over and over and over again—Martin Luther King's speech at the Washington Memorial. Dad, whose first published article (at the age of eighteen) was about "the crime of racism in the South," was adamant about human rights, working on the edges for change and conscientious objection to war. Dad introduced me to Passolini, Tarkovsky, and Andrei Roublev.

At the center of it all lay history. (No wonder John Oyer, a Mennonite history professor, and Dad enjoyed such a warm relationship.) History! I discovered as a child that history is not simply facts but rather what happens, and how, and why.

Dad revels in sifting through causes and consequences. He often imagines himself to be like the little Dutch boy in the story, the finger in the cracked dike, the grain of sand in the gear. Dad probes the changing patterns, the evolving thought, always ready to decipher the signs of the times, feeling the wind shift the very moment it shifts, watching where and how it blows, reading the future in the margin, never bypassing the margins, seeing the potential of the diamond in the rough. No wonder some find him too idealistic and unswerving in his views. His eye is set on a diamond larger than the Cullinan, and he plans to mine it himself.

Crissie Judith Buckwalter

I was eight years old and in the third grade. I remember it was that year, because I had just gotten off the shuttle bus that had taken the students in my class from our off-campus classroom (in a house on Rue Haute) back to the main school (on Rue Croy). I had school in that house only when I was in Mademoiselle Marneffe's third-grade class.

It was a hot day—Belgian hot, at least—so it could have been May or June. And it was a Wednesday, since school ended at midday and Daddy would never have been late on a Saturday, the other midday school day. At least, I'd like to think he wouldn't have been late on a Saturday.

I met up with my brother Stephen, who was in the fifth grade. Michael, our older brother, biked to school and would have already been heading home. Stephen and I were to wait in front of the school for Daddy to pick us up.

We waited and waited. And then, as some friends headed home on foot, and others got on their buses for home, and still others were picked up by their parents, Stephen and I got tired of waiting and took off on foot. Our idea was that we would meet up with Daddy along the way.

Our school, l'Athénée Royal de Rixensart, was five kilometers away from our home in Ohain. The road home crossed the Avenue Franklin Roosevelt, passed through the town of Rixensart, passed the butcher shop and our store-front church building, passed the lot that was to become the property of the Temple Protestant de Rixensart (where a "proper" building would be built and Dad would be pastor till he left Belgium), and down the hill in front of the Pensionnat de Filles (the girls' boarding school).

We walked, we sang, we talked, we got thirsty and kept on walking, wondering as the road bottomed out at the swimming resort of the Lac de Renipont, two kilometers into our trek, whether we had missed Daddy in the car. The road now ascended for a short kilometer up the steep hill on Rue de Renipont, then flattened out on the plateau for a long kilometer until, tired, thirsty, and almost home, we reached the turn-off onto the cobblestone Ruelle Crollé.

Then, with relief, we saw Daddy's car, the old grey Peugeot. We stopped and waited for Daddy to reach us. But suddenly he turned into a small driveway. We ran toward the car, but Daddy backed up and headed down the road in the other direction! I don't remember the rest of the walk home. I do remember Mom telling us that she had been try-ing to get Daddy off the phone and out the door, and that it seemed he had just left when he came back with an empty car. "Where are Crissie and Stephen?" "They're already at the Ruelle Crollé, 300 meters from home."

Rachel A. Shenk

As the youngest child in my family, I breathed in much information at the dining room table, not only about food and manners, but also about community, values, faith, the world around me, and parenting, to name only a few. There was always a table to sit down to. Rarely did we eat on the run.

The table was where we gathered as a family at the end of the day. Being the daughter of a pastor meant that often my father's seat was empty because he had been held up by a lengthy meeting, by a parish-ioner needing a listening ear, or by a phone call from someone asking for assistance. I remember answering the phone for him and saying that I was his secretary and would the caller like to leave a message. Or writing him a note in my childish script—"Dinner is ready!"—to put down in front of him while he was on the telephone in his office. Dur-ing our meal together I didn't want to share him with someone on the phone! When these delays happened, we waited as long as we could and then would sit down, four children and their mother, to not only eat but also share the stories of the day.

When my father would join us, I always knew there would be something to learn. The lively conversation would seesaw from English to French and back again. A discussion about politics and war, a critique of a news story, a detailed review of a historical event, a briefing on philosophy, an explanation of a religious view, a talk about art—these were all part of our supper table conversation, often requiring us to pull out the big encyclopedia to ascertain a date, a spelling, or a definition.

Sometimes my father would play the devil's advocate to help us understand both sides of an issue. One year we were going to Italy on vacation, so every night we would learn an Italian word or two before we started in on the food. Music was also a part of the picture. We sometimes sang our prayer or had a record playing on the stereo. The music of Vivaldi, Dvořák, Handel or Bach, Harry Belafonte, Mahalia Jackson, and Peter, Paul and Mary became the background of my childhood.

I also learned that others were always welcome at our table. Sundays after church, guests would often accompany us back to our house for dinner. During the week, my father would often come home with an unexpected guest. We didn't always know who might be coming, but my mother seemed to know how to make the food stretch, so no one would leave hungry. Roasts would be cooking in the oven while we were at church, and as we came home, the smells would welcome us in.

At my family's table, I met people from all over the world and from all walks of life, and I observed how everyone was fed and treated with warmth and acceptance. My mother's hospitality was the perfect backdrop to my parents' involvement in other people's lives. At her table I learned that food does more than feed the body. From these guests, I discovered that the world was more than just mine. I also found out that different people eat different foods, as I saw my mother planning a meal for a vegetarian visitor.

And then there was the food. My mother made meals with love and lots of planning. The food she put on our table created an atmosphere of sharing and enjoyment. Her menus combined flavor, color, and nutrition all in one big package that said *bon appétit!* Sometimes a simple meal of soup, cheese, and bread gave us all the nourishment we needed. Colorful tablecloths, luminous candles, and fresh flowers contributed to an overall feeling of comfort and pleasure.

Today, when I host guests, if I can offer half of what my parents did, I will feel that I've done a great job! Thanks to them for being role models of a world where good food coupled with caring conversation brings out the best in people.

Michael H. Shank

Early on, I got the clear sense that my parents, and Dad in particular, were available and open to many people. In Brussels, when I was no more than a kindergartner, we shared an evening meal in our home with a man I had never seen before. This was not unusual in itself, but I remember that Dad carried a largely one-way conversation as the man himself (and the rest of us) had little to say. Only after he had left did I learn that my parents did not know the man either. I discovered this by asking Mother why she was boiling the man's plate and silverware, something I had never seen her do before. She explained that it was a precaution since she knew nothing about the man or his health. He was a hungry stranger that Dad had invited in from the street. I have never forgotten this spontaneous act of kindness.

Other occasional dinner guests that I recall vividly included André and Magda Trocmé, the full significance of whose wartime courage in Le Chambon, France, did not hit me until I was an adult and read Phillip Hallie's *Lest Innocent Blood Be Shed.* I also remember being in awe of André Vandermensbrugge, a conscientious objector who was repeatedly jailed after World War II for refusing to serve in the Belgian army; he lost teeth and bone density on account of a prison diet lacking in calcium. Not least, he repeatedly refused induction and was returned to prison until a law allowing conscientious objection passed in Belgium.

I was impressed that these were not only friends of my father's but also other people who sought his advice. My parents were just as likely to share a Sunday dinner with Mr. Champenois, a gentle, disheveled, and impoverished church member who walked with a shuffle and wore a brown moth-eaten winter coat. I enjoyed riding in the car and would sometimes go along when Dad drove him home after the meal.

As an engineer's son who had done his share of farm chores, Dad was versatile and good with his hands. When I was very small, I admired him for being able to fix and rewire lamps, for knowing how to mix concrete and lay bricks, for the fact that he had operated bulldozers and supervised an earth-moving crew in Civilian Public Service. It took me many years to figure out that there were some things he did not know how to do.

Once I remember with particular fondness that he not only gave me good advice on how to achieve a smooth final finish on a bicycle frame that I was restoring from the bare metal up, but also helped me with some of the sanding—all by hand, of course. Since we all knew that he was busy, such moments seemed particularly precious. The upside of his busy-ness was that I had direct, and mostly unsupervised, access to many of his tools. Thanks, Dad!

I have fond memories of Dad's office, with its large oak roll-top desk and the book-lined walls. The desk had a special little shelf where he kept paper that had been used on only one side. When Stephen and I were small, it was a special treat when Dad would make us little drawing booklets by stapling together ten or fifteen scrap half-sheets of used mimeographed paper and old letters. We would fill the little booklets with our stories and drawings, and then we would go back to ask him to make more. Much later, when I was a teenager, we moved to a smaller house in Genval and I was especially pleased to inherit that desk. We dismantled it and moved it to my attic room. I remember doing a lot of high school homework there. At the time, I don't think either Dad or I was aware of how fond I was of those desk-related memories and their continuity with him and my childhood.

Earlier, when our family had moved to a large house surrounded by lawns in the village of Ohain, we were finally allowed to have a dog. Dad had learned about her from an acquaintance whose dog had recently had a litter. Our prized dog was a beautiful, small, black-and-white mutt with sensitive eyes and brown eyebrows—some kind of terrier blend with a fine nose and the head and feathered tail of a small setter. Mother named her Rita, but we called her Rit. Although Dad picked her out, she was not officially his dog and he did little to care for her. The one exception was that when he stopped at the butcher shop, the butcher would sometimes give him a beef lung for Rit. We kids would cut it into small chunks and feed them to Rit, who seemed to snarf them down whole.

As dogs will do, Rit picked out Dad as the alpha male. When he came home, no one else mattered, meat or no meat. On those occasions, Rit expressed her joy in extravagant wagging and wiggling and rolling on the floor, sometimes with loss of bladder control if Dad had been away on a trip for a few days.

But the most extraordinary thing about Rit was her acute perception of Dad's return. When Dad was out with the car—often late at night—Rit would be lying on the living room floor. Suddenly her head and ears would perk up. She would stand, give a little cough-like bark, and go to the door. Several minutes later, we would hear the tires of the gray Peugeot 403 crunching the gravel in the driveway. Admittedly, traffic was light in the village at night, but Rit did not react to any other cars; she reacted only to the specific far-off sound of her master's engine.

During my last year or so at home, when I was about sixteen, Dad took me aside one day and told me that the two of us were going into Brussels to see a very disturbing film. I was now old enough, he said, to learn in some detail about the horrors that human beings had inflicted on their fellows. The film was a documentary on the Holocaust, assembled from newsreels, from personal photos and films shot by the Nazi Schutzstaffel (SS) as well as by Allied cinematographers and photographers present at the liberation of the concentration camps in 1945. It was indeed profoundly shocking and sobering, but I have always been grateful to Dad for his guidance in this part of my ethical and historical education.

3

Apprenticeship in Blokosso

James R. Krabill

In the final stages of preparing this volume for print, I made a quick early morning phone call to David Shank to clarify a few details—place names, bibliographical sources, etc.—about which only he had the required information. But before we could get to the jots and tittles, Dave had a question for me. "Do you subscribe to *Books & Culture*," he wanted to know. "You *don't*?" He responded with surprise and what seemed like a tinge of disappointment in his voice. "Well, you *should*! It's one of the best ways to keep up on current literature."

Never missing a beat

Whenever Dave has made a reading recommendation to me over the years, it has generally served me well to pay attention. And I knew at that moment that I really *should* subscribe to *Books & Culture*, for failing to do so would surely deprive me of the broad perspective I need in order to be fully equipped for the work I do.

"There's an especially important book review on the church in China in this month's issue," Dave continued. "I can't read the whole thing to you—it's four pages long—but listen to this paragraph."

> China-watchers in the church should now be looking for another book, one that cannot quite yet be written, namely a study of the rapid growth of Christianity in the intellectual and governing communities over the past twenty years. By a great irony of history, "true-believer Marxism" has been a precursor, a John the Baptist, to Christianity among cultural élites.

James R. Krabill served for fourteen years in West Africa as a Bible and church history teacher among African-initiated churches. He is the author and editor of numerous articles and several books and currently serves as senior executive for Global Ministries at Mennonite Mission Network in Elkhart, Indiana.

In these circles one finds an increasingly vibrant, intelligent faith that has more in common with the Christianity of Roman antiquity just before Constantine than it does with anything currently Western.[1]

"Do you understand the importance of this?" Dave asked me with excitement. "This is a major new development worth following. Here, let me read the quote to you again: 'China-watchers in the church should now be looking for another book, one that cannot yet be written. . . .'"

When Dave and I finished our conversation ten minutes later, I hung up the phone and chuckled to myself about what had just happened. David A. Shank. Eighty-five years old. Still going strong. Never missing a beat. The phone exchange had ended with Dave's promise to send me the full issue of *Books & Culture*, though he *did* want it back because "you never know when a good quote like that might come in handy."

A flood of memories

Working through some of David's key writings in preparing this book for publication has reminded me how much his thought and general approach to missions have shaped me over the years. I first became aware of David in the early 1970s when he and his wife, Wilma, were still serving as Mennonite mission workers in Belgium. But our lives would soon become more intertwined when we both accepted assignments to work among the Harrist people of Côte d'Ivoire, West Africa.

From 1976 to 1978, my wife, Jeanette, and I had several face-to-face encounters with the Shanks, at Overseas Seminar (a weeklong orientation for North American workers preparing for international assignments); in Aberdeen, Scotland (where Dave was completing his doctoral thesis on the Prophet Harris); and in Paris, France (where Jeanette and I were doing French-language and African studies and where the Shanks came to visit us in the context of David's dissertation research).

But it was in the spring of 1979 that things intensified considerably when Jeanette and I embarked on a three-year adventure with the Shanks of sharing a one-floor, several-room apartment in the village of Blokosso-Abidjan, Côte d'Ivoire. Part of living together meant negoti-

---

[1] The book under review was Lian Xi's new release, *Redeemed by Fire: The Rise of Popular Christianity in Modern China* (New Haven: Yale University Press, 2010), and the quote is from reviewer David Lyle Jeffrey, "Christianity in China: An Irreducible Complexity," in *Books & Culture*, September/October 2010, 23.

ating space and the use of a common vehicle, as well as establishing a rhythm of food shopping, cooking, and clean-up.

What I remember most of that time were the neighborhood home Bible studies, the frequent Sunday visits to Harrist villages, the significant relationships we established at the nearby Catholic institute and among Protestant missionaries and local church leaders; and the rich daily conversations the four of us had around the evening dinner table as we attempted to process all the incredible things happening to us. Our children, two of whom were born during this period, came to know the Shanks as "Uncle Dave" and "Aunt Wilma," and have continued to maintain contact with them ever since those earliest days spent together in Blokosso.

It is impossible to capture in a few pages the many ways the intense conversations and unforgettable experiences shared with David and Wilma in Côte d'Ivoire shaped and oriented our ministry as a couple in the years to follow. But as junior colleagues living with the Shanks—veteran mission workers with almost thirty years of experience in Europe and the U.S.—the impact on us was appreciable, to say the least.

What follows is but a small window into a few of the ministry principles that guided David's mission thinking and practice as I witnessed him at work—principles that I in turn have found helpful in my own ministry and which I believe are worth considering by *anyone* choosing to participate in God's reconciling mission to the world.

Ten principles I have learned from David's life and ministry

1. Ground ministry and theology firmly in scripture.

David feasted on a more diverse menu of reading material than almost any person I had ever met, all the while maintaining an absolute commitment to the Old and New Testament scripture as the principal text given to God's people for matters pertaining to faith and practice. His was no cavalier approach to God's word; he gave only the highest respect and deepest devotion to understanding and applying the inherited text, in the original Hebrew and Greek languages and in the multiple English and French translations with which he worked throughout the course of his teaching and preaching ministry. Several chapters in this volume attest to the primacy David attributed to the biblical text and the seriousness with which he studied it.

2. Keep focused on God's mission in Jesus.

With all the potential distractions and detours that can result from the study of scripture, David kept his eye carefully tuned to the grand meta-narrative of God's reconciling mission to the world in Jesus Christ. Central to that mission is certainly Jesus' earthly ministry as evangelist, healer, exorcist, prophet, teacher, and man of protest. Yet this ministry, David constantly reminds us, opens up as well to broader christological understandings and perspectives and leads us in faith to Jesus who is also the Messiah, or Christ, the one who has come and is yet coming, the Creator and Sustainer, the resurrection and the life—our Savior and Lord. Again and again in the pages of this volume the reader will encounter Shank's impassioned conviction that it is only in Jesus the Messiah that our deepest personal longings—and indeed History itself—will ever find ultimate meaning, direction and purpose.

3. Recognize the church as primary model and messenger of God's work in the world.

The church has not always performed well as a representative of God's reconciling mission. Nor is God limited in time or space to the witness of the church with regard to that mission. Yet none of this changes the fact that God has called forth a people, a "messianic community," following after and empowered by the Messiah to embody and proclaim the good news of God's already-yet-still-coming reign. Part of that message is that individual believers can be reconciled to God in Christ. But the broader biblical message is that those believers are invited to be part of a new and transformed people as God's ambassadors of reconciliation, committed to God's ongoing and as yet unfinished plan to set things right with the world. David's repeated warning to us not to spiritualize or politicize our calling as God's people becomes a central theme throughout his writings.

4. Embrace the Anabaptist stream of history.

Some preachers and evangelists believe it is important to play down the details of church history in order to focus on the more generic "core" affirmations of the gospel. Only when believers mature in their faith, it is held, can they truly understand and appropriate the theological nuances of the past. David Shank could not disagree more. Shank has never promoted preaching the "gospel of Anabaptism;" he knows full well that the gospel is, and always must be, focused solely on the Christ event of history. But he also knows that various streams of thought and practice have emerged throughout history regarding that event and that some, he believes, are more faithful to the biblical witness than others. He is not arrogant about this belief. Nor is he unaware of the many times and places where the direct descendents of Anabaptism have failed miserably to live up to their own understandings and commitments. But he will challenge readers of this volume to take another look at the Anabaptist lens and to consider what it has to offer to contemporary would-be disciples of Jesus.

5. Be prepared to take the cultural plunge.

The church has always struggled with what it means to be *in* the world, yet not *of* it. First-century believers—and Anabaptists and others following their example—were empowered by the Holy Spirit to create faith communities that both surprised and intrigued their neighbors, and to invite them to be a part of the new reality that those communities represented. David Shank has always believed that building bridges of gospel communication to friends and neighbors in a given culture would require taking seriously that culture, mastering its language, reading its poets, viewing its films, studying its art and history—in short, "becoming all things to all people . . . for the sake of the gospel" (1 Cor. 9:22–23). One of the fascinating aspects of this collection of writings is observing how Shank worked diligently at this challenge in two very different cultural contexts, the first in Europe (Belgium) and, the second, in West Africa (Côte d'Ivoire). Readers will learn valuable lessons from his relentless efforts in this regard.

6. Adopt a mentor from within the local culture.

Early on in his European ministry, David became well acquainted with the spokespersons from the culture in which he found himself. In his article, "A Missionary Approach to a Dechristianized Society,"[2] written when he was a twenty-eight-year-old only eighteen months after his arrival in Belgium, Shank cites the works of A. Ryckmans, Henri Godin, André Gide, Simone Weil, François Mauriac, Jacques Maritain, and many others in developing his presentation. Later on, David came to appreciate the insightful cultural-religious analysis of Jacques Ellul and literally purchased and devoured every major publication this French philosopher-ethicist ever produced. In the 1970s, studying the life and thought of Liberian Prophet William Wadé Harris became Shank's preoccupation in preparation for his ministry in Africa. In one of the many conversations I had with David during our early years in Blokosso, he

---

[2] This article appears as chapter 8 in the present volume.

told me: "You need at least one good cultural mentor to help you as an outsider understand the context in which you are working. Ellul played that role for me in Europe, and Harris did much the same in West Africa."

7. Keep looking for the big-picture paradigms that give meaning to the details.

One of David's strengths is finding the larger overarching paradigms on which to hang the innumerable stories he loves to tell. One such paradigm is Harold Turner's description of the types of new religious movements that emerge as a result of the encounter between traditional "primal" religions and Western Christianity. Another is the itinerary experienced by many African Christians as they journey from the beliefs and practices of traditional religion toward a fully embraced New Testament faith. Yet another comes from the insightful work of French sociologist Henri Desroche in his analysis of the processes and stages of the messianic dynamic. Such movements throughout history and in our world today abandon the initial impetus and leadership of their founding messiah and spin off into some kind of spiritualized or politicized version of the original vision. Shank comes back to these themes again and again in his writings to explain "the story behind the story" in settings as diverse as first-century Palestine, sixteenth-century Switzerland and twentieth-century Nigeria.

8. Strike a balance between being a scholar and a pastor.

David has spent much of his life in academic pursuits, studying cultural trends, doing literature reviews, teaching religion and theology, and completing original research for a doctoral dissertation. But he has also served for many years as a pastor, a small-group Bible study leader, a personal counselor for new believers, and an actor—representing the Rabbi of Bethlehem in his congregation's annual Christmas pageant, for example. David's life energies and commitments have been directed at building the body of Christ, offering whatever gifts he has at his disposal for that purpose. He once told me: "Had I known I would be spending an extra year in Aberdeen finishing my PhD thesis, I would have tried harder to plant a church there." Really? Who *does* that? Well, someone who believes that the church is the primary model and messenger of God's reconciling mission in Christ to set things right with the world.

9. *Never stop learning.*

In the Shank children's essay found in chapter 2 of this volume, daughter Rachel describes what she remembers of the ambience at the evening family dinner table. "The lively conversation," she writes, "would seesaw from English to French and back again. A discussion about politics and war, a critique of a news story, a detailed review of a historical event, a briefing on philosophy, an explanation of a religious view, a talk about art—these were all part of our supper table conversation, often requiring us to pull out the big encyclopedia to ascertain a date, a spelling, or a definition." In Blokosso, some twenty years later, the conversation was most certainly of a different nature and on topics not even imagined many years before. But the curiosity, the passion for understanding God's world and our place in it, remained the same. It is that same spirit that has made my journey with David such a fascinating one, never boring or predictable, always moving forward to some place I had not anticipated.

10. *Take life seriously enough to laugh about it.*

As seriously and intensely as David takes his life commitments, there is always room for hearty laughter, not as a polite accommodation to some awkward social situation, but because laughter is in the very nature of things, a healing balm for the soul, a requirement for surviving some of life's most challenging conditions. There were many times in our life with the Shanks that laughter was all we had—when loud music during holiday celebrations in the village of Blokosso made it impossible to hold a conversation around the table, or when heavy rains washed out country roads making it difficult to complete our journey for an anticipated Harrist village visit. It was in such situations that one could count on Dave to carry us beyond the presenting problem to a place of levity and perspective that reminded us that ultimately this was not *our* work and we were not in control but rather in the hands of God who has promised to be with us and sustain us wherever we find ourselves engaged in the kingdom purposes of God's anointed one, Jesus, the Messiah, the Christ.

Section II Personal pilgrimage

David Shank (right) with cousin Lowell Hartzler (middle) and
brother Ernest ("Ernie") (left) in 1933

4

On the margins
My pilgrimage in mission

David A. Shank

In January 2000, when the Association of Anabaptist Missiologists recognized my "contribution to mission thinking and practice during the past few decades on three continents," I was taken aback. Missionary, yes! But missiologist? Then when Editor Jonathan Bonk asked me to offer my "pilgrimage in mission" for the *International Bulletin of Missionary Research*, I was even more astonished. I have read with pleasure the pilgrimages of stalwarts of Christian mission, without it ever having occurred to me that mine would merit recounting.

But I am willing to tell my story. I intentionally include the names of many people whose contributions to my pilgrimage have been significant. And the many details mentioned are required in order to hold the story together and make sense of it.

My roots

I come from a marginal Christian people. At least as far back as the 1560s, my Shank ancestors were a part of a *Taüfer* (Anabaptist) community of faith who had taken refuge at Eggiwil in the mountainous Langnau district of Switzerland. The local official Reformed clergy often insisted that their own people should take their lifestyle cues from the heretics. But the mission of the *Gemeinde*—the *Taüfer* community— was too attractive and effective; it won over many members of the Reformed state-church population. The civil authorities saw it as such a threat that its members deserved banishment and even death in the pope's galleys at Venice.

In order to escape such punishment, a certain Christian Shank fled with others in 1671 in total destitution to the Palatinate, and from there in 1717 his descendant Christian Shank and son Michael migrated with their families to Quaker William Penn's colony in what is today Lancaster County, Pennsylvania. With the son of Mennonite bishop Hans Herr, their closest neighbor, they helped build the Herrs' house, where they worshiped and where their Indian neighbors are said to have often come in by the unlocked door to sleep on the hearth of the open fireplace.[1] In 1816, a century later, Jean Neuhauser, an Amish miller in the French Alsace on my Yoder mother's maternal side, emigrated as an indentured servant to Canada to avoid conscription in Napoleon's army. He later arrived in Lancaster County, too.

Preparation

Early years

I requested baptism at age eleven in the Orrville (Ohio) Mennonite Church, in order to receive forgiveness from Christ for having taken money from my younger sister Esther's piggy bank, and in order to make sure that I would not be "left behind." (I had heeded the warnings of Mennonite evangelist Brother Roy Otto from Pennsylvania.) I was right with God and the universe, a member of the church of Christ, and committed "to walk in newness of life" and "to give and receive counsel from the brotherhood."

I knew nothing of other churches, except that—unlike Mennonites—"they" were said to not practice the "all things" that Jesus told his apostles to teach to all nations. In addition to baptism on confession of faith, and the Lord's Supper, these things included the holy practices of foot-washing; the kiss of fellowship; the rejection of violence, oaths, divorce, and jewelry, including wedding rings. The sisters were to dress modestly, with long hair and prayer coverings for worship. In addition, "separated" or "non-conformed" living meant that we did not dance, use tobacco or alcoholic drinks, swear, or go to the movies or theater. If people divorced, they left our church and went to worldly churches that didn't believe the "all things." The possibility of being kept back from communion somehow lay behind the twice-a-year services of preparation for communion, which accented the importance for the brotherhood of "keeping the all things," and of first "making things right" with the brothers and sisters "of like precious faith." As an eleven-year-old, I found it awesome, and saw it as the true church.

---

[1] The Hans Herr House is today the oldest house in the region and has become a museum. It is located at 1849 Hans Herr Drive, Willow Street (Lancaster County), Pennsylvania.

Yet, I was the only Mennonite in my class in school in North Canton, Ohio. We were a marginal people. I was learning that *the true church is a marginal reality.*

My parents had been Mennonite missionaries from 1915 to 1919 in Dhamtari, in what was then the Central Provinces of India. Both were first-generation college graduates of the denomination's young Goshen (Indiana) College, with my father having also spent a year at Purdue University studying mechanical engineering. Both had been deeply influenced by the student Christian missionary movement of American Protestantism: missionaries of different denominations were all involved in a similar calling that was somehow—a serious contradiction!—much greater than membership in the Mennonite Church. In Dhamtari, my father, Charles, had directed carpentry and rope-making shops for orphan boys saved from the great famine that had taken Mennonites to India for famine relief at the end of the nineteenth century. My mother, Crissie (Yoder), worked with Bible Women, who were engaged in grassroots colportage and evangelism. After having buried their first child "under the mango tree" by the grave of the first Mennonite missionary to die in India, their mission was cut short when their second child developed rheumatic fever and her life was threatened.

The "missionary call" was so sacred that it seemed as if my father lived the rest of his life under the burden of being seen by fellow missionaries as having abandoned the call because he was unwilling to pay the price of staying. He never spoke of India in public. In 1929, when I was five years old, my mother died from complications surrounding the birth of their eighth child. From the early 1920s until her death, she had been the literature secretary for the Mennonite Women's Missionary Association. She had been the first American Mennonite woman author, of a book on India,[2] published the year of my birth. She often spoke of missions and India in the churches—from behind the pulpit!— at a time when Mennonite women didn't generally speak in worship services. Along with the book and its pictures, there were my folks' India photograph album to peruse again and again, and an "India trunk" in the attic full of exotic mementos that never ceased to provoke my wonder and curiosity. Former colleagues on furlough from India would visit our family. They seemed to be another breed of Mennonites.

---

[2] Crissie Y. Shank, *Letters from Mary* (Scottdale, PA: Mennonite Publishing House, 1924).

Ours was not a typical Mennonite family. Yet it was one where breakfast started with the oldest to the youngest child memorizing and repeating the Golden Text of the next Sunday's Sunday school lesson, the reading of a Bible text, and a prayer that said more than just "thanks for this food." My father's next-older brother had pioneered a new Mennonite missionary endeavor in Argentina, and later pioneered from within the new Argentine Mennonite church a mission to the Indians in the northern Chaco. Stories from correspondence and furlough visits of Uncle Joe and his family were a normal part of our family life.

Further, my father's oldest brother was a rural, horseback-riding missionary to the mountain folk in the Ozarks of Missouri. To top it off, when Papa was remarried in 1939 to Lydia F. Shenk, French professor at Goshen College, her twin sister was Dr. Lillie Shenk, a missionary in Tanganyika. Lillie was establishing a grassroots clinic there. Our ex-missionary family was plugged into missions in India, Argentina and its Chaco, and Tanganyika—the only foreign "mission fields" of the (Old) Mennonite Church at that time.

We attended at the time the Canton Mission, one of several city mission efforts of Mennonite Board of Missions (MBM). In addition to my own future ministry in Europe and Africa, an older brother was to work in China, an older sister and her husband would give twelve years to ministry among Palestinians and then in Zaire, while a younger sister and her husband would spend their lives as missionaries in Brazil. We were a missionary family.

When my father lost his job as research engineer for the Hoover Sweeper Company because he could not in good conscience work for its government-contracted war industry, he moved the family to Goshen, Indiana, in order to offer his children the opportunity to go to Goshen College, his alma mater, and make out financially by living at home. Mission, peace, and education were always intimately tied together in our family.

I was in my senior year at Goshen's public high school at the time of the Pearl Harbor attack. I had been actively involved throughout my high school years in orchestra, chorus, and "worldly" drama and debate, and I was thinking seriously about going into law, even though Mennonite church life and values at that time told me that this would be an inappropriate life vocation. In my first year of college, I not only met my future spouse, Wilma Hollopeter, but took a challenging pre-med chemistry course taught by Glen Miller, and managed to earn an A-. This success suggested to me that perhaps science and chemistry might be in my future.

In preparation for the oncoming war, the college congregation in Goshen was intimately involved in the development of a Civilian Public Service alternative to military service, through the efforts of professors Guy Hershberger and Harold S. Bender. I ultimately spent time in four CPS units during three years of "public service of national importance." These experiences included two relief training units, since I had envisaged voluntary postwar relief service overseas. At Grottoes, Virginia, I dug postholes in a soil conservation project and did lookout duty for forest fires. In Denison, Iowa, I was foreman of a terracing crew working with soil conservation.

In both camps I learned biblically about the importance of creation care. But I also learned that there existed other, earthy Mennonites who did not practice the life of separation, and that there were Methodists, Episcopalians, Presbyterians, Baptists, Pentecostals, and Catholics who were Christian conscientious objectors. Our experience together was a grassroots ecumenicity—before the word became common in broader church circles.

At Hudson River State Hospital in Poughkeepsie, New York, I was a ward attendant. Our relief training unit had an informal theology professor, Donovan Smucker, a Mennonite student at Princeton Seminary. He stirred in me a deep theological interest, as well as a growing awareness of the significance of historical Anabaptism.[3] To my naive biblicism he added his comparison of Anabaptist thought and practice to the contemporary theologies of Reinhold and H. Richard Niebuhr, Karl Barth, and Emil Brunner, and Paul Minear's "biblical realism." I began making comparisons with the Mennonite Church.

With the earth-shaking events of World War II, the late Holocaust discoveries, and Hiroshima/Nagasaki, I decided that scientific and technological transformation had crossed a line, and that my own life contribution would be in the domain of *human* transformation. I consciously moved beyond "churchianity" to a serious personal commitment to Jesus Christ, following John Baillie's *Invitation to Pilgrimage*. I realized fully—and shared with my parents—that in one way or another Christian mission was my future. But I was far from convinced that the

---

[3] See Smucker's just then published "The Theological Triumph of the Early Anabaptist-Mennonites" in *Mennonite Quarterly Review* 19, no. 1 (January 1945): 5–26, which he gave as off-print copies to each of us. Bender both published and commended Smucker's work.

Mennonite denomination was ideally suited, since I had now become acquainted with other options. I decided that after a term of postwar relief work overseas, I would study under Paul Minear at Andover Newton Seminary, and go on in faith from there.

I was invited to make a CPS transfer to Mennonite Central Committee's headquarters at Akron, Pennsylvania, where I was asked to edit the *C.P.S. Bulletin* for the Mennonite CPS units. There in mid-1946, Harold S. Bender organized a conference on Anabaptism. He invited Frank Littell, a young Methodist scholar at Yale, to speak. Littell presented a chapter of the doctoral dissertation he was writing on the missionary dynamics of the sixteenth-century Anabaptists. I saw, as Bender did, that this missionary dynamic was an essential part of Mennonite roots—to be added to Bender's own earlier identified threefold "essence of Anabaptism."[4] The church was thus to be seen more accurately as essentially *fourfold*:

1. *disciples of Jesus*, responding to the good news of God's reign,

2. in a *community* of mutual support,

3. committed to God's service through *nonviolent love*, and—following Littel's added insights—

4. the *mission* of sharing the good news by inviting others into the fellowship.

When I subsequently discussed my future with Bender, he explained to me that following the various relief ministries in Europe, the Mennonite Church might well have need of church workers with this kind of Anabaptist vision, well trained in Bible and theology. Persuaded by him, I ended up back at Goshen College to earn a BA in sociology under Guy Hershberger, and then to enroll in Bender's young and mod-

---

[4] As incoming president of the American Society of Church History, Harold S. Bender gave his presidential address just two-and-a-half years earlier as "The Anabaptist Vision"—seen as the fulfillment of the Reformation impulse and intention. See Harold S. Bender, "The Anabaptist Vision," in *Church History* 13 (March 1944), and also "The Anabaptist Vision," in Albert N. Keim, *Harold S. Bender, 1897-1962* (Scottdale, PA: Herald Press, 1998). Bender's "Anabaptist Vision" would play a dominant role in the reorientation of significant parts of Mennonitism during the next half century, and largely through John Howard Yoder would influence both Protestant and Roman Catholic thinkers. It would also influence missiological thought worldwide, through Dr. Wilbert Shenk, among others. See James R. Krabill, Walter Sawatsky, and Charles E. Van Engen, eds., *Evangelical, Ecumenical, and Anabaptist Missiologies in Conversation* (Maryknoll, NY: Orbis Books, 2006).

est Goshen College Biblical Seminary, where I was thoroughly "Bender-ized" for two years.[5]

Between college and seminary, Wilma Hollopeter and I married, and Wilma has been ever since not only the mother and co-educator of our four children but also my in-depth collaborator. With independent personal calls to India, we easily decided to go there to work in what had been my parents' unfinished mission.

Preparatory mission

During those years of college and seminary, I was a member (with other former CPS men) of the Vesper Quartet—a singing group that traveled all over the Mennonite Church in the U.S. and Canada. This touring gave me additional understandings of Mennonitism. Once a week, our quartet also became "Your Worship Hour Quartet," broadcasting from South Bend, Indiana, as a part of the radio ministry of the Mennonite Brethren in Christ pastor Rev. Quinton Everest.

At the same time, under the structures of Goshen College's Young People's Christian Association, I became the superintendent of a student church-planting effort near Syracuse, Indiana, which I called the Wawasee Lakeside Chapel. A number of other future missionaries—Albert and Lois Buckwalter, Chaco, Argentina; Eugene and Louella Blosser, Japan; and Anna Kay Massanari, Puerto Rico—were co-workers. Each Sunday we picked up children, including the three young sons of the local coiffeuse, Virginia Bornman. Others followed through after us, and we were recently surprised to learn that three of Virginia's grandsons are involved in Christian ministry—in Oregon, in a mission effort to Mexico, and in leading the Friends of the Wolof in Senegal, West Africa.

Our sense of call to India was seriously challenged when Mennonite Board of Missions Overseas Secretary J. D. Graber told of the changing postcolonial context in India, with Western missionaries no longer in demand in what was later to develop into the time of "Missionary, go home!" Instead, Graber asked, would we be open to a postwar follow-through to relief service in Belgium? But missionaries to Europe, the heartlands of Christianity? When I hadn't yet completed my BD program? Bender had earlier spoken of such a possibility. But what kind of ministry? And why?

Immediately after the war, American Mennonite relief workers in Belgium under Mennonite Central Committee (MCC) were involved via YMCA with German prisoners of war. Later, under the Mennonite Relief

---

[5] I had eight semesters of courses under his tutelage.

Committee through the military chaplaincy of the national Union of Protestant Churches, Mennonites served families of imprisoned Nazi collaborators and Eastern European and Slavic refugees through Latvian Baptist pastor Charles Grikman.

There had, on one hand, been major distributions of canned meat, milk, and cheese, and on the other, of soap and clothing—often to children's homes such as the evangelical[6] Home of Hope, which was also served by a Mennonite monitor for two years. Further, a Builders' Unit had helped reconstruct the village of Bullange in the German-speaking part of eastern Belgium. There the village priest often commended the lifestyle of the Mennonite youth to the youth of the village. The government's reconstruction support for wages was voluntarily poured into a village "Mennonite Fund" for people in need—a fund that outlived by several years the departure of the Mennonite relief workers.

Belgians, of course, asked about Mennonites and learned that these were a Christian people of peace and service who had been at the forefront of the Reformation in Flanders. Belgian historian A. L. E. Verheyden's recently published research[7] indicated that Mennonites had furnished more martyrs than all other groups, and that Mennonites had been in more than fifty locations in Flanders prior to the rise of Calvinism. Some people, including Catholic leaders, asked American Mennonite relief workers whether there should not be a new beginning for Mennonites in Belgium. Indeed, after four hundred years and as a consequence of the Spanish Inquisition, all Protestants combined totaled fewer than 50,000 people, less than one-half of one percent of the total population. A traditionally dominant, highly cultural Catholicism was hotly contested by liberal, socialist, and Masonic structures and pressures.

Our assignment would be to build on the presence and contacts of the American Mennonite postwar relief workers, and to reestablish an Anabaptist witness among Belgians. Wilma and I were both ordained by Bishop S. C. Yoder, after passing the local Indiana-Michigan Mennonite Conference's ministerial committee and the Mennonite Board's personnel committee. One committee member asked whether we were

---

[6] In this chapter I will use "evangelical" with a small "e" as a word of description, and "Evangelical" with a capital "E" as a partisan distinction from others it opposes.

[7] See A. L. E. Verheyden, *Anabaptism in Flanders, 1530–1650: A Century of Struggle* (Scottdale, PA: Herald Press, 1961), translated by John H. Yoder and others from the original Dutch, *Geschiedenis der Doopsgezinden in de Zuidelijke Nederlanden in de XVIe Eeuw* (Brussels: Paleis der Académiën, 1959).

ready to work hard and see only meager results. We responded by asking if they would continue to support us if that were the case, and they affirmed that they would. With this kind of trust and support, we were ready to go—after a summer serving as assistant to Pastor Roy Koch in the Mennonite congregation at St. Jacobs, Ontario, waiting for our visas for Belgium to come through.

Mission I: Belgium (1950–73)

Transition

In September of 1950, at twenty-six years of age, I sailed for Belgium with Wilma and our nine-month-old son Michael. We saw ourselves most simply as servants of Jesus Christ, to whom we wished to introduce others. We were open to and trusted the leading of the Spirit of God. Our immediate task was to close out the American Mennonite relief program and to orient ourselves to our situation and assignment.

Five American Mennonite relief workers remained in Belgium: Pastor Isaac and Laura Baer, with their teenage daughter Mary, involved with Eastern European refugees; Howard Rush, serving as chauffeur for Latvian Baptist pastor Charles Grikman in his ministry to Slavic refugees and immigrants in miners camps of the Hainaut, the Borinage, and around Liège and Hasselt; and Esther Eby, who was concluding her assignment as monitor in the Home of Hope for babies and children of war. There was still a considerable stock of food and clothing, with more scheduled to arrive.

We were introduced to each of these contexts, as well as to the relevant authorities and various personal connections. These included the authorities of the nationally recognized and subsidized Union of Protestant Churches, the various governmental ministries, the village officials at Bullange, the WCC's Service for Refugees, the office of the Congo Missions, and the American-supported Belgian Gospel Mission. The latter was an aggressive post–World War I Evangelical institution with active anti-Catholic evangelism and its own Bible school with clear and disciplined doctrinal positions. It had many Flemish and Walloon congregations, and saw itself as a counterweight to the "liberal" union which was affiliated to the World Council of Churches, recently formed in 1948. In addition, the Baers introduced us to the small minority of Luxembourg Mennonites less than a day's drive away.

A Mennonite center

Within several weeks the American Mennonite workers had left for the U.S. and we were on our own. We soon transferred to a larger, spacious "center" where we could live, have an office, stock the incoming relief goods, receive people, and eventually have meetings. It even had a garage for our inherited Skoda station wagon. For the first period of time, we followed through with receiving Eastern European refugees and immigrants and served as chauffeur for aging Pastor Grikman in his ministry to scattered temporary refugee and immigrant Slavic congregations. This work took me into labor camps in Germany and Austria, and even as far as Trieste. I often found myself teaching or preaching there with Grikman interpreting. People were coming to faith in response to the simple ministry of the gospel, and for a while I was simply happy to be Grikman's close colleague.

Little by little, though, we realized that this work was not really Belgian work but rather work among foreign marginals in Belgium. Over the years, however, we continued fellowship with Pastor Grikman, participating with him in his annual conferences and in the ordination of young Vasil Magal, who assumed leadership after his death. On occasion, I would visit and preach in one or another of the congregations related to the ministry, even as Magal eventually took up an important radio ministry to people behind the iron curtain—"The Voice of a Friend"—supported by Mennonite Broadcasts. Until the death of "Sister" Olga Grikman, our mission supported her remarkable deaconess ministry among the continuing influx of Slavic refugees, hundreds of whom emigrated to Canada. But for the long haul, we needed to orient ourselves more directly to the Belgian culture and context.

The big scene was one of slow postwar recovery in Belgium, taking place in a dense and industrialized population of nine million people in a Maryland-sized nation that was undergoing rapid dechristianization and secularization, with competing, highly politicized socialisms, from communist to Catholic. There was at the time a strong class consciousness, a permanent cultural/linguistic conflict between the Catholic Flemish in the north and socialist Walloons in the south, a bicultural Brussels located in between the two, and all in the context of a European continent devastated and divided. Belgium was also a colonial power, and mission was understood as work among the various tribes in the Belgian Congo, Rwanda, and Burundi, *not* work among the Belgian people themselves![8]

Within the first year after the arrival of MBM colleagues Orley and Jane Swartzendruber, we hired French teachers and took courses in Belgian history and literature at the Free University of Brussels, where all the talk was about Freud and Marx. Orley and I also took a course at the very young Faculté de Théologie Protestante de Bruxelles, in the philosophy of Émile Boutroux, taught by the aging and "old-school" liberal professor Dr. Mathieu Schyns, president of the Synod of the Union of Protestant Churches and pastor at the prestigious chapel of (Lutheran) King Leopold I. I took another course as well, in historical method, with Dr. Verheyden, so helpful for my thesis in 1977–78, and was able to transfer some of the credits earned from this work back to Goshen Biblical Seminary to complete the requirements for my interrupted bachelor of divinity program.

During that same year we studied the whole situation of Belgian Protestantism, with its diversity, attempting to see what contribution Mennonites might make to that picture. Our experiences at the secular Free University of Brussels made it clear that there was no Protestant student ministry of any kind, so we imagined a student house close to the university as a center for meeting, talking, gathering, sharing, and studying with other students. We went with our proposal to the Federation of Protestant Churches, composed of the Union, Methodists (we attended the Methodist church in order to hear Pastor Descamp's slow and careful French), the Belgian Christian Missionary Church (initiated as a mission by the Swiss Free Reformed Church and later to become the Reformed Church of Belgium), the Dutch Reformed and Re-reformed Churches, and a small Baptist Union.

Our proposal for a student center fell flat. The sentiment was straightforward and simple—"Why would this federation of proper and respectable churches want Belgian Protestantism to be officially represented at the Free University by a sect such as the Mennonites . . . and *American* Mennonites at that?" Pastor Schyns, who knew us as students at the faculté, clearly did not support us. We were later to learn the extent to which some Protestant leaders were involved in the Masonic lodge, which had a dominant voice at the university as well as in the

---

[8] French Dominican Henri Godin and colleague had nonetheless published a modest volume, *La France, Pays de Mission?* (Paris: Éditions du Cerf, 1943), nearly a decade earlier. The same publication appeared in an English translation (*France, a Mission Field?*) in 1949.

anti-Catholic political machines. And so we found ourselves pushed to the margins. A number of years later, however, I was to sit ex officio on the federation's council, because of a social ministry that had developed among immigrant laborers. Not long after that, with ecumenicity in the air, the federation disappeared altogether, when most of the member churches simply joined the Union of Protestant Churches, a move that also transformed them.

After Swartzendrubers' reassignment to Paris at the request of the French Mennonites, we were to understand better the marginal groups found within the broader Protestant family in Belgium, groups that included the Salvation Army, several kinds of Baptists, "open" and "closed" (Plymouth) Brethren, and even more closed Darbyists, as well as emerging Pentecostals of various stripes and origins. All of these—plus the Evangelical churches founded by the Belgian Gospel Mission between the two world wars—constituted a miscellany of free-church reality wholly separated from the state-recognized and subsidized Union of Protestant Churches.

In January 1952, a group of eight American Mennonite men living in Europe—former relief workers, missionaries, university students—got together in Amsterdam. I was among them. The purpose of the gathering was to listen to the wisdom and experiences of Dutch Mennonite historians and theologians; to assess in some depth the European postwar spiritual, ecclesiastical, and religious situation; and to reflect on our own Mennonite calling and vocation in that setting. Some members of the group were studying under renowned scholars—Karl Barth, Emil Brunner, Walther Eichrodt, and Karl Jaspers. Several in the group had had experiences with the varieties of Dutch, German, French, and Swiss Mennonite minorities, and others with leaders of Swiss, French, or German Protestantism in the budding World Council of Churches movement. Each of us had agreed to bring a paper describing what we were working on at the time. My presentation was "A Missionary Approach to a Dechristianized Society."[9]

Most of our conversation seemed to turn on the relevance of H. S. Bender's "Anabaptist Vision" for European Christianity in the postwar ecclesiastical and spiritual context. But we also asked about its relevance for American Mennonitism, then seemingly evolving into a conventional American denomination. John Howard Yoder was given the lead assignment among us to publish a couple of our presentations in

---

[9] H. S. Bender published it in *Mennonite Quarterly Review* 28, no. 1 (January 1954): 39–55. It is reprinted as chapter 8 in the present volume.

Concern, a series of occasional pamphlets launched as a result of this gathering and appearing for more than ten years with the intent of contributing to church renewal among American Mennonites.[10]

I was deeply marked by the Amsterdam meeting, which made it clear that the fruits of our Belgian Mennonite work would not look like the sending Mennonite denomination in the United States. Rather, we understood that our ministry would emerge out of a grassroots understanding that the Spirit works with people beginning where they are, and that the church develops wherever Christ is present with "two or three gathered in his name." Any emerging faith community, however, would also be consciously shaped on our part by the four broad Anabaptist accents of discipleship, fellowship, the service of nonviolent love, and mission.

After that year shared with the Swartzendrubers, during which time we followed together an early morning daily liturgy from the Taizé community for personal nourishment and to become more accustomed to using religious French, it seemed to us that *our* program was over. After that, the *Holy Spirit's* program kept coming at us and challenging us as it opened up perspectives while we simply did our best to keep up. The following pages recount the story of what happened.

The Brussels-East congregation

We were sought out by Jules and Madeleine Lambotte, who were informed of our presence by a French Mennonite elder and neighbor of Madeleine's parents. Jules was a Flemish evangelist of the national Protestant union's Flemish-focused home mission organization. As a catechumen of Pastor Schyns, Lambotte had at first been attracted to Nazism, and then rejected it entirely as he came to pacifist convictions following a conversion experience resulting from the street-preaching ministry of the Belgian Gospel Mission. Jules was looking for a spiritual home that would recognize his pacifism, and he and Madeleine—a Lutheran, "born again" in the nearby French Mennonite assembly at Montbéliard—became our first members.

More than we realized or understood at that time, the Lambottes brought with them a whole polarizing Evangelical program, including scouting activities, a youth center, a budding publishing effort inherited from Jules's father, a personal monthly newsletter with a partisan

---

[10] See J. Lawrence Burkholder, "Concern Pamphlets Movement," in *The Mennonite Encyclopedia* (Scottdale, PA: Herald Press, 1990), 5:177–80.

vision of unifying the nonfederated Evangelicals *against* both Roman Catholics and the "liberal, ecumenical" union and federation. Indeed, Jules would be moderately successful in achieving his goals in this regard.

The Lambottes were our first members, and with them came two "converts." One was a former member of the Third Order of the Franciscans, and the other was a scout from traditional bourgeois Catholicism, fully determined to refuse military service and accept imprisonment as the price of Christian fidelity. These relationships eventually got us connected to the ecumenical Belgian Fellowship of Reconciliation which was working to create legal recognition for conscientious objection to military service and war. The considerable publicity in the press about the trial of our Mennonite conscientious objector highly encouraged those efforts, and such legislation was eventually passed, though only after our friend had served a prison term that had lasting effects on his health. While in prison, our friend was persuaded by the Reformed chaplain that he should not be "Amish," and he subsequently became a pastor in the Reformed Church, eventually in Switzerland. These events had the effect of pushing us further toward the margins, both in relation to the federated churches and to the Evangelicals in Belgium.

For our initial congregational endeavor, we chose a parish area of East Brussels where there had never been a Protestant church of any kind. There we created Foyer Fraternel, with Lambotte ordained as evangelist working under my pastoral leadership. We tried as a team to concentrate especially within a given geographical area, while remaining open to anyone interested in attending.

We began with the public installation of Jules Lambotte in the presence of the union's President Schyns and representatives from some of the other churches. Then followed a week of "good news" lectures by schoolmaster and elder Pierre Widmer, the most important leader of the Mennonite Church in France. A desperate retired opera singer caught hope during the meetings, and a Belgian Mennonite congregation of seven was underway.

Because of the one-by-one character of congregational growth in our ministry context, and especially later at Bourgeois-Rixensart, I would become deeply impressed with the ways the singular Christ event is similar to a diamond, variously seized, trusted, appropriated, and believed through its different facets by different individuals with their different personalities, experiences, gifts, and needs. The Christ event as I came to understand it included various facets: eternal Word, creation, incarnation, anointing, temptation, obedience (with proclaiming, calling, teaching, praying, healing, reconciling, exorcising, forgiving, promising, etc.), cross, descent, resurrection, ascension, reign, and consummation.

The light reflected by each or any or several of the facets of the diamond often serves for a particular individual as an entry point to faith in Christ and a beginning appropriation of the fullness reflected by all the other facets. The pastoral recognition and honoring of this diversity of entry points to faith, and the various personal itineraries in the Spirit toward fullness, became for me a permanent challenge.[11] This was clearly a different approach than that of my Belgian colleague Jules Lambotte with his doctrinal skirmishes. On the other hand, Lambotte was the future connection—via George Thompson, an independent Ghanaian pastor-evangelist—to MBM's eventual mission work in Ghana.

In the mid-1960s, Lambotte established his publishing enterprise in a spacious property at Flavion in the Belgian province of Namur. There he published many Evangelical novels and histories, while seeking to put Mennonites back into Belgian history. He also established a congregation that met in his Flavion center, and another across the French border at Givet, where renewed French Mennonites would later continue the work.

In 1965 American colleagues Robert and Wilda Otto arrived and gave continuity to the Brussels-East congregation, thrice moving its location and establishing Belgian leadership for the group. Close to the Palais de Justice, the congregation currently serves many Christians from the global South living in Brussels, the "capital of Europe."

The Home of Hope at Ohain
We were approached by the wife of the pastor-administrator of Home of Hope, asking us as Mennonites to take over the establishment, which had been abandoned by her husband who had returned to Switzerland with a single mother of a small child placed in the home. After prayer and consultation, we decided to accept the challenge, following the positive MCC postwar experiences with children's homes in France.

---

[11] I articulated this idea more fully in "Toward an Understanding of Christian Conversion," *Mission Focus* 5, no. 2 (November 1976): 1–7. It is reprinted as chapter 12 in the present volume.

This decision would require us to relocate the home and move our family into it, assume administrative responsibilities, and find competent people to manage it. Several babies and very young children were to live in the home. The collaboration with our first director was instructive and fruitful, for professional insights and those related to grassroots Protestantism. Mademoiselle Gabrielle Révélard had volunteered out of her retirement as director of a school of puericulture, but needed to be replaced after a serious fall down the basement steps.

We had been concerned lest an institution sidetrack us from our main purpose of planting congregations in a post-Christian society. We learned, though, that evangelism, as a social raison d'être, was hardly culturally appropriate, but administering a children's home was. It thrust us into Belgian life, forcing us to speak ordinary French and not the bookish kind we had been learning. We had to deal with personnel, children, social workers, commune administrations, banks, postal services, merchants. And because the home had been supported in part by some of the marginal, miscellaneous free-church groups of Belgian Protestantism, it also led to contacts in those circles.

One of those contacts was with an open Brethren industrialist who was a member of the administrative council of Home of Hope. He also held house meetings for worship and Bible study, but found no one among his Brethren for a church-based follow-up with people who showed interest. When he learned of our purpose for being in Belgium, he invited me to attend one of his home meetings with the intention of just such follow-up, which I undertook. The children's home at Ohain was a forty-minute drive from the East Brussels congregation. During this initial period we worked closely with the Lambottes, preaching every other Sunday to the small but growing faith community taking shape.

Ultimately, since the Protestant community did not produce enough of the Christian caretakers we needed for Home of Hope, we eventually closed down the infant section, stopped taking new children, and turned the older children over to a Walloon/French couple, Ursmer and Suzanne Lefebvre, and eventually to a new Christian family of a former police commissioner. The Home of Hope property saw continued use for children's summer camps, serving the children and youth from Vasil Magal's Slavic ministries and many other youth encounters and weekends, interchurch activities, and celebrations. With time we moved to the town of Genval to pastor the emerging Bourgeois-Rixensart congregation next door. The Home of Hope property in Ohain has since become the *Maison Communale*, of reportedly one of the wealthiest communes in the country.

The Bourgeois-Rixensart congregation

The Aimé and Marie Debroux family had had Catholic origins, but during the war became deeply involved in the *Résistance* through the Communist Party's underground. Aimé's name is on a wall of the infamous Breendonk Nazi prison where such captured people were imprisoned, tortured, and sometimes executed. Their daughter Georgette was a courier for the underground and spent time in the Prison de Forest (Bruxelles) after capture and arrest.

It was in their home at Bourgeois, only fifteen minutes from Ohain, that the Home of Hope board member held his house meetings for worship and Bible study on Sunday afternoons. The group that met included the Debroux couple; their son Norbert and family from the neighboring village; their daughter Georgette and her adolescent son; and the Vanderlindens, a mixed Flemish/Walloon couple. I went along for a first encounter, and then participated more fully, as did others, and ultimately on Easter Sunday 1955, began a second grassroots congregation, with eight baptisms. The flavor of the group was seasoned by Brethren piety and informality, with the Lord's Supper celebrated every Sunday. As with Jules Lambotte, I ordained the congregational leader as evangelist under my pastoral leadership.

Our family left on a furlough in the summer of 1955, accompanied by our industrialist colleague looking for American equipment for his shirt factory and visiting in our churches. We left two growing congregations back in Belgium, with the Home of Hope in the good hands of the competent and well-trained Mademoiselle Gittens, who had been baptized in our home. She had been much impressed with the postwar ministries of Mennonites to children's homes she had helped supervise for the official Oeuvre Nationale de l'Enfance.

During our furlough, the evangelist returned, organized a nonprofit Belgian Mennonite Mission, and bought an old store-front house as a meeting place for the growing fellowship of working-class people. When his serious moral indiscretions became known, the young congregation was shaken, and several important people left the group. On our early return, I was saddled with the pastoral task of putting the pieces back together.

Ursmer Lefebvre had studied at a Baptist Bible school at Nogent, near Paris, where French Mennonite evangelists were also in training. Lefebvre was ordained for the Bourgeois congregation while studying at the theological faculty. When Ursmer and his wife, Suzanne, later followed a missionary call to Burundi, I again assumed pastoral responsibilities for the congregation and sought to associate the congregation with the French Mennonite Church across national boundaries, and a long day's drive away.

The congregation was the only non-Catholic church in the area, and the members eventually erected a meeting place—a *temple*, in French—that looked more like a church building than what they had had before. The group called themselves the Église Évangélique[12] de Rixensart and began to attract Christians of all kinds living in a five- to ten-kilometer radius around the area, a growing suburb of Brussels. These included Jehovah's Witnesses, Friends of Man (a J. W. offshoot), Pentecostals, Christian Science, Belgian Christian Missionary, Union Synod, Methodist, Baptist, Salvation Army, Catholic, Anglican, Swiss Reformed, Assemblies of God, and German Lutheran. It became a cross section of Belgium's divided Protestant family, pastored in this case by a Mennonite from America.

I found myself involved in an experience in ecumenicity far beyond that of a typical North American Mennonite congregation. And it put me in contact with various pieties, practices, and theologies as they had been appropriated and were at the time en route. An alcoholic woodsman rubbed elbows with the right-hand man of the government's minister of French cultural affairs. A half-blind Pentecostal widow rubbed elbows with the niece of the president of the new European Common Market. A Swiss professor of New Testament rubbed elbows with a Flemish factory worker, who later dropped out because of the shifting social-class reality within the congregation. And of course, the congregation's piety was influenced considerably by that varied population.

What held the group together was a biblical theology reflecting the fourfold "Anabaptist" thrust described earlier. Yet any open Anabaptist or Mennonite references were exceptional, for we were perceived locally to be the local Protestant church. My own preoccupation no longer turned around being the true church of Christ, but rather around truly being the church of Christ in this place.

We organized the congregation into groups who led worship. Students from the theological faculty started attending our congregation to learn about church renewal, and I was invited for a year to be their chaplain. Along with our French Mennonite affiliation, we ultimately asked for an associate relationship with the Belgian Reformed

[12] Intended as descriptive, not partisan.

Church. This was an ecclesiastical novelty, created for the first time. The French Reformed Church's latest liturgy provided for an optional service of presentation of a newborn, on the one hand, and a service of baptism on confession of faith, on the other hand. It was an Anabaptist/ Reformed congregation, and I was invited to both participate in the Reformed synod and be a consultant for its biweekly publication, *Paix et Liberté.* I was also invited to hold series of renewal meetings for Reformed consistories, as at Brussels-Belliard, Mons, La Louvière, and Charleroi. It was an exceptional part of their program. During this time I was inspired by the emerging writings of Jürgen Moltmann.

Despite all the renewal, I felt like I was getting involved in churchianity all over again, though at another level. It was sometime during those years that I came across Jacques Ellul's *False Presence of the Kingdom*, leading me to one of his earlier works, *Presence of the Kingdom,* and ultimately to a shelf of some fifty of his substantial publications dealing with Christ, the church, and the world. These writings were pivotal in my formation and kept me going more or less on what seemed to be the right track.

Amid the influences of the World Council of Churches, the transformations of Vatican II, and the Protestant/Catholic cooperative French translation of the New Testament, our congregation at Rixensart initiated Protestant/Catholic Bible studies. The local Catholic priest and two Benedictine Sisters from the local convent participated. During the annual Catholic time of "prayer for unity" I was invited to preach in the neighboring Catholic parish of Limal. Rixensart's second priest invited me to lead a weekend of spiritual renewal for some fifty parish youth leaders. I asked him if he had a sense of how many of them were believers. He reported knowing of one young woman who believed in the resurrection, and a second—a friend of hers—who "maybe/probably believed."

By 1971, I was thinking seriously about handing the leadership of the Rixensart congregation over to a Belgian pastor, so we could be released for mission among students at the newly established French-language university of Louvain-la-Neuve, only eight kilometers from Genval, where we were living. Wilma and I talked in jest about the possibility of putting up student housing on Rixensart church property. It was a period of transition both for us and for the congregation. Later when an emerging ministry assignment in West Africa seemed likely, Wilma and I took a course in social anthropology at the University of Brussels.

When we left Belgium in 1973, a Reformed pastor claiming to be sympathetic to our approach to ministry assumed the pastorate but did not pursue any Mennonite connections or Anabaptist accents. Rather, he guided the congregation into the Belgian Reformed Church, eventually joining the union. The congregation is today *the* Protestant Church of Rixensart, with "Temple Protestant" on the façade of the meeting place we had built. Willy and Annie Hubinont, a couple from the congregation, inspired by Mennonite ways and wishing to work at the Anabaptist-Mennonite contribution to the Belgian Protestant ethos, later initiated a Mennonite Center in Brussels. There a team ministered long after our departure. Team members included our son Stephen and his wife Jean, who were active in the center for a dozen years.

European Mennonite Bible School and the French Mennonites

For three years during the early stages of our time in Belgium, I taught three- to four-week classes annually in the French section of the European Mennonite Bible School at Basel and later at Bienenberg, Liestal, Switzerland. John Howard Yoder, working with the French Mennonites in postwar MCC ministries, was a teaching colleague for those sessions.

The assignment took me away from the Belgian work temporarily, but was an excellent orientation to parts of the French, Swiss, and German Mennonite youth and resulted later in leading French youth camps and holding Bible Weeks in Mennonite congregations, such as at Pfastatt, Mulhouse, Montbéliard, and Boucq. It further led to a cooperative publication with John Howard Yoder and Pierre Widmer, since there was virtually no Mennonite literature in Belgium at the time.[13] Later I met regularly with the elders of the French Mennonite Church, and they agreed to expand their official name to include Belgian *assemblées* (congregations). Two of our churches in Belgium affiliated officially with them, but distance always remained a problem.

Algeria

I became involved in Algeria when John Howard Yoder invited me to do three study visits with him and others to explore ministry possibilities in that late-colonial situation merging into the Algerian war of liberation. Yoder had earlier worked with Pastor André Trocmé of the French Fellowship of Reconciliation to initiate overseas service oppor-

---

[13] Pierre Widmer and John H. Yoder, *Principes et Doctrines Mennonites* (Montbéliard and Brussels: Publications Mennonites, 1959).

tunities for conscientious objectors from countries that did not legally recognize them, including Switzerland, Germany, France, Belgium, and Spain. This led to the creation of Eirene[14] and an MCC Pax service unit for post-earthquake reconstruction in Algeria.[15] Many Americans in Pax service studied French in Belgium as preparation for their assignments in North Africa.

The Algerian consultations introduced me to a broader world beyond Europe—to French colonialism, Muslim poverty, Christian mission by French Pietists and American Methodists in Islamic contexts, and to the Protestant presence among the resident French population in North Africa. Two youth from our Brussels and Rixensart congregations eventually served for a year or more in Algeria.

Mauro Sbolgi and the Social Service for Foreigners

In 1956, the director of the Belgian Gospel Mission's Bible Institute called and asked me to assume some responsibility for a "very troublesome Italian Mennonite student." I interviewed the youthful, ex-communist, Florentine Mauro Sbolgi, and decided to encourage his approach to the Italians in the Belgian mines and mining camps. Sbolgi had been sent to Belgium with support from an American Mennonite industrialist, Lewis Martin, who met him during a visit to Dr. Luciano Monti's radio ministry in Florence.

Sbolgi's work was formed into the Social Service for Foreigners (SSE) and eventually led to the gathering of a temporary Italian congregation at Chapelle-lez-Herlaimont and two Spanish congregations in Brussels for which I assumed oversight. Spanish prospective deaconess Sister Gabrielle Fernande, Baptist pastor Daniel Campderros, and Puerto Rican Mennonite pastor Samuel Rolon all worked for a time with this emerging reality. It led ultimately to the ordination of two young men as pastors—José-Luis Suarez, who married Gabrielle, and José Gallardo—both of whom are currently carrying on ministries in different congregations in Spain. Many of the Spanish children living in Belgium were "Belgicized" through the schools and melted into Belgian congregations. Partly in response to this phenomenon, a third Spanish preacher was ordained for the congregation at Brussels-East.

---

[14] Eirene is a European service agency initiated by André Trocmé and others, together with the historic peace churches, to provide service outlets for conscientious objectors to military service from countries where such objection was not then legally recognized.

[15] The whole Algeria story is well told by Marian E. Hostetler in *Algeria: Where Mennonites and Muslims Met, 1955–1978* (Elkhart, IN: Marian Hostetler Edition, 2003).

The SSE expanded with our support—for a time under the sponsorship of the Federation of Protestant Churches through Reformed Pastor Pierre Regard—and in 2000 was carrying on a major autonomous program with a staff of more than a dozen persons and a budget of $1.5 million.

Congo missions, Congolese, and Kimbanguists

Belgium was a colonial power, and we related to Mennonite missionaries from two different North American Mennonite mission boards as workers were going and coming to and from the Belgian Congo.

These workers came to Belgium to study French, to take courses in the Belgian colonial school, and if they were medical personnel, to study at the colonial medical school in Antwerp. Here was interaction that we had not foreseen, but that would have significant implications, especially after 1960, with Congolese independence and the increased presence of Congolese people in Belgium and in our congregations.

The Lambottes were invited, as Belgian Mennonites, to visit the (Mennonite) Congo Inland Mission; this had a definite influence on Jules's future publishing efforts. In the Congo Pavilion at the Brussels World's Fair in 1958, a Mennonite choir from the Congo Inland Mission filled an important role and gave a public concert at our own center at Ohain. Two Congolese leaders from Mennonite missions in the Congo were students in Belgium. Our Rixensart congregation had three Baptist Congolese students and an Anglican Rwandan wife and mother from an ex-colonial Belgian family. We received two Mefalessi sisters in our home during school holidays. Ex-colonials, with their many stories, were members of our Bourgeois congregation.

Ursmer Lefebvre's contacts at the theological faculty led to relationships with theology students Jean Bokaleale and Bernard Ntontolo, both of whom I would later meet as leaders in the Protestant Church of Zaire following its unification under Bokaleale's lengthy term as head bishop. At the Zaventem airport we met Mennonite missionaries who had just fled the dangerous territories in light planes shot at by the rebels. We had socialist literature describing the illegitimate parallel sociopolitical structures in the colony, and our missionaries could not believe that there were names of some of their own schoolteachers in those clandestine structures. Ex-colonial military chaplain M. Vandezande and his wife found lodging in our center for a month while seeking to get resettled in the mother country. All this interaction provided us with exposure to issues of missions and colony, missions and power, and Western missions and Africanity.

But most important of all there was the telephone call in 1966 from Jean Van Lierde of the Mouvement de Réconciliation, putting us in touch with two Kimbanguist leaders returning via Brussels from Copenhagen where they had attended the world gathering of pacifists. These leaders, too, claimed to be pacifist, but as part of a "sect" they were not received by Belgian Protestant pastors whom Van Lierde had contacted. We had them in our home for dinner, heard their story—which I immediately likened to that of the sixteenth-century Anabaptists—and wished them well.

It was my first contact with the phenomenon of African-initiated churches (AICs), though I had had some exposure to Bishop Ed and Irene Weaver's experiences in Uyo, Nigeria.[16] As a result of this encounter, MCC placed Pax workers and Eirene teachers in schools and on an experimental farm owned and operated by Kimbanguists. As a further result, I was invited in 1971 by the Head of the Church, Kuntima Diangienda, to the fiftieth anniversary of the founding of The Church of Jesus Christ on the Earth by the Prophet Simon Kimbangu.[17] At the holy city of Nkamba, some 400,000 Kimbanguists were present for the celebration, but most missionary colleagues and agencies in Kinshasa had no idea that it was going on, a fact that illustrates the distance between Western mission-founded and African-initiated churches. I was deeply impressed with what I saw and heard, and it opened up for me a whole new dimension of mission.[18] In addition to this important encounter with the Kimbangust Church reality, this trip also afforded me the opportunity to visit a few of our Belgian Volunteers for the Third World.

Professor of Protestant religion

With a growing congregation at Bourgeois-Rixensart, the director of the socialist-initiated, pre-university Athénée Royal de Rixensart asked me—in the name of the inspector of religious instruction of the Union of Protestant Churches—if I would assume the role of professor of Protestant religion for the Protestant children attending the school. I accepted and thus began earning a government salary, teaching Bible and church history to my own children and others, and learning to know

---

[16] See Edwin and Irene Weaver, *The Uyo Story* (Elkhart, IN: Mennonite Board of Missions, 1970).

[17] Simon Kimbangu was Kuntima Diangienda's father.

[18] I reported some of my observations in "An Indigenous Church Comes of Age: Kimbanguism," *Mennonite Life* 27, no. 2 (June 1972): 53–55.

various scattered Protestant families who were not related to our local congregation.

The school was *marxisant* (promoting Marxist thought) and anti-Catholic in a still dominantly Catholic region. Here were largely secular professional contacts and opportunities for witness, and I created the school's first Parents of Pupils Association. Through these educational connections, I was also invited during a two-year period to teach in a preparatory school for teachers of Protestant religion in the elementary schools of the country.

But this assignment also offered adequate proof that a Belgian pastor—should one hear and accept the call—could eventually replace me and earn a living teaching religion, serving as a self-supporting leader of the Rixensart congregation with its Sunday attendance of about seventy-five individuals.

The Belgian Mennonite Council

In the late 1960s, I called together about every three months a Belgian Mennonite Council with the hopes of moving our various ministry efforts—ethnicities, cultures, theologies, interpretations, languages, mentalities—toward a common vision. The members of the council included me, an American Mennonite; the Flemish Evangelical Jules Lambotte, somewhat isolated geographically at Flavion; the American Mennonite Robert Otto, working with the East Brussels congregation and a Protestant foyer for African students; the Walloon Ursmer Lefebvre, from the Belgian Gospel Mission, representing Home of Hope, the theological faculty, and the Bourgeois-Rixensart congregation; the Italian Mauro Sbolgi, baptized in Dr. Monti's bathtub, now with a service ministry to foreigners and spin-off Bible fellowships over much of the country; the Spanish ex–Dominican novice José Gallardo, converted through translating my French sermons into Spanish at Ixelles-Brussels; and the Carpathian pastor Vasil Magal, with his radio ministry behind the iron curtain and his autonomous Baptist, Slavic congregations in Brussels, La Louvière, Charleroi, and Liège. We shared plans and projects, counseled one another, and discussed our budgets. And we tried to connect our work to other European grassroots Anabaptist/Mennonite ministries, in London, Paris, and elsewhere. But no permanent Belgian fellowship of congregations developed out of these efforts during our time in Belgium. And I consider it to be one of my important failures.

Diverse activities in Belgium

When Mademoiselle Vandenitte, a retired social worker from the Belgian Christian Missionary Church, made an appeal to all Brussels's Protestant churches to create a Protestant Social Center in Brussels, I responded and became a founding board member of what was to develop into an amazing interchurch instrument of service to the public. For a while, we Mennonites rented a house in Ixelles that provided Sunday worship space for Italians in the morning, Spaniards in the afternoon, and a Slavic group in the evening. On the second floor of the building we lodged the Protestant Social Center and its offices, and on the third floor, Sbolgi had his Social Services for Foreigners offices, while retaining modest living quarters for himself on the fourth.

After Belgian law began to recognize conscientious objection to war and military service, I helped to create and presided over the Association of Protestant Volunteers for the Third World, which effectively sent many volunteers into African missionary contexts, before universal conscription was abandoned by the Belgian government. Five youth from our Bourgeois-Rixensart congregation served in such alternative service.

For a year or more, we sponsored a people's clinic in the working-class area outside Liège and held midweek home meetings, with the hope of beginning a congregation. It never materialized, however, just as other such efforts at La Hulpe, Limal, Braine-le-Comte and (Flemish) Ruysbroek never developed into anything permanent.

Our mission board supervisors from 1950–73 were three: J. D. Graber, ex-missionary to India, followed by theologian John Howard Yoder, who was then replaced by missiologist Wilbert R. Shenk. It was Shenk in particular who urged me to record and submit my findings from our European ministry for the *Mission Focus* journal he edited. Each of these administrators contributed particular gifts to our pilgrimage, and we were deeply enriched by their questions, guidance, and relationship with us.

North American assignments

For our first furlough, in 1955, we settled in Blooming Glen, Pennsylvania, so I could attend Eastern Baptist Seminary in Philadelphia, as recommended by H. S. Bender. I was particularly enriched by courses with Professors Edward R. Dalglish (Old Testament), Norman H. Maring (church), and Cuthbert Rutenber (Kierkegaard). I had hoped to eventually complete an MA in theology, but the work in Belgium was too demanding. In 1968, without a thesis, Eastern granted me an MDiv degree.

During our 1968 furlough, my main occupation was to study in the doctoral program at the University of Notre Dame. There, I was particularly enriched through work with professors John L. McKenzie (Prophets), John Dunne (faith and doubt), John H. Yoder (free church history) and Josephine Ford (Revelation). All this study eventually proved to be useful background for my later research work on the Prophet Harris.

In addition, John Dunne impressed me with the significance of the changing *myth*—answering the question of what it means to live—of the *successive*, rather than *progressive* cultural times between antiquity and the modern myth of self-fulfillment. People, according to Dunne, either *believe* the myth, *see through* the myth, or *see beyond* the myth to the next one, or as I prefer to put it, to the coming kingdom of God Jesus incarnated and preached, while anticipating the church as a sign of it.

This study was important for me in understanding and dealing with the West's more-than-millennial paradigm shift from "duty" to "desire," underway since the Depression and World War II, which was creating a wholly new Western hermeneutic. Unrecognized by Christian scholars among the baby boomer generation, the Christ event was being submitted to that new hermeneutical canon—How does Christ help me fulfill myself?—rather than being the canon for critique of the cultural ethos with its moral and ethical shifts. We were later to become most aware of these dynamics through going back and forth between Africa, Brussels, and North America.

Further at Notre Dame, John Howard Yoder helped me understand how the sixteenth-century breakup of Christendom led to a Reformation quadrilateral, consisting of Tridentine Christendom, spiritualism, theocracy, and free church (Anabaptism and others). According to Yoder, "free church" renewal, grounded in apostolic faith and new covenant discipleship and fellowship, just keeps happening within history, over and over again, and constitutes another kind of apostolic succession.

At Goshen College during that year, I gave the campus spiritual life lectures focusing on culture shifts, later to be published in book form as *Who Will Answer?*[19] The tragic assassinations of Robert Kennedy and Martin Luther King cast long shadows over that year, though our perceptions of these and other events may have been somewhat differ-

[19] David A. Shank, *Who Will Answer?* (Scottdale, PA: Herald Press, 1969).

ent since we had for almost two decades been conditioned to view the whole Black freedom movement through European eyes.

Back in Belgium in 1971, I experienced a time of spiritual renewal and refocusing through the ministry of Nelson Litwiller, longtime missionary to Latin America, retired, who was passing through Brussels. I was subsequently invited back to the States by Wilbert Shenk to give a series of mission forums on the Holy Spirit and mission, later published with a response by Shenk, under the title *His Spirit First*.[20]

In 1973, Shenk invited Wilma and me to accompany Dr. Marlin Miller across the West African coast to explore whether we would be open to a ministry among African-initiated churches, as Bishop Ed and Irene Weaver had done in Uyo, Nigeria, and Accra, Ghana. Weavers' program was one of reading and studying the scriptures with emerging leaders of African-initiated churches (AICs), and relating them to the resources of the "old" stream of mission-planted realities.

Following Weavers' trail with Miller across French West Africa,[21] we received two direct and poignant calls. The first was from a dozen leaders of diverse AICs in Cotonou, Dahomey, to create a Bible-training program for their ministers. The second was at Petit Bassam, near Abidjan, from Spiritual Head John Ahui of the Harrist Church in Côte d'Ivoire to "help me water the tree" for which he had been responsible ever since the Prophet Harris gave him that charge in 1928. Harrist Head Preacher Cyril Abueya of Abobo-té had at an earlier formal dinner explained that "God is white [in West Africa, the color of 'spirit'] and you are white, so you are the older brother, and you have received from our Father the patrimony to share with your younger brothers. Not to do so would be a betrayal of our Father."

A prominent Ivorian Methodist consultant, of Harrist parents and a member of the all-powerful Bureau Politique of President Félix Houphouët-Boigny's one-party regime, told us that this Harrist opening to us was not only unique but scarcely believable, and urged us to follow through. Without some kind of internal renewal, he assured us, the largely coastal Harrists—as simple monotheists—would surely in time be swallowed up by integration into Islam, increasingly descend-

[20] David A. Shank, *His Spirit First* (Scottdale, PA: Herald Press, 1971).

[21] The Weaver and Miller earlier contacts with the Harrist Church led, at the Harrists' request, to the translation by Mennonite Marie-Noëlle Faure of Gordon Haliburton's important historical volume, *The Prophet Harris* (New York and London: Oxford University Press, 1973); abridged edition. The French version of Haliburton's text appeared under the title *Le Prophète Harris* (Abidjan: Les Nouvelles Éditions Africaines, 1984).

ing from the north. We were in transition, but at neither West African location was the local context ready for our presence. We would not in fact arrive in Abidjan until April of 1979.

A good summary of my faith understandings at fifty, when we left Belgium after nearly a quarter of a century of service, would have been much as follows: The One Spirit Creator of all things—by the covenant of grace and peace fulfilled through the life and teachings of Israel's Messiah and his cross, resurrection/ascension, and reign—is reconciling alienated humans to their unique Source, to different others, and to creation, as disciples of Jesus with a new, shared, renewing Holy Spirit empowering them for living out such reconciliation in hope and love in new messianic faith communities as signs of God's reign and the coming reconciliation of all things.

Within the catholicity of the static Apostles' Creed, this statement implicitly recognizes all kinds of diversity in the expression "alienated," in the reconciling work, and in the shaping of the accented new messianic communities. But it also accents the life and teachings of Israel's Messiah, disciples of Jesus, and the kingdom both now and coming, along with ongoing fulfillment and Spirit empowerment, in a way the Apostles' Creed does not. Whether or not it was biblical or apostolic or Anabaptist or Mennonite or holistic or charismatic or ecumenical or catholic, or whatever other nomenclature one might apply, it had become my understanding of mission, reflected in my upcoming teaching ministry and the context of my further preparation for ministry among AICs. But I could in no way perceive it to be sectarian, even if I found myself on the margins. I simply worked on the assumption that this was the Christian mainstream.

Mission II: Interim in the United States and in Aberdeen, Scotland, 1973–79

While our youngest daughter was finishing secondary school and college, I was invited by Dean John A. Lapp at Goshen (Indiana) College to teach as assistant professor in the Bible, religion, and philosophy department. There I taught the standard junior-senior course on Christian faith, one required of two options, and a last chance to have students take a long, serious look at Christ, faith, and the church. I focused on the covenanting God of grace and the fulfillment of divine purpose through the Messiah Jesus, a diamond for faith. I used John Howard

Yoder's just released *Politics of Jesus*[22] as a text for new covenant ethics, and taught the dynamics of messianism as discerned largely by former Dominican Henri Desroche, who had become the esteemed dean of French sociologists of religion. I was able to work at two other courses relevant to our future work in Africa: New African religious movements, inspired largely by anthropologist Gottfried Oosterwal's recent *Modern Messianic Movements as a Theological Challenge*,[23] and New Testament charismatic issues, because the Holy Spirit was then also culturally "in" within American Christianity. Ten students, having learned of my interest in Jacques Ellul, asked for a course in his thought, which I co-taught with professor of physics Robert Buschert.

During that first year, I was also asked to be the speaker on The Mennonite Hour, a weekly broadcast that included a fifteen-minute message. I found the preparation of these messages one of the hardest assignments I had ever done—a month ahead of time, for an unknown context and an invisible audience, with eventual response arriving a month or more afterward.

In the second year, President J. Lawrence Burkholder asked me to consider serving as campus minister, in addition to my teaching assignments. I presided over a new Campus Ministries Team, including several students. The team guided a several-year experiment of campus worship into an experimental congregation called The Assembly that was being initiated by a few of us in an intercongregational small group that wanted to work at a more nearly authentic twentieth-century "Anabaptist" gathering.

Here there was personal recovenanting, every member's participation in both the assembly and in small-group interaction, congregational continuity and more stable eldership than students could provide in their own planned worship during nine months of academia. I was named "Keeper of the Vision," and though asked to stay on as Goshen's campus minister, I was committed (as was Wilma) to the openings in Africa represented by those earlier calls.

We visited many Mennonite congregations during this period, explaining the phenomena of African-initiated churches and the call by AICs for the ministry of Westerners, just at a time when many missionaries were going home at the insistence of the West's denominational churches which its missions had planted in Africa. The Mennonite

---

[22] John H. Yoder, *The Politics of Jesus* (Grand Rapids, MI: Eerdmans, 1972).

[23] Gottfried Oosterwal, *Modern Messianic Movements as a Theological Challenge* (Elkhart, IN: Institute of Mennonite Studies, 1973).

Board of Missions—and we!—wanted Mennonite supporting congregations to understand what we would be doing, modeled after the innovative work in Uyo, Nigeria, and Accra, Ghana, carried on by Ed and Irene Weaver since the late 1950s. Our best outcome, as we then imagined and explained it, would probably be much like that of Priscilla and Aquila at Ephesus in apostolic times. These two workers simply invited Apollos to their home and explained "the Way of God more adequately." We, of course, never forgot the challenging reality of the Pauline church in Corinth.

So we left in late summer of 1976, this time without our four children, to begin a graduate study program at the University of Aberdeen in northern Scotland. It was in Aberdeen that Professor Andrew Walls had established his Institute for the Study of Christianity in the Non-Western World; it was there that Dr. Harold W. Turner had set up his New Religious Movements (NERMS) research and documentation program, with scholar-assistant Dr. Jocelyn Murray; there, that Dr. Adrian Hastings was working on the Oxford Press "History of Christianity in Africa"; and there that we thought we could maximize our chances for relationships and exchanges with English-speaking doctoral students from all over the African continent.

Another source of enrichment during our time in Aberdeen would be the fellowship of a small group to which we were invited by Dr. Murray. In addition to Murray, the group's members included Paul Ellingworth of the British Bible Society, former missionary with the evolved 1924 Methodist spin-off of Harrism in the Ivory Coast; I. Howard Marshall, professor of New Testament; and Ruth Edwards, Greek professor and Anglican deaconess, and her husband Patrick. In these rich, stretching exchanges, they always took an interest in our exceptional Mennonite participation.

At the university we were oriented to the centuries of Christian mission: to the Europe of traditional "primal" religions, to sub-Saharan and traditional Africanity and its religions, to missionary origins and interactions with that traditional life, to colonial and postcolonial religious movements in Africa, and to the phenomenon of African-initiated churches with all their amazing diversity. We learned the dynamics of primal religion, within the Hebrew/Christian scriptures and beyond, and came to recognize and appreciate the work of God in it. Independently of Western missions and missionaries, sub-Saharan Africa knows—despite its many ethnic names and intermediaries—the reality of one Creator God and his law, the priority of the spiritual over the material, the necessity of sacrifice and mediation, and the experience of covenant.

Since we were planning to accept the invitation from John Ahui, the head of the Harrist Church in Ivory Coast, I began an in-depth study of the Prophet Harris himself, and discovered texts and manuscripts from his times that opened up new perspectives and appreciation for his self-understanding. I completed a three-volume doctoral thesis[24] documenting and reflecting on these understandings, their roots, their expressions, and their interrelationships. Dr. Murray eventually assisted me in publishing an abridged version of the thesis, *Prophet Harris, the "Black Elijah" of West Africa*[25]—a publication Dr. Andrew Walls has generously referred to as "a landmark volume."

The Harrist Church was the result of a messianic movement, rightly so-called, which led me to further study the phenomenon of messianism itself, nearly universally dependent on the Judeo-Christian scriptures. Henri Desroche's dictionary[26] with its massive research helped me see to what extent the messianic dynamics involve essentially four directions of movement inherent in Christianity of whatever name, age, size, place, or history. These four directions really constitute a much larger, universal context and typology than that of Yoder's Reformation quadrilateral which, nevertheless, illustrates the same phenomenon perfectly.

Indeed, Yoder's *Politics of Jesus* had for the title of its first chapter "The Possibility of a Messianic Ethic." The growth of two-thirds world messianic movements ultimately led in Vatican II to the insertion twice of *populus messianicus*—a novel, latinized creation out of the Hebrew—in *Lumen Gentium*, no. 9. The French Catholic theologian Yves Congar also tried to get it inserted into *Gaudium et Spes* and in no. 5 of *Ad Gentes divinitus*, but it was erased during editing. In 1975, Congar came out with *Un Peuple Messianique*,[27] followed in 1977 by theologian Jürgen

---

[24] "A Prophet of Modern Times: The Thought of William Wadé Harris, the West African Precursor of the Reign of Christ" (PhD diss., Aberdeen University, 1982), 3 vols.

[25] David A. Shank, *Prophet Harris, the "Black Elijah" of West Africa*, abridged by Jocelyn Murray (Leiden: E. J. Brill, 1994).

[26] Henri Desroche, *Dieux d'Hommes: Dictionnaire des Messianismes et Millénarismes de l'Ère Chrétienne* (Paris: Éditions Mouton, 1969). See also his *Sociologie de l'Espérance* (Paris: Calmann-Lévy, 1973).

[27] Yves Congar, *Un people messianique* (Paris: Éditions du Cerf, 1975).

Moltmann's volume on ecclesiology as "a contribution to a messianic ecclesiology."[28]

Within the larger revelation to the Hebrews of the unique, compassionate God of covenanting grace, and its fulfillment begun already with the servanthood of shalom in the Messiah Jesus and his Spirit-led people, I came to understand that my own Mennonite/Anabaptist story was really one of a type of messianic resurgences. There were many others similar to it before the sixteenth century, and the Kimbanguists, Harrists, and some other AICs in Africa were similar to it in non-Western contexts four centuries later. Messianic movements are constantly pressured by worldly realities into either spiritualist religion or theocratic politics, or into a return with time to a religiopolitical affirmation of worldly power, success, and dominance, as in Christendom—which Vatican II finally renounced as a way forward.

I had personally experienced the call and the various pulls from the variety of traditions in my experiences with the Bourgeois-Rixensart congregation, but I had no way to describe it. Now I better understood what I had been doing all along, and had a tool for better understanding Christian phenomena in whatever time or place.

The messianic challenge and pull of the Holy Spirit is, for those who name the name of Christ, to continue in Christ's messianic way, despite the pressures of the world. In the organized ecumenical movements, all the churches are seen to be confessing Jesus Christ as Lord. In the messianic perspective they are also all within the same messianic circle. But, in contrast to typical ecumenical understandings, within that circle all are not necessarily going—or even seeking to go—in the same messianic direction, "the Way" of peaceful servanthood as fulfilled by Messiah, at the price of the cross and with the promise of resurrection. Hence, within the *missio Dei*, resurgences out of the worldly status quo, the spiritualist or the theocratic impulses and tendencies continue to happen, because Jesus' gospel of the kingdom in its fullness clearly addresses those three deviations. These appear to be constants, as they too renew themselves within history.

I shared these insights with Mennonite missiologist Wilbert Shenk, who was committed to working on a messianic missiology. An entire volume on this matter appeared much later as a collaborative effort in

---

[28] Jürgen Moltmann, *The Church in the Power of the Spirit: A Contribution to Messianic Ecclesiology* (New York: Harper, 1977).

a work Shenk edited, *The Transfiguration of Mission*, to which I contributed two chapters.[29]

Between 1973 and 1979, Wilma and I made two more trips to West Africa, following through on earlier contacts and carrying on research related to Prophet Harris's story and work in Sierra Leone, Liberia, Côte d'Ivoire, and Ghana (Gold Coast). Our calls were confirmed by these visits, but time was not of the essence, which allowed for the preparatory study reported above.

Mission III: French West Africa (1979–89)

Côte d'Ivoire

When we left in my fifty-fifth year for Abidjan, Côte d'Ivoire, in April 1979, we hoped for a last decade before official retirement from ministry under Mennonite Board of Missions. I spoke fairly good French in a country where French was the official language, among some eighty others, and where the younger generations were most typically school trained and literate in the French language. I thought I had a pretty good sense for what God was doing—and wanted to do—for humanity and creation, by reconciling all things through the good news of peace and righteousness by means of Israel's Messiah and his cross, the whole Christ event. I still had a lot to learn, however, about how that all happens.

I had been given abundant experiences with the gift of the word to teach, to preach, to lecture, and to engage in dialogue. I had learned in Belgium to work with and relate to a wide diversity of faith understandings and ecclesial patterns, while seeking to enable the messianic dynamic of my own tradition and experience and just letting whatever seemed irrelevant fall by the way. I had become ecumenical with a messianic free-church stance. I had become catholic through the apostolicity of new covenant scriptures. I had functioned much like an overseer without any episcopal title and without thinking about it in those terms.

In Côte d'Ivoire, we and our younger American colleagues, James and Jeanette Krabill, along with a couple of French Mennonites working in French Evangelical missions, were the only Mennonites in the

---

[29] See Wilbert R. Shenk, ed., *The Transfiguration of Mission: Biblical, Theological and Historical Foundations* (Scottdale, PA: Herald Press, 1993). My chapters were "Jesus the Messiah: Messianic Foundation of Mission," 37–82; and "Consummation of Messiah's Mission," 220–41. They are reprinted as chapters 5 and 6 in the present volume.

country. With the great variety of foreign missions and African-initiated churches, we had no intention of making publicity about Mennonites or creating an Ivorian Mennonite church! In contrast to our original assignment in Belgium nearly thirty years earlier, we were now committed to *not* create a Mennonite denomination.

But we did not seek to hide our identity. When asked, we explained that we were Mennonite Christians, but freed by our American churches to learn about developing African Christian life and understandings and to be available to share and further enable African churches in their various itineraries.

We were *disponibles* ("available") through conversation; dialogue; hospitality; pastoral ministry; or teaching Bible, Christian history or theology as requested by anyone interested. We called ourselves the Group for Religious and Biblical Studies, implying that we were learning as well as teaching. We were open to acknowledging God's work amid those who did not share our understandings. At the same time, our special concern was to respond to the best of our abilities to the call of the Harrist Church, and eventually that of the dozen AIC leaders at Cotonou. Our hope was that we would find ourselves over and over again, in different places, as a part of a circle of Harrist preachers or other AIC leaders simply reading and studying the Bible together.

From orientation studies in Paris, the Krabills preceded our arrival in Abidjan by some six months and were temporarily studying at the Catholic Institute of West Africa. We established ourselves with them in the Ebrié village of Blokosso-Abidjan, a popular quarter of the city surrounded in every direction by urban sprawl. We lived together on the second floor (*première étage*) of the residence of village schoolmaster Félix Diagou and his family, near the entrance to the village down by the lagoon.

We had to go through the family courtyard to get to the steps leading up to our lodging. Because of the wall cutting it off from the luxurious, Parisian-style Hotel Ivoire property just ten minutes' walk away, the naturally expanding village could only grow by adding floors. We were eventually to move up to the third floor, more open to the breezes from the lagoon and farther away from insects, open sewers, animal droppings, and the natural latrine in the brush on a knoll between Blokosso and the neighboring village of Petit Cocody. We made full use of the flat roof at the top of our building for hanging out laundry and seeking protection from the sun under an *apatam*, a thatched-roof shelter built by the Krabills, where we could casually receive visitors and guests in an outside atmosphere, just as they did for us, in their court-yards.

Blokosso, with its population of some 2500 villagers, was one of several traditional Ebrié villages around which the larger metropolitan area of Abidjan had grown. Yet with modernization happening at a diz-zying pace, the Ebrié people tried hard to retain their traditional social structures and customs—chief, elders, age classes, and celebrations. Ebrié villages were nevertheless perceived to be "Christian" villages since the meteoric passing of the Prophet Harris in 1914. Members of traditional village families all attended one of three available churches, Harrist, Methodist, or Roman Catholic. The foreigners, mostly Mus-lims from the north, also had their prayer grounds. We and the Krabills were one of only three white (*toubabou*) family units in the village. We lived there near the entrance to Blokosso because we wanted to be able to observe and eventually participate in Harrist life, practice, and wor-ship at its grass roots.

As participant-observers for ten years in Blokosso, we were ex-posed to most of the realities of this village, caught between traditional life, Christianity of various kinds, more of Islam, and the rapid speed of modernization *à la française.* The latter had been happening ever since the inception of the colony just before the turn of the twentieth centu-ry. Political independence happened *from* France, but also *with* France, beginning in 1960 and carrying on throughout the 1970s and '80s. Abi-djan itself was a French-looking modern metropolis, "the pearl of West Africa," largely dependent on its *pétrole vert* of coffee, cocoa, rubber, pineapple, and the logging industry.

For almost three years, we and the Krabills shared space and daily noon and evening meals, until at the request of Head Preacher N'Guessan Légré Benoît of the Dida Harrists, the Krabills moved to the interior Dida village of Yocoboué to establish a Bible study program for the church's preachers and youth. In Blokosso, we set up a Docu-mentation and Research Center related to African religious phenom-ena, change, and history, and opened it up to any interested visitors. Wilma managed the center, and word got around that we had valuable resources. So, visitors we had, including many Harrists, interested par-ticularly in the documentation and resources that I had collected about their prophet.

From the beginning of our arrival, Harrist Church Spiritual Head Ahui welcomed us, blessing and supporting the biblical work of the Krabills among the Dida. However, among the older, largely illiterate

Ebriés in charge of the Harrist National Committee, some leaders were not in agreement with Ahui's openness. But the newly literate youth in the Union of Harrist Youth *were* open, thus putting us in the middle of a built-in generational conflict.

With time the conflict became more than generational. Within the larger Harrist community, two parallel interpretations of the Prophet Harris had been operating simultaneously. The first was consigned in the Harrists' first published catechism in 1956. That oral tradition, which we heard many times, proclaimed that God loves all the peoples of the earth. When a people in distress cry out to God, he responds by sending them a prophet: Moses for the Jews, Jesus Christ for the whites, Mohammed for the Arabs, William W. Harris for the Blacks. God sent the Prophet Harris to deliver Black Africans from their idols and fetishes, and to teach them to live in peace with one another.

The second tradition in circulation went something like the following: God loves all the peoples of the world. When they cried out in their distress, God sent his Son, Jesus Christ, to deliver them. But the whites killed him before he could ever get to Africa. Yet God did not give up on Africa. He sent the Prophet Harris to tell people about Christ and to do Christ's work among Africans. Harris delivered us from our fetishes and idols, taught us God's law, and made peace between our different tribes.

The Krabills learned that the Dida people largely followed the second tradition, hence their eagerness for biblical instruction. On the other hand, the Ebrié and Attié peoples, to whom we Shanks most closely related, followed the first tradition. Harris was thus "their" prophet; and Christ was "the white man's" prophet. When Raoul Aby, president of the Attié Harrists, invited us to his home for a Christmas dinner, it was in honor of *our* holiday and *our* celebration of *our* prophet Jesus Christ—a holiday that Raoul and his Harrist friends would not ordinarily have celebrated. Yet the published Ebrié hymnbook for the different *koya* ("choirs") had songs for the celebration of Christmas, despite the contradictory tradition of the Ebrié *vieux* ("elders"). And the sign in front of the Ebrié Harrist village churches in Abobo-Doumé and Abobo-Té read "Christ Church"—an expression used by Harris himself during his preaching ministry. It was this ambivalence in the Abidjan region that made our ministry problematic, despite the invitation of Ahui.

While the Krabills were able to carry out a program of biblical teaching largely for youthful future preachers among the Dida people, our mission in Ebrié and Attié territory became primarily one of sharing what we had learned from our research about the Prophet Harris and his thought. It was to become a ministry of the gospel through the work and understandings of the Prophet Harris himself—*their* prophet.

Who was the Prophet Harris? In Liberia, colonized by American Blacks, just west of Côte d'Ivoire, Western multidenominational missionary efforts during an eighty-year period had not created peace between Harris's Glebo people and the Black American colonists who claimed the settlers' right to rule in the area around Cape Palmas. As a Methodist convert, former lay preacher, and later as an Episcopalian catechist, schoolteacher, and master of a boy's boarding school, Harris had spent time in prison in 1910 for having fought for that peace. A vision in prison changed him from a former agent of Western missions—wearing patent-leather shoes and coattails—into an Elijah-like, barefoot African prophet, calling for conversion, the destruction of fetishes, and baptism of all Africans in view of Christ's coming reign of peace with its judgments on idolaters and unbelievers.

Harris saw himself as Spirit inspired and Spirit endowed, a pentecostal before he met any Western Pentecostals.[30] He labored first in Liberia in 1911, then along the coast of Côte d'Ivoire to mid–Gold Coast in 1913–14—with more than 100,000 persons exorcised and baptized—before being forcefully repatriated by the French colony back to Liberia. There he continued to minister and went three times to Sierra Leone, working to establish peace in the hope of that coming peaceful millennial reign of Christ. He openly declared himself to be a prophet of Jesus Christ and his imminent reign. This is an obvious confirmation of the second tradition among the Harrists (noted above), and a highly significant correction of the first. The prophet's intention was a universal, Christ-centered movement involving all the churches and missions under Christ's reign.

During our Ivorian decade, we shared this simple understanding from the documentation—through conversations in Harrist homes and in ours; at meals following our visits to Harrist Churches; to youth congresses; to preachers and other leaders who came to our sun shelter up on the roof; and through Sunday afternoon lectures for whole villages, organized by Harrist leaders under thatch-roofed *apatams* located *beside*, not *in*, the local Harrist church building.

---

[30] I underscore this point particularly in "Le Pentecôtisme du Prophète William Wadé Harris," in *Archives de Sciences Sociales des Religions* 105 (January-March 1999): 51–70.

But more than this, I shared about Harris's Christian faith and ministry through a pamphlet[31] that sold—largely to Harrists—more than 6,000 copies through local Christian bookstores. Because of the demand, it was printed and reprinted again and again. The content of the piece was essentially a résumé of Harris's Christian thought which I wrote at the request of the editor of the French-language missiological journal *Perspectives Missionnaires,* in order to inform and correct understandings of Western missionaries in Côte d'Ivoire, who often perceived Harris to be a charlatan.

But as an off-print, the pamphlet fulfilled the unanticipated function of informing thousands of Harrists in the generations of the newly literate and, as they themselves reported, of freeing Christ-oriented apostles and preachers within the church to expose more boldly Christian accents. It may well be the most efficacious piece I ever wrote, unintentionally contributing—along with other influences, of course—to the possibility of the Harrist movement growing in affirmation of a self-understanding more nearly like that intended by its founder. In 1998, less than ten years after our departure from Côte d'Ivoire, the Harrist church officially affirmed itself to be a Christ-confessing church as it was accepted as a member of the World Council of Churches.

During our own decade of ministry, we visited some forty Harrist congregations in ten different ethnic groups, usually in response to an invitation. But except during our initial contacts, I was never invited to speak *in* a Harrist church, not even among the most open and brotherly Dida. We visited some congregations several times, and a few quite often, where our presence always appeared to please, as in the villages of Petit Cocody, Anono, or Petit Bassam, the mother congregation of Ahui.

We always dressed in white, like the Harrists themselves, to attend their churches. We accepted invitations to festivals where we would be received as honored guests and danced through the village streets behind the singing Honor Girls, as we were shown off to the village. We celebrated events with Harrists, visited occasionally in their homes, invited some of their leaders for meals, all the while aware of resistance to our presence behind the scenes. We observed and listened, asked questions, checked and rechecked answers, listened to stories, heard their understandings of problems, and listened to interpretations of their sermons and their life, generally valuing their experiences. We

---

[31] "Bref résumé de la pensée du prophète William Wadé Harris," which first appeared in *Perspectives Missionnaires* 5 (1983): 34–54.

took copious notes and compared notes from one day to the next, from one place to the next.

What we found was a remarkable autonomous African religious community and institution of somewhere between 100,000 and 200,000 people, expressing many Old Testament understandings and some from the New, depending on the congregation and ethnic group involved. The Harrist movement saw itself involved in a spiritual contest against "fetish," not unlike that of Elijah and the priests of Baal, or the spiritual conflicts that Harris himself had confronted during his ministry. The movement was spontaneously suspicious of any outside intervention or help, yet desirous of relationships in view of being acknowledged, recognized, and validated. It had its own distinctive church architecture, prophet-inspired white dress, structures and ordered hierarchy, patterns of meeting, liturgy, festivals, hymnody with calabash accompaniment, and traditions. This was *their* religion, given to them by God through the Prophet Harris.

In Harold W. Turner's five-dimensional descriptive typology of those African religious movements situated somewhere between traditional African religion(s) and Western Christianity, there were *neotraditional, synthesist*, and *Hebraist* groups, and *independent* and *mission-planted* churches.[32] We found that the Harrists included all of the middle three, with the *Hebraist* type largely dominant and some growing tendencies toward an *independent* Christian church.

The belief system for most Harrists involved accepting one sovereign God, the church building as a holy place, a kind of priesthood, religious commandments, and necessary ritual. Carved out of at least fifteen different ethnic groups, "Harrism" had become—under the typical radar screen—a most remarkable grassroots socioreligious unity celebrating the same God, the same prophet, the same book, the same holy day (Sunday), the same color for worship (white), the same clerical garb *à la Harris*, the same annual Flood Festival, and the same taboo (no sexual relations outside on the ground).

Nevertheless, in contrast to the dynamic, eschatological, kingdom-of-Christ orientation of Harris during his original impact, the Harrist movement had become ritualized and hardened into an institution seeking recognition. Yet it was still winning people out of their traditional religions into a fetish-free, law-restrained (that is, it's only "sin"

---

[32] See Harold W. Turner, "New Vistas, Missionary and Ecumenical: Religious Movements in Primal (Tribal) Societies," in *Mission Focus* 9, no. 3 (1981): 45–54.

when caught) monotheistic faith, experienced as a break with and major advance over *paganisme.*

Côte d'Ivoire's Western mission-planted churches—Roman Catholic, divers Baptists, Methodist, Christian and Missionary Alliance, Adventist, various independent Evangelicals, Assemblies of God, and several Pentecostals—had all profited, largely unconsciously, from the remarkable and unique 1913–14 spiritual breakthrough of the Prophet Harris. This foundation for the mission-planted churches is a unique phenomenon among AICs, which typically are split-off reactions to the Western character of the mission-planted churches.

Yet the Harrist Church has generally been seen by the missionary churches as an illiterate, fetish-enspirited, marginal African sect, from which people need to be converted. Most missions could not recognize the major break from traditional religion that had taken place with collective exorcisms and with prayer replacing blood sacrifices. They ignored the further evolution of the movement through Bible possession and various other Christian influences and accents via neighbors, literature, and modern media. Finally, they appeared not to understand—even for themselves—the implications of the necessary religious itinerary between African traditional religion and the full-orbed faith of the apostles found in the New Testament.

Study at Aberdeen permitted us to see things differently. Here was an African grassroots, monotheistic, anti-fetish movement, with the law of God and the Lord's Prayer, begun by a Bible-inspired Christian prophet, and currently en route with the scriptures, Christian symbols, and the Spirit of God working to develop authentic African Christians. The ministry of the gospel in a context where Christianity was just emerging out of the all-encompassing, ethnic, oral, ritual, and sacrificial religions of African tradition and spirituality was clearly a totally different missionary assignment than that of planting churches in a dechristianizing Western society with more than fifteen hundred years of interaction with Christendom and the gospel.

Interactions with Harrists

We were present not only amid the Harrists but also among a wide variety of Christians in settings where I often shared what I was learning about the Harrists. Many outsiders saw the Harrists with a closed, symbolic Bible; we, however, heard the scriptures read and commented on in every Harrist worship service we attended for ten years. Some mission-taught Christians called Harrism a fetish religion; but we observed a powerful anti-fetish thrust, while we learned that many Methodist and Catholic church members frequently appealed—sometimes in secret—to traditional sources of protection.

During our ten years of visiting among the Harrists in and around Abidjan, we always sensed reservations behind the scenes about any religious input from us. First of all, as noted above, there were the occasional popular echoes that this was after all a question of Black, African identity, and their ownership of the genius that Prophet Harris had demonstrated among them, creating their religion, even as Jesus had done for the whites. When a special public anniversary celebration of the Prophet Harris's mission of 1913–14 was scheduled by Methodists at Cocody-Abidjan, a Methodist scholar and I were asked to give public lectures on the prophet. But protest from some Harrist quarters was so intense, though far from unanimous, that the lecture had to be called off, with the police sealing the entrance to the Methodist church where the lecture had been scheduled. The understanding behind it all was simple: Harrists are the only persons authorized to speak publicly about the Prophet Harris; absolutely no one else is qualified or authorized to do so.

Second, from an influential former Catholic and Western-trained Harrist *intellectuel*, a consultant to the elders of the National Committee, there was also consistent, formal opposition to any Western religious input. There was the perceived need to keep this African religious reality pure—unspoiled by the West, especially France, and what it was doing to the Ivorian people. The Harrist (non-Christian) catechism of 1956 was reported to be the work of this intellectual, and he carried significant weight because of his effective engagement of the Harrists during the struggle for independence from France in the late 1950s, which had given the church national visibility and acceptance by Ivorian officialdom. This leader's sympathies aligned with and encouraged those currents opposing Spiritual Head John Ahui's invitation to us in 1973. Other persons or forces in opposition included the influential, illiterate head preacher, cross carrier, and self-designated "Cardinal" of the Harrist Church, and the non-Christian dynamics of highly regarded prophet-healer Albert Atcho's popular exorcist ministry. All of this represented opposition to our involvement in a Bible-teaching program with the Harrists in Ebrié and Attié country.

The Union of Harrist Youth presided over by university-trained Tchotche-Mel Félix understood our potential for its program from the beginning. But when the youth adopted us and our commitment to Ahui's invitation, it brought on severe opposition from other sources.

We were caught in the middle of a traditional generational conflict which was intensified by the pro-white/anti-white considerations related to the greater context of historical white missionary interaction with the Harrist Church.

Back in 1926, French Methodist missionary Pierre Benoît had officially visited the Prophet Harris in his home in Liberia and took with him back to Côte d'Ivoire a "testament" signed by Harris, encouraging "his people" to join the Methodist church. As a result, hundreds of Harris's disciples joined the Methodists in what was experienced by other Harrists as sheep-stealing. In fact, Harris had encouraged this, though he was unaware of the Methodist position on polygamy. But in 1929, when he learned from John Ahui that the Methodists required monogamy, he felt betrayed by them and sent the consecrated Ahui back to carry on his work, with the full approval of polygamy.

In reality, the betrayal by the Methodists—not so understood by Harrists, however[33]—was that of knowing full well from Benoît's visit that Harris opposed enforced monogamy, yet they carried on that policy as if it were that of Harris himself. In any case, the deep Harrist tradition about white missionaries is that they act cleverly to steal Harrists for their own mission. This justified the permanent break between Harrists and Methodists, and it was inevitable that for many Harrists that tradition was an important lens for understanding our presence.

Despite these various currents which we learned about little by little, we were available for the Harrists *first*—present as Christian whites, open to learning about them, sympathetic to their situation, appreciative of certain dimensions of their religion, and students of their prophet with documentation they had never seen, ready to share in discussion and study of the Bible.

This open posture gave us a wide variety of opportunities for building relationships. Harrist youth, for example, in several of the secondary schools of the capital met as Harrists, at the same time that Methodist and Catholic youth met for free-time religious study. At the request of the Harrist youth I gave a series of biblical and historical studies, with the full approval of Pierre Anin, then president of the Harrist National Committee. The large Harrist *koya* ("choir") of the congre-

---

[33] Copies of these documents with a Harrist interpretation are found in Appendices 2 and 3 in Paul William Ahui's book, *Le Prophète William Wade Harris: Son message d'humilité et de progrès* (Abidjan: Les Nouvelles Éditions Africaines, 1988). Ahui, the son of the church's spiritual head, shared documents with us and was able to use some of our work for his own study (see Ahui, *Le Prophète*, 206, 285).

gation in Yopougon, a popular village in greater Abidjan, asked me to give choir members a series of studies introducing them to the Bible. In another instance, I spent many hours with a recently ordained head preacher and cross carrier, discussing Harris's story, thought, and understandings, and exposing biblical motifs. And in a typical week in Blokosso, there was always a trickle of one or two Harrists interested in the collections in our Documentation and Resource Center.

On more than one occasion we asked ourselves about the appropriateness of our open availability for the Harrists. Indeed, on one earlier occasion, Wilma and I met—discreetly, at his request—with the (then) new president of the National Committee, accompanied by its secretary. We asked them frankly about the appropriateness of our remaining in Côte d'Ivoire for the Harrists. The secretary immediately responded without hesitation or reflection, "I see absolutely no reason whatsoever for you to remain; you are really free to leave at any time." The president then took his turn, responding with, "It's just like my secretary says, we need a historian; you can be very helpful to me, particularly in these times when we lack clarity among us. You should indeed stay, and I will be grateful to you." We chose to heed the president's invitation rather than the secretary's, and it was the president who later encouraged our work with the Harrist youth meeting in the various secondary schools.

When the youth did ultimately take over authority in the National Committee, they had to make a clean break with us in order to have the full acceptance of the elders of the old National Committee. They needed to prove that they were not influenced by us or connected with us, even formally opposing the work of the Krabills, whose ministry had been thoroughly accepted by Dida Harrism and blessed by Ahui. At the time, James was not only doing Bible instruction in six village centers but was also helping save a rich patrimony of Dida hymnody[34] and assisting church leaders in programming Harrist music on Dida-language broadcasts played on national radio.

When we left Côte d'Ivoire in 1989, we went to the national offices at the large national church at Bingerville in order to officially turn over to the church a full copy of our collected documentation about the Prophet Harris. Our former friend who had been president of the Union of Harrist Youth had become president of the National Commit-

---

[34] Krabill ultimately did a doctorate on Dida hymnody; see James R. Krabill, *The Hymnody of the Harrist Church among the Dida of South Central Ivory Coast, 1913-1949* (Frankfurt: Peter Lang, 1995.)

tee. He symbolically made us wait for three-quarters of an hour before finally receiving us. He wore a scowl during the whole proceedings and then hindered us from giving parting protocol greetings to Spiritual Head Ahui, who had originally invited us and supported us during our Ivorian stay. It was the ultimate affront, a necessary political stance, which enabled the president to maintain his authority. It was a peculiar *au revoir* for us, after ten years of living in Côte d'Ivoire for and among members of the Harrist Church. Yet we understood.

Our style of ecumenical availability

As a Group for Religious and Biblical Studies, we also made ourselves available to and learned from other Christians in Côte d'Ivoire. Each week we attended Bible studies at the Cocody Methodist Church led by a Methodist layman, Minister of State Mathieu Ekra,[35] and his wife. Since she was the daughter of a Togolese prophetess, Akofala, who was instrumental in Minister Ekra's conversion, we received comparative African perspectives for appreciating Harrist understandings and biblical interpretations. Several times I was asked there to adjudicate differing interpretations or to present the Bible study of the evening.

I was also occasionally asked to fill the pulpit at the Cocody Evangelical Church, or the Plateau Methodist Church with its Reformed liturgy, or the Senufo Baptist congregation, or elsewhere. I was invited to give a lecture for Father Pénoukou and his students at the Catholic institute (ICAO) and another for the Jesuits involved in social and economic development (INADES). I was also privileged to take Father Pénoukou's insightful course at the institute, on African theology.

Several times I was invited to lecture for the Summer Institute of Linguistics (SIL) translation group. I was also asked to offer a course for Centre Évangélique de Formation en Communication pour l'Afrique (CEFCA), to give a series of lectures at the Yamoussoukro Evangelical Bible Institute, and another series and a youth retreat for the Bible Institute of the Worldwide Evangelism Crusade. In addition, I was invited a number of times to lecture for the Groupe Biblique Universitaire (InterVarsity Fellowship) in Abidjan. On three occasions, that included being the keynote speaker at their triennial convention in Lomé (Togo), Jacqueville (Côte d'Ivoire), and Ouagadougou (Burkina Faso), with university students and professionals coming from fourteen French-

---

[35] Ekra's particular African biblicism, inspired by prophetess Akofala, "my master teacher," is reflected well in his work, *L'Echelle sans fin* (Paris: France-Impressions; and Abidjan: Nouvelles Éditions Africaines, 1977). I reviewed Ekra's book in the *Journal of Religion in Africa*, 11, no. 3 (1980): 225–31.

speaking countries—a larger francophone population than that of France. Other contacts and involvements during our years in Abidjan included:

- consultancy work and orientation for the Navigators, Campus Crusade, the Nazarene Church, and the Church of Christ. For the latter, I was asked to open up a ministry through a Bible seminar for some seventy Ghanaian independent churches living and ministering in the greater Abidjan area, all churches largely ignored by the Western missionary community.

- rich exchanges with the Catholic institute's Jesuit professor Meinrad Hebga, a Cameroonian healer with three doctorates, who made good use of our documentation center on a number of occasions;

- recording a series of messages for Monrovia's Radio ELWA;

- consultancy work for the BBC's Dr. Charles Elliot in his filming of "Sword and Spirit"—a documentary on AICs in West Africa;

- providing teaching sessions for the Christian and Missionary Alliance church's annual retreat in the Banco Forest;

- lecturing on mission for Muslim secondary school professor colleagues of the Association of Evangelical Professors in Korhogo, northern Côte d'Ivoire;

- organizing on behalf of our own Groupe d'Études Bibliques public lectures in Abidjan by Mary Oyer, Tite Tienou, and colleague James Krabill, among others.

An African itinerary to New Testament faith

Through all these rich contacts and relationships, I was able to get a feel for what was going on not only among the Harrists but also among the mission-planted churches. It became clear to me that just as there were many Harrists whose personal itineraries had led them to a vital faith in Christ, there were also many in the mission-planted churches who were struggling with faith issues, even though they had learned all the proper language and practices of faith as members of recognized churches. These Christians did not yet have, in the words of Catholic missionary Jean-Paul Eschlimann, "the same confidence in Jesus that their brothers have in the customs of their ancestors and the Koran."[36]

---

[36] This assessment by Eschlimann was made of the more than 11,900 Catholics in his parish among the Agni people. His comments appeared in the occasional newsletter *Afrique et Parole*, Letter No. 10 (1984), edited by Dominican Father René Luneau.

The study of many African Christian faith pilgrimages led me to understand that just as there were all across Africa various typical religious movements between traditional religion and the Western mission churches, so also individual African Christians had typical itineraries. These spiritual journeys moved progressively toward fuller understandings of God, Christ, and the life of faith, as the Spirit gave more and more clarity to understandings of the gospel and the New Testament writings.

One of the most important learnings and eventual spin-offs of our ministry in Africa was getting a sense of this African religious itinerary from traditional religion to Christian faith. Based on the religious experiences of Africans themselves, I suggested such an itinerary and then on numerous occasions checked its validity in different geographical regions with Africans who both undertook critique of the analysis and then confirmed it in their own self-understandings.[37] It underwent extensive verification and some adaptation before I offered it for publication in the festschrift for Dr. H. W. Turner following completion of our term of service in Africa.[38]

All-Africa conferences

During our time in Africa, Mennonites were more involved than any other Western mission in ministry with AICs, though a few others also had deep commitments to this work—for example, Dr. Marie-Louise Martin with the Kimbanguists; the Canadian Baptists in Kenya; the Christian Reformed among the Bassa in Liberia; researcher G. C. Oosthuizen in Durban, South Africa; Anglican T. John Padwick in Kenya; and researcher Fr. Joseph Chakanza in Malawi. Dr. Harold Turner kept a list of the names of such persons and made it available to our Mennonite Groupe Biblique in Côte d'Ivoire. From that list, we organized a conference in Abidjan in 1986,[39] for the purpose of comparing notes and

[37] Locations for testing included the Abidjan-based Groupe Biblique Universitaire (InterVarsity Fellowship), Wycliffe Bible Translators' assistants, personal conversations in Abidjan, students at St. Paul's seminary at Nairobi, Kenya, and a study conference at the University of Zululand, South Africa.

[38] "African Christian Religious Itinerary: Toward an Understanding of the Religious Itinerary from the Faith of African Traditional Religion(s) to that of the New Testament," in *Exploring New Religious Movements: Essays in Honour of Harold W. Turner*, ed. A. F. Walls and Wilbert R. Shenk (Elkhart, IN: Mission Focus Publications, 1990), 143–62. It is reprinted as chapter 13 in the present volume. See also the French translation of the same text in *Perspectives Missionnaires* 31 (1996): 30–52.

[39] See David A. Shank, ed., *Ministry of Missions to African Independent Churches* (Elkhart, IN: Mennonite Board of Missions, 1987).

learning from the experiences of others working in this unusual kind of mission.

The gathering was so helpful and fruitful that in July 1989 we organized a second such encounter, with the help of Dr. Marie-Louise Martin, held at the Kimbanguist Center in Kinshasa. This time, though, we also invited African leaders of AICs with whom the various missioners were collaborating. It was a remarkable exchange, and as with the first such conference, the presentations were brought together in a published volume for the purpose of contributing to ongoing missiological reflection in this area of ministry.[40] Several similar conferences in more recent years have augmented those resources. In addition, at the suggestion of our colleague James Krabill, a *Review of AICs* was also begun for exchanging experiences and learnings following the Kinshasa consultation. It was subsequently published for a decade and a half, thanks largely to its dedicated editor, Dr. Stan Nussbaum.

The call from Cotonou

In 1983, our mission administrator, Wilbert Shenk, was passing on his role to our next supervisor, Ron Yoder, and the two of them visited us and our work in West Africa. Their visit led us to take up contacts again with AIC leaders in Benin. Since our last visit, the Marxist regime had taken over Christian schools and opposed the churches' work, in anticipation of closing them all down. But the various churches, including AICs, held shared prayer meetings for deliverance, and the one Marxist in the junta who most opposed the church's work died suddenly. The regime decided abruptly to seek the churches' cooperation and asked them to organize themselves so that the regime could deal with one Protestant ecclesiastical organization, rather than with many.

Pastor Harry Henry, president of the oldest Methodist church and later of the All African Council of Churches, presided over the new Interconfessional Protestant Council of Benin. The Council received us and took up the offer to AIC leaders that Dr. Marlin Miller and Bishop Edwin Weaver had earlier made and accentuated with a Bible seminar back in 1969–70. On this more recent trip, I was invited for a one-week seminar in the fall for AIC leaders, with the proposed theme "The Shepherd and His Flock."

At that first seminar we were told in the open discussion that the major problem perceived by these leaders was the mutual sheep-steal-

---

[40] See David A. Shank, ed., *Ministry in Partnership with African Independent Churches* (Elkhart, IN: Mennonite Board of Missions, 1991).

ing taking place between them. We were also told that we fulfilled two conditions absolutely necessary in order for the seminar to succeed. The first was that we needed to be from outside the context, since any teachers from within the Benin setting would be perceived as also working to win people to their church. The second condition was that we should have no denominational ambitions for Benin, that the church of Christ was already present there in so many forms that an additional denomination was not needed.

We were in fact committed to *not* planting a Mennonite church but sought only to build up the churches already at work, in the light of the kingdom of God recognized—in some sense—as already present in their midst, and yet still coming. It was this "kingdom present *in some sense*" that President Harry Henry recognized in the African-initiated churches, that permitted him to encourage our initiative in a way that other leaders of Western-initiated churches were apparently incapable of doing.

Henry provided the locale for the seminar and presided over the event. The study pattern proposed was simple. A time of singing and prayer would open the day. In the first part, I was to present a study. In a second part, students would ask questions about the study and then in small groups would seek to find answers to their own questions through the scriptures. In the third part, the small groups would report back on their work, and then I would respond with additions, corrections, suggestions, and concluding remarks.

This was the pattern for each morning and afternoon for an entire week. Seminar participants decided the experience was so fruitful that it should be repeated the following year. And so it went for seven years—first, a dozen participants, then some thirty, then seventy, and by the seventh year, a full 140 participants, most holding some form of leadership within twenty-some different African-initiated denominations. The period of Marxist repression had been productive for AICs. And this was happening more or less under the radar screens of the Western-initiated denominations, which—when they *were* aware of these fast-paced developments—saw them largely as problematic.[41]

The variously initiated, divided, and mutually contesting "denominations" in Benin were really a remarkable grassroots phenomenon with African piety, structures, music, and other popular African forms

---

[41] See Rodney Hollinger-Janzen, "A Biblical Teaching Program by the Interconfessional Protestant Council of Bénin with Mennonite Cooperation," in *Ministry in Partnership*, ed. Shank (1991), 161–70, especially n27.

of expression—and with some problematic dimensions and abuses, indeed! In one seminar study of 1 Corinthians, an AIC leader asked, "How could God have known all these things about us and put them in the Bible to correct us?" What, I thought, if one were to understand these churches as a broad grassroots movement emerging and rising out of traditional religion on an itinerary toward the faith of the apostles? Would not watering such a *"movement en route"* with a solid, Christ- and kingdom-oriented biblical theology of the covenanting God of grace and peace enable a highly creative and salutary power within Beninese society?

Here were largely self-taught, charismatic, mutually jealous, and contesting leaders who were now singing and praying together; reading, studying, and absorbing the same word together; and after two or three years, incorporating catechists, evangelists, and occasional pastors from the Western-initiated churches into their midst! Bishop Edwin Weaver's threefold strategy in Uyo, Nigeria, was being fulfilled in Benin, in ways that we could never have anticipated.

After two or three years of seminars, the AIC leaders requested unanimously that our Mennonite mission should go well beyond the annual seminars to (1) not only help create a permanent, fuller program of study in a Bible training school, (2) but also provide training for grassroots health workers from their churches, and (3) offer training in village development. Every year from 1973 to 1979 I spent ten days in Cotonou for the annual Bible seminar of the Interconfessional Protestant Council of Benin. In the later years of this period, three Western Mennonite couples—two American and one French—each with developmental skills in one of the requested areas—were brought in to build on the solidarity developing through the study seminars.

But this is only the beginning of broader amazing story. For there is now an Institut Biblique de Benin in Cotonou which, under the early initiative of Rod Hollinger-Janzen and Steve Wiebe-Johnson, has become the shared territory of four unions of churches with their many and various congregations. And there is, second, with the assistance of French Mennonites Dr. Daniel and Marianne Goldschmidt-Nussbaumer—physician and midwife/psychologist—and nurse Dorothy Wiebe-Johnson, the grassroots development of "Bethesda," an initiative that grew rapidly from house to clinic to hospital. In the third place, under the structures of Bethesda, Mennonite development worker Lynda Hollinger-Janzen initiated and helped develop what has become the official governmental program of garbage collection—largely by AIC members—not only for the one million people in the city of Cotonou, but also for other important cities of the republic. And, fourth, village development workers Phil and Christine Lindell-Detweiler developed a small-loan program that has lifted many families out of poverty. Following my interpretation, this all emerged out of the powerful upward and forward dynamics of Jesus' messianism freshly at work within Beninese Christianity. How different from the Harrist reality of hardened rituals and institutions seeking public recognition—yet with a potential openness to a resurgence, should the word of Christ become fully alive to members of this once-vibrant movement. Each of these contexts, I have come to realize, is at a different place within the messianic circle.

Elsewhere

Such absences from Côte d'Ivoire helped underline for Harrists the fact that we were also available to respond to other calls and were not imposing ourselves on them.

The research I worked on among the Bassa AICs in Liberia for Christian Reformed missionaries was another illustration.[42] Also, twice during the decade we were absent for month-long teaching sessions at the Faculté de Théologie Évangélique de Bangui [FATEB] in Central African Republic. There were in addition two missions to Zaire, the first for a peace seminar for Zairian Mennonite pastors, followed by a retreat for the MCC workers in the Congo; and the second, for a similar retreat for Western MCC workers and missionaries. That trip also included a return visit to the Kimbanguist mother village of Nkamba in the Lower Congo.

A fruitful three weeks' visit hosted by Dr. G. C. Oosthuizen in South Africa during the apartheid era was instructive; Oosthuizen had written extensively about AICs in South Africa and had attended our pan-African AIC conference in Abidjan. The trip included other features, involving a visit to the son of Prophet Shembe of the Nazaretha church and some time spent with North American AIC workers in Lesotho, Transkei, and Botswana. En route via Nairobi, we visited with church leaders from two significant Kenyan AICs—The Brotherhood Church and African Christian Schools and Churches. The bishop of Brotherhood explained to us how the gospel of Christ fulfills the local African "Old Testament" tradition.

---

[42] Summarized in my analysis of their work, "An Approach to Understanding 'Mission' to 'Independent Christianity' among the Bassa People in Liberia, West Africa." Unpublished manuscript (1981), in my personal archives.

Mennonite Board of Missions asked me to do a study of the Good News Training Institute that Ed and Irene Weaver had launched in Accra, Ghana. The Ghana Mennonite Church also asked me to teach a seminar for them. The GMC struck me as being similar to local AICs in Ghana, yet since it was a "proper church," it clearly did not want to be identified with them. It almost seemed that for the local Mennonite leadership, a proper church was one that had non-African origins.

On two occasions, my colleague James Krabill and I held Bible seminars similar to the Benin ones, for some forty AIC leaders in Monrovia, Liberia. Two Mennonite missionary couples were ultimately placed in Liberia, but then terminated quickly because of the onslaught of civil war.

Wilma and I had settled in Blokosso-Abidjan, Côte d'Ivoire, but we were much more informed and enriched by all those various visits, exchanges, and ministries in Liberia, Ghana, Dahomey/Benin, Zaire, Kenya, Central African Republic, South Africa, Transkei, Lesotho, and Botswana.

Activities and ministries in retirement (1989–)

For our retirement from Mennonite Board of Missions, we decided that we would simply continue our policy of being *disponibles* ("available") for whatever the Lord would put on our path. When nothing else would be on the horizon, there would be ongoing work with a translation into French of an abridgement of my doctoral thesis on the Prophet Harris. We returned to our experimental congregation in Goshen, Indiana, only to discover that culture shifts during our absence had effectively led it deeply into what we considered to be an alien hermeneutic and which we had hoped to help clarify.

We had a home built on the side of a hill overlooking Lake Perrin and Amigo Centre, a Mennonite retreat center near Sturgis, Michigan. There we were able to receive all four of our children, their spouses, and nine grandchildren, for a time of bonding. After forty years, there was to be more time available for an expanding family. Eventually, we began attending the nearby Mennonite church, a rural congregation called Locust Grove, only eight miles from home. There I was asked to preach the occasional sermon and to teach the Sunday school class of my peers. Three times I was in the lot for elder without being called. Other activities included presiding over the Church Life Commission for two terms, helping organize congregational small groups, serving on the pastoral search committee, and volunteering to play the role of Rabbi of Bethlehem for the annual Christmas drama, eight years running. Occasionally we were also invited by Mennonite Mission Network to visit other congregations to tell of our work in West Africa.

During this time I was invited to southern Florida by Southeastern Mennonite Conference as "scholar in residence," speaking, consulting, and teaching at the conference's Southeast Institute. I was also asked to replace Dr. J. Denny Weaver at Bluffton College (Bluffton, Ohio) for two semesters. At Goshen College, I was asked to teach a course on missions, to co-teach another, and then later yet another at Associated Mennonite Biblical Seminaries in Elkhart, Indiana.

For a year Wilma and I were invited to serve Indiana-Michigan Mennonite Conference as visiting ministers to marginal congregations that were often neglected by the "center" around the cities of Goshen and Elkhart. Eventually we were ordained as overseers for three Elkhart congregations: Prairie Street, Fellowship of Hope, and Belmont.

For four months, Wilma and I accompanied Carroll and Nancy Yoder of Eastern Mennonite University, with students from French and missions classes, through French-speaking Europe and on to Côte d'Ivoire. After the collapse of the Marxist regime in Benin, a second trip to West Africa (and in Cotonou for some two months) saw us interviewing one by one some forty leaders of Benin's AICs. We wanted to get their sense about the future, in order to help clarify structures and relationships, if there were to be an ongoing Mennonite mission in Benin.

The political climate after the establishment of a liberal, democratic government called for adaptations to the spontaneous, voluntary, and legal changes that ensued. A third trip to West Africa saw me teaching the Old Testament Prophets in the Benin Bible Institute that had grown out of the earlier Bible seminars. I spent a further week lecturing on the African religious itinerary at the Centre Évangélique de Formation en Communication pour l'Afrique (CEFCA) in Abidjan. That was followed with lectures on the uniqueness of Christ for the triennial conference of the Groupes Bibliques Universitaires in Ougadougou, Burkina Faso. These presentations were later published as *L'Afrique en crise: Quelles perspectives?*[43]

As strange as it might appear, during our second visit to Cotonou in 1992 we were surprised at our residence by the visit of the president of the National Committee of the Harrist Church. It was he who had so

---

[43] David A. Shank, *L'Afrique en crise: Quelles perspectives ?* (Abidjan: Presses Bibliques Africaines, 1999).

rudely spurned us at the time of our departure from Côte d'Ivoire. He was there in Benin, accompanied by a choir and church officials of all kinds, with the nearly 100-year-old Spiritual Head of the Church John Ahui, for an evangelistic mission trip in Benin. The president was warm and friendly, just as if there were no reason for things to be otherwise. We invited him and two colleagues for a meal. It was the week before Easter, and we accompanied the dancing chorus through the streets of Cotonou, attending the president's lectures and evening meetings, as well as the Easter Sunday service—a Christian service, appropriately celebrating the resurrection of our Lord with an excellent resurrection sermon by a preacher whose weekday occupation saw him serving as a German-language professor.

For the worship service, the president's protocol had placed Wilma with his own wife on the front bench of the church to the left in front of the women chorists, and placed me—with several preachers—on the right front row, in front of the men chorists and calabash players. Toward the end of the service, the president gave a special word of recognition, acknowledging our presence, thanking us profusely for our presence with them during the week of witness, and on the occasion of the Easter celebration and the meal to come, which he referred to as "a sort of communion meal."

At the end of his speech, the president concluded with reference to "the Shank family who has given us unconditional support for twenty years." And for the meal, he again had us seated at the table of honor with Spiritual Head John Ahui at the head, with the president and me on the right, and First Head Preacher and Cross Carrier Léon Akpé on the left with Wilma. During the solemn meal, conversation was typically absent, and concluded with the aged Ahui's ceremonial exit. Wilma approached him, extended her hand, and greeted him with "Bonjour, Papa." He stopped and held her hand very warmly at length, as he smiled and repeated several times, "Ahh, Madame, Madame!" just as he had done on previous occasions when we had visited him at his home in Petit Bassam.

Our astonishment could not have been greater. Yet from the beginning of our African decade, we lived with the fundamental messianic hope that all things will eventually be reconciled in Jesus Christ. But the ways that happens, and are yet to happen, have not been fully elucidated. Toward the end of the twentieth century—sometimes referred to as "the African century"—in which more people moved into the stream of Christian faith than at any other time in history, Africans

showed us ways and means of which we had known nothing on the
other two continents where we had ministered.

During our time of attending the Locust Grove congregation in
Michigan, I was asked to represent Mennonites as a member of the in-
terdenominational executive board of Thurston Woods Village, a retirement community in Sturgis under the sponsorship of Mennonite
Health Services. My particular contribution was an insistence on the
establishment of a permanent chaplaincy. For two years I have also
served as a consultant for African Projects for Peace and Love Initiatives, through its president, Rev. Titus K. Oyeyemi, and his action for
peace education in Nigeria.

In 2000, Wilma and I were invited to Belgium for the celebration of
the fiftieth anniversary of the beginning of our work in Belgium, and
the twentieth anniversary of the current Brussels Mennonite Center.
Presentations from Catholic and Protestant authorities affirmed the
importance of the ongoing Mennonite presence and witness in Belgium. On that occasion, Fr. Thaddé Barnas of the Catholic National Office for Ecumenism delivered a written apology for past Roman Catholic actions against Anabaptist-Mennonites four hundred years ago.[44]

In October 2003, we sold our Michigan home, downsized with an
auction sale, and moved to Greencroft, a retirement center in Goshen,
Indiana. There we transferred our church membership to Berkey Avenue Mennonite Fellowship. Once again, I was asked to teach the Sunday school class of our peers and bring the occasional sermon during
pastoral vacations. We are members of a congregational small group
of a dozen brothers and sisters and meet regularly with another small
group of persons from our past. In addition, I have a regular Tuesday
breakfast with a handful of other retired men, along with a coffee time
every Thursday morning with a fellow dialysis patient.

Third Way Café of Mennonite Media has requested my services in
dealing by e-mail with "difficult questions" asked by visitors to the web
site. This has occasionally led to extensive correspondence. And I've
also done some other writing all along the way, including the ongoing
work of translating into French my book on the Prophet Harris.

---

[44] See "Culte de Reconnaissance pour les 20 ans du Centre Mennonite de Bruxelles et
les 50 ans du retour des Mennonites en Belgique," Eglise Protestante du Botanique-
Bruxelles, 10 octobre 2000 (Brussels: Centre Mennonite, 2000).

Conclusion

During our nearly forty years of ministry under Mennonite Board of Missions, we were always conscious of the fact that there were congregations and a church who believed in us and supported us, and that in a real sense we were in continuity with them, even though the anticipated "meager results" at the outset of our ministry never really resembled those sending bodies to any great degree.

The *missio Dei* and the gospel are one. But the differences between missions remain enormous, accentuated even more by the various parochialisms we face, whether a secular American imperialism claiming to be the light on a hill, or the dechristianization within a European union whose constitutional project chooses to ignore its Christian millennium.

These differences include the major contextual ones between *Western individualism* ("I think, therefore I am"), where faith and religion are seen to be strictly private matters and people respond to the gospel one by one, and *African solidarity* ("We are, therefore I am"), where faith is conditioned by the extended family and peoplehood. These differences include the crucial distinctions between a people shaped, on one hand, by modern science, technology, and media, and on the other, a people adapting to the fruits of both an alien secularism and a liberating Christian worldview.

Into such significantly different human and geographical contexts, the good news of the word of God is fulfilling its purpose as people are introduced to Jesus Christ. As I still see it, The One Spirit Creator of all things—by the covenant of grace and peace fulfilled through the life and teachings of Israel's Messiah and his cross, resurrection/ascension, and reign—is reconciling alienated humans to their unique Source, to different others, and to creation, as disciples of Jesus with a shared, renewing Holy Spirit empowering them for living out such reconciliation in hope and love in new messianic faith communities as signs of God's reign and the coming reconciliation of all things. It is a perception of what is going on in the world that I take to be biblical, apostolic, Anabaptist, Mennonite, holistic, charismatic, ecumenical, catholic, missionary—and still marginal.

Section III Selected Essays

Shank family at home in Genval, Belgium (1966).
Clockwise: David, Stephen, Michael, Crissie, Wilma,
and Rachel

Section III Selected Essays

A Theology of mission

Farewell celebration for the Shank
family at the Rixensart church, Belgium
(1973)

5

Jesus the Messiah
Messianic foundation of mission

Christology is traditionally the study of the doctrine of Jesus Christ as it has been pursued in the life of the churches of Christ since the crucifixion and resurrection of Jesus of Nazareth. It covers the rich expressions of apostolic understandings as well as the post-apostolic developments leading up to the so-called ecumenical creeds, including the perceptions that these eliminated. It includes high scholastic developments and the fivefold Reformation and its scholastic Protestant outgrowths. It involves the modern critical developments of the nineteenth- and twentieth-centuries' scholarship on "lives of Jesus," as well as contemporary post-dogmatic approaches.

Today, at least for churches originating in the West, Christology involves not only the critical studies of the canonical texts of the New Testament—especially the four Gospels; it also includes an effort to translate the results of these studies into Western understandings that have been shaped by the thought and technology of modern sciences—physical, biological, historical, psychological, sociological, anthropological, and religious. Nothing is more noticeable today than the great variety of understandings and interpretations that constitute christological thought in the churches, including those well beyond the West, to say nothing of references to the past. The diversity is understandable and justifiable from a biblical point of view[1] as well as from the

---

Reprinted, with editorial changes, from *The Transfiguration of Mission: Biblical, Theological and Historical Foundations,* ed. Wilbert R. Shenk (Scottdale, PA: Herald Press, 1993), 37–82. Used by permission.

[1] There is the pluralism of names and titles and their meanings (for example, John 1). There is the pluralism of time-events within the biblical telling of one Christ event: pre-existence, conception, birth/presentation, temple at 12, baptism/endowment with Spirit, temptation, ministry, suffering, death, burial/descent into hell, resurrection, ascension, Spirit baptizing at Pentecost, sitting at the right hand, Parousia—each has its potential for theological interpretation and accent. For example, "descended into hell," based on limited biblical evidence, had great importance for first-gen-

highly diverse human, cultural, and worldview contexts from which that material comes. This chapter sketches a framework for the Christology inherent in the mission and life of the churches of Jesus Christ throughout the world today.

Professor Andrew Walls presents an excellent periodization of the history of the churches "based on the dominant cultures with which Christianity has been associated at various times."[2] Nevertheless, he says, "There is no simple 'Christian civilization,' but an endless process of translation into various languages and cultures and subcultures within them."[3] His schema is as follows:

Jewish phase	ca. 30–70
Hellenistic-Roman phase	
(includes Eastern Orthodoxy)	ca. 70–500
Barbarian phase	ca. 500–1100
Western phase	ca. 1100–1600
Phase of expanding Europe	ca. 1500–1920
Southern phase	since 1920

With this historical framework before us, three observations are significant for our christological reflection at this juncture in Christian mission.

The foundations of understanding and interpretation, including the canonical writings of the churches, are grounded in the first forty years—the Jewish phase.

---

eration Gentile Christians; today, however, it is nonexistent in many evangelical statements of faith. Each event of the total Messiah event has lent itself to new and different insights as cultural, social, and political changes offer different prisms for reading scripture. As we shall see, even the pluralism within the ministry of Jesus opens up different christological perspectives: evangelist, healer, exorcist, prophet, teacher, man of protest. In a society where healing is traditionally controlled by spirit powers, the healing ministry of Jesus opens up to a Christology quite different from that in the usual Western context. Then there is the pluralism of images for faith appropriation of God in Christ: be born again, drink water of life, bear the yoke. Even the biblical language descriptive of Christ's work is pluralist: redemption, justification, adoption, regeneration, election, reconciliation. Each has known its own theological and christological formulation. The argument of this chapter is that the foundational messianic dimension must be seen as the context for any and all the varieties; the diverse approaches—to be valid—must at the least be within a nonnegotiable messianic context.

[2] Andrew Walls, "Christianity," in *A Handbook of Living Religions*, ed. John R. Hinnels (Harmondsworth, Middlesex: Pelican Books, 1985), 58.

[3] Ibid.

Up until about 1920, the Christian scene, from the standpoint of culture and civilization, has been dominated and conditioned by the Hellenistic-Roman phase. It was initially extended into the phase of "barbarian" syncretization, then into the Western phase with its European expansion until the post–World War I period. During this latter period, the Greek-Latin filters for understanding Christ and his work dominated the scene through the colonial and missionary expansion of Christianity.

In the current—Southern—phase, a result of Christian mission, churches in non-Western cultures read and interpret the scriptures and understand Jesus Christ from their own cultural/civilizational perspectives alongside that of Western christological reflection from AD 70 to 1920.

For centuries, the dominant and imposed Christology in the churches, evolving within the Greek language and cultural ethos, was discussed almost exclusively in the Greek mode. "Christ" is, of course, the English transliteration of the Greek *Christos*; but beyond that, the Greek-Latin categories of reason, law, spirit and matter, nature and substance and person could practically drown out other dimensions and perceptions.

To illustrate, if one speaks of a Messiah doctrine today, it has a different feel to it than speaking of Christology, which literally means the same thing. The term *Messiah* implies a specific historical personality who poses as effective redeemer and liberator in a given context of oppressive alienation. Yet the term *Christ* in the Greek tradition often ignored the holistic Hebrew dynamics, with their social, economic, and political implications for faith, all of which are inherent in the language of *Messiah*.

Kenneth Cragg makes this point forcefully, and his word needs to be taken seriously.[4] In reality, by AD 500, the good news of Jesus the Messiah had spread into various Mediterranean cultures with scriptures existing not only in Greek but also in Syriac, Coptic, Latin, Ethiopic, Armenian, Gothic, and Slavonic. Yet the dynamics of imperial unity, first invited by the Donatist controversy, co-opted the "Christ" and ultimately commanded a uniform Greek-Latin understanding—cutting off traditional Hebrew roots—of the Hebrew Jesus of Nazareth, first confessed by Jewish apostles as Israel's Messiah for the world. This

---

[4] Kenneth Cragg, *Christianity in World Perspective* (New York: Oxford University Press, 1968), 57–58.

engendered a knowledge/life dualism that led to a separation of faith and life.

In the 1,500 years since the crystallization of the Orthodox and Roman Catholic creeds within Constantinian imperial Christianity, Christology has majored in the static and ahistorical dimensions of divine-human relationship and mediation. Except for the heterodox, sectarian, millennial, and monastic traditions, much less concern and attention has been given to the human, temporal dimensions of the divine-human relationship of Messiah Jesus—hence a vacuous neglect of their implications for mediation between the future and the present as well as between people, peoples, and institutions in the present.

However, allowing for some important exceptions, this accent has shifted significantly in the West under the pressures of the Hegelian and Marxist preoccupations with the dynamics of history, the demise of the Constantinian synthesis, and the contemporary apocalypse of the technological cul-de-sac as demonstrated in World War II and subsequent wars. Indeed, the horrors of the Holocaust within Hitlerian messianism forced Western Christianity into a new encounter with Judaism and a rediscovery of its own Hebraic roots. All of this change has implications for christological reflection at a time when there is a Western consensual reaching out for a more humane way into a more humane future.

On the one hand, the logical Western problem-solving approach is that of squarely facing the human problem, looking for a way out, and then concocting a Christology as an ideology of salvation. There is, on the other hand, the quite different approach of grasping the fundamental roots of apostolic messianic understandings during that beginning forty-year formative period, taking them seriously as foundations for faith, and then facing the world, its problems, and the future in that light. One suspects that the two approaches may have some parallels and similar accents, yet crucial differences may be as important as that between Messiah and anti-Messiah, even as those differences came to be experienced by Anabaptists in the beginnings of the unraveling of the great sacral construction of Constantinian Christendom.

Despite the later Greco-Latin cultural imperium, it is clear that the early churches in Judea were Jewish, with Hebrew language and thought patterns, albeit deeply affected by the culture of exile and the contemporary Hellenist influences. There remained an essential, nonethnic, nonparochial, and nonnegotiable foundation of Hebrew thought. A divine/human dialectic and travail is engaged in fulfilling history,[5] with the beginning of a new realization of God's goodwill and blessing for Israel and all the nations with the fulfillment of a universal messianic hope through Jesus of Nazareth.

But the early Greek-inspired shift from the "horizontal," temporal, historical mediation of the future to a largely "vertical," ontological mediation played down the earthly accents and the social, economic, and political preoccupations of the biblical Messiah's work of salvation, redemption, and restoration. Instead, it favored the divine/heavenly (spiritual, eternal, immortal) preoccupations and accents of the Greek cultural ethos. This shifted the holistic thrust of the biblical message and gospel of the Messiah to accentuate spiritual good news about the eternal heavenly hereafter. The old covenant was seen to be earthly and temporal and filled with "types" of spiritual realities of the new covenant that fulfilled them. The exodus/liberation of Israel was a typological forecast of inner spiritual salvation from the earth and sin to heaven's promised land through the heavenly Savior. And in that journey, the church of Christendom, during more than a millennium, was recognized and charged with the spiritual side of the empire.

Happily, in some circles in the West, a theological thrust oriented to the kingdom of God has served to pull together the earthly and the heavenly, the material and the spiritual, in a more nearly holistic understanding of messianic mission. But the flywheel of the past has often limited effects on the Christology of the same circles.[6] On the other hand, the various liberation theologies (Latin American, Black, feminist) have emerged as a theological mainstream starting with the particular oppression—social, economic, political, sexist, racist—along with a materialistic dialectic as the instrument of analysis and strategy. Then, accenting certain elements of biblical concern from within the prophetic and messianic tradition, these theologies have brought to the fore the exodus, the political dimensions of Jesus' mission, and his identity with the marginal ("God's option for the poor," as made

---

[5] The best biblical scholarship indicates the uniqueness of Israel's faith as over against that of other sacral nations of the time.

[6] "There is no reasonable doubt that Jesus rejected the ideas of political messiahship. His teaching regarding his mission was not cast in this mold. He eschewed the idea of violence and advocated an approach that would obviously have been a political nonstarter [as in Martin Hengel, *Was Jesus a Revolutionist?* trans. William Klassen (Philadelphia: Fortress Press, 1971)]. No political revolutionary could ever have exhorted people to love their enemies. The Sermon on the Mount is intelligible as a spiritual directive, but makes nonsense as a political manifesto" (Donald Guthrie, *New Testament Theology* [Downers Grove, IL: InterVarsity Press, 1981], 241).

explicit by liberation theology), thus challenging the whole Western church's notion of salvation and Christian mission.[7] But this is clearly a thrust different from that of the vigorous pietism and evangelicalism of the eighteenth and nineteenth centuries that had an aggressive sociopolitical agenda, so well illustrated by the antislavery campaigns or the Blumhardts of Bad Boll, Germany.[8]

In this current context, does the so-called sectarian tradition, perennially outside the theological mainstream, have anything to offer on Christology in view of mission? With the openness in the West, and the new approaches in the non-Western cultures despite the major Western influence through missionary activity, it is perhaps not inappropriate to look again—from the sixteenth century's left-wing perspective—at the early christological accents of the first messianic communities centered on Jesus of Nazareth. This tradition emerged out of the rejection of the Constantinian synthesis and, like the messianic communities within the Roman Empire, bore with the Jews and Muslims a major brunt of the triumphant temporal power—Christendom structured on a spiritual, heavenly Christology. In any case, the intention in this study is to underscore elements from the first forty foundational years of messialogical thought, as well as from the Anabaptist tradition of the sixteenth century, as part of a catalytic brew within which locally accented Christologies may ferment.

Given the cultural pluralism of the churches in the world today, a variety of Christologies is quite understandable and almost unavoidable, regardless of the main traditions in which the mission-planted churches have been immersed. This has been heightened by the World Council of Churches' encouragement and support of theological "contextualization" worldwide—the context as a starting point for theology. In evangelical circles it is well illustrated by Vinay Samuel and Christopher Sugden in *Sharing Jesus in the Two-Thirds World;*[9] for conciliar and Catholic circles, *The Bulletin of African Theology* is a prime illustration. The concern raised by the present chapter is related to the question of whether there are traditionally neglected sine qua non dimensions of

---

[7] "Salvation Today" was the theme of the conference of the Commission on World Mission and Evangelism held in Bangkok, Thailand, in 1973.

[8] The Blumhardts of Bad Boll, Germany, were the forerunners to the Christocentric theology of Karl Barth and Emil Brunner and the founders of the Evangelical academies of the German Protestant Church.

[9] Vinay Samuel and Christopher Sugden, *Sharing Jesus in the Two-Thirds World* (Grand Rapids, MI: Eerdmans, 1984).

Christology that ought not to be ignored in any of the current diverse formulations.

One of the lesser but more noticeable elements in this study will be the use of *Messiah* rather than *Christ*. Meanings associated with Christ—often with anti-Jewish overtones in those years between AD 70 and 1920—shift not only the original intent but also the impact. Thus, this text will use Messiah, messianist, messianic, messianism, messianity, and for Christology, messialogy. The implications, however, if taken to their inherent conclusions, are important.

The first is that using these terms frees and encourages Christians/messianists outside the West to do their own messialogical reflection with a knowledge of the ways one's cultural history can encapsulate and domesticate Jesus and the apostolic faith, to its own detriment as well as that of others.

Second, use of these terms enhances the validity of plural accents in Christology, in the West as in the rest of the world, while recognizing an essential framework within which the divergences are fully and correctly honored and valued.

Third, for Western churches caught up in the fruits of the secular reaction to Western Hellenized Christology, it is important for them to see themselves again from within the framework of the essential apostolic messianism, rather than to judge and criticize the latter from the latest evolved perspective of modern Western consciousness, with the domestication and parochialism that that involves.

Finally, in a time when the religious pluralism of the world continues to challenge the truth of God in Jesus the Messiah, particularly in religious circles with atrophied Christian roots, it may be helpful to restate the essential content of messialogical thought with its parameters.

The present writing is from a perspective that has emerged from within the history of that Anabaptist messianic community that knew the intense suffering, persecution, and martyrdom of nonresistant powerlessness at the hands of the sacral Christendom it challenged in the name of Christ and experienced as antichrist. Although that community inherited from the Christology of the Western creeds an authoritative mediating Christ, the Jesus in the Gospels—as taught by his apostles in the New Testament writings—had more authority than the creeds and their formulations.

The community thus had a strong commitment to the normative importance of Jesus' life patterns and teachings on forgiveness, love, and service for all human life and institutions. Baptism was a covenant with Jesus Christ in the mutuality of life together in the assembly of his followers. There was a clear vision of eschatological triumph that called forth a childlike obedience like that of Jesus, despite humiliation and suffering. The Holy Spirit was experienced as freedom, capacity, and mission for a human transformation that challenged the cultural canons of the day.

Such a tradition, so at home in the scriptures and so much en route in the world, is intuitively suspicious, not only of the world pressures that oppose the life of God in Jesus the Messiah, but also of passing theological and christological fads that emerge from within the religious life of that world. Yet, in these efforts of one more Westerner to suggest for world mission an essential understanding of Messiah, it is only honest to admit also that if in this essay he cannot avoid reading the scriptures from a Western perspective, it is one that in its infancy at least challenged Western Christianity—unto death.

So it is correct to call this perspective "neo-Anabaptist," even though this has its own requirements. First of all, it must be biblical. Second, it must allow biblical understandings to critique the current ones (whatever those might be) rather than to project those back into the biblical understandings, admittedly a difficult task. Third, its conclusions are taken as a position on which to stand independently of its effectiveness or its relevancy; it does not need to be justified before the world to whom it witnesses, because it only seeks to be justified by God.

First Thessalonians: The earliest clues

One good point at which to peg early understandings about Jesus is the oldest and first New Testament canonical writing, the missionary letter written by apostles Paul, Silas, and Timothy to the new gathering (*ekklēsia*) of believers and disciples in Thessalonica, a principal metropolis of Macedonia. Written about AD 51–52, scarcely more than twenty years after Jesus' death and resurrection, the letter came from a group headed by one who some seventeen years earlier had officially led a violent persecution of the new movement within Israel. While on a mission to the nations/Gentiles, Paul was accompanied by both an official representative and a leading brother (Mark) of the original Jerusalem gathering, along with Luke (his personal physician), and a young Greek, Timothy, born of a Jewish mother. Paul was fully qualified by more than fifteen years of service in the new movement, and fully authorized by the mother assembly in Jerusalem for taking that movement into areas where it was still largely unknown.

From the story written by Luke some twenty or thirty years after the mission to Thessalonica (Acts 17:1–9), we are told that it was a relatively brief mission because of open opposition. Paul argued from the Jewish scriptures in the synagogue for three Sabbaths, proving that it was necessary for the Messiah to suffer and to rise from the dead, and saying, "This Jesus, whom I proclaim to you, is the [Messiah]" (17:3).[10] As a result, some Jews believed in Jesus as the Messiah and attached themselves to the apostolic team, suffering the jealousy of fellow Jews who openly opposed the movement. The apostolic team was accused of "turn[ing] the world upside down" (17:6) and "acting against the decrees of Caesar, saying that there is another king, Jesus" (17:7). Even if the accusation had been false, the political overtones of the messianic message are evident in that if there were none, the dead Jesus could represent no threat, either to Jews accused of rebellion or to the local authorities under Roman rule.

In addition to the Jews who believed, there were a great many pious Greeks and not a few of the leading women, possibly also from among the Greek population. These were the highly divergent religious and social roots of a new *ekklēsia,* a word also used for a Greek political formation. A new messianic gathering, or assembly, had emerged as a consequence of a messianic proclamation by a team endowed with a messianic consciousness, naming Jesus of Nazareth the present acting transcendent Messiah-king with universal authority—higher than the head of the Roman Empire.

The messianic content of 1 Thessalonians

Titles. The salutation and the final greetings of the letter are like a parenthesis, opening with "To the [*ekklēsia*] of the Thessalonians in God the Father and the Lord Jesus [the Messiah]: Grace to you and peace" (1 Thess. 1:1), and closing with an anticipation that "the God of peace himself [will] sanctify . . . wholly" (5:23) the believers in view of "the coming of our Lord Jesus [the Messiah]. . . . The grace of our Lord Jesus [the Messiah] be with you" (5:24–28). In those two parameters, God is confessed as relationally intimate (Father)—something unusual for the

---

[10] Scripture references in this essay, unless noted otherwise, are from the Revised Standard Version. I have replaced "Christ" with "Messiah" for reasons given earlier in my text.

Jews of the time—and as effecting a reign as "God of peace,"[11] while the man Jesus is confessed as Messiah and Lord. Both are in intimate association as the effective source of essential manifestations of God's reign. In this brief letter "[Messiah] Jesus" appears two times, "[the Messiah]" is found three times, "Lord Jesus [the Messiah]" is found five times. "Jesus" is used three times; "the/our Lord Jesus," six times; "the Lord," thirteen times; "[God's] Son," only once.

Confession and proclamation of faith. "Lord Jesus the Messiah" is here much more than a name or a title; it is, in fact, a double confession of faith: "Jesus is the Messiah," and "The Messiah Jesus is Lord." It is the full confessional identification of Jesus of Nazareth with the promised and awaited Messiah of Israel's prophets and with God and his purposes. "Messiah" appears ten times in 1 Thessalonians; "Lord" (*kyrios*) appears twenty-four times. Indeed, "Jesus is Lord" rapidly became the most-used confession in the new Hellenistic assemblies, but it must be seen as an apostolic usage meaning "Jesus [the Messiah] is Lord."[12] In fact, two decades after his crucifixion and resurrection, "Jesus" within the movement was already wholly identified with the title and function of Messiah.

The only scriptures at Thessalonica, beyond this authoritative apostolic letter, were those of the synagogue, but they were now interpreted in the light of what the letter calls "gospel" (1 Thess. 1:5), "gospel of God" (2:2, 8–9), "gospel of [the Messiah]" (3:2), "the word" (1:6), "the word of God" (2:13), or "the word of the Lord" (1:8; 4:15). This proclamation can surely be summarized by this primary confession that we have seen, but there are other suggestions of brief formulas of proclamation and confession of faith:

> You turned to God from idols, to serve a living and true God, and . . . wait for his Son from heaven, whom he raised from the dead, Jesus who delivers us from the wrath to come (1:9–10).

---

[11] The expression "God of peace," appears only once in pre-Christian literature (Testament of Dan 5:2), but is used repeatedly by Paul (Rom. 15:33; 16:20; 1 Cor. 14:33; 2 Cor. 13:11; Phil. 4:9) and is found in Hebrews 13:20, reflecting a new and important usage. See William Klassen, "The Voice of the People in the Biblical Story of Faithfulness," in *The Church as Theological Community,* ed. Harry Huebner (Winnipeg: Canadian Mennonite Bible College Publications, 1990), 144. Klassen also notes this as a "redefinition of God in a community where it was all too easy to visualize God as a God of war" (ibid., 153).

[12] Vernon H. Neufeld, *The Earliest Christian Confessions* (Grand Rapids, MI: Eerdmans, 1963), 141.

For since we believe that Jesus died and rose again, even so, through Jesus, God will bring with him those who have fallen asleep (4:14).

[According to] the word of the Lord, . . . the Lord himself will descend from heaven. . . . And the dead in [the Messiah] shall rise first; then we who are alive, who are left, shall be caught up together with them in the clouds . . . and so we shall always be with the Lord (4:15–17).

God has not destined us for wrath, but to obtain salvation through our Lord Jesus [the Messiah], who died for us that whether we wake or sleep we might live with him (5:9–10).

One cannot but be struck by the core of faith: Messiah's dying and rising again is to effect already a human salvation, which is to be wholly fulfilled in his end-time appearance, Parousia (1 Thess. 2:19; 3:13; 4:15; 5:23) and final gathering of the faithful, of which the Thessalonian gathering from among Israel and the nations (Jews and Gentiles) is already a part.

Self-described apostolic impact. If there was clarity of conviction and proclamation in power in the Holy Spirit (1 Thess. 1:5) by the apostolic team, as indicated above, there was also, from their point of view, an equally vital collective demonstration of the gospel in their lives (2:4–10) that made them, with Jesus, worthy of emulation (1:6). The apostolic team was itself clearly a validation of the message and an integral part of its impact.

Salvation in the Thessalonian gathering. As cited above, salvation already known was that of "turn[ing] to God from idols, to serve a living and true God, and to wait for his Son . . . Jesus who [now] delivers us from the wrath to come" (1 Thess. 1:9–10). The letter speaks of "your work of faith and labor of love and steadfastness of hope in our Lord Jesus [the Messiah]" (1:3). As indicated, they had become "imitators" of Messiah's apostles and Jesus himself, receiving the word "in much affliction, with joy inspired by the Holy Spirit . . . and became an example" to other believers in the area (1:6–7). They "became imitators of the churches of God in [the Messiah] Jesus that are in Judea" (2:14), knowing with them the suffering implicit in their calling with Messiah (3:3). Finally, the "word of the Lord sounded forth from you . . ., your faith in God has gone forth everywhere" (1:8).

The salvation outworking anticipated by the apostles in the assembly included leading "a life worthy of God, who calls you into his own kingdom and glory" (1 Thess. 2:12); steadfastness in affliction (3:3); and "instructions we gave you through the Lord Jesus" how to live and please God (4:2–12). The manifestation of mutuality is already at work in love (eight uses of *agapē* or derivatives) as taught by God (4:9), but it is anticipated in mutual comfort (4:18), mutual encouragement and mutual edification (5:11), mutuality of peace (5:13), mutual kindness and refusal of repaying evil for evil (5:15), and patience for everyone (5:14). There is to be respect and love for their leaders and concern for the idle, the faint, and the weak. Self-control regarding sexual practice and personal life is to be received through faith, love, and hope of salvation (5:8). But beyond the confines of the gathering itself, love (3:12) and kindness (doing good) is for all, with no resisting of evil with evil (5:15). They are to live with bodies disciplined, by working with their own hands, being self-supporting, quietly minding their own affairs, and thus commanding the respect of outsiders. And all this while their faith is going forth everywhere (1:8) and in the face of great opposition (2:2).

Résumé of messianic understanding

Within the letter is a fourfold understanding of "the Lord Jesus, the Messiah." First, Jesus suffered in the line of the prophets (1 Thess. 2:15) when he lived a pattern of life that is imitated (1:6), having given clear instructions on how to live and please God (1:5) and a clear word of eschatological promise (4:15), which all ended in his death at the hands of fellow Jews.

Second, Jesus rose from the dead, and he now sends out apostles with the good news of his messiahship: he died and rose again and is coming to fulfill salvation of a gathered humanity in the midst of coming judgment (wrath). The Holy Spirit through the apostles creates assemblies of the great messianic ingathering that learn from the apostles, Jesus, and one another. Called into the kingdom and glory of God by the Messiah, they suffer opposition and the temptation to turn aside, but they live in the grace and peace given by him and the Father, kept by their faith, love, and hope in him, whose full ingathering they await. They become notorious sharers of their faith and the gospel they received. They are to work out their salvation in their gathering/assembly/*ekklēsia*/church in a common life of love and mutuality. In the larger society, in spite of opposition and affliction, they are to show love and kindness to all, refusing to render evil for evil, in line with instructions from Jesus through the apostles.

Third, the coming "day of the Lord" (1 Thess. 5:2) is to begin with the unannounced "coming" of God's Son Jesus (1 Thess. 1:10; 2:19; 3:13; 4:15; 5:23) to command both the resurrection of the faithful who lived and died in the Messiah and the final gathering together with them of the transformed, living faithful.

Finally, the ultimate salvation of all from the coming wrath is to be fulfilled in an ongoing life with the Lord, Jesus the Messiah, in the reign of God without end.

An early transcendent Messiah understanding

If little is given in 1 Thessalonians about Jesus' life, it is apparent that much of the description of the Thessalonian *ekklēsia* cited above is a result of such sharing during the mission. Most important, clearly the life, teachings, death, and hope of Jesus are the historical foundation of all the rest, even though the "coming of Messiah" for the final ingathering has now become the focal point of orientation for the time since Jesus' death and resurrection. But most of the letter concentrates on that present time of Messiah and his church—time of the Holy Spirit, time of grace and peace, time of service (like Jesus) to the true and living God, with its testing through opposition and suffering; its work of faith and witness; its mutuality in faith, love, and hope.

The fourfold messianic understanding portrays a picture of human history under the reign of God with culminating events fulfilled and articulated by the life, death, resurrection, present ministry, and coming of the Messiah Jesus as he gathers together God's people (for the moment, in smaller scattered gatherings) in view of the salvation of humanity into the service of God. There is the event of Jesus' life, teaching, sufferings, and death; there is the event of the resurrection; there is the event of exaltation lived in fellowship with the apostolic gathering sent out on the mission of assembling disciples; there is the eschatological event to come, of the full ingathering of the people of God with the appearing of Messiah.

The close relationship of God as Father with Jesus the Son/Messiah is further enhanced by the repeated, almost regular, use of *kyrios* ("Lord") for the Messiah. This was the word used in the Septuagint for Yahweh in his sovereignty; since the Greek usage itself accented such sovereignty in divinities and those rulers seen to be divine; it clearly stressed the kingly sovereignty of the Messiah Jesus in relation to that of God's kingdom (see 1 Thess. 2:12). To the extent that the Messiah is so associated with God's sovereignty, one can speak of an early transcendent Messiah understanding (that is, Christology), even though the concern is that of the mission and function of the Messiah and not the precise nature of the association or relationship. But there can be no doubt that Jesus the Messiah is fulfilling his kingship from a position of transcendence in God.

The fact that all within the letter hinges on singleness of faith in that messianic transcendence of Jesus, and his finalizing mission in human history, is further underlined by the absence of language and ideas so prominent in later canonical writings (for example, fellowship, eternal life, justification, redemption, adoption, regeneration, sacrifice, justice/righteousness, atonement, reconciliation, blood, election) and no mention of baptism or the Lord's Supper. Indeed, all these terms will be used later to explain, interpret, expound, or explicate and apply the simple message: Jesus, whom you imitate with joy in the midst of severe suffering, suffered and died for you, and is risen and exalted as Messiah-king to give you the call of God into his kingdom and glory, delivering you from sin and the coming wrath, as you live in the Holy Spirit with faith, love, and the hope of life with him forever, when he will appear in the midst of all his gathered people. Your gathering in Thessalonica is a manifestation of his messiahship, as you stand firm in him and follow his instructions.

The message is one of redemption more universal than that to the Jews in Palestine living under Roman oppression. But since Paul possibly had no contact with Jesus before his death and resurrection, one can rightfully ask whether this was his own interpretation and understanding that he projected back on the Jesus story. Or was it Jesus' own self-understanding as he communicated it to the Twelve who fully authorized the mission to the Gentiles as led by Paul? In any case, there is no doubt about the character of the movement as messianic. Is it the one intended by Messiah himself? This is the question that naturally throws us back to the Gospels, written later, and perhaps even reflecting some of this understanding. We should, nevertheless, observe that Paul had worked closely at Antioch with Mark, one of the Jerusalem church's recognized ministers of the oral tradition about Jesus and his mission. And Luke was Paul's close friend and companion.

But before looking at the Gospels, we should first recall the general context of Jesus' and Paul's messianism.

The context of Jesus' messianism and service

The covenants of God

The ongoing creative work of God and its redemptive fulfillment, as seen within the unique perspective of Israel's inspired writers, can be briefly summarized in the progressive covenantal self-commitments by which God is tied and bound, within creation, to humanity and its condition. The successive covenants are God's sovereign and compassionate acts of grace and faithfulness to all of human creation, even when they are given to and through Israel; to them, Israel and humanity are expectantly invited to respond by choosing to serve God, according to this self-revelation.

1. After chaos, there is from God the Spirit both *good creation and blessing* for the primeval couple made in the divine image, in view of dominion over the earth for God.

2. With the disastrous consequences of the primal apostasy in its wish for absolute autonomy and freedom "as God," there is given the *promise of a posterity* that will crush the primeval seducer, liar, bringer of death and alienation.[13]

3. After the corruption and violence that ensued, followed by flood and destruction, there is the universal *covenant of providence* for the emerging and expanding nations, with a clear limitation of vengeance/violence within the human family—made in God's image indeed, yet now with an evil-inclined heart from childhood, and so recognized by God.

4. After the nations' collective heaven-grasping with its Babel confusion and dispersion, *a covenant of call (election) with blessing* is promised to Abraham and Sara and their posterity in view of blessing for all of the nations (*pars per ommes*).

5. After Israel's experience of God's liberation from pharaonic oppression and slavery, without their own use of violence,[14] God makes a kingly *covenant of law* of priestly service to and for the nations.

---

[13] No African myth, says the African theologian John Mbiti, offers a solution to the ever-present primeval loss. See John Mbiti, *African Religions and Philosophy* (New York: Frederick A. Praeger, 1969), 99.

[14] This oft-neglected part of the story has been best exposed by Millard Lind in *Yahweh Is a Warrior: The Theology of Warfare in Ancient Israel* (Scottdale, PA: Herald Press, 1980).

6. With Israel's constant disobedience and abandonment of God's covenant and kingship, God grants Israel a "king like the nations" with a later *royal covenant* of Father/Son love for an heir ("anointed"/*mašiaḥ*/Messiah/Christ) of King David. The reign of blessing and peace (*šalom*) over God's people would know no end.

Henceforth, the people of Israel, the kingdom of Israel, and the Messiah from within Israel's Davidic dynasty are seen to be inseparable because all result from God's covenantal commitment and are tied to the faithfulness of God to the covenant. But Israel neglects the divine intention that this promise, these actions, and fidelity of God are in view of the blessing and peace (*šalom*) of salvation for all the nations' service to the Creator and creation.

The movement in history has been from creation to humanity, followed by alienation from God and his purposes; from salvaged but alienated humanity to Abraham and Israel, for all of humanity; from unfaithful Israel to a faithful remnant, for all Israel; from the remnant to the one anointed—the Messiah. According to the prophets, when Messiah comes, he is for the remnant, the remnant is for all Israel, Israel is for all humanity, and humanity is for all the earth as creation.[15] Henceforth, Israel in the midst of foreign oppression, exile, dispersion, and the return of many to Zion is constantly confronted with the bitter facts of that yet-unrealized messianic fulfillment.

With the hellenization of the Near East, the Syrian persecution of Israel in their own land, and later control by Egyptian overlords, an unsuccessful Hasmonean (non-Davidic) dynasty's confusion invited in the Roman Empire with an ultimate military occupation, and forced integration into the empire. Smoldering hopes for a national liberator—the Messiah—were constantly stirred and fanned through the presence of Roman imperial rule, taxes, military legions, and imposition of a pagan culture and lifestyle.

The messianic problem

The central issue of hope in God's covenanted promise, with its questions, debates, and reflection in Israel, is what one can call "the messianic problem." The problem can be summarized briefly in three questions: When shall Messiah be revealed to Israel? Who is Messiah? How

---

[15] The simple naive reading of the Bible and the significance of the theological narrative of creation, fall, redemption, and consummation as hermeneutical keys are both objects of theological reflection and the epistemological means by which that reflection is controlled, as has been incisively formulated by Henry Van der Coot in *Interpreting the Bible in Theology and Church* (New York: Edward Mellen Press, 1984).

shall Messiah's reign come into existence and be carried out in the face of pagan imperial domination of Rome, disputing Jewish vested interests, and contradictory religious parties?

These were the troubling unanswered questions for the circles in Israel, by then purified of idolatry and deeply chastened by its history of being dominated, oppressed, and continually harassed by the occupying foreign power and its Jewish collaborators.

The socioreligious particularity of Jesus of Nazareth

In this context, Jesus of Nazareth appeared in Israel's life with his baptism by John the Baptist, and in the history of the nations when he "suffered under Pontius Pilate." His unique stance, which took place within a socioreligious/political context, has been well described as "quadrilateral."[16]

Sadducees. Jesus was not a part of—or identified with—the Jewish Sadducean religious and social establishment, or with priests and scribes, or with the Sanhedrin rulers who had determined a collaborative modus vivendi with Rome. On the contrary, he expected and proclaimed radical change and transformation in view of the coming kingdom of God, the prophesied and awaited final consummation of God's purpose for humanity in creation. Could he be the Messiah?

Zealots. But neither was Jesus a part of the revolutionary Zealots with their armed resistance in view of restoring King David's theocratic kingdom of Israel. They believed firmly in the God-sent plenipotentiary liberator/Messiah who would forcibly remove pagan domination. While Jesus did not have a takeover program for social or political action, he was clearly in touch with Zealot disciple "Simon the Zealot." Yet he called for a revolutionary turnaround, or repentance (*metanoia*), in light of the kingdom of God; he acted in the light of its presence in himself for those about him, for Israel's salvation, in view of the full consummation of God's purpose for humanity.

Thus, Jesus rejected the pressures of his being acclaimed the Zealots' national Messiah, and called for a renunciation of violent force— not resisting the evildoer, but offering goodness, blessing, and prayer for those who hate, curse, and persecute. He was more revolutionary than the Zealots. He represented "a decidedly nonviolent revolution . . . emerging from man's most innermost and secret nature, from the

---

[16] This is an adaptation from Hans Küng, *On Being a Christian* (New York: Wallaby Pocket Books, 1978), 177–79; see especially 211.

personal center, from the heart of man into society . . . a conversion away from all forms of selfishness toward God and his fellow man."[17] Society, in Israel and the nations, had to be transformed through transformation of people's inner being (see Mark 7:20–23). Could this be the manner and strategy of Messiah?

Essenes. Was Jesus then for social withdrawal? There was just such a movement in his time, a kind of Jewish communal reality, the Essenes, about which we know more as a result of the Qumran manuscripts found in the late 1940s. If there was any connection between their ritual baths, understandings, and hopes, and those of Jesus, it was quite possibly indirectly through John the Baptist. However, Jesus was not isolated from the social world of his day but was in the very midst of it, rejecting the notion of cutting oneself off from the "sons of darkness" as did the Essenes. Could this be the way for the Messiah to be recognized? He was not a fanatical ascetic as they were, since he was free to reinterpret certain traditional practices of the law, defending his disciples for not fasting and even facing charges of being a glutton and a drinker. Indeed, Jesus' alternative was not for an elite in separated communities but for all people everywhere. He was in touch with people from all walks of society, including non-Israelites.

Pharisees. Both the violent Zealots and the communitarian Essenes had attempted radical responses to the unfaithful and accommodating socioreligious establishment they faced. Both accepted the rule of God as they understood it, and were ready to assume its full consequences in a life-or-death commitment, yet with opposing strategies. However, if unlike them, one did not accept a break "at the roots," what other possibility was there? It was the way of the devout or pious—cheerfully, inconsistently working out diplomatic adjustments and attempted harmonizations of God's law, yet quite obviously involving moral compromise—the way of the Pharisees. Their hope for a restoration of Israel through law by keeping with its external, legal, and ritual preoccupations was clearly not the approach of Jesus. He was not a pious legalist, and he opposed self-righteousness; yet he did not ignore the law of God. On the contrary, he called for a higher understanding and deeper commitment to it in its source in the Creator-Redeemer God, whom he called Father with a provocative familiarity! But since he freely broke the detailed, stringent Sabbath laws that had developed with interpretations of creation's story, how could this be the Messiah?

---

[17] Ibid., 191.

The description of these current options leads us to a fuller examination of Jesus' self-understanding, from the traditions in the Gospels.

Messianism in the Gospel tradition: Conceptual elements of Jesus' messianism

The earliest Christian confession in the midst of Israel—"Jesus is the Messiah"—was a response to at least four major strands of thought within Israel's life: (1) the universal reign of God, believed in (prayers were addressed to the "king of the universe"), but clearly not yet wholly realized; (2) Israel's calling—and betrayal—of its holy priestly mediation of God's mercy and justice to the nations, as it had been experienced in the exodus from Egypt; (3) the prophetic denunciations of the ruling elites' political, social, and economic oppression that accompanied their apostasy from Yahweh; (4) the promised restoration of Israel and its world mission through the royal covenant with David and his dynasty in the *mašiaḥ*, the God-anointed one, the Messiah (the Christ).

For these strands to come together, focused in one personality incarnating them all, required the merging of several prophetic images and titles: (1) the son of David/Son of God fulfillment of the royal covenant; (2) the Son of Man of Daniel 7:13–14, the heaven-borne restorer of universal dominion under God; (3) the servant of Yahweh, the Spirit-anointed messenger of God who calls Israel and its elite back to God in a new covenant, then takes the message of redemption to all nations in view of a universal redeemed community with God in its midst; (4) the suffering servant who incarnates mediation in a life and death that transcends the failed sacerdotal and sacrificial system in Israel. We review each of these strands to see how in the Gospel tradition their contents fill out the messianic image in Jesus of Nazareth that we have already seen in the letter to the Thessalonians.

The Messiah

The open identification of Jesus and the Messiah, so central to the Thessalonian epistle, should in one sense come as a surprise, since it is quite clear from the text of the Gospel of Mark, with its many stories, that there was a great deal of reluctance on Jesus' part to use the title and language of Messiah. Following Peter's confession, the Twelve are warned specifically not to tell anyone (Mark 8:30). This fact has been called "the messianic secret"[18] in scholarly circles, from which the following conclusions can be summarized:

Jesus never spoke openly of himself as the Messiah. At the same time, everything he said and did had messianic significance, particularly the proclamation of the kingdom of God as being decisive for the present and the future, and his interpretation of his ministry as an effective sign of the kingdom, already present. He thus awakened messianic expectations and encountered faith that believed him to be the Messiah. Yet he seems to have done everything possible to discourage the propagation of that title as applied to himself.[19]

How shall we explain this fact? On the basis of contemporary Jewish writings and history, we know that the messianic expectations generally centered on a strong national leader who, as a powerful military instrument of God's righteous cause, would violently defeat and dominate the Roman oppressor, recreate national independence, and restore the Davidic kingdom to its former glory, all as a vindication of Yahweh before the nations who did not accept his kingship.[20]

Jesus, in his life and ministry, was constantly confronted with that conception. This becomes clearest when Peter, in response to Jesus' question about his identity, openly confessed Jesus' messiahship but just as openly refused Jesus' own clear understanding of his ministry, rejection, betrayal, suffering, and crucifixion (Mark 8:27–38). For Jesus, that refusal was satanic; it was the crucial issue he had faced and dealt with in the desert temptations following his baptism/presentation to Israel.[21]

---

[18] See Christopher Tuckett, ed., *The Messianic Secret* (Philadelphia: Fortress Press, 1983), who brings together in this helpful volume recent scholarly thinking on the question.

[19] My summary of Tuckett.

[20] The ideal, which dealt mostly with questions of race, land, and boundaries, was the "restoration of national independence and the installation of a new kingdom of Israel called to become a political and religious center of a society of nations bowed beneath the yoke of Yahweh and his people." See Joseph Coppens, *Messianisme Royal: Ses origines, son développement, son accomplissement* (Paris: Éditions du Cerf, 1968), 176; my translation.

[21] "Jesus believed himself to be the Messiah, but his conception of the Messianic role was an unexpected and unpopular one. Because the title had such different connotations for Jesus and for those who heard him, he never used it of himself or unequivocally welcomed its application to him by others. And when his actions or words seemed to encourage the to him false conception of messiahship, he tried to prevent it by commands to silence. Nevertheless, he did not deny his right to the title, but attempted to reeducate his hearers to the significance of it for him. And the claims

The words of the prophets in Israel had made it clear that Messiah would bring the kind of redemption and blessing that would overcome social ills, economic injustice, and political oppression; this was inherent to the mission of Messiah. He was to bring his people back to God and the law, and bring God's full salvation to his people and to the nations. Thus, the content of the messianic mission was not in question; what was at issue was the nature of that mission. How would Messiah fulfill his God-anointed mission to Israel and the nations? Was there another option besides that of narrow nationalism, violent repression, and domination from the summit of human hierarchy by forcing and imposing the kingdom with human power and prowess in the name of Yahweh?

Jesus' answer to that question has ever since been a part of the concern for understanding the specificity of Jesus' messianism, as well as the nature of the redemption he brings and the salvation he fulfills. Unfortunately, Western Christianity, with the dualism so characteristic of Greek thought, has at this very point generally misconstrued the issue as one of political Messiah versus religious Messiah, heavenly kingdom versus earthly kingdom. The great biblical scholar Oscar Cullmann is a well-known recent representative of such thought, constantly distinguishing between the political Messiah of Judaism and his own understanding of what he called the "spiritual messiahship" of Jesus. "Jesus knows that the specific ideas relating to the Jewish Messiah are of a political nature, and nothing is more foreign to his conception of his calling."[22]

The elimination of the political, social, and economic concerns from Jesus' understanding of his messiahship simply vitiates the holistic restoration and salvation thrust of Israel's prophets "when predicting the sufferings of [Messiah] and the subsequent glory" (1 Pet. 1:11b) as "indicated by the Spirit of [Messiah] within them" (1 Pet. 1:11a). Perhaps the most striking illustration is the typical interpretation of Jesus' word to Pilate, "My kingship is not of this world; if my kingship were of this world, my servants would fight, that I might not be handed over to the Jews; but my kingship is not from the world" (John 18:36). In the

---

he made to messiahship and Messianic authority were of a parabolic sort whose significance was there, plain for all to see whose eyes were not blinded and whose ears were not clogged by misconceptions." See James D. G. Dunn, "The Messianic Secret in Mark," in Tucket, *Messianic Secret,* 128.

[22] Oscar Cullmann, *The Christology of the New Testament,* trans. Shirley C. Guthrie and Charles A. M. Hall (Philadelphia: Westminster Press, 1963), 121.

Western spiritualist tradition, the word has been construed to mean a dominion "not on earth" rather than as a reference to a non-worldly (not conformed to God's will) ethos or quality of dominion. However, Jesus' own insistence is on being "in the world" and is contrasted with being "of the world," not with being "out of the world" (John 17).

The issue is the nature and quality of the mission of Messiah, who is political by definition.[23] The issue is not whether political, social, or economic concerns are included in Messiah's agenda, but rather how they are to be dealt with. And here we must turn to other dimensions of Jesus' understanding.

Son of God

As was already indicated, "Son of God" is a royal title, but it was applied first of all to Israel itself when the first-born sons of Pharaoh and Egypt were lost in order to save Yahweh's "first-born son," Israel (Exod. 4:22–23). Later in the time of Israel's kingship ("like the nations" and only permitted by God), the term was applied to the king in Israel as a title (see Ps. 2:7) for one who fully represents all Israel and who yet receives authority and unction/anointing as God's representative, ruling for God.

Especially did that title become meaningful as a future hope because of the Davidic covenant earlier referred to and given through the prophet Nathan: "I will establish the throne of his kingdom forever. I will be his father, and he shall be my son. . . . Your kingdom shall be made sure forever before me; your throne shall be established forever" (2 Sam. 7:13, 16; see also 1 Chron. 17:11–15). The Chronicles text adds, "I will not take my steadfast love from him" (1 Chron. 17:13). The Davidic covenant was foundational to the Jewish kingdom's identity, and in times of exile and non-Davidic rulers, it was foremost in Israel's thought.[24] Later, particularly in the Greek context, Son of God became perhaps the most-used title for Jesus apart from Lord and Christ, but it had lost its messianic functional impact.

---

[23] John H. Yoder has effectively pointed out that there is a political stance of Jesus with a remarkable consistency between the earthly and transcendent Messiah; see *The Politics of Jesus* (Grand Rapids, MI: Eerdmans, 1972).

[24] It is difficult to accept some scholars' rejection of the connection between Messiah and Son of God, particularly when important synoptic texts make the connection explicit. The question of the high priest to Jesus, "Are you the [Messiah], the Son of the Blessed?" (Mark 14:61), and Peter's confession in the Matthean eye-witness account, "You are the [Messiah], the Son of the living God" (Matt. 16:16), must be accounted for, along with some important textual readings of John 6:69.

What seems most important is that beginning with this Jewish royal understanding and title, Jesus demonstrated the messianic Father/Son unique relationship and intimacy in a way that makes it a reality that moved well beyond the scope of nationalist preoccupations but not beyond the political ones. Indeed, that intimacy and sense of uniqueness would ultimately be associated with the later Greek emphasis on the divinely "substantial" Son of God. Yet this sense of uniqueness and intimacy does not eliminate the messianic dimension but gives it a scope in God that reaches well beyond Israel to a fuller universal messianism and dominion. The title Son of God must not be extracted from that messianic meaning and context.

In the last week before his death, Jesus himself tried to make the Jerusalem leaders more sensitive to this reality during his open discussion about Psalm 110:2. "How can the scribes say that the Christ [Messiah] is the son of David? David himself, inspired by the Holy Spirit, declared, 'The Lord said to my Lord, Sit at my right hand, till I put thy enemies under thy feet.' David himself calls him Lord; so how is he his son?" (Mark 12:35–37). Indeed, how can the Davidic dynasty have a scion who is higher than the founder of the national dynasty? Yet does not David himself recognize it to be true? This very real transcendent political preoccupation was in Jesus' consciousness just a couple of days prior to his crucifixion . . . and resurrection. Was he not calling Israel to readiness for that answer so soon to come?

Son of Man

It is most significant that Jesus clearly preferred to give himself the title "Son of Man." We find it fifteen times in Mark's earliest written presentation of the oral tradition. Indeed, it is found some sixty-nine times in the synoptics and a dozen times in the Gospel of John, with practically no other use of the title in the New Testament writings (see Acts 7:56; Rev. 1:13). However, despite that fact, as one recent christological study notes in dismissing its importance, "it has never played a major role in the theological definition of Christ's person" because it is "associated with—if not synonymous with—the title 'Son of God' (Mark 14:62 and parallels)."[25] Eclipsed in that manner by many theologians, its meaning—so significant for Jesus—has nevertheless appeared to have had continuity in the thought of Paul, which we have already seen (1 Thess.

---

[25] See C. Norman Kraus's discussion in *Jesus Christ, Our Lord: Christology from a Disciple's Perspective* (Scottdale, PA: Herald Press, 1987), 93n15. In fact, "son of the blessed" and "Son of Man" are titles that each give different content to Jesus' unique understanding of his messiahship.

4:15) in his understanding of the yet-to-come eschatological ministry of the Messiah Jesus, to which we will later return.

It is not possible here to develop the ancient Jewish and non-Jewish roots of the title, which was current in some circles in Jesus' time.[26] Suffice it to say that it referred to a heavenly or ideal man, representing on the one hand the beginning of humanity with Adam's dominion, and on the other hand the "end times" (*eschaton*) when such dominion would again appear with humanity under God. Both deal with the representative human, "man" called to be faithful to his divine destiny to be the image of God.[27] In Daniel 7, he appears in the eschatological context "with the clouds of heaven" (7:13) and is presented to the Ancient of Days; dominion, kingdom, and glory were given him "that all peoples, nations, and languages should serve him" (7:14) in an "everlasting dominion, which shall not pass away, and his kingdom one that shall not be destroyed" (7:14). The expression is interpreted as being a personal representation of the collective "saints of the Most High;" it did not escape integration into the self-understanding of one who proclaimed the kingdom of God as present in his words and ministry.

The use of the title by Jesus must have carried some ambiguity, however, for in Job and the Psalms the expression is often used to refer to humankind generally, and peculiarly to human frailty in responsibility before the eternal Creator God (see Ps. 8:4). Further, in the writings of Ezekiel, the term is found more than eighty times in reference to the prophet. In the opening vision, seeing himself only as a "child of man" in the face of the glory of the transcendent God, the prophet falls on his face (Ezek. 1:28); called to his feet, he is given the Spirit, with strength to proclaim the message of God (2:1–2; 3:1–2). Thus, he becomes a messenger of God's word of judgment and salvation to a rebellious people. Not as a "son of Israel" to Israel, but as a "Son of Man" (son of universal humanity) to Israel and all the nations, the prophet is called to judge both Israel and its enemies for their salvation.

---

[26] See Cullmann, *Christology of the New Testament,* 151–53, and particularly Rudolph Otto: "The phrase ['the figure that you saw in human form' (see Dan. 7:13: 'one like a Son of Man')] bore such emphasis in circles of readers familiar with this [Book of Enoch] and similar books, that when mention was made of 'the man,' with association of judgment, the coming world, the right hand of God, the coming with or on the clouds of heaven, the words 'Son of Man' had the force of a title; and when an eschatological preacher spoke of the coming of the Son of Man and of his judgment it was known what he meant, viz., the king in the coming world"; see Otto, *The Kingdom of God and the Son of Man* (London: Lutterworth Press, 1938), 226, and 176–218.

[27] Cullmann, *Christology of the New Testament,* 151.

In the early part of Jesus' ministry, the title he used could easily have been understood as open acknowledgment of such a prophetic ministry, and was recognized as such (see Matt. 16:13; Mark 6:15; John 6:14). And Jesus could also use it for himself in the sense of frailty and humiliation. The very question to Peter, "Who do people say that the Son of Man is?" (Matt. 16:13, NRSV), indicates the ambivalence of the term, for if it had clearly meant the transcendent, eschatological king, there would have been no reason to ask the question. But there can be no doubt that after Peter's confession, such an orientation became unambiguous.

Henceforth, Jesus' use of the title referred to the eschatological "man" in his exaltation, thus accenting the more his betrayal, rejection, suffering, and death. It is the judicial dimension of the Son of Man in his exaltation that is most often underlined in Jesus' words and understandings. Matthew 25, with the judgment between sheep and goats, is the most striking; here, the nations are judged in relationship to their responses to the needs of "these who are members of my family" (Matt. 25:40, NRSV). We see it again in Matthew 24:29–31 where the tribes of the earth will mourn as "his elect" are gathered under the authority of the Son of Man. In Luke 17:22–37 the "days of the Son of Man" are compared to those of the flood in the time of Noah and the judgment of Sodom and Gomorrah. Most striking, of course, is Jesus' startling response to the high priest: "You will see the Son of Man sitting at the right hand of Power, and coming with the clouds of heaven" in answer to the question "Are you the [Messiah]?" (Mark 14:61–62).

Here is open acknowledgment by Jesus that he is not only the son of David/Messiah of particular Jewish national concern but also the universal Son of Man/Messiah of present-day and ultimate eschatological significance. It is indeed the image of Daniel 7 on the one hand, yet tied clearly to the righteous ruler of Psalm 110 who executes judgment and high priestly mediation among the nations, with universal authority far beyond that of the high priest of Jerusalem before whom he appears. The combination illustrates Jesus' consciousness of a coming magistracy to be exercised prior to the fulfillment of God's universal eschatological reign—a political function and mission much greater than that of the simple messiahship of national Israel and its imperial interests, of which he is accused.

What is unique in this understanding of the Son of Man is the earthly humiliation of this ideal, heavenly man—the image of God—in an earthly testing, as a prerequisite to the exaltation of universal magistracy. Indeed, the Son of Man to whom judgment is to be given is not an ideal man in the heavenly world; he is rather one who on earth, in the flesh, in the world, struggles and agonizes in his human calling of righteousness and love to be faithful to his identity and destiny as the true and faithful image of the Father-Creator of humanity who sends him.

The testing of the cross must happen as an ultimate test of that faithfulness: only he is worthy of exercising eschatological judgment who has suffered in death the loss of his freedom, precisely because of his free and faithful obedience in love, while continuing to love and forgive his enemies, respecting even their freedom to kill him. It is this image of God that Jesus the Son of Man demonstrated before the coming day was over. On the one hand, it was the fullest human response to God's covenant of grace and faithfulness; on the other hand, it became the new covenant of God to all humanity (*uno per omnes*).

The ideal or prototypical and representative humanity as image of God, with its fulfillment in an ultimate humiliation because of human faithfulness to God as a condition of glory, are inherent in Jesus' appropriation of the title Son of Man, and his understanding of its ultimate eschatological importance. That orientation and its tension in which he lived is well depicted in a later commentary that had recognized that representative role so well: "looking to Jesus . . . , who for the joy that was set before him endured the cross, despising the shame, and is seated at the right hand of the throne of God. Consider him who endured from sinners such hostility against himself, so that you may not grow weary or fainthearted" (Heb. 12:2–3; see also 2:6–10).

Servant of Yahweh and the suffering servant

The servant (*'ebed*) in the Servant Songs of Isaiah (42:1–4; 49:1–9; 50:4–11; 52:13–53:12) is in the Septuagint translated as *pais*, which can in turn be translated either as "servant" or as "child" (as in Acts 4:27, 30, AV).

It is important to note that in Jesus' time this "servant of Yahweh" was identified either with the coming Messiah or with corporate Israel. This identification was both in the Qumran writings and in the Targum of Isaiah, but all the traces of suffering and humiliation had been removed from that understanding, as being incompatible with Messiah and his mission. What was significant for Israel was that he was the anointed one—the one to whom God's Spirit is given (Isa. 42:1), that is, the *mašiah*, the Messiah—who is to "bring forth justice to the nations" (42:1), persevering in his universal mission "till he has established jus-

tice in the earth" (42:4). This is, of course, an eminently political function given as the basic calling, mission, and purpose of the servant,
the context of all of his activity—as well as in the collection of Servant
Songs. In his person, the servant is a "covenant to the people [Israel], a
light to the nations" (42:6) as the bringer of God's justice.

If, from the womb, the servant of Yahweh was chosen to bring about
the restoration of Israel, his ultimate mission through Israel was to be
that light so "that my salvation may reach to the end of the earth" (Isa.
49:5–6). Contrary to Judaism's understandings, it is as the servant of
rulers (49:7) that he will attract the homage of rulers! Prior to the song
of Isaiah 52:13–53:12, the task of the servant is given as that of bringing
good tidings (gospel) of peace, goodness, and salvation—of proclaiming
to Jerusalem the kingdom of God, "Your God reigns" (52:7). Through
the redemption of Jerusalem "before the eyes of all the nations," all
the ends of the earth will see the salvation from Israel's God (52:7–10).
All of this had clear import and significance for Judaism in Jesus' time.

Thus, from the perspective of the texts themselves, it would appear that Oscar Cullmann overstates the case when he insists that "the
principal function of the servant of God is found in his sufferings and
his substitutionary death."[28] Rather, it is in the context of this principal,
political function of bringing justice to the ends of the earth through
Israel—and only in the perspective of this mission—that the servant
becomes despised (Isa. 49:7), smitten, and spat upon (50:6), becoming
indeed the suffering one, wounded, bruised, chastised, oppressed, af-
flicted as an offering for sin. But even after the self-giving unto death,
the mission is not terminated, although the death itself becomes also
a means of justice-making—making "many to be accounted righteous"
(53:11). Indeed, as the song of Isaiah 52:13 begins, "He shall be exalted
and lifted up, and shall be very high."

The mission of the servant is the restoration of Israel by preaching
the peace of the reign of God, in view of the establishment of justice
among all the nations. Thus, the servant's "sufferings and substitutionary death" to which Cullmann refers are first of all the consequences
of a prophetic preaching mission of persuasion for justice and peace,
with only God to justify him before those who reject and oppose that
mission (Isa. 50:7–9) in which he "poured out his soul to death" (53:12).

It was just such a reception at the hands of those opposed to God's
reign that was unacceptable and impossible for the Messiah as understood by Judaism. But the vicarious suffering and death were also a

---

[28] Ibid., 55.

function of the servant as "offering for sin" (53:10), "for the transgression of my people" (53:8), "[bearing] the sin of many . . . [with] . . . intercession for the transgressors" (53:12); their first consequence was a posterity that would also be made righteous. The servant's place as one who is great and who divides the spoils of victory is also a consequence of his first giving his life in that mission faithfully unto death. His exaltation is a consequence of his faithfulness despite rejection, suffering, and death.

In the perspective of the whole—both that unacceptable to the Judaism of Jesus' time and that marginalized by Cullmann in our time—the Messiah is a prophet-king who is God's chosen servant for justice to Israel first, and thus through Israel is servant to the nations. In that mission he suffers and dies at their hands, fulfilling a priestly service of reconciliation as the one who representatively suffers and dies for all. But the mission continues: The servant "shall prosper, he shall be exalted and lifted up, and shall be very high" (Isa. 52:13), "till he has established justice in the earth" (42:4), for that is the mission.

Independently of current Jewish understandings, Jesus fully assumed the *ebed*-Messiah alternative, including the suffering unto death, starting with the Spirit-empowering at his baptism by John. There, the servant-king messianic commission is explicit (Mark 1:11 and parallels, in the light of Ps. 2:7 and Isa. 42:1), and in the Gospel of John (1:36) the "Lamb" of God of Isaiah 53:7 is also made explicit in the language of the Baptist. Thus, as already indicated, Jesus knew himself to be the chosen Messiah of Israel for the nations, with the high calling of reestablishing peace through justice through the appeal and persuasion of the proclaimed word of God by a faithful servant—without self-defense, violence, or deceit (Isa. 53:9). Jesus said it clearly in one important statement in Mark's Gospel: "For the Son of Man also came not to be served but to serve, and to give his life as a ransom for many" (Mark 10:45). The declaration is made in the context of contrasting Gentile ("the nations") lordship, rule, and authority with that of Israel's calling as the faithful covenant partner in the kingdom of God, of which Jesus was the supreme instance.

This manner of ministry was dramatically represented and symbolized in Jesus' washing the feet of the disciples at the Last Supper, "an example, that you also should do as I have done" (John 13:15). Here again the reference is to a political style, a servant-Messiah: "The leader [should be] as one who serves. . . . I am among you as one who serves" (Luke 22:26–28). The high point of Jesus' ministry, the paschal celebration in view of the coming final sufferings and death, is specifically set forth in explicit servant language and action. The references to death "for many" (as in Isa. 53:12), in Mark 14:24 and parallels, in that context confirm this self-understanding as suffering servant.

It is not strange, of course, that this self-understanding would be confirmed in other Gospel writings.[29] The Gospel of Mark, and especially the Passion narrative, has been seen by scholars to have been written in the light of the servant messialogy as it was known and expressed in the oral tradition that emerged from Jesus' own self-understanding.[30] This motif appears as well in the earliest reported preaching in Jerusalem where the servant (or "child") theme is accented in the context of Peter's ministry (Acts 3:13, 26; 4:25, 30). Indeed, the "righteous one" of Isaiah 53:11 was clearly a part of the current language of the early days (Acts 3:14; 7:52; 22:14). Significantly, both remain important in the much later epistle of Peter, where the "servant" (1 Pet. 2:21–25) and "the righteous one" (3:16–18) are appealed to as the example for the disciples' daily way of life as well as the way to God.

One also recalls the important application of Isaiah's suffering servant to Jesus in the ministry of Philip to the Ethiopian minister of Queen Candace (Acts 8:32–40). The very early homologic that Paul exploited in his exhortation to the Philippians (Phil. 2:1–11) describes Jesus' earthly ministry as the "form of a servant" (v. 7; compare "form of God," v. 6), who as man, "humbled himself and became obedient unto death" (v. 8). And most significantly, the apostle exposes it as the mind-set of the Messiah Jesus to be appropriated by his disciples (v. 5). Finally, this is also most obviously reflected in the apostles' early self-designation as "servants" in juxtaposition with Jesus' servanthood (Acts 4:29), or in the usual way of describing themselves and their associates (Rom. 1:1; 1 Cor. 4:1; 7:22; Gal. 1:10; Phil. 1:1; 2 Pet. 1:1; Jude 1:1).

The evidence indicates that probably the earliest messianic understanding of the post-resurrection community, informed by the risen Jesus (as reported by Luke 24:26–27 and 45–46), was that which experienced and knew Jesus as ʿebed Yahweh and the servant-Messiah.[31] Although the language and understandings were eventually to become marginal in the Greek contexts that eclipsed those of Judaism, even there they nevertheless retained some importance both for liturgy (see

---

[29] Matt. 8:16 (compare Isa. 53:4); Matt. 12:18–21 (compare Isa. 42:1–7); John 12:38 (compare Isa. 53:1).

[30] See Cullmann, *Christology of the New Testament*, 63.

[31] Ibid., 79.

Didache 9:2; 10:2; 1 Clement 59:3; 61:3) and for life pattern (for example, 1 Clement 16) as in 1 Peter.

One could, of course, ask why this servant Christology, which was so important both in Jesus' consciousness and in the early life (Andrew Walls's "Jewish phase") of the church, was later to lose vital significance. Was the servant/slave language culturally unacceptable for the context of the Greek world? Was it seen as inappropriate ideology for the empire? Here we simply stress its singular importance, for this is in fact the essential revolutionary turnaround in the disciple-community's messianic consciousness. This is the itinerary from Peter's confession of Jesus as Messiah, through his sword-carrying and sword-wielding defense of Jesus in the garden, to the authoritative apostolic word that gives the Messiah Jesus' nonresistant suffering in doing good as the supreme example to be followed in the vocation of his disciples (1 Pet. 2:21–25).

This servant Christology was present also in the oldest document, addressed to the Thessalonians, by one who made exactly the same conversion as Peter and was ultimately preaching and practicing that same servanthood. But in our earlier examination of that epistle, this concept was not then seen so clearly, nor was its significance and its source well understood.

> To the church . . . in God the Father and the Lord Jesus [the Messiah]: Grace to you and peace. . . . You became imitators of us and of the Lord, for you received the word in much affliction . . . so that you became an example. . . . The word of the Lord sounded forth from you. . . . You turned to God from idols, to serve a living and true God. . . . We exhorted each one of you and encouraged you and charged you to lead a life worthy of God, who calls you into his own kingdom and glory. . . . You . . . became imitators of the churches of God in [the Messiah] Jesus . . . for you suffered the same things. . . . We live, if you stand fast in the Lord. . . May the Lord make you increase and abound in love to one another and to all [people], as we do to you. . . . For you know what instructions we gave you through the Lord Jesus. . . . Be at peace among yourselves. . . . See that none of you repays evil for evil, but always seek to do good to one another and to all. . . . May the God of peace himself sanctify you wholly. . . . The grace of our Lord Jesus [the Messiah] be with you. (1 Thess. 1:1–5:28)

There are, of course, deep roots for this servanthood in the vicarate given to the first human couple as God's servants in and over creation and in God's liberating Israel from Egypt ("that they may serve me").[32] This theme is clearly repeated in their God-given mediating vocation as a "kingdom of priests" (Exod. 19:4–6) in the midst of the nations. Through Torah and the prophets, we know of a created humanity and a redeemed Israel for the service of God in and over earthly creation. But where is that servanthood and service visibly realized? It is promised by the word of God through the prophet Isaiah as a specific character- istic of God's anointed, the Messiah, the one for the many; it was self- consciously fulfilled by Jesus of Nazareth.[33] But even as it was unaccept- able to official Judaism, it was also not congenial to the later dominant Greek mentality or to the barbarians among whom their Christianity spread and extended itself worldwide.

Yet then and now, inside and outside Israel, Jesus' fulfillment re- mains a permanent provocation and corrective to current and popular misunderstandings of messianism, giving a new and definitive mean- ing to the title "the Messiah," the Christ. But thus appropriated, it in no way whatsoever eliminates the full dynamics of messianic hope and fulfillment for humanity restored in community; there, goodness and blessing, love/mercy and righteousness create peace through the anointing by Jesus the anointed one/Messiah and give evidence of God's salvation, holy presence, and reign in the midst of and for the nations that know no such hope.

Servant elements of Jesus' messianism

The relationship to God as Father

There seems to be little doubt that the book of Deuteronomy had con- siderable influence in Jesus' personal training. The accent therein on Israel's covenant response of service to God is repeated over and over again (see Deut. 6:13; 10:12, 20; 11:13; 13:4). And it is to this basic call to Israel that Jesus turned in the inaugural desert confrontation and temptation: "Away from me, Satan! For it is written: 'Worship the Lord your God, and serve him only'" (Matt. 4:10, NIV; see also Luke 4:7–8).

---

[32] Strangely, liberation theology, based also on the exodus as founding event, gener- ally gives scant attention to this closure in God's service, so integral to the penta- teuchal account (see Exod. 4:23; 5:1; 7:16; 8:1, 20; 9:1,13; 10:3, 7–8).

[33] See Deut. 6:13; 10:12, 20; 11:13; 13:4; from one of the sources most cited by Jesus. For this consciousness of literal fulfillment, see Luke 22:37, where his asking for swords is to fulfill the word of Isa. 53:12 ("He . . . was numbered with the transgressors").

The way Jesus understood that service to God is, however, not according to the types of slave to master, of subject to royalty, or even of creature to Creator. It is, rather, in an intimate parent-to-child-to-parent relationship of mutual love (see Deut. 6:5, quoted in Mark 12:33) and trust in which a common identity and destiny prompts in the one a willful, active, and obedient reflection of the life, character, purpose, and will of the other whose shared identity is thus totally disclosed. The idea of obedient sonship was not a new one for Israel;[34] it only lacked full embodiment. That was promised, as we have seen, in the royal posterity of David, the Messiah, when he would come.

Without question, Jesus impressed those about him with the fact that he lived his inherited sonship in Israel in a unique way, as he spoke of and to Abba with an intensity and familiarity previously unknown.[35] It became public at least at the time of his baptism by John, when that affinity was confirmed with the word (Ps. 2:7; Isa. 42:1) to the ʿebed of Yahweh: "You are my Son [ʿebed, pais], whom I love; with you I am well pleased" (Mark 1:11, NIV). This central dynamic relationship expressed itself in an ethos of God's presence, the Holy Spirit, which for others henceforth characterized Jesus' life and service.[36] And this life core of anointed/messianic sonship was seen by Jesus also as a future reality and measure of judgment, beyond the crucifixion to the time of the eschaton when "the Son of Man is to come with his angels in the glory of his father" (Matt. 16:27). Jesus' sonship was acknowledged by his apostles as an exposed "exegesis" of God (see John 1:18), fully identified with the eternal (John 8:58, "before Abraham was, I am") creating Word (John 1:1–2) and Wisdom (1 Cor. 1:30) of God.[37]

The relationship to Israel

Jesus' basic messianic approach. Jesus began his public ministry within the stream opened up by John the Baptist's ministry in which he called

---

[34] E. J. Tinsley, "The Way of Sonship," in *The Imitation of God* (London: SCM, 1960).

[35] "No Jew would have dared to address God in the manner. Jesus did it always. . . . This term *abba* is an *ipsissima vox* of Jesus and contains *in nuce* his message and his claim to have been sent from the Father" (Joachim Jeremias, *The Lord's Prayer* [Philadelphia: Fortress Press, 1964], 20). With reference to the current discussions of patriarchy, and God as Father, see John W. Miller, *Biblical Faith and Fathering: Why We Call God "Father"* (New York: Paulist Press, 1989).

[36] See Paul W. Newman, *A Spirit of Christology: Recovering the Biblical Paradigm of Christian Faith* (Lanham, MD: University Press of America, 1987).

[37] The wisdom theme follows that of Prov. 3:19 and 8:22–31. Jesus spoke of wisdom in Matt. 11:19 and 12:42; Paul used the theme in 1 Cor. 1:18–2:16.

all Israel to repentance and righteousness of obedient faith in view of the kingdom of God (Luke 3:8; Matt. 3:9). Jesus, in accenting the kingdom of God and its justice, followed with that same call to all Israel in a way that has sometimes astonished. It can even appear that he strictly limited his ministry and that of his missioners to "the lost sheep of . . . Israel" (for example, Matt. 10:6; 15:24), even when he allowed for Samaritan and Gentile exceptions. In any case, it has been well shown that his constitution of the Twelve was an eschatological witness and a prophetic sign to the "twelve tribes of Israel," as illustration or demonstration of his intent to reassemble, to re-gather, to reconstitute, and to restore the people of God that all Israel was called to be.[38] How poignant that becomes in the Matthean-cited plaint: "O Jerusalem, Jerusalem, you who kill the prophets and stone those sent to you, how often I have longed to gather your children together, as a hen gathers her chicks under her wings, but you were not willing" (Matt. 23:37, NIV).

It is quite clearly the particular strategy of beginning again radically with the message and reality of God's reign at the grass roots as yeast or seed, with the gathered remnant as the base, in order to gather all of Israel. Yet Israel's salvation is ultimately in view of and the means of the Gentile nations' salvation (John 11:51–52).[39] It was in Israel first that God's messianic sonship needed to be recognized, sanctioned, and heeded. But it was a clear political strategy, in view of the assembling group (Hebrew: *qahal*; Greek: *ekklēsia*; English: assembly/church) of God's faithful people for their calling in the midst of and for the nations. Jesus was clearly not totally misunderstood when he was crucified as the "King of the Jews."

The little apocalypse of the Gospels indicates both Jesus' sense of foreboding about the future of Jerusalem, and his deepest desire to arrest that doom, even as Jonah in Nineveh (Matt. 12:41–42). Indeed, more than a half millennium earlier, Jerusalem's destruction and Israel's exile under Babylon were seen to be precipitated (Jer. 34:17–22) by its overt disobedience in reneging on the Jubilee covenant of justice and liberty that the law of God had prescribed (see Lev. 25) as a sign of God's justice and mercy in the Passover and exodus.

---

[38] See the important gathering theme in Ezek. 34–39, with Messiah fulfilling that role as king (37:24–28). See also Gerhard Lohfink, *Jesus and Community: The Social Dimension of Christian Faith,* trans. John P. Galvin (Philadelphia: Fortress Press, 1984); and John E. Toews, *Jesus Christ, the Convener of the Church* (Newton, KS: General Conference Mennonite Church, 1989).

[39] See Joachim Jeremias, *Jesus' Promise to the Nations* (London: SCM Press, 1958).

Thus, at the very beginning of his ministry in Nazareth, Jesus, following King Zedekiah, began with a royal call to that practice of economic justice and liberty (Luke 4:16–30) in fulfillment of the Isaianic servant's vocation (Isa. 61:1–2; 58:6) and in view of Israel's salvation; it nearly led to his death. Nor did Israel as a whole heed the call, although the exception is clearly observable in Zacchaeus (compare Luke 1:9) who repented and in obedient faith received the salvation offered only days before Jesus' death at the hands of those who refused it. But his proclamation of Jubilee makes it clear that Jesus, in his preaching of the kingdom and the call to repentance and obedient faith, was concerned about the total human welfare (*šalom*) of Israel: "Would that even today you knew the things that make for peace! . . . They will not leave one stone upon another in you; because you did not know the time of your visitation" (Luke 19:42–44).[40]

The messianic ways and means. In observing the ways and means with which Jesus carried out his messianic sonship and God-revealing service, we may often find grounds for the later development of particular, local, contextual Christologies, each of which makes a contribution to a fuller understanding.[41]

The manner or ways of Jesus' servanthood cannot be separated from his identity; these were the ways of the Son. Father-oriented communion/prayer was a fundamental characteristic that has inspired mystical Christologies. His freedom in obedience to the Father has inspired Christologies of freedom. His victory over Satan in the desert, in later temptations with Peter's confession or in the garden, over evil spirits, and on the cross have contributed to Christologies of Christus victor. Jesus' gathering of a disciple community has inspired strategies of congregation planting. When the compassion of his freedom became a contestation of the established powers, he fully assumed the consequences of their hostility; it has inspired Christologies of contestation or revolution. He accepted suffering as inherent in his calling of doing and fulfilling God's justice, with forgiveness of enemies and the refusal of violence against them; it has inspired pacifist Christologies.

Jesus' total openness to persons of all social classes inspires Christologies of relationship and personhood. His rejection of power has

---

[40] See André Trocmé, "Jesus and Jubilee," in *Jesus and the Nonviolent Revolution,* trans. Michael H. Shank and Marlin E.Miller (Scottdale, PA: Herald Press, 1973).

[41] This composite Christology can be seen much in the same way as the "body and its members" image, which Paul used in 1 Cor. 12, when writing of the different spiritual gifts in the life of the church.

contributed to kenotic Christologies. Because all his filial service to God was seen as love (*agapē*) for others, including the enemy, it has inspired Christologies of love and the "man for others." Indeed, such love humanly fulfilled God's law without diminishing its intent; hence, Christologies of fulfillment. One cannot but be impressed with Jesus' preoccupation with service to the marginal and the poor, inspiring a Christology oriented to "God's option for the poor;" to women, inspiring a feminist Christology ("Jesus was a feminist"); to publicans and harlots, with a "Christ for the outsiders." His "set at liberty those who are oppressed" (Luke 4:18), has inspired a Christology of liberation. All of them together indicate the way of the Son, the Messiah. Each is one part of the way. God's liberation is for the service of God.

The means—or techniques—of Jesus' servanthood reveal the many methods of articulating his messiahship with the various manifestations of alienation in the people among whom he moved and served. Beginning with his proclamation of the kingdom and the call to repentance, Jesus the preacher inspires a kerygmatic conversionist Christology, or a kingdom Christology. Thereupon follows his personal call to follow him, inspiring ethical Christologies of Master-disciple, discipling, discipleship; Jesus can become a human model to follow. His response to those who are sick, lame, blind, deaf, and ill with leprosy is one of healing and wholeness; it is not strange that Christologies of healing and care for the sick should develop from this dimension of his ministry. Where he meets those who are demon possessed and totally alienated from others, he confronts and casts out evil spirits, manifesting the victorious power of the kingdom of God; given the context, this dimension of his ministry has often inspired Christologies of exorcism and power confrontation.

As a recognized rabbi/teacher among his fellow Jews, Jesus taught, often effectively with parables, as he reinterpreted the law of God and the prophets, often in the light of his own work. He did not hesitate to confront prophetically the oppressive legalism and religious formalism and exploitation of his time. Both of these latter expressions have provided inspiration for prophetic and teaching Christologies of the word. Jesus openly entered the domain seen as that of the divine and gave the priestly proclamation of forgiveness of sins; this has inspired Christologies of mediation of grace. His blessing and promises of blessing have certainly been exploited in Christologies of prosperity.

These summaries can perhaps be more fully completed with others. But all these ways and means of Jesus' life, action, and service were expressions of his obedient sonship and a servant exegesis-revelation of the Father. He saw them to be, in fact, the very signs of his God-sent messianity: "Go and tell John what you hear and see: The blind receive their sight and the lame walk, lepers are cleansed and the deaf hear, and the dead are raised up, and the poor have good news preached to them. And blessed is he who takes no offense at me" (Matt. 11:4–6). What is important here is the recognition of all these dimensions of Jesus' life and service as a fuller revealing of the Father by the Son. Each was a true—even as it was a partial—revealing of the Father.

Each partial understanding needs to be understood and critiqued in the light of the fuller one. Yet it was all implicit in the Jewish apostles' gospel ministry and life together in Thessalonica, when they lived and preached Jesus the Messiah two decades after his death, and two decades prior to the destruction of Jerusalem, which he had tried to save. They were indeed taking up the servant mission of Israel to the nations (see Acts 13:46–47) as they participated in the messianic end-time gathering of the peoples into the universal *ekklēsia* of God.

It is not clear that all those who experienced personally that revelation of God and those signs of divine sonship, messianity, and the kingdom of God, received them as such. Neither is it clear that they came—without offense—to faith in Jesus as the Messiah, the Son of God. Nor is it clear that through Jesus they all came to know God as Father, living out the child-stance of obedient trust and love that would reflect God's life and reign, even as Jesus had taught and done. Nor is it clear that they all identified with Jesus' new community in Israel. (Only about a hundred and twenty people were in the Jerusalem circle in the days after Jesus' resurrection ministry.) But ways and means into that possibility had been present as a revealing of the Father—for those who would hear and see. Indeed, each means had been a potential path into the "way" of Jesus' divine sonship and messianity, and thence to the Father who was thus made known for the salvation of Israel, itself the chosen instrument, the "kingdom of priests," of such ways and means of making God known for the blessing and salvation of the nations.

The suffering servanthood of Jesus' messianism

The disproportionate amount of space given to the betrayal, trials, sufferings, and crucifixion of Jesus in the four Gospel accounts has focused particular attention on that death and its meaning, not only for the ordinary reader, but also for theologians. Classical theology referred to this as the passive obedience of Jesus: that which he endured in his acceptance of death and which happened to him; he was crucified by others (passive mode). Not enough attention was given to the active obedience of Jesus: that which he freely took on as task and calling, which he fully assumed, and which led to his death ("became obedient unto death" [Phil. 2:8]; "by the obedience of one shall many be made righteous" [Rom. 5:19, AV]).

What has been correctly stressed much more in Western Christianity in recent years is Jesus' inaugural presentation in Nazareth in which he publicly proclaimed and defined his messianic mission: "The Spirit of the Lord is upon me, because he has anointed me to preach good news to the poor. He has sent me to proclaim release to the captives and recovering of sight to the blind, to set at liberty those who are oppressed, to proclaim the acceptable year of the Lord" (Luke 4:18–19). The immediate reaction to that proclamation, with the death intent, indicates that Jesus' death was first of all the consequence of his Spirit-anointed mission of righteousness and freedom for the peace of Israel, in view of the nations.[42]

"It is written" indeed that the servant of God would suffer and die, but we have already seen in Isaiah's songs that it was because the servant fully assumed the task of bringing forth "to the nations" the justice of obedience to God. And this meant that all the forces of oppression and injustice in their disobedience to God would pit themselves against such a mission. It was the taking on of God's struggle with disobedient and sinful humanity as of old, as well as his covenant commitment to it.

It was Jesus' active and faithful filial obedience in that mission that brought on the opposition that inflicted suffering and ultimately his death; it was "written," given his mission and its context of disobedient humanity, both in Israel and among the nations. At any point Jesus could have turned away from that mission and avoided the wrathful outworking of that disobedience in violent opposition and its consequences. But his calling was to absorb that injustice and persevere, to assume the consequences and persevere, vicariously to take on himself that wrath.[43]

In his freedom of obedience to the Father's steadfast love, Jesus would also in steadfast love (*agapē*) respect the freedom of others to

---

[42] See the section "Jesus removes the idea of vengeance [on the Gentiles] from the eschatological expectation," in Jeremias, *Jesus' Promise to the Nations*, 41–46.

[43] The prophetic word for the violent rebellion against God absorbed by Israel was "Assyria, the rod of my anger" (Isa. 10:5). See also Guy Hershberger, "The Wrath of God in the Old and New Testaments," in *War, Peace and Nonresistance* (Scottdale, PA: Herald Press, 1969, rev. ed.), 17–20.

reject his appeal by word and life for repentance. Yet, in love, he totally respected such refusal and offered forgiveness, even when it meant his own death. He was indeed "obedient unto death, even death on a cross," as the oldest Christian hymn says it (Phil. 2:8) and as the Isaiah song had indicated (see Isa. 50:4–9). As the Son of Man, the one for all, he had offered to the Father the "living sacrifice" of his free and total obedience. As the servant/Son he had freely sacrificed his own free life in death and thus revealed the Father and the extent and fullness of his love.

Even more, he had paid the price of forgiveness and atonement in fully assuming and absorbing the wrathful disobedience and injustice of humanity alienated from God; "the Lord has laid on him the iniquity of us all" (Isa. 53:6).[44] God's work as Creator-Father of humanity was fulfilled ("it is finished") in the human servant Jesus, the fully obedient child—the Messiah, son of Israel's David, Son of God, but also the Son of Man—the one-for-all and once-for-all paradigm for humanity. Both his life and his death were essential to his unique work of justice for peace.[45]

Thus, in addition to the Gospels' description of that God-purposed humanity, the space and attention given to Jesus' sufferings, crucifixion, and death served to underline once for all the fundamental and unique nature of Jesus' messianism when compared to other messianic pretenders during the last times (Mark 13:22). It further displays the events in Jesus' pouring out his life in self-giving as a full revelation of the sacrificial love of God, with free access to that love—and the new humanity in God—through the forgiveness offered in Messiah who lived and died in such manner. Messiah Jesus is God's new covenant solidarity with humanity for the elimination of all its alienation and its restoration.

The vindication of the servant-Messiah: The resurrection

If there had been any doubt that Jesus was the Messiah—and his death had dramatically reinforced those doubts—the disciples' experience of

---

[44] For a fuller discussion of "Vicarious Suffering" and nine other major biblical images used in New Testament understandings of the death of Jesus, see John Driver, *Understanding the Atonement for the Mission of the Church* (Scottdale, PA: Herald Press, 1986), especially 87–100.

[45] "This chapter is unique in the history of religion, and expresses an experience that is wholly irrational and not elucidated by any theory. A group of disciples experience atonement and sanctification in the humble voluntary suffering of their master in obedience to God"; see Otto, *The Kingdom of God and the Son of Man*, 261.

Jesus' resurrection from the dead not only finally erased them but absolutely confirmed that he was the Messiah, victorious over the powers that opposed him with death. The steadfast love that had conquered the temptations from disciples and the powers was totally vindicated. It had fully borne unto death the betrayals and the assault of the powers' injustice and sin without becoming like them or wiping them out. And now Jesus' resurrection vindicated that triumph of love and the sacrificial obedience of sonship. When humanity does its worst and kills the Son who reflects the image of God, Jesus' resurrection becomes the triumph of divine love and life. On the other side of death, Jesus explained the scriptures to the disciples, showing them that "the [Messiah had to] suffer these things and enter into his glory" (Luke 24:26).

Jesus' messianity of servanthood in sonship newly revealed God, as well as a new Israel and a new humanity. The obedience of *agapē*/love unto death defined the nature of the messianic mission, and the bearing of sin with the forgiveness of the cross fulfilled the way into the new humanity. The resurrection confirmed this fulfillment for the disciple witnesses, and assured them of the risen Messiah's ongoing mission and magistracy in view of the restoration and salvation of all Israel and all the nations. Moreover, they were themselves commissioned by the risen Jesus for this mission with him through the preaching of the good news of his messiahship, his mission of governance, and his coming for its fulfillment. Starting from the new alternative human space of their Jerusalem assembly, they were assured of the presence of the Holy Spirit in their own relationships and mission as children of God through faith and fellowship in the Messiah, the Son of God.

Christological understanding

The implications of the servant theme for our christological reflection and understanding are important. Understanding must include the messianic means, yet not be limited to any of them, since it must move beyond them to the heart of Jesus' messianity—the *agapē* servanthood of faithful filial obedience as the mark and manifestation of God's reign and purpose in the midst of the people in God's service. The Messiahking is freely and wholly in the service of God at the same time that he is freely and wholly in the service of God's people. He lives his sonship with God, fully trusting in the Father and his steadfast love unto death. He lives his kingship with the people as a fully obedient reflection of the Father and his steadfast love unto death. He is indeed a mediatorking, a priestly king.

In that mediation, the history and destiny of Messiah's people are inextricably bound to two factors. They are bound, on the one hand, to Messiah's fidelity in loving trust in the Father, and his faithfulness in obedience to the Father's steadfast love. But they are also bound to their own measure of faithfulness in identification with him, as the mark and manifestation of God's reign and purpose. Jesus' obedience to the cross is the demonstration and historical guarantee and nonretractability of that fidelity ("The death he died he died to sin, once for all" [Rom. 6:10]); and his resurrection/exaltation is the guarantee of its living continuity ("the life he lives he lives to God" [6:10]). That human fulfillment in God—as son of David and Son of Man—becomes the nonvariable determinant of Israel's and all the nations' history and destiny.

And this message was the essence of Paul's messianism as he preached it at Thessalonica. At Athens only a few weeks later, he proclaimed it clearly: "While God has overlooked the times of human ignorance, now he commands all people everywhere to repent, because he has fixed a day on which he will have the world judged in righteousness by a man whom he has appointed, and of this he has given assurance to all by raising him from the dead" (Acts 17:30–31, NRSV). Because of the unique character of this Messiah event for all human history, every people and each person is invited to turn forward in identification and solidarity with him and his community that lives in expectation of its fulfillment. It is that community's strength or weakness of identity/relationship to the servant-Messiah Jesus that ultimately becomes the major variable determinant in its history and destiny. But it is that unique, crucial, and nonretractable role for all human history and its fulfillment in God that is the nonnegotiable dimension of Jesus' servant messianism.

The mission of the servant-Messiah as Lord

Whatever its strength or weakness, the identification with Jesus the Messiah by the community that bears his name is indeed that which testifies to the ongoing character of the Messiah event. It is an event in continuity, still in process, in fulfillment within the times of the Messiah until he comes. Exalted in God's glory, Jesus is henceforth the mediator of access to the Father-child-Father relationship in God he so fully demonstrated, having personally fleshed out God's eternal Word and Wisdom.

The apostolic witness to that ongoing event and mission comprehends several important dimensions of mediation.

1. The anointed one becomes the anointing one, the mediator of the fullness of the Holy Spirit. Hence, the interpersonal presence of God in the relationship between the community of Messiah and the Father, as between its disciple(s) of Messiah and the Father, is experienced also as the same interpersonal *ekklēsia*-edifying power and dynamic known in Jesus: "You shall receive power when the Holy has come upon you; and you shall be my witnesses" (Acts 1:8). In the Pentecost event, the community that was gathered together by the Messiah received the same endowment that Jesus had received in his sonship, the endowment he had promised. The church was henceforth identified with him in his messianic mission as the messianic community, potentially in the fullness of the Spirit and now universally so.

2. The sent one becomes the sending one, not only to all the cities of Israel, but now in a mission universalized with the exaltation/ glorification of the Messiah exalted in God. The followers are sent out; that is, the disciples become apostles. The focus of mission is now "to all nations," "all the world," "all creation," "to the ends of the earth" (Acts 1:8 et al). "Repent and be baptized . . . in the name of Jesus [the Messiah] for the forgiveness of your sins" (Acts 2:38) is to be proclaimed as the key to access to God the divine parent, and it is the covenant of adoption into the family of the gathered *ekklēsia*, now fully identified with Messiah as the community of the Holy Spirit (love, joy, justice, and peace) in the midst of the many nations with their divergent cultures and politics.

3. Jesus' gracious priestly proclamation of divine Fatherly forgiveness and acceptance was localized in the days of his flesh. Now those gifts are universally accessible, even if not known, in a universal intercessory mission, since "when he had made purification for sins, he sat down at the right hand of the Majesty on high" (Heb. 1:3). In his obedient life, Jesus perfectly fulfilled the will and intention of God for humanity. "And by that will [unto death], we [his church identified with him] have been made holy through the sacrifice of the body of Jesus [the Messiah] once for all" (Heb. 10:10, NIV). Thus, his *ekklēsia* is the unique witness to a new universal reality-as-possibility of sure confidence in the still-invisible but more fully revealed liberating God, Father. There is access into "the Most Holy Place by the blood [that is, his life freely poured out in sacrificial love unto death] of Jesus, by a new and living way opened for us through the curtain, that is, his body" (Heb. 10:19–20, NIV).

4. The humiliated Jesus has become the exalted Messiah with dominion over and in the world. Victorious in life over the powers
of the world in his obedience unto death (see Col. 2:15), with continuity and confirmation of that life in his resurrection from the
dead, he pursues that same triumph through his church (note the
question, "Saul, why do you persecute me [the church]?" [Acts 9:4])
with reigning glory "at the right hand of God . . . until his enemies
should be made a stool for his feet" (Heb. 10:12–13). The messianic
riddle of the cross-bound Jesus to the ruling Sadducees ("David . . .
calls him Lord; so how is he his son?" [Luke 20:44]) is answered by
that triumph and in that of the free obedient service of his oft-hu-
miliated community that is called to live "in love, as [the Messiah]
loved" (Eph. 5:1), to "follow in his steps" (1 Pet. 2:21), and to "walk
in the same way in which he walked" (1 John 2:6).[46]

That apostolic consensus of faith is thus openly proclaimed in the
earliest reported public confession of the church (Acts 2:34–36) and
is found in different authors' writings (1 Cor. 15:25; Rom. 8:34; Eph.
1:20; Col. 3:1; 1 Pet. 3:21; Heb. 10:12–13; 12:2–3; Rev. 5:5–6). In the
perspective of that faith, the destruction of Jerusalem (Rev. 11:2, 8)
and the future doom of Rome and all it typifies (Rev. 18) are sans
repentance sealed and fulfilled in virtue of the triumphant freedom of the "Lamb who was slain" (Rev. 5:12; compare Isa. 53:7). The
faithful and the true one, whose name is the Word of God, pursues
prophetic war with the nations with the sharp sword that comes
out of his mouth (Rev. 19:11–16). It is the ongoing combat of the call
to repentance and the freedom of obedient faith that the servant
in Isaiah 40–66 was to fulfill "till he has established justice in the
earth" (Isa. 42:4).

5. In his universal magistracy and dominion over the world, Jesus the
Messiah saves, restores, and heads a universal human community
of many local assemblies. The free obedient servanthood to God
and humanity in Jesus the Messiah, the Son of God, has become
the divine measure and criterion of human freedom and historical fulfillment (Rev. 7:9–17; 22:3–5) of this universal community of
humanity (Rev. 5:9–10). With and through his community of the

---

[46] See Willem Adolph Visser t'Hooft, "The Kingship of Christ in the Bible," in *The
Kingship of Christ: An Interpretation of Recent European Theology* (New York: Harper, 1948).
Unfortunately, the generally good exposition of the theme does not tie it, as does the
New Testament, to the earthly life of Jesus as paradigm for the glory of the church in
its members. Hence, the constant risk of distorted triumphalism.

Spirit, he is working out his purposes that everyone everywhere shall be given that offer and space of salvation to become together in time and eternity, on the earth and beyond, all that God the Creator intended. "See, the home of God is among mortals. He will dwell with them as their God; they will be his peoples, and God himself will be with them [and be their God]. . . . I am making all things new" (Rev. 21:3–5, NRSV).

6. Yet in ways that are strange beyond our understanding, the Messiah in his faithful fulfillment of his *agapē* mission sorrowfully respects the freedom of those who reject his love. As when he wept over Jerusalem in its refusal of his rule (Luke 19:41), his magisterial triumph must clearly bear all those marks as he actively bears the outworking of wrath in all human history, even as he once bore it on the cross. There can be no doubt of great suffering in the midst of triumph, especially when the community of those who openly bear Messiah's name turns aside and betrays him, or turns away and abandons him in the way he is (Heb. 6:6), thus emptying the good news of the cross (1 Cor. 1:17) and distorting the perception of God whom he had revealed by his combat in life and death. "As it is written, 'The name of God is blasphemed among the Gentiles because of you'" (Rom. 2:24; compare Isa. 52:5). Again, strangely yet realistically, Jesus foresaw this turning away when he proclaimed the good news of the kingdom of God and allegorically saw it as seed falling into different soils—along the beaten path, on rocks, among thorns, and only a small portion in productive earth (Matt. 13:1–23).

7. Though the apostolic writers bear witness to Israel's, Jesus', and their own faith in cosmic restoration through Messiah, which is made explicit in his triumph over death and victory over the powers, little attention could be given in this study to this dimension that is nevertheless fully shared in faith. Except for some discussion of the sovereignty of Jesus, we have offered little comment about the Creator's ways and means in this regard.[47] Here, we offer only this witness to the conviction that a most significant part in future developments must come also through the humanity that has been at fault in its alienation from God in his self-revelation, that is, his Wisdom, his Word, and his Messiah.

---

[47] This subject is dealt with more extensively in chapter 6 of the present volume, "Consummation of Messiah's Mission."

But ultimately what comes must be through that community gathered and restored by Messiah and with which he is fully identified. It knows itself to be in, with, and under him, the servant Son of God, who wills to do the Father's saving will in and for creation in the Father's way and time. In that willing and doing, he fully revealed the purposes of God, which yet await ultimate fulfillment.

Mission Now: God's purpose revealed and fulfilled

It is quite obvious that it is impossible to deduce from the reading of the letter to the Thessalonians all that we have seen above. Yet all that we have gleaned from the tradition of the Gospels, and occasional references to the broader apostolic witness, is wholly consonant with—if not implicit in—that early apostolic document. It appears urgent to this writer that the human-fulfilling, community-fulfilling, and history-fulfilling (that is, sociopolitical) features of the mission of Jesus the servant-Messiah be seen as essential dimensions of an adequate Christology.

But foundational to those dimensions of apostolic understanding are the Son of Man and servant embodiments of messianism, so fundamental to Jesus' own understanding of his identity and mission, and yet traditionally so neglected by the dominant theological traditions.[48] Without them, the distortions that Christian world mission in the Constantinian mode has offered to history are inevitable. They are analo-

---

[48] One contemporary Western mainline Protestant systematic theologian had given noticeable attention to these themes in his earlier writings, before he renounced his own "deductive" method; but in that he also recognized its distinctiveness as rooted in the sixteenth-century Anabaptist critique of Western Christianity; see Gordon D. Kaufman, *Systematic Theology: A Historicist Perspective* (New York: Charles Scribner's Sons, 1968). Note especially the following sections: God's being as "servant" is revealed in the historical Jesus ("God's Coming into History," 167–75); Jesus' servanthood is described (not negatively) as "technically developed in the so-called adoptionist Christology " (195), with a suggestion, nevertheless, for understanding the metaphysical claim about the unity of God and Christ, while rejecting "Messiah" as explicatory of the meaning of Jesus, implying (for him) "that one must become a Jew in certain respects before one can become a Christian" (192n2; see also 190–97); the "nonresistance of God" as revealed by Jesus is seen as "divine perfection" and "the only way he can maintain the full integrity of those creatures to whom he has granted genuine freedom," and is expression of both power and love (219–21). See also in *Compassion: A Reflection on the Christian Life,* by Don McNeill, Douglas Morrison, and Henri Nouwen, the excellent pastoral chapter on "Servant God" (New York: Doubleday, 1983).

gous to Peter's messianic confession which Jesus rejected as not being the "things of God, but the things of men" (Matt. 16:23, NIV).[49]

Finally, there is something extremely ironic in the fact that Jesus, who came to liberate Israel with a view to the nations' salvation, never openly attacked what the Jews perceived to be the enemy and source of their oppression, the pagan Roman Empire. Yet everything that Jesus incarnated was opposed to the alienating powers there at work. His political strategy of grassroots building of messianic communities ultimately overcame the power of the empire. But it is also ironic that at one level that victory should lead to a human change of strategy and the nature of those communities. The homeopathic cure of human servitude through servanthood of and for God shifted to that of human power.[50]

Indeed, the extension of time, in the patience of God, with human and material development well beyond that anticipated by the Twelve and Paul, oblivious to the expanses and potential of earth and its peoples with the leaven of the messianic good news, raises again and again questions about the ongoing mission of the *ekklēsia* within the societies of the world where wheat and tares grow together. Yet in, with, and under the servant-Messiah Jesus, at least the die is cast: "For no other foundation can anyone lay than that which is laid, which is Jesus [the Messiah]" (1 Cor. 3:11). Indeed, it was no accident that Anabaptist communities found it important to celebrate the washing of each other's feet in conjunction with the Lord's Supper as described in John 13. The disciples' experience of the "full extent of his love" (John 13:1, NIV) was when the Lord and Master had washed their feet, setting for them

---

[49] More recently, the "powerlessness of God" has taken on some importance in theological reflection in the West as self-directed criticism of the distorted triumphalism of Western Christianity. Here we have attempted to indicate that the weakness has been in a failure to recognize the suffering servant as servant-Lord with his servant people, and in the Zealots' omnipotent Lord who elevates servants through whatever means are necessary to make them lords. My article here was written in 1990 before the appearance in English of Jürgen Moltmann, *The Way of Jesus Christ: Christology in Messianic Dimensions* (San Francisco: Harper and Row, 1990), where the basic preoccupation of this chapter is dealt with more completely.

[50] This point has been most helpfully demonstrated in a thorough analysis of the patristic literature by Jean-Michel Hornus in an adaptation of his doctoral thesis, translated from the French as *It is Not Lawful for Me to Fight: Early Christian Attitudes Toward War, Violence, and the State*, trans. Alan Kreider and Oliver Coburn (Scottdale, PA: Herald Press, 1980).

an example of practical earthy servanthood as a parable of his life and death.[51]

When using the personal analogy in speaking of God and the *missio Dei*, one might well refer to the coherency of being, agency, and purpose. The purposive Creator God of peace, the loving parent who sent and inspired the child-servant Jesus and whose image he fully reflected, may best be understood as Being. The Holy Spirit may be understood best as Agency, effecting that historical purposiveness first in all creation, then more fully in Abraham's Israel with prophets, priests, and kings, and finally bodily in Mary's Jesus,[52] son of David, fully anointed Messiah, prophetic and priestly king, as well as the new restored community he gathers. But the purpose itself is only clearly revealed and understood in the human obedience of Jesus, God's faithful, suffering servant Son, embodying God in his Wisdom and Word and perfectly fulfilling his saving work in the gathering of a universal people who share his service of love.

Whether the foundation and parameters indicated by this study will be heeded in continuing theological reflection about Jesus the Messiah, one cannot know. It can only be noted again that now is a propitious time in God's mission and world for them to be appropriated.

---

[51] Avery Dulles in his useful *Models of the Church* (Garden City, NY: Doubleday, 1974) also discusses one modern servanthood model of the church and concludes with: "The modern notion of the 'servant church' therefore seems to lack any direct foundation in the Bible. Yet it may not be out of place to speak of an 'indirect foundation.' The so-called Servant Songs in Isaiah are applicable to the Church as well as to Christ" (1974, 93). The apparent contradiction is a result of the model he criticizes, in which the church in conciliar circles was seen to be strictly governed by the "agenda of the world," submitting to the world-defined needs as servant to master. The critique is fully justified. Indeed, that was the thrust of an early section in the introduction to my chapter here. It is most unfortunate that Dulles does not follow through with the full implications of the applicability of the Servant Songs to the church via Jesus' self-identity and the church's solidarity with him. It is indeed direct biblical foundation, that of the pre-Pauline churches, to which Paul refers: "Your attitude should be the same as that of [Messiah] Jesus, . . . taking the very nature of a servant" (Phil. 2:5–7, NIV).

[52] This messianic activity and sign (see Isa. 7:14; Matt. 1:23) in the midst of entropy is seen by apostolic faith to be the first visible expression of servant messianism. The human embodiment in Jesus of the image of the self-revealing Father is seen to be the equivalent of the slave's mark of a pierced ear (see Ps. 40:6–8; Heb. 10:5–10). It is the full acceptance of the created human role of obedient and faithful servant in creation (Phil. 2:7). Apparently, only the full implications of the resurrection made the sign retrospectively understandable (seee the "How can this be?" Luke 1:34, NRSV): all God's work, from God, initiated by God.

6

Consummation of Messiah's mission

What is the significance of the "last (*eschatos*) days" (Acts 2:17, from Joel 2:28; 2 Tim. 3:1; Heb. 1:2; James 5:3; 2 Pet. 3:3), "the end of the times" (1 Pet. 1:20), "the last hour" (1 John 2:18), or "the last time" (Jude 18), for the dynamics of the messianic mission of Jesus and his people? This is the concern and preoccupation of eschatology as it relates to the essential mission and calling of the messianic community.

Here we recall the importance of eschatology in the first apostolic epistle to the Thessalonians, the earliest missionary document.

The "coming of Messiah" for the final ingathering has now become the focal point of orientation for the time since Jesus' death and resurrection. . . .

The fourfold Messianic understanding portrays a picture of human history under the reign of God with culminating events fulfilled and articulated by the life, death, resurrection, present ministry, and coming of the Messiah Jesus as he gathers together God's people . . . in view of the salvation of humanity into the service of God. There is the event of Jesus' life, teaching, sufferings, and death; there is the event of the resurrection; there is the event of exaltation lived in fellowship with the apostolic gathering sent out on the mission of assembling disciples; there is the eschatological event-to-come of the full ingathering of the people of God with the appearing of Messiah.[1]

Reprinted, with editorial changes, from *The Transfiguration of Mission: Biblical, Theological and Historical Foundations*, ed. Wilbert R. Shenk (Scottdale, PA: Herald Press, 1993), 220–41. Used by permission. Scripture references in this essay, unless noted otherwise, are from the Revised Standard Version.

[1] David A. Shank, "Jesus the Messiah: Messianic Foundation of Mission," in *The Transfiguration of Mission*, ed. Shenk, 49–50. This essay is reprinted as chapter 5 in the present volume.

The "day of the Lord" (1 Thess. 5:2) was an old expression of Israel's hope, which the writing prophets took up with fuller content (Amos 8:9; Isa. 2; Mic. 1:2–5; Zeph. 1; et al.), including coming historical, political, and cosmic changes involving both salvation and judgment. It came to signify the ultimate fulfillment of the saving purposes and reign of God as sovereign over humanity both in Israel and in the nations. In Jesus' language in the Gospels it has become the "day of judgment" (Matt. 10:15; 11:22; 12:36), the "day of the Son of Man" (Luke 17:24, 30; John 8:27–56), the "last day" (John 6:39–54; 11:24; 12:48). Finally, in the apostolic language, as in the Thessalonian letter, that day is totally identified with the exalted Jesus Christ and his return in glory. Hence "the day of our Lord Jesus Christ" (1 Cor. 1:8), "the day of the Lord Jesus" (1 Cor. 5:5; 2 Cor. 1:14), or "the day of Jesus Christ" (Phil. 1:6).

Basic New Testament understanding

But this apostolic accent on the coming of Messiah as that which is yet to come (1 Cor. 11:26) dare not remove from our minds the more fundamental idea that the day of the Lord has already come in the life and work of Jesus (John 8:56; Luke 4:21). Salvation with its inherent judgment has come in Jesus of Nazareth (see John 3:16–21). In scripture this eschaton, or final fulfillment, must be seen from the perspective of the prophets of Israel looking forward to it (1 Pet. 1:10–12), from that of Jesus incarnating it (Matt. 12:28; Luke 9:10–11), and from that of the apostles who experienced and lived it (2 Cor. 6:1–2) and looked forward to its culmination with Jesus' universal manifestation (*epiphaneia*) or coming/appearing (*parousia*) in glory.

The nearly 2,000 calendar years that have passed since the death, resurrection, and exaltation of Jesus do not change that latter perspective, which we share with the apostles, even though the chronological time span tends to distort the reality of the time of our Lord in the ongoing Christ event by giving an impression of distance from the death and resurrection and/or rapprochement to the Parousia. One biblical critic has stated it well:

> The clue to the meaning of the nearness of the End is the realization of the essential unity of God's saving acts in Christ—the realization that the events of the Incarnation, Crucifixion, Resurrection, Ascension and Parousia are in a real sense one event. The foreshortening, by which the Old Testament sees as one divine intervention in the future that which from the view-

point of the New Testament writers is both past and future, is not only a visual illusion; for the distance actually brings out an essential unity, which is not so apparent from a position in between the Ascension and the Parousia.[2]

With the coming of Messiah, the end times have come; we are in that position today, and we live in the hope and expectation of its ultimate fulfillment, as announced by the prophets, incarnated and taught by Jesus, and interpreted by the apostles with a rich variety of understandings.

New Testament eschatological understandings

When the New Testament writers wrote of the "last things"—the *eschaton*—they used a wide variety of expressions to portray its meaning. The following summary indicates the universality, totality, and comprehensiveness of that reality, the outcome of the *missio Dei*:

- "The time is fulfilled, and the kingdom of God is at hand" (Mark 1:14: Jesus);

- "To restore [*apokathistanēmi*] all things" (Matt. 17:11; Mark 9:12: Jesus, referring to the Malachi end-times promise re: Elijah redivivus);

- "The renewal [*palingenesia*] of all things" (Matt. 19:28, NIV: Jesus, in reference to the glorious reign of the Son of Man);

- "Everything must be fulfilled [*plēroo*] that is written about me in the Law of Moses, the Prophets and the Psalms" (Luke 24:44, NIV: the resurrected Jesus);

- "The . . . restitution [*apokatastasis*] of all things" (Acts 3:21, AV: Peter);

- "To bring [*anakephalaioō*] all things in heaven and on earth together under one head" (Eph. 1:10, NIV: Paul);

- "To reconcile [*apokatallassō*] to himself all things, whether on earth or in heaven, making peace [*eiranopoieō*] by the blood of his cross" (Col. 1:20: Paul);

- "'For God has put all things in subjection [*hypotassō*] under his feet' . . . that God may be everything to every one" (1 Cor. 15:24–28: Paul);

---

[2] C. E. B. Cranfield, "St. Mark 13," *Scottish Journal of Theology* 7 (1954): 283; cited in *The Presence of the Future: The Eschatology of Biblical Realism,* by George Eldon Ladd (Grand Rapids, MI: Eerdmans, 1974), 323.

- "And every tongue confess [*exomologeō*] that Jesus Christ is Lord" (Phil. 2:11; pre-Pauline hymn?);
- "A salvation [*sotērion*] ready to be revealed in the last time" (1 Pet. 1:35; compare Rev. 12:10; 19:1);
- "The end [completion/consummation/*telos*] of all things" (1 Pet. 4:7);
- "A new heaven and a new earth [*kaina poiō*]" (Rev. 21:5; compare 21:6; 2 Pet. 3:13);
- "The kingdom of the world has become the kingdom of our Lord and of his Christ, and he shall reign forever and ever" (Rev. 11:15).

When Jesus spoke of the kingdom of God, regeneration, restoration, or fulfillment of all things, he was clearly referring to the end-times promises in the prophetic writings, of which John the Baptist was the harbinger. Jesus himself was the inaugural manifestation, whose full actualization he expectantly anticipated. Whether it was the promise of the messianic banquet (Isa. 25:6–8) or the restored kingdom (Jer. 23:5–7; Ezek. 37:20–28; Dan. 7:13–14; Isa. 11; 49:8–11; 60) with its promises of peace and justice and prosperity (Isa. 65:17–25; Joel 2; Mal. 4), in Jesus' perception their fulfillment had begun definitively since the Spirit of God had begun to break into Israel's life in his life and service.

Peter, John, and Paul used the language of restitution, recapitulation, reconciliation, making peace, subjection, consummation, renewal of all things, or the kingdom of God in the light of the same promises; but they had the new perspective of Jesus' life of service, crucifixion, resurrection, and messianic exaltation, as well as their own Spirit-anointing by the anointed. Their mission anticipated, participated in, and contributed to those immediate and long-range consequences. They knew for a certainty that the end-time fulfillment promised by the prophets had begun in Jesus; sent by Christ/Messiah, their mission was a participation in that free Spirit-movement of love and grace within Israel and the nations that manifests God's ultimate purpose.

They were to expose and declare it to the world as they shared in that apocalyptic in-breaking. The end near, they knew, for they were participants in it already; the reconciliation of all things was nigh, for they experienced it; the submission of all things could not tarry, since they lived out daily their own obedience to Messiah, who had already united them under his headship. Indeed, the resurrection of Jesus was the first fruits of the coming harvest (1 Cor. 15:20), and the gift of the Spirit was down payment of that which was yet to come (Eph. 1:13–14.).

This diversity of language should not, however, overshadow the one reality that is expressed: that Jesus, God's Messiah, reveals and fulfills God's purposes in and for creation. That one reality is a certainty that clearly orients life in the midst of all the present uncertainties. It is a vision that takes on actuality in the present. But it is above all an experience of participation "in God the Father and the Lord Jesus Christ" (1 Thess. 1:1)—the personal, vital, dynamic power who is bringing it to pass, who gives the certainty and assures the vision.

Thus it is not strange that the personal faith-within-community appropriation of that ultimate prophetic hope is itself also expressed in terms of regeneration (John 3:3–6; 1 Pet. 1:3, 23), reconciliation (2 Cor. 5:18–19), peace or peacemaking (Rom. 5:1; Eph. 2:14; Matt. 5:9), renewal (2 Cor. 5:17–18), perfecting (Matt. 5:48; Phil. 3:12–15; 1 Cor. 13:9–13), subjection (Eph. 5:21–24), salvation (Eph. 2:5-8), confession (Rom. 10:9–10), or kingdom (Col. 1:13). That future that is promised by God through Israel's prophets is already really, truly, and effectively known in Christ, even if only in part (1 Cor. 13:8–13). Thus, for example, Paul wrote to the Colossians of God's purposes through Christ "to reconcile to himself all things. . . . And you . . . he has now reconciled" (Col. 1:20–22). It is that "now"—used so consistently in the apostolic writings[3]—that emphasizes strongly what George Ladd has characterized as the "presence of the future."[4]

The ultimate ending-out, completion, or perfecting of God's purposes is—to use Paul's expression in relation to "subjection"—when "God [is] everything to everyone" (1 Cor. 15:28). John's Revelation uses similar language to say the same thing about this ultimate end: "See, the home of God is among mortals. He will dwell with them as their God" (Rev. 21:3, NRSV). What is significant is that this is not new language but that of Moses and the prophets (Exod. 6:7, 25:8, 29:45; Lev. 26:12; Jer. 31:1, 33; Ezek. 37:27) expressing God's intention and purpose. The apostles are simply expressing what has already become true in Jesus (John 1:14) and now in the churches (2 Cor. 6:16–7:1; Heb. 8:10–9:28). There is a continuity of intention but an ever-greater fulfillment of

---

[3] See G. Stählin, "The NT Now," in *Theological Dictionary of the New Testament,* ed. Gerhard Kittel; trans. Geoffrey W. Bromiley (Grand Rapids, MI: Eerdmans, 1967), 4:1112–23.

[4] See Ladd, *The Presence of the Future.* This idea is also spelled out by John Driver, "The Kingdom of God: Goal of Messianic Mission," in *Transfiguration of Mission,* ed. Shenk.

that purpose, with its ultimate completion yet coming; that is nothing more—or less—than God fully present in humankind, and humankind fully in the service of God (Exod. 8:1, 20, et al.; Lev. 25:42, 55; Deut. 6:13; Matt. 4:10; Rev. 22:3).

To speak of God's intention for humankind in this way is to speak most certainly of spiritual reality; the intention is also certainly so-cial (interpersonal) and political (ordered/governed)—a reign, the kingdom of God, "on earth as it is in heaven" (Matt. 6:10). Whether in heaven or on earth, within history or beyond history, it is an eminently social and political spiritual reality. Hence the *ekklēsia* "in God the Fa-ther and the Lord Jesus [the Messiah]" (1 Thess. 1:1) is the gathering of those now/already called together "into his own kingdom and glory" (1 Thess. 2:12).[5] The church of the Messiah is a manifestation of the last times, of the kingdom of God come and coming. It is eschatologi-cal, an end-times reality; its collective interpersonal life is ordered by the Holy Spirit (1 Thess. 4:8) of Messiah in view of his coming (1 Thess. 3:11-12) when he brings all things to fulfillment.

The content and character of the eschaton in the New Testament

The consensus of the writers of the New Testament is that in Jesus the Messiah, God is revealed as active love (*agapē*) and grace (*charis*). We recall that in the oldest apostolic and missionary document—to the Thessalonians—Paul can say of this young church that they "have been taught by God to love one another" (1 Thess. 4:9). It is not teaching as precept but the teaching given through God's self-revelation in the life, death, and resurrection of Jesus the Messiah, who, when trusted and obeyed, reproduces such love in the life of whomever thus participates in his Spirit (Rom. 5:5-8). John saw the full manifestation of that love of the Father for the Son (John 17:24-26) and of the only begotten Son (John 3:16) for the Father (John 17:4) in his obedient service for hu-mankind, even unto death, and for the expiation of sin. The end-time (1 John 2:18) revelation is that "God is love (*agapē*)" (1 John 4:8).

In the last times, the righteousness/justice (*ṣedeq/dikaiosynē*) of God, so fundamental to Israel's existence and understanding, is re-vealed in the Messiah Jesus to be an expression of the one true God

---

[5] Jürgen Moltmann portrays this reality correctly and effectively with the expression "the church of the kingdom of God," in *The Church in the Power of the Spirit: A Contribu-tion to Messianic Eccesiology* (New York: Harper & Row, 1977).

of love that the gospel proclaims (Rom. 1:16–17, 3:21–26). The peace of God (šalom/eirēnē), so dominant a theme in Israel's life and hope,[6] is revealed in Jesus the Messiah to be an expression of the one true God of love (Eph. 2:14; Phil. 4:7) who takes on himself the injustice and strife of sinful humanity in order to restore it. The joy of the Lord and rejoicing in God, so spontaneous in Israel's worship of God, in response to God's acts of mercy and compassion, are revealed in the Messiah Jesus to be expressions from the presence of the one true God of love (John 15:11) and intrinsic to life in the Spirit in his service (1 John 1:4; Matt. 25:21–23; John 16:22–24).[7]

Within the context of Messiah Jesus' ultimate revelation of love, its full, complete end-time manifestation is expressed necessarily in the eschatological dimensions of covenant justice, peace, and joy. The classic Pauline text and locus of the Protestant Reformation's *solo fide* reports this eschatological appropriation of covenant justice, peace, and joy (Rom. 5:1–2) as a consequence of God's love (*agapē*) in the Messiah Jesus "while we were yet sinners . . . [or] enemies" (5:8–10). Toward the end of that same letter, Paul insists that the end-time (13:11–12) understanding of the kingdom of God is precisely "righteousness and peace and joy in the Holy Spirit" (14:17). These are fundamentally categories of personal relationships and of ordering of human life (social and political) that now become functional within the church of the kingdom of God (Rom. 14:19; Col. 3:15; 1 Thess. 5:13; Rom. 6:17–19; Phil. 4:4) at whatever cost (1 Pet. 2:20–25) as it is scattered within human society (Matt. 13:37–38.; 2 Tim. 2:22; Heb. 12:14; Phil. 2:15–16; Rom. 12:17–18). The Messiah is the example, even as he taught those who confessed his messiahship (Matt. 16:24–28).

The content of the eschaton, when "God [will] be everything to everyone" (1 Cor. 15:28), will be divine love within the gathering of God's people in the Messiah Jesus "from every nation, from all tribes and peoples and tongues" (Rev. 5:9); it will be expressed in that reign as justice, peace, and joy over and among this new humanity with and under God. But most significantly, it is already to be found in the communities of the Messiah and in societies where disciples of Messiah Jesus discern

---

[6] See Perry B. Yoder, *Shalom: The Bible's Word for Salvation, Justice, and Peace* (North Newton, KS: Faith and Life Press, 1987).

[7] "The new life under his [Messiah's] influence cannot be understood merely as new obedience, as a reversal of life's direction and as an endeavor to change the world until it visibly becomes God's creation. It is also, and with equal emphasis, celebrated as the feast of freedom, as joy in existence, and as the ecstasy of bliss" (Moltmann, *The Church in the Power of the Spirit,* 109).

their true calling and freely live it out. It recalls Jesus' parable of the kingdom of God: "It is like leaven, which a woman took and hid in three measures of meal, till it was all leavened" (Luke 13:21).

The itineraries of messianic communities in the end times

There is a certain paradox in the juxtaposition of Jesus' parable of the leaven with the early one (Mark 4:3–20) of the sower whose seeds fell along the path, on rocky ground, among thorns, or into good soil where it "brought forth grain, growing up and increasing and yielding thirty-fold and sixtyfold and a hundredfold" (Mark 4:8). The first speaks figuratively of an action that is totally fulfilling: "till it was all leavened" (Luke 13:21). The second speaks figuratively about receptivity to the messianic word of the kingdom of God; in contrast to the first, only a part—apparently a minority—of those who hear become fruitful. Indeed, a majority are apparently not fruitful for the kingdom.

The mystery of the satanic taking away of the word leaves some hearers outside the range of receptivity; Jesus appears to have been conscious of their loss. But he is also conscious and concerned about those who, like young plants in rocky ground that wither in the heat of the sun, receive the word and fall away "when tribulation or persecution arises on account of the word" (Mark 4:17). He is no less conscious of those who, like plants choked out by thorns, are unfruitful because of the choking effect of the "cares of the world, and the delight in riches, and the desire for other things" (Mark 4:19). The hearers of the good news of the kingdom of God in the last days go their four ways. Those who receive the word of the kingdom and are under its influence nevertheless go three separate ways. The ones who bear fruit are those who hear and accept or "understand" (Matt. 13:13, 19, 23) or "hold . . . fast in an honest and good heart" (Luke 8:15) the word of the kingdom; they are the ones who are oriented to and by the kingdom of God as they walk the "way of Messiah."[8]

Near the beginning of his ministry, Jesus interpreted the parable of the sower and the soils for the Twelve that he had called together to form the new Israel, the new messianic community where the end-

---

[8] This theme is particularly well developed in the Gospel of Mark, as has been shown by Willard M. Swartley in his helpful analysis of the evangelist's use of *hodos* ("the way"); see Willard M. Swartley, *Mark: The Way for the Nations* (Scottdale, PA: Herald Press, 1979).

times content was to take social and political shape. Thus, he openly informed them of the possible sidetracks that their community—and others called together through and after them—could take. And he clearly accented the eschatological path of the coming kingdom of love ordered in justice, peace, and joy. On another early occasion, he had insisted: "Seek first [God's] kingdom and his righteousness, and all these things shall be yours as well" (Matt. 6:33). And during the week of his Passion, in the Olivet discourse, he continued to insist: "Take heed that no one leads you astray" (Mark 13:5).

Insofar as Jesus the exalted Messiah is himself the mediator between the times of the apostles and the future fulfillment of the kingdom, with historical hindsight we may become more and more aware that these potential itineraries have indeed been played out. Much has depended on how the communities that have borne his name have understood or misunderstood him and his mission in relation to the kingdom and his church.

The itinerary of faithfulness

From the Olivet discourse (Mark 13) we grasp Jesus' understanding of the itinerary of the fruitful church of the kingdom of God;[9] it is along a way in which:

- false messiahs will indeed lead many astray (13:5-6);
- wars and rumors of wars are part of the agenda before the end (*telos*), with nation rising against nation and kingdom against kingdom (13:7);
- earthquakes will occur in various places (13:8);
- there will be famines (13:8);
- the disciples will be delivered up to councils and beaten in synagogues (13:9);
- the disciples will bear witness for the sake of Messiah before governors and kings, the Holy Spirit giving them what to speak (13:11);
- the gospel must be preached to all nations (13:10);
- family members will deliver disciples up to death—brother turning against brother, father against children, children against parents (13:12);

---

[9] Hendrikus Berkhof has pointed out this trajectory so well in *Christ, the Meaning of History* (London: SCM Press, 1966); see especially page 70, where he deals with the *Fernerwartung* (distant expectation) in Jesus' eschatological thought.

- disciples will be hated for the sake of Jesus' name, but salvation is in endurance (13:13);
- a desolating sacrilege will be set up, no doubt in the temple at Jerusalem, leading to a time of terrible, unequalled tribulation (13:14–20);
- false messiahs and false prophets showing signs and wonders will seek to lead disciples astray (13:21–23);
- "powers in the heavens will be shaken" in a context of cosmic disturbances affecting sun, moon, and stars (13:24–25); and
- the powers will see the Son of Man coming in the clouds with great power and glory, as he sends his messengers to complete the gathering of his people from out of all the earth and heaven (13:24–27).

All these things are to be seen as signs of the nearness of the Son of Man, the mediator of the end, and the eschatological Savior and judge of humankind (Mark 13:29).[10] Watchfulness (13:33–37) is the order of the times, because of the uncertainty of the day and the hour of the end, which are known only by the Father (13:32–37).

The prophetic "I have told you all things beforehand" (Mark 13:23) is fully in harmony with the prophetic "Take heed" (13:5, 9, 23, 33), given in the context of a perceived ongoing history. The apocalyptic dimensions of cosmic shaking of the heavenly powers—who see the glory of the Son of Man in his calling together a humanity from the four corners of the earth and heaven—portray a telescoped history fully consonant with the prophetic proclamation of Daniel 7:14: "To him was given dominion and glory and kingdom, that all peoples, nations, and languages should serve him; his dominion is an everlasting dominion, which shall not pass away."

Today we find the telescoping at least partially undone and opened, with a continuing projection of the signs of the nearness of the Son of Man on the screen of human history. Here Messiah's call in view of the end of the end times is to watch; to take heed; to endure or persevere unto the end; to witness to authorities under the leading of the Holy Spirit; and to suffer in the face of the opposition from the religious, political, and ethnic powers.

This call is in a context of earthquakes and famines, nationalistic wars and uprisings, false messiahs and prophets with their signs and wonders, where the necessity of proclaiming the good news of

---

[10] See the "Son of Man" section in chapter 5 ("Jesus the Messiah") of the present volume.

the kingdom to all nations thus remains a messianic priority. This response, from Messiah Jesus, is the way of fruitfulness and salvation for the community he calls, which is ordered by God's love in justice, peace, and joy in the Holy Spirit, as we have seen.

The deviated itineraries[11]

How striking is Jesus' awareness of those who in the midst of opposition and difficulty—or preoccupied with cares of the world—would not persevere in the way of the word of the kingdom of God. That is also Paul's major preoccupation with the young assembly at Thessalonica (1 Thess. 3:1-5); he tries to prepare the church there for suffering from opposition as an inherent dimension of life in the Messiah. He is concerned that they not abandon the faith. What he probably does not (yet) anticipate is the way a faith community bearing the name of Jesus the Messiah could maintain the name yet lose both its meaning and the faith and life of the kingdom he reveals. Yet he does later discover this to be true in Galatia, Corinth, and Colossae; and before the end of the century, "Christian" churches addressed in Revelation 2-3 are maintaining the name but are also being called to repent. In the epistle to the Hebrews it is clear that zeal is cooled, and "the Day drawing near" (Heb. 10:25) is the appeal for stimulation. The second book of Peter makes it clear that the not-yet-fulfillment of the eschatological hope is bringing the scoffers with their reference to nonfulfillment: "All things have continued as they were" (2 Pet. 3:4); it is necessary to restore assurance in the prophetic vision of the new heavens and new earth (3:13) beyond the judgment of the worldly system and those involved in it (3:1-13).

The "last days" have come; the new age has broken into the old, with a real salvation yet to be totally fulfilled with judgment of the old (see 2 Cor. 5:17). Yet the power of the old age continues to impinge on the communities of Messiah, either through direct opposition and persecution or through seduction, in its various and devious forms. In the former case, the lines are often clearly drawn, as becomes more apparent with those of Israel who reject Jesus' messiahship and with Rome's Caesar, which cannot bear the "Messiah is Lord" claims as over against its own lordship (see Eph. 1:21). More difficult is the mainte-

---

[11] Throughout this section, I will use the present tense, writing of what is past as present in these last days of Christ. Perhaps the best discussion of the shift from messianic movement to Christian religion is by Christopher Rowland, in *Christian Origins: From Messianic Movement to Christian Religion* (Minneapolis: Augsburg Publishing House, 1985).

nance of clarity in the midst of seductive pressures, often heightened, paradoxically, through the leavening effect of the gospel of Messiah and his church on surrounding society, where the lines become fuzzy.

Moreover, since the Gospel of Messiah is a proclamation of God's saving truth for all peoples, it must first be interpreted from Aramaic, the popular Hebrew of Jesus and his circles, and appropriated in popular (koinē) Greek, which is already such a dominant influence in non-Palestinian Judaism. The same is true for Latin, Syriac, Armenian, Coptic, Gothic, and Ethiopic as the circle of mission expands and the need for translation of the scriptures arises. But it becomes necessary also to attempt to save that truth from competing understandings, perceptions, and systems of thought that function as truth for many peoples. Hence, the truth of the simple confession "Jesus the Christ is Lord" is perceived to be "saved" by the successive confessional councils and their creeds.

However, we have already noted that the intent of the Messiah is to save and restore humanity, to gather a people whose life together bears the sociopolitical signs of the eschatological God being "everything to everyone:" loving service; ordered in justice, peace, and joy; as incarnate in the servant-Messiah, at any cost. The perseverance given to preserving the truth of the confession of faith is not always paralleled with perseverance in the itinerary of community (that is, sociopolitical) fidelity traced by Jesus, the servant; yet endurance in the obedience of faith in love, as a sign of the last days, is also essential truth (Eph. 4:14–15; 1 John 2:4–6; 3:18). "The love of many will grow cold. But the one who endures to the end will be saved" (Matt. 24:12–13, NRSV). Such a community is what Origen, in the times of imperial persecution more than two centuries later, could call "another sort of country created by the Logos of God."[12] But within another century and a half, things changed rapidly.

"The glorious City of God pursues its pilgrimage through the times and impiety [of the earthly city], living here below by faith," writes Augustine of Hippo in 413 as he begins The City of God. "With patience she awaits the eternal sojourn where its justice in its turn will be judge, and its holiness will be in possession of the last victory and of inalterable peace."[13] Like Paul sixteen generations before him, Augustine

---

[12] Origen, Contra Celsum, trans. Henry Chadwick (Cambridge: Cambridge University Press, 1965), 3.

[13] Augustine, De civitate Dei 1.1; translation by David A. Shank, from Augustin, La Cité de Dieu, annotated by G. Brady (Paris: Bordas, 1949), 1.

also states his eschatological hope of justice and peace, but in different terms. From within the perspective of a couple of generations of Rome's imperial tolerance and cooptation of the messianic movement, he also adds at the end of Book 1, given the difficulty of knowing who is a Christian: "The two cities are entwined and intermingled in this age until the last judgment separates them. It is [only] on their origins, their progress, and the end which awaits them that I wish to develop my thoughts."[14] Indeed, between the two statements is found his classic word on divinely authoritative exceptions to the interdiction of killing: "Sometimes God orders murder either by a general law or by a temporary and special command. He is not morally homicidal who owes his ministry to the authority; he is only an instrument, like the sword with which he strikes. Thus they have not transgressed the precept, those who by order of God have made war; or in the exercise of public power have, following its laws, that is to say, following the will of the most just reason, punished criminals with death."[15] Here the social and political orientation is based not on the servant Messiah but on the "just reason" of Roman public power and its laws, and is illustrated by Abraham, Jephtha, and Samson from the Old Testament.

This is not the place to trace the churches' generations of experience or to offer a critique of their various sociopolitical stances. But it is important to illustrate an end-times itinerary other than that which Jesus and the early apostolic church lived and taught. For now, imperial reason with its legal system and legion-imposed Pax Romana orders the life of the church bearing the name of Messiah Jesus, while his justice, holiness, and peace will come only at the last judgment. In such a perception, the full force of the eschatological "now" in the messianic community is gone; the future is not yet present but is wholly future; old things have not passed away, for it is the old era (illustrated by the Old Testament) that has overtaken the new that is come in Jesus the Messiah.

Yet in fact the church sees itself as over and above the rest of society, consciously ordering it with Roman and Old Testament ways as a theocratic millennial reign of Christ. But the illustration of Augustine is intentional, for there can be no doubt that this eschatological perception has dominated the Western Christian mission in ways that

---

[14] Augustine, *De civitate Dei* 1.35.

[15] Augustine, *De civitate Dei* 1.21.

are parallel to that indicated for Christology, following Andrew Walls's cultural history of Christianity.[16]

This dominant but deviant itinerary makes it considerably easier to explain the ever-recurring alternatives in the so-called sectarian reactions to this so-called mainstream. One recalls the Waldensian movement, the Wycliffe influence through the Lollard mission and its social impact, the early Hussite movement with the Moravian Brethren spinoffs in missionary pioneering, the Anabaptist Mennonites and their nonresistant free-church alternative with its missionary impact, the Pietist ecclesiolae in ecclesia with its strong social mission, the Quaker mission with its creative peace and social thrust, the Methodist awakening, the Adventists with their holistic gospel, and the nineteenth-century Blumhardt revival, or the Pentecostals with their accent on the Spirit of the last times.

A common thread of perseverance—at whatever cost—appears in the beginnings of these various efforts to take the spirit of the New Testament and the Christ of the Gospels as the last and definitive word. That thread is the rediscovered messianic mission of Jesus Christ,

---

[16] See Andrew Walls, "Christianity," in A Handbook of Living Religions, ed. John R. Hinnells (Harmondsworth, Middlesex: Pelican Books, 1985), 58–73. Note also F. L. Cross's assessment: "Augustine's influence on the course of subsequent theology has been immense. He molded the whole of that of the Middle Ages down to the 13th century, and even the reaction against Augustinianism with the rediscovery of Aristotle in the 13th century . . . was less complete than has widely been supposed. The Reformers also appealed to elements of Augustine's teaching in their attack on the Schoolmen. . . . Without Augustine's massive intellect and deep spiritual perception, Western theology would never have taken the shape in which it is familiar to us"; see "Augustine, St. of Hippo," The Oxford Dictionary of the Christian Church (New York: Oxford University Press, 1958), 107. For an Anabaptist perspective on Augustine, see particularly Walter Klaassen, "The Anabaptist Critique of Constantinian Christendom," Mennonite Quarterly Review 55, no. 3 (1981): 218–30. A brief critique from another Anabaptist perspective is offered by Harold S. Bender: "In fact the church is equated with the kingdom of God in which Christ reigns. (It should be noted that Augustine was the first to make this identification.) . . . The contrast between the splendor of the church and the fast-decaying Roman empire is such that Augustine was convinced that the millenium [sic] forecast in the Revelation of John was already in effect; it had begun with the first coming of Christ upon the earth and would continue until his second coming. (Augustine was the one who put the death knell to the millennialism of the Ante-Nicene age.)" (Harold S. Bender, "Augustine's Doctrine of the Church and Its Influence on the Reformers," in Conference on Augustinian Thought [Wheaton, IL: Wheaton College Department of Bible and Philosophy, 1955], 48). Two other significant critiques, the first Anabaptist and the second Reformed, are John H. Yoder, "The Meaning of the Constantinian Shift," Christian Attitudes to War, Peace, and Revolution (Elkhart, IN: Goshen Biblical Seminary, 1983); and Leonard Verduin, The Anatomy of a Hybrid (Grand Rapids, MI: Eerdmans, 1976).

Spirit-anointed and anointer, as the one who transforms, restores, rec-
reates, and regenerates humanity into a new spiritual/social community with its new life as a challenge and alternative to the old. In it is
an implicit—and sometimes explicit and apocalyptic—eschatological
orientation that seeks to bring about in the present the promises of the
end time.[17]

From such a perspective we must observe that the reappearance
of such movements of mission within Christendom points out a line of
continuity in these last times, from which the Augustinian eschatology
and its sociopolitical shaping is itself a deviation.[18] Indeed, the great
evangelical missionary movement of the nineteenth and twentieth
centuries emerges from such movements often in the face of opposition from the mainstream churches. The eschatological dynamic is a
most important dimension in that movement, although the motif was
later shifted to "while there is yet time"/"before it's too late." More recently, the major holistic and biblical eschatological motif of the kingdom of God is there again coming to the fore.

Also in recent years, messianic dynamics as sociopolitical phenomena are being studied by scholars, precisely because of their social and
political creativity. Particularly helpful is the work of Henri Desroche
indicating the sociological directions taken within so-called messianic

---

[17] See particularly Christopher Rowland, *Radical Christianity: A Reading of Recovery*
(Maryknoll, NY: Orbis Books, 1988). Reinhold Niebuhr also indicates how in his judgment the doctrine of the second coming of Christ has been particularly fruitful of
error (which he attributes to a chronological illusion making it a "point in history"
rather than a transhistorical reality symbolized by time): "It has led to fantastic
sectarian illusions of every type. Yet it is significant that the dispossessed and disin-
herited have been particularly prone to these illusions, because they were anxious
to express the Christian hope of fulfillment in social as well as in individual terms.
Sectarian apocalypticism is closely related to modern proletarian radicalism, which is
a secularized form of the [former]. In both, the individualism of Christian orthodoxy
is opposed with conceptions which place the corporate enterprises of mankind, as
well as individuals, under an ultimate judgment and under ultimate possibilities of
fulfillment. In these secular and apocalyptic illusions the end of time is a point in
time beyond which there will be an unconditioned society. But there is truth in the
illusions" (Reinhold Niebuhr, "As Deceivers, Yet True," in *Beyond Tragedy: Essays on the
Christian Interpretation of History* [New York: Charles Scribner's Sons, 1937], 22–23). Is
the truth not also in Niebuhr's own underestimation of the biblical witness to the way
history's consummation comes by way of the peaceful kingdom of Christ "on earth as
it is in heaven," of which the messianic community is the visible sign?

[18] In the language of the French sociologist Georges Gurvitch, as used by Roger Bastide, "the history of Christianity is that of a discontinued continuity or a continued
discontinuity" (see the preface to Martial Sinda, *Le messianisme congolais* (Paris: Payot,
1972), 8; my translation.

movements when the holistic restoration of the promised kingdom does not intervene as or when expected.[19]

In the midst of oppression, domination, injustice, and alienation a personality appears as God's instrument for bringing about a new humanity, interpreted as a coming new creation/kingdom/order and visualized as the promise of a holistic reality encompassing religious, social, economic, and political aspects of life. Those who break with the old order to follow the leader form new communities that become a critique of the old order and a foreshadowing of the new when it will be wholly fulfilled.

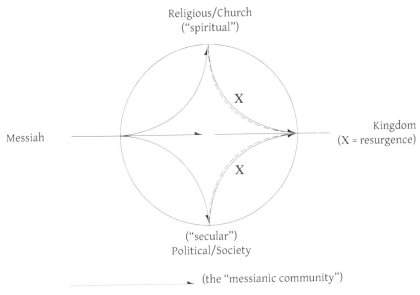

Figure 1. Processes and stages of the messianic dynamic

When the promised order fails to appear in the world, the initial impetus wanes and the movement undergoes fission, one part veering in a religious direction and the other taking on a political shaping. The breakup thus denatures the original holistic thrust; each deviation

[19] Henri Desroche, *Dieux d'hommes: Dictionnaire des messianismes et millénarismes de l'ère chrétienne* (Paris: Éditions Mouton, 1969). The interpretative introduction has been expanded into a volume translated into English: Henri Desroche, *The Sociology of Hope,* trans. Carol Martin-Sperry (Boston: Routledge and Kegan Paul, 1979). The work grew out of the author's concern to understand how so often the Christian faith expressed in alternative movements was not Marx's "opium of the people" but a renewing ferment. Indeed, the role of persecuted Christians in Eastern Europe must surely be seen in this perspective along with the demise of the communist system in 1989–90, itself functioning as a veritable opium.

from the initial intent becomes itself a movement that reinterprets the hope event from a reductionist perspective, playing down the other accents found in the original vision, and reacting to their shape in the sidetracked itineraries.

Under new conditions, the initial event may be newly appropriated by either or both of these parts. The original holistic thrust is rediscovered, thus provoking a messianic resurgence that picks up and draws on the original eschatological vision and dynamic, with recreation of holistic alternative communities.

One cannot but be struck with the manner in which the cycle discerned by Desroche has been played out not only in so-called sectarian movements but within Western Christianity as a whole, during this continuing age of our Lord; the Augustinian synthesis is now being fully critiqued by renewal in the midst of its demise, and eschatology has been a major dimension in that renewal. One has only to recall the Evanston meeting of the General Assembly of the World Council of Churches.

But Latin Europe was also affected. Vatican II itself was a call for a more eschatologically oriented church.[20] Indeed, one of the leading French Catholic theologians influential in Vatican II, Yves Congar, later wrote a volume on the church as a messianic people,[21] in which he fully exploits the expression *populus messianicus* (with the intentional latinization of the Hebrew), which is found twice in the text of *Lumen Gentium*, the Dogmatic Constitution on the Church, no. 9, at his insistence.[22] One of the leading European Protestant theologians, Jürgen Moltmann, wrote his volume on ecclesiology as "a contribution to Messianic ecclesiology."[23] And John Howard Yoder's *The Politics of Jesus,* published a few years before Moltmann's work, further defended the possibility of messianic ethics.[24]

It would appear that an important part of that corrective—messianic resurgence—is also a spinoff of the worldwide mission of the nine-

---

[20] The eschatological dimension of this shift in Latin Europe has been well described by Étienne Fouilloux in "Une vision eschatologique du christianisme: *Dieu Vivant* 1945–1955," *Revue de l'Histoire de l'Église de France* 57 (January-June, 1971): 47–72.

[21] See Yves Congar, *Un peuple messianique* (Paris: Éditions du Cerf, 1975).

[22] Second Vatican Council, *Lumen Gentium,* no. 9. Congar also attempted to insert it into a passage of *Ad Gentes,* no. 5, but it was erased during corrections and editing; see Congar, *Un peuple messianique,* 93n50.

[23] See Moltmann, *The Church in the Power of the Spirit.*

[24] See John Howard Yoder, *The Politics of Jesus* (Grand Rapids, MI: Eerdmans, 1972), chap. 1.

teenth and twentieth centuries already referred to. The World Council of Churches is itself a direct outgrowth of that movement. The insertion of *populus messianicus* in Vatican II documents is a result of the earlier influence of theologian M.-D. Chenu, who is particularly sensitive to the religious messianic dynamics developing in the two-thirds world, where the missionary movement is carrier of a new worldview with an ending-out of history.[25] Moltmann indicates clearly that his own volume does not grow out of his study or the lecture rooms at Tübingen University:

> The experiences of Christians in Korea, their missionary zeal and their suffering in political resistance; the charismatic experiences of the independent churches in Kenya and Ghana, their prayers and exuberant dances; the work of Christian communes in the slums of Manila, and the villages of the campesinos in Mexico, their life among their people and their persecution by the police—all these things impressed me more vividly than I probably realized myself. They have at least shown me the limitations of the church in Germany.[26]

This incursion from the two-thirds world into the West is also a recall to Western Christianity, where the kingdom of Christ is generally interiorized, spiritualized, or privatized, if not put simply into a millennial future in the plan of God. And it is a recall to the Western theocratic hangovers from Augustine, which easily can reject Jesus Christ's sociopolitical significance as an irrelevant model since he is indeed presented only as personal, religious, inner, and private. Indeed, the new messianic community in which Jesus is followed takes its sociopolitical cues from the servant-Messiah often more spontaneously than self-consciously and deliberately. The latter becomes necessary where Christianity has become a cultural given.

In a colloquium of Catholic scholars studying the possible current understandings of the return of Christ, sociologist Jean Séguy observed that theologians, exegetes, and philosophers presented it as being quite problematical, as a part of the human "imaginative"; instead of the return being a real historical future, they represented it quite flatly as strictly a question of here and now. How, he asked the intellectual elite,

---

[25] See M.-D. Chenu, "Libération politique et messianisme religieux," in *Parole et Mission* 19 (1962): 529–42; and "Un peuple messianique: Constitution de l'Eglise," in *Nouvelle Revue Théologique* 89 (1967): 9. His conversation with Desroche is reported in Desroche, *The Sociology of Hope*, 5.

[26] Moltmann, *The Church in the Power of the Spirit*, xv.

does that relate to the traditional affirmations—"stupidly traditional, foolishly traditional"—of the creeds, which clearly make it a question of the real return of Christ?

There is a whole density of history in which one sees the Christian people in its diverse forms await that return (with a realism that is very moving in the failure—each time renewed—of the expectation), love that return, fear that return. [Where others in the colloquium saw these as "aberrations," "temptations," or "mirrors of temptations," he responded:] I observe very simply that thousands, hundreds of thousands of Christians across the centuries, even today in numerous countries, await the return of Christ; and this helps them to read things, to situate themselves in the world where they live, to get a real hold on the world. Then, they will not transform it perhaps in the manner that certain others speak of transforming the world, but in their own particular way, and around them they will certainly transform it in a certain manner. . . . I am certainly much more moved by the expectation of a Brazilian tribe seeking for the earth without evil and the return of Christ; by the waiting of an Adventist, of a Darbyist; by the expectation of a Joachim de Fiore watching for the opening of the Third Age; or even by the expectation of Newman (to cite a cardinal of the Holy Roman Church) in his two famous sermons on, precisely, "Waiting"; much more moved by that attitude than by that which consists in relativising that value of expectant waiting. . . . In speaking of imaginative, one should observe that it is what permits one to go beyond oneself. It is that which permits one to consider oneself other than what one is; that is to say, to conceive another reality, and eventually to start moving to bring it to pass. . . . There are several ways of conceiving the expectation. But it is always active, either by prayer and holiness in the type of church that wishes to be renewed according to the old, or else peacefully but already in a concrete way in a messianic community, or else by taking up arms.[27]

The sixteenth century, which has so much conditioned the shape of Western Christianity, experiences the same resurgence and the same fission. In response to the oppressive sacral *corpus Christianum* resulting

---

[27] Jean Séguy, in *Le retour de Christ*, ed. Charles Perrot et al. (Brussels: Facultés Universitaires St. Louis, 1981), 181–88; my translation.

from Augustine's synthesis, the Reformation reaction appears, moving in several directions: the Lutheran religious orientation, with certain Spiritualists (such as Sebastian Franck or Caspar Schwenckfeld) pushing it even further; the theocratic/political direction of the Calvinists as earlier on a smaller scale with Thomas Müntzer or the infamous Münster kingdom; or the direction of free communities of witness and suffering and mission,[28] with Jesus the Messiah as sovereign Prince of Peace and example, as over against the ruling prince of the times.

In these last times, then, directions differ in relation to the eschatological mission and itinerary shaped and taught by Jesus the Messiah and his early apostles as they lived out the foolishness of the cross in the light of the experienced coming and future fulfillment of the kingdom of God.

The different eschatological scenarios

If we have observed different itineraries, we must also observe that they are partly at least the result of differently perceived scenarios of the penultimate end times. The different apostles with their different influences, emphases, and accents write of Jesus' resurrection being the first fruits of an end-time resurrection of humanity. Or they may refer to that resurrection as the presence of and struggle with the antichrist (anti-Messiah); deliverances from divine wrath—a final judgment of the nations, of individuals, of death and Hades; the binding of Satan during a thousand-year reign of Christ with his martyrs; the salvation of all Israel; the new Jerusalem; hell and the lake of fire; Christ's victorious combat; his coming with the saints, or the so-called rapture.

There appears to be no end of image, symbol, analogy, and metaphor used to portray and represent the necessary changes, threats, surprises, crises, outcomes, conflicts, interventions, tribulations, transformations, testings, judgments, and deliverances that must inevitably be effected in time, in history, in the church, in the world, in Israel, among the nations, and in the universe before the complete fulfillment of the kingdom of God, when "God will be everything to everyone." All the resources of language of the prophets of Israel, of Judaism's apocalyptic writers, and of then-current reality are used by the Spirit to prepare, to save, to proclaim, to exhort, to win, to forewarn, to strengthen, and

---

[28] See Wilbert R. Shenk, *Anabaptism and Mission* (Scottdale, PA: Herald Press, 1984).

to console the churches and the disciples in their perseverance and faithfulness in mission under the rule and in the service of Messiah.[29]

It is in the interpretative arrangements of those descriptions and events that the greatest divergences have been found in countless scenarios purporting to portray a precise history of the end times. We have only alluded to Augustine's, where, following the influential Origen, the "thousand years" was interpreted symbolically (amillennial) as the time of Christ's dominion over the world through the church. This interpretation was in contrast to clear, future, earthly expectations of some earlier writers such as Justin and Irenaeus. But later millennial scenarios did not agree about whether Christ would return before or after an earthly millennial reign. It was indeed the latter postmillennial view that predominated during the great missionary century after 1800.

Among those who agree that Christ's return would be before (the premillennial scenario), there is not agreement on whether it will be before or after a great tribulation to which Jesus and John's Apocalypse refer. Since the historicizing eschatological writings of the Chilean Jesuit Manuel Lacunza at the end of the eighteenth century, much disagreement about the role, restoration, and timing of the salvation and mission of Israel is reflected in the scenarios of Irvingites, Darbyists, Adventists, and other so-called dispensationalists.

These scenarios grow out of the following situations and states: the natural desire to know ahead of time; the new lenses provided by political changes and opposition to the gospel in a given time span; the literal, predictive character imposed on all prophetic and apocalyptic writings in scripture; the cultural distance from the scriptural texts; and the imaginative and speculative character of human understandings. These and others may combine with the great diversity already mentioned, to accentuate unduly the importance of penultimate scenarios and debate about them, to the detriment of the basic eschatological thrust of scripture. That thrust is the shaping now through the gospel, in and through the Holy Spirit in the churches, God's ultimate saving purpose as revealed through Israel in Jesus the Messiah's life, death, resurrection, magistracy, and coming. And that purpose fea-

---

[29] A balanced examination of these materials is found in David Ewert, *And Then Comes the End* (Scottdale, PA: Herald Press, 1980).

tures divine *agapē* love ordering human life, existence, and service in justice, peace, and joy on earth as it is in heaven.[30]

The present on-the-earth, in-the-world faith participation in that salvation in the Spirit of Christ is already the service of God of the end times. It is out of love for the servant Lord, Jesus the Messiah; and "whether we live or whether we die, we are the Lord's" (Rom. 14:8). Being gathered in, by, and for him, and gathering with him others in this mission, is sufficient personal eschatological knowledge beyond the hope that his own resurrection is the "first fruits of those who have fallen asleep" (1 Cor. 15:20–28), and that he "will change our lowly body to be like his glorious body" (Phil. 3:21).

Proclaiming the fulfillment of time

This brief study has not addressed the precise nature of the relationship of the church to and in society where the old order protests the call of the new. Both in history and geography the temporal, cultural, political, and socioeconomic contexts in which the churches find themselves vary considerably, and thus we cannot here venture into such developments. But it is essential that the church as human community express concretely in its existence that the last days of God's fulfilled purpose for humanity in the Messiah Jesus are taking shape in temporal, cultural, political, and socioeconomic patterns. And wherever in the world that is not to be found, the church is called to an apostolate of teams—cells of salt and light—that proclaim: "The times are fulfilled, the kingdom of God is at hand; repent and believe the good news of the king, the Messiah Jesus." This is indeed the meaning of the so-called Great Commission found in the four Gospels and the Acts of the Apostles, the very heart of the churches' calling between the ascension and the Parousia.[31]

---

[30] An excellent accent on the major thrust of scripture in the face of different scenarios is found in Paul Erb, *The Alpha and the Omega: A Restatement of the Christian Hope in Christ's Coming* (Scottdale, PA: Herald Press, 1955).

[31] The exaggerated use of "obedience to the Great Commission," as a motivation for modern Western missions under the imperialism of European colonialism, has caused some contemporary missiologists, starting with Roland Allen's reaction, to play down its importance. For example, Lesslie Newbigin—often quoted—goes so far as to say that after Christ gave the mandate, it was no longer cited in the apostolic writings. This, of course, completely ignores the command and empowered obedience to it as confirmed by the exalted Lord's messenger (Acts 5:20) to Peter, and the latter's—"We must obey God rather than men"—as related to that command. It obviously overlooks the command's central place in Peter's Caesarean summary of the christological

event (Acts 10:42, an early and important Anabaptist text), and its most significant reiteration by the exalted Christ (Acts 26:17–20) to Paul, who most significantly ties it to the servant-Messiah of Isaiah 42:6 and 49:6, as at Antioch in Pisidia. Its structured significance for the ending-out of history within the freedom of the Christ event was fully grasped by the sixteenth-century free churches of the Anabaptists, precisely in the context of an imperial Christendom. Franklin H. Littell has spelled out this dynamic in "The Anabaptist Theology of Mission" (published first in 1946; later reprinted in Shenk, *Anabaptism and Mission*) and pointed out its implications for mission and history in "A Response" to the pivotal Roman Catholic Vatican II "Religious Freedom in the Light of Revelation," in *The Documents of Vatican II*, ed. Walter M. Abbott (New York: Association Press, 1966). It is true that this foundational dimension of the mission of the messianic community becomes functional only after Pentecost, as Harry Boer insists; see *Pentecost and Missions* (Grand Rapids, MI: Eerdmans, 1961). But, contrary to Newbigin and others, as the above references indicate for three important turning points in the apostolic period, the relationship in the messianic movement between mandate and Spirit-anointing after Pentecost is one of ongoing interdependence. Within the *missio Dei*, Lamin Sanneh has insisted, for the planting of Christian faith in West Africa, the nineteenth-century missionary transmission of the message (that is, obedience to the Great Commission) was both marginal and crucial "even if in practice it may have been prosecuted by uncouth means;" see Sanneh, *West African Christianity: The Religious Impact* (Maryknoll, NY: Orbis Books, 1983), 247.

7

The shape of mission strategy

As a technical military term, *strategy* speaks about the deployment of people and materiel in order to defeat and force capitulation of the enemy. In the context of the mission of the people of God, the term is loaded and its use is fraught with danger. There is first of all a built-in notion of conquest, of triumphal imposition, of imperialism. But in it also inhere the ideas of planning, structuring, and commissioning of "special forces" for the jobs of conquest. It seems that although God works in history through a comprehensive people-nation, and strictly speaking not through a missionary army, the latter must be organized for the avant-garde work of the total people.

This second danger is illustrated by Christian history and by our own times. That history is replete with the exploits of Christian crusaders and their conquests, proof abundant of an effective strategy. Whether the results were those sought by the servant of the Lord who is to "bring forth justice to the nations" (Isa. 42:1; see also Matt. 12:18) cannot be examined here. The subtle dangers inherent in the term, however, lead us to expect distortion, and amply justify a new look at the shape of strategy for Christian mission.

How does one avoid distortion? What precedents are valid for today? To what do we turn for criteria? What is the understanding that governs our discernment of a strategy?

The cross as strategy as well as message

The Abrahamic pilgrimage of faith was fulfilled in the lordship of the life-giving Spirit released through the crucial ministry of Jesus of Nazareth. From his ministry emerged a new people from and in the midst of all nations. Through that strategy of persuasion through his suffering servant, God created a like-minded people who are servant to all peo-

Reprinted, with editorial changes, from *Mission Focus* 1, no. 3 (1973): 1–7. Used by permission.

ples for their blessing and salvation. The strategy of Christian mission is nothing more—or less—than participation in carrying out God's own strategy. Its shape is that of a cross.

Paul's appeal to "Christ and him crucified" (1 Cor. 2:2) is essential to the missionary thrust. Even more basic as a clue to strategy is the apostle's appeal to the mind-set of the crucified one. Any note of triumph or conquest or empire based on the essential and primitive confession of faith that Jesus is Lord must be seen in the light of that prior mind-set which conditioned that lordship and shaped its strategy.

The shape of strategy that you should have is the one that Christ Jesus had: He always had the nature of God, but he did not think that by force he should try to become equal with God. Instead, of his own free will he gave it all up, and took the nature of a servant. He became like a man, he appeared in human likeness; he was humble and walked the path of obedience to death—his death on the cross. For this reason God raised him to the highest place above so that in honor of the name of Jesus all beings will openly proclaim that Jesus Christ is Lord to the glory of God the Father (Phil. 2:5–11).

The persuasive appeal continues to be addressed to the church of Christ in the world today as the sine qua non of mission strategy. If, as Emil Brunner once wrote, "The church exists by mission as fire exists by burning," we can add—with 2,000 years of history to substantiate the apostolic word—Christian mission is shaped by the cross as both strategy and message. The lordship of the life-giving Spirit is the same as the incarnate servanthood of the self-denying, obediently humble, crucified one. Our strategy should also be shaped by the same understanding. The Johannine great commission parallels the Pauline appeal: "As the Father has sent me, even so I send you" (John 20:21, AV). The appeal addresses the whole people of God, both in the Philippians letter and in the resurrection word given to the disciples. The whole people of God is the special force to accomplish God's mission by the cross strategy.

The elements of a cross strategy

Self-denial, the prerequisite

The normal mind-set behind the strategy of the individual, the social group, the institution, the religious body, the nation, is fundamentally: What do I get out of this? How will this enhance my existence? How does this participate in my sense of fulfillment? How will this permit a more perfect self-realization? How shall I use privilege for my development? But all these questions are in contradiction to the cross mind-set of Jesus, who "always had . . ., but of his own free will he gave it all up."

"Go from your country and your kindred and your father's house to the land that I will show you." "And he set out, not knowing where he was going. . . . For he looked forward to the city that has foundations, whose architect and builder is God" (Gen. 12:1; Heb. 11:8–10). Abraham's faith was the self-denial of pilgrimage, not the adventure of self-fulfillment. This is the place where the Babel confusion of primeval history opens into the strategy of a new people. "If any want to become my followers, let them deny themselves . . ." (Mark 8:34). The people of God learn to renounce privilege. Being "baptized into his death" (Rom. 6:3) is their point of departure.

The call to renounce and give up what constitutes a basic cultural identity (country, family, home) leads to the disturbing cross-cultural experience of discovering new identity. This new identity comes through faith in God who promises the creation of a universal family of those with a faith like that of Abraham. The test of that faith through the sacrifice of Isaac—the denial of his identity and continuity in the future descendants—is evidence of his reaffirmation of that mind-set, his readiness for God's newness and mission.

The evidence of that readiness in God's people will always be their no to legitimate privilege. Without that strategic denial, their mission will always be haunted by the specter of a smothering paternalism. "Look what I gave up for you" really means that nothing was given. "Why don't you appreciate what we are doing for you?" is always blurted from a standpoint of privilege. As is "bringing them up to our level." The greater the apparent sacrifice—giving without giving up—the greater will be the paternalistic follow-through. The imperialism is to be found in the attitude.

The kingdom will break through the mission of God's people in the faith discovery of new life in new forms, not in a reproduction of the false absolutes of human privilege that have been renounced, whether economic systems, ideologies, political institutions, nationalism, racism, ethnic religions. The posture of Abraham is completely opposite that of the people of Jacob who are his descendants, when the latter said to Samuel, "We will have a king over us, that we also may be like all the nations, and that our king may judge us and go out before us and fight our battles" (1 Sam. 8:19–20, AV). The apostle Paul—the greatest of the church's missionaries in the Abraham-Jesus tradition—expressed the cross strategy when he wrote: "Yet whatever gains I had, these I have come to regard as loss because of Christ" (Phil. 3:7). This is the cross in life, where the medium is the message.

The basic strategy is a no to privilege, without which all other strategies become expressions of a betrayal. It is not a once-for-all denial. As with Jesus, the tempter returns ever again seeking a more appropriate season.

Servanthood, the stance

Without a fundamental no to privilege, the self-giving yes leads to self- (group, institution, nation) exaltation and lordship. But the self-denying no opens the door to a yes of servanthood. It was to this that Abraham's descendants were called as a light to the nations. The prophetic word in the Isaiah Servant Songs points to that intention. But this servant is always seen first as the servant of the Lord. Without the relationship to the Lord of justice and peace, the servant to the nations would only serve the nations' own self-exaltations, ambitions, and lordships. The oft-quoted phrase "the world writes the church's agenda" is a faithful reading only when the church—in the steps of Jesus—is the suffering servant of the Lord. With this important condition laid down, servanthood is best understood, it is true, in terms of availability, the second important element of mission strategy.

Servants allow others to dispose of them; they turn themselves over to the ones being served. In this they are completely vulnerable. The ones being served define the situation, the condition, the need, the ambitions. They write the agenda for the servants of the Lord who serve with the Lord's strategy. "I am a free man, nobody's slave; but I make myself everybody's slave in order to win as many as possible" (1 Cor. 9:19, Good News Bible). The basin and towel of the servant who washes the other's feet is without doubt a foretaste of the cross and an essential part of its strategy.

Now it is clear that the doctor is not a crippling master but a true servant when she performs an appendectomy on the patient who pleads with her for a laxative. But even where doctor knows best, the diagnosis is based on the patient's complaint, a thorough examination of the patient, and a thorough consultation with him. Such a parable helps us see how servants of the Lord are clearly oriented and qualified by him in their service to the nations. But this orientation does not make them ipso facto experts with all the answers to every situation. In the service of the church to the world, it is expert only in that in which it is the most vulnerable—in its own faith, hope, and love expression which it maintains only as it gives them away as servant.

Another parable? The maidservant from Israel who attended Naaman's wife, and the prophet of God, Elisha, give an image of a people who are servants of healing to the leadership of one of the nations, because they are first of all servants of the Lord. The leper Naaman provides the agenda, the servants are available—in the Lord. The leper refuses the word of the Lord's prophet and dictates his own terms in the light of his own understandings. The servant is still available, but he has shown that that availability is not subject to the personal whims of the leprous master. Other servants will persuade the Syrian officer to listen to the prophetic word; his obedience will bring the Lord's healing through his servants who served him. This is what men and women saw in Jesus of Nazareth, who took the nature of a servant. The apostle Paul who said that he was nobody's slave will unashamedly call himself the slave of the one who reoriented his service. This is elementary to all of the people of God.

Identification, the risk

The servant–Son of God put himself in the human situation and "became like a man." Thus by virtue of this identification with humanity, the strategy of the people of God is also defined as putting oneself in the other's place. For Jesus it meant experiencing Zealot ambitions to reestablish the Davidic kingdom, violently struggling with Pharisaic desire for purity that could choke out the human, and knowing the Sadducean appeal to compromise and conformity as his own. This could be a risky thing, but Jesus was the servant of the Lord.

"Sitting where they sit" will be fundamental to mission strategy if it is a cross-strategy. We never have a guarantee that the risk will not fail! Israel was a part of God's risk when they settled in Canaan and lost out in the midst of the land's national Baals. The artist Vincent Van Gogh took the risk as an evangelist in the mining area of the Belgian Borinage, and lost. The worker priests of the Paris Mission took the risk, until the Roman hierarchy intervened and said the risk was too great. But precisely this risk makes servanthood possible. Identification with the ones being served, living faith, temptation, and love in this context and from their perspective is the hallmark of service. The writer to the Hebrews understood incarnation as meaning that we have "one who in every respect has been tested as we are, yet without sin" (Heb. 4:15). This kind of servanthood is at the heart of God's strategy.

One of the classical heresies with regard to the incarnation was docetism, which taught that Jesus appeared to be a man, that for all practical purposes he seemed to be a man, but he was not really human. The doctrine presented Christ as one who was only "playing man." In a similar way we must face the fact that much of what we have traditionally called missions has been heretically docetic. Missionaries seemed to want to identify, but they didn't really. Often by definition they were structured into the place of privilege from which they came. Factory workers in Paris told the worker priests that they were just playing being workers, because at any moment they could decide that they had had enough of a life of a laborer and return to parish church or convent. For true workers in Paris this was not possible, for they had no other place to go.

This docetic missionary stance—apparently almost inevitable—only points more clearly to the way the total body of the people of God is called to mission. In fact in the deepest sense of the word it is the Everyman of the church that is in true identification—in the shop and factory, in the school and classroom, in the office and business. It is the so-called special forces sent into new and strange and other-cultured contexts that are docetic. This is the reason they work as rapidly as possible to create a new people of God in this place, so that there will be authentic identification. It is the docetic character of this pattern that should more than ever make missionaries suspicious of automatic transfer of their own cultural values to other people. It reduces the people's identification with their own milieu, and thus reduces the heart of God's strategy—incarnation—to a docetic, nonredemptive mission.

Naaman said to Elisha, "For your servant will no longer offer burnt offering or sacrifice to any god except the Lord. But may the Lord pardon your servant on one count: when my master goes into the house of Rimmon to worship there, leaning on my arm, and I bow down in the house of Rimmon, when I do bow down in the house of Rimmon, may the Lord pardon your servant on this one count." [Elisha] said to him, "Go in peace." (2 Kings 5:17–19).

And what if the risk should fail? It is no worse than that of refusing to take the original risk Christ took in identifying with humanity. At the same time the docetic threat is always there. As a mobile and flexible missioner, the apostle Paul was aware of this threat, yet he worked hard at overcoming it. "To the Jews I became as a Jew, in order to win Jews. To those under the law I became as one under the law (though I myself am not under the law) so that I might win those under the law.

To those outside the law I became as one outside the law (though I am not free from God's law but am under Christ's law) so that I might win those outside the law. To the weak I became weak, so that I might win the weak. I have become all things to all people, that I might by all means save some" (1 Cor. 9:20–22).

Was Paul "playing" Jew or Gentile or weak? He was anxious to see that the bridges of God in cultural identification not be absolutely broken through cultural transfer. "This is my rule in all the churches," he wrote. "Was anyone at the time of his call already circumcised? Let him not seek to remove the marks of circumcision. Was anyone at the time of his call uncircumcised? Let him not seek circumcision. Circumcision is nothing, and uncircumcision is nothing; but obeying the commandments of God is everything. Let each of you remain in the condition in which you were called (1 Cor. 7:17–20).

We always risk failure, docetic or otherwise, when we seek to identify with others. Yet the people of God take the risk. "The Son of Man came eating and drinking, and they say, 'Look, a glutton and a drunkard, a friend of tax collectors and sinners!' Yet wisdom is vindicated by her deeds" (Matt. 11:19).

Humble obedience, the contradiction

The servant of the Lord is characterized by obedience to the Lord. The servant in the midst of the nations is characterized by humility—submission to the human context of need, learning from it, and obedience to that situation. The description of the servant stance has already pointed out in passing what is here underscored—the contradictory situation of the person who commits himself or herself to people in their situation. Yet in spite of identification with them, the servant obeys the Lord in another Spirit, with another word, with another means, with another strategy. And this latter can often be interpreted as being the opposite of humility.

We must admit that docetic missions have often—and this is the perennial problem—confused the "will of the human context from which I come" with the will of the Lord. Thus what has been honestly discerned as "obedience to the Lord" by the servant has often been "obedience to my own points of reference." The people of the nations often correctly discern that this is not a humble obedience but a proud imposition of the foreign.

Yet, taking into account this serious distortion, a true obedience to the Lord, the life-giving Spirit, can and will still be interpreted as a proud intrusion of the foreign. This foreign element of Spirit and word is, however, the real reason for being and has ultimate meaning. This contradiction is built into the heart of mission; it can be no other way. Docetic missionaries, because of the possibility of these facile distortions, will therefore do their "sorting out" *with* the new people of God and not *for* them. It may be that the missionaries' sense of identity and integrity will require of them that they cannot accept for themselves that discernment. Nevertheless, they will not impose their commitment to their own sense of identify on those of the new people of God who have discerned otherwise, even in a learning process. One can be a true servant of the Lord, fully respectful of his other servants in mutuality and humble obedience.

The cross, the consequence

This built-in contradiction leads to the cross—the consequence of faithful obedience to the Lord. Those who are still moving in the stream of self-fulfillment, rather than the fulfillment of the Lord's purposes, oppose God's servant. Their opposition may take forms of mistrust, rejection, persecution, or liquidation. This rejection is not in any sense to be confused with a false cross of bearing up under necessary deprivation, or with the lot of suffering humanity (war or famine), or with the consequences of a bad character and temperament or national identity. The cross is the consequence of obedience in identification, particularly when obedience is revealed in the refusal to use self-fulfillment and its offensive and defensive tools as a strategy—either for the servant's sake or by "profiting" from that stream in others "for the sake of the gospel."

The servant announces and works for the salvation of justice and peace—reconciliation in community—that Christ gives, in the way that he did, as a suffering servant. Results and effectiveness must always disappear in the dust behind the movement toward faithfulness and the cross, experts on church growth notwithstanding.

Final remarks

A strategy of the cross is fundamentally personal and derives meaning through personal commitment. It explains the personal character of this description. "Israel" is a personal reality; "the servant" is a personal reality; the "body of Christ" or the "new person in Christ" is a personal reality, even when they imply collective personalities. The individuals who symbolize or represent such collective reality, even though plagued by the contrast of their personal cross strategy with that of the rest of the group, can resolve the conflict only by putting that too in the light of the cross. For this the Spirit is given—but that would be another chapter. And should the strategy mean failure before men and women—well, that too is another chapter, also written by our Lord, a chapter called Resurrection.

Section III   Selected Essays

B   Mission in the European context

Following Sunday worship at Rixensart, Belgium (1956).
David standing at center.

A missionary approach
to a dechristianized society

Before discussing a missionary approach to a dechristianized society,
permit me to clarify for you my own relationship to the problem.

Introduction

Our Lord Jesus Christ has laid on me a compulsion to be an agent of his
reconciliation—a means of presenting him to the world. It is a compulsion I cannot deny or suppress. On the basis of my testimony to this
effect, the "Old" Mennonite Church—a small, 70,000-member Christian
group—with European roots in the radical left wing of the Reformation
and a contemporary American rural sociological expression, has sent
me to Western Europe, to Brussels, Belgium, to give expression to that
compulsion.

It is now eighteen months since my arrival in Europe. Half of that
time is spent in religious social work with all levels of European society,
where I have met dechristianization at its grass roots. The other half
of that time has been spent in study with a view to orienting myself to
my mission field and to finding ways and means to function as a servant of Christ in that area. The problem presented by the title of this
paper is therefore real to me, and the paper itself is in a sense a result
of my time in Europe—an elaboration and more comprehensive understanding of my answer to my mission board when it asked me what I
conceived our task to be in Europe. The response to that question was
simply, "To introduce men and women to Jesus Christ."

The problem will be analyzed and studied according to the following pattern or outline: an analysis of dechristianized society, followed
by an analysis of the message to be brought to bear on that society, and
the methods to be employed in that presentation. Finally, we will look

Reprinted, with editorial changes, from *Mennonite Quarterly Review* 28, no. 1 (1954):
39–55. Used by permission.

briefly at the implications of these analyses for the church that sent me. We have, then, the problem, the message, the method, and Mennonitism.

The problem

The statement of the question for discussion assumes from the outset the fact of dechristianization. Whether it is a "revived" Belgian parish priest who writes of the "accelerating process of the dechristianization of the masses" and the "necessity of the 'rechristianization' of the masses of adults";[1] or whether it is the French Catholic founder of the Mission of Paris, with its increasing numbers of worker priests, who entitles his book *France, a Mission Field?*[2] or whether it is the English historian Toynbee who describes our society as a "post-Christian secular civilization";[3] or whether it is the editor of the literary journal *Synthèses,* who says frankly that "one of the errors of the church is to believe that the problems which trouble men the most during our era are still those of individual survival, fear of death, and the beyond"[4]— whether it is one or the other, I say—all voices unite to announce the dechristianization of contemporary society, where God, according to Nietzsche, is dead. This fact is clear. The church announces it nostalgically, the liberals announce it triumphantly, the historians announce it objectively, and we of the sects accept it—and today ask what we should do about it.

But what does this fact mean? Dechristianization is the undoing of that which has been Christianized. A civilization can be dechristianized only after it has once been Christianized. Central Africa is unchristianized, the forests of the Amazon are unchristianized, parts of China, India, Japan, and Tibet are unchristianized. But Europe is dechristianized. The difference between prefixes cannot be overemphasized. Here are descendants of people who constituted Christianized society, whether it be Russian or English, French or German, the Low Countries or the Balkans. A Christianized society is one in which the total life (political,

---

[1] A. Ryckmans, *La Paroisse Vivante* (Tournai; Paris: Casterman, 1950); quoted in the *Revue Générale Belge,* July 1951, 444, in "La Paroisse Vivante," by Francois Declairieux.

[2] Henri Godin, *La France, Pays de Mission?* (Paris: Union Générale d'Éditions, 1943).

[3] Arnold Joseph Toynbee, *Christianity and Civilization* (London: Student Christian Movement Press, 1940).

[4] Editorial in the journal *Synthèses,* January 1952.

social, economic, religious) is submitted to a moral, cultural order and expression evolved from the gospel of Christ.

The word I use is *submission.* Kenneth Scott Latourette in his classical study on the expansion of Christianity describes this process of Christianization in a dramatic manner.[5] Constantine at the beginning of the fourth century; Clovis, king of the Franks, in the fifth century; Charlemagne on Christmas Day of the year 800; and Vladimir, king of the Russians, in the tenth century—these mark some of the steps of the process of the Christianization of a society. Christianization meant the formal dropping of a pagan culture and religion, and the adopting of and adapting to a Christianized Roman culture and religion—or Byzantine, as the case happened to be—usually through military, political, or strong social pressures.

The power of this politico-religio-cultural relationship is seen clearly only four hundred years ago in the political formula of the sixteenth century, *cuius regio, eius religio.* More recently, our own century has seen remnants of this reality in the formula, "a Russian is an Orthodox." Spain under General Franco remains perhaps the best contemporary demonstration of the Christianization reality.

This does not say, however, that a Christianized society has something merely superimposed on it, that this process of Christianization is an external one. On the contrary, Christianization means that the individual in society is literally saturated with a "Christian" point of view and interpretation of life. So complete is this saturation that there is no other point of view from which to consider life, its meaning, its source, its goals. The Crusades of the Middle Ages were a powerful expression of such a society.

Probably the first real beginnings of dechristianization—that is, the possibility of a non-Christian worldview in the midst of a Christian society and culture—began with the Renaissance, which made people conscious of Greek culture and philosophy, of the individual capacity for creation and science. Recall only that paper, gunpowder, and the printing press were introduced into this society in the fifteenth century. What began as a "Christian" renaissance initiated the process of dechristianization; Karl Jaspers calls it the "conscious secularization of human existence." The fact that there were admitted values in non-Christian philosophy, art, and culture introduced the possibility that one could be other than a Christian in a Christian culture and society.

---

[5] Kenneth Scott Latourette, *A History of the Expansion of Christianity* (New York: Harper & Brothers, 1937–45).

The sixteenth-century upheaval in the church brought a demand that people be Christian in a Christian culture, something that could be accomplished at that time only through a separation from the centralized ecclesiastical-political authority. The combination of developments—Renaissance and Reformation—helped lead to a rationalistic-political expression which reached its apex for a time in rationalistic revolutionary France. An epoch had arrived when people were going to take their own lot in hand and base it on rational principles. Thus was presented to members of Western society the beginnings of an "era-consciousness," the feeling that this particular era might be better than eras past, and even that their own era might achieve a betterment they themselves had predetermined and outlined.

Georg Wilhelm Friedrich Hegel only emphasized this whole trend through his dialectic, which described the effects of consciousness on itself in producing a more and more intense view of itself and its environment and the inherent possibilities of itself and its environment. Karl Marx hardened this dialectic and his consciousness into a material absolute or necessity predetermined by history. The failure of this determinism, used as metaphysic as well as method, put an end to people's hopes in a rational order, and leaves them where Friedrich Nietzsche and Søren Kierkegaard saw them—confronting the abyss of nihilism. This outlook is well summed up by a word of Karl Jaspers:

> Since the world, of which we have become very conscious, is not necessarily settled in the condition in which we find it, the hope of man, instead of seeking its rest in the transcendence, is placed in the world. This hope knows that the world can be transformed, and thus it becomes a faith in the possibilities of an earthly accomplishment. But the individual even in the most favorable situation is able to attain only very limited realizations, and must recognize that the effective results of his activity depend a great deal more on general circumstances than upon his own intentions and plans.

> That leads him to take account of his own narrow field of action when he compares it to the possibilities he has envisaged. Finally even the course of the world—whose global aspect results definitely from no will in particular— is questioned. All of this provokes a specific sentiment of powerlessness. Man feels himself led about by the course of things, whereas previously he believed himself able to direct them. The religious attitude, insofar as it is self-denial in the face of the transcendent, was

not able to be disturbed by the spectacle of change in a world given by God. Change took care of itself and was not necessarily resented as an opposition to another possibility. On the other hand, the pride of contemporary man, which claims to attain a universal understanding of the world, and to make himself the master of it in organizing it according to his own will after an ideal which he considers the best and the truest, is transformed by contact with all of these limits that it meets into a crushing sentiment of powerlessness.[6]

After Jaspers had written this in 1930, the German people faced the nothingness with this feeling of powerlessness and jumped according to the formula of Nietzsche, only to find themselves before a worse abyss than before. And the other nations of this dechristianized society do not find themselves in a better position. If the German state followed the formula of Nietzsche, where are those who have followed the formula of Kierkegaard in the presence of the same apparent nothingness and powerlessness?

That feeling of powerlessness is expressed so well by a foot soldier in an autobiographical account of the recent war, written by Sidney and Samuel Moss. This poor Joe, after having been through the worst of the war, waiting only for an opportunity to quit fighting and go home, reenlists in the United States occupation army in Germany because he cannot see any basic difference between fighting as a civilian or as a soldier, and he prefers to take his "straight."

"It seems to me," Wagner argued, "that you'd at least get out of the army to avoid being used as an instrument of force."

"You see the war as an isolated thing, Wagner, like an earthquake. You forget that it's only a culmination of events deep rooted in society. Yet you've only got to look around to see that the war is all-pervading. The struggle of man against man prevails all through our civilization. War is everywhere. There's not and never was any peace. The struggle is the sordid struggle for existence. The war's not something that arises out of nowhere. Look, if a man's body breaks out in a syphilitic rash, we know the disease that ravages his whole system. When the

---

[6] Karl Jaspers, *La situation spirituelle de notre époque* (Paris: Desclée de Brouwer, 1951), 9; my translation. Originally published as *Die geistige Situation der Zeit* (Berlin: Walter de Gruyter, 1932).

body politic erupts all over with war, what conclusion shall we draw from that symptom?"

He paused to let us answer. But his words had stirred in us a desolation we had rather lie dormant, and we were silent.

But Wagner speaks, breaking the silence. "If that's the state you think the world's in, why don't you do something to change it?"

Fred looked at him. "Listen, buddy. I've been in the war for four years. I've hated every minute of it, and I've shot off my mouth about it wherever and whenever I could. And nothing happened. I wasn't able to speed it up or retard it—the war. How do you think I'm going to change the world?"[7]

This cry—How do you think I'm going to change the world?—is the cry of a dechristianized society and is what best characterizes it. In this sense, we as Americans are not yet dechristianized, for our confidence has not yet subsided. But the very fact that we are meeting together in these weeks to gain perspective on our task in our day in a conference entitled "Christianity and the Decline of the West" is one of the evidences that we ourselves as Christians are participating in or being strongly influenced by that spirit of dechristianization. However, the fact that we do this as Christians reminds us that dechristianized society is not all non-Christian or anti-Christian, but that a segment of society looks at it hopefully and redemptively, seeing it as the biblical "world" to which the gospel must he preached, because it stands condemned, and from which God calls out a people. As Herbert Butterfield writes,

> Indeed after a period of fifteen hundred years or so we can just about begin to say that at last no man is now a Christian because of government compulsion, or because it is necessary in order to qualify for public office, or the way to procure favor at court, or because he would lose customers if he did not go to church, or even because habit and intellectual indolence keep the mind in the appointed groove. This fact makes the present day the most important and the most exhilarating period in the history of Christianity for fifteen hundred years; and the removal of so many kinds of inducements and compulsions makes nonsense of any argument based on the decline in the numbers of professing Christians in the twentieth century. We

---

[7] Samuel and Sidney Moss, *Thy Men Shall Fall* (Chicago: Ziff-Davis Publishing Company, 1948), 315–16.

are back for the first time in something like the earliest centuries of Christianity, and those early centuries afford some relevant clues to the kind of attitude to adopt.[8]

But of what is this society composed? What are its elements? First of all there is the church itself, in its Roman, Protestant, and sectarian expressions, which faces the "world." These elements recognize in general that they no longer have the automatic option on people's allegiance. To a dechristianized society in general, these elements represent reactionary conservatism. It is they who are "sitting on the lid." These who have claimed to have the truth, we are told, support social conservatism, moral expediency, religious opportunism and formalism, and medieval political strategy, and do not in general apologize for their position. Happily, there are elements within the churches that, taking a more nearly Christian view of social, political, and economic questions, are able to draw nigh to many dechristianized elements. But the fact remains that the church, which by nature, origin, and calling is a dynamic creative force, has been more conservative than creative, and it has required a shock like that of dechristianization to call forth in our day the truly creative elements within it.

Within the church we see a hopeful return to the sources of life. The undercurrents of biblical emphasis and liturgical reform within the Catholic church, and the whole trend of Protestant theology to a more nearly biblical position, have implications for the creation of new life within the lifeless clay. But it is little, and it is late. Nietzsche had pronounced that "God is dead" in a practical sense already a century ago, when the Catholics were creating papal infallibility and the Protestants were immersed in rationalism and the sects were just starting to wake up.

Within Protestant circles this change has tremendous implications for unity both organically and organizationally. For the left-wing sects of the Reformation there must be a recognition that our point of view is gaining ground in high places. It is in part a matter of contingency—a world that offers more than one object of faith requires faith decision. But the biblical influence in this "return" must not be overlooked. I merely mention the fact of these elements within society today to point up the necessity of sharpening and clarifying our own relationship to these elements, as missionaries within this society.

---

[8]   Herbert Butterfield, *Christianity and History* (London: Bell, 1950), 135.

Another significant element of this world is its strong reaction to the social expression of the church and to its vaunted supernaturalism. This includes of course, among other elements, the communist wings, which in Western Europe are a significant political and social power. It is this element that has constantly prodded the social and economic weaknesses of our age, either without offering cures or with offering only unacceptable ones. Many in our day have tried communism and found it wanting but continue to follow the easy road of reaction and criticism.[9]

Perhaps a more important element is the one of reaction which is seeking a new morality. Whether we consider Sartre and Heidegger with their atheistic existentialism, or their first cousin Camus with his "pagan," "pre-Christian" intellectual climate, we can perhaps best understand this total point of view through the attitude of their influential spiritual father, André Gide, who "made oscillation the foundation for a new ethic."[10] I will simply summarize this position with a quotation from Harvard's Albert Guerard in his study of Gide, "A Crisis of Individualism."

> Gide wanted to be a destroyer of pragmatic prestness, of abstract or inherited authority, and of flattering, self-delusion. He wanted to throw open all questions which men are tempted to consider closed; to challenge all received opinions, all restrictive institutions, all a priori notions concerning the nature of man. He had the Puritan's horror of spiritual inertia, the scientist's skepticism of conclusions, and the optimist's faith that man achieves a higher destiny if he works it out unaided. Perhaps his most characteristic gesture is to refuse to profit from the "élan acquis;" from the acquired momentum of what others have discovered and codified, or of what one has himself discovered in the past. The ardently critical spirit thus advances into an always fresh, perilous, and unpredictable future, though constantly menaced by nostalgia for a comfortable and an inherited past. The shadow of Renan and Nietzsche and Blake may appear to hang over this attitude and effort, though Gide sharply criticized the dilettantism of Renan and the pseudo-scientific relativism of Rémy de Gourmont.

---

[9] See Arthur Koestler et al, *The God Who Failed: Six Studies in Communism* (London: Hamish-Hamilton, 1950).

[10] Albert Guerard, *André Gide* (Cambridge: Harvard University Press, 1951), 5.

Temperamentally Gide was inclined both to mysticism and to rationalism; to destroy both therefore required an unusually severe effort. He was harried as often by the nemesis of every institution which depends upon compromise or submission and which is rooted in ancient habit; the church, the family, and home most obviously, but also all political and intellectual "parties," the Cartesian and kindred traditions, and the elaborate ethics of custom. Gide believed in progress, but where others sought progress through provisional order, he preached provisional anarchy. Like Nietzsche he offered a startling parody of the golden mean. Rather than seek the midpoint between two extremes, man should cultivate both extremes and hold them in precarious harmony. Suppression and fear may paradoxically induce comfort; the comfort of mediocrity and ignorance.

But only the most ruthless and most adventurous exploitation can create new energy. "Descend to the bottom of the pit if you wish to see the stars." Gide called this a "proverb of Hell" which by no means implied disapproval. Why did he insist on the educative value of what men normally call "evil?" Primarily because the "evil act" is often independent and insubordinate, and sometimes as spontaneous as to appear gratuitous. However dangerous in itself, it promises a possible progress to a different state of being. The lawless individual, if he does not rest in lawlessness, has a chance to transcend himself.[11]

Such is Gide's ethics of movement and politics of evasion. Unlike the dilettante or casual skeptic, Gide understood as well as any of his contemporaries the comforts of identification and commitment, the enormous relief that comes from referring all questions to a higher authority. But stronger still was his distrust of comfort, inertia, and compromise. He refused to settle down and thus dramatized, half unwittingly, the moral and political dilemma of the twentieth-century individualist.

One other element of this society I should like to characterize as one of reaction to the moral and social expression of the church without explicit denial of the supernatural: "I don't go to mass—the church is nothing but a business and a theater—but I believe in God." This voice of the person of the street has found in the past few years a highly

---

[11] Ibid., 30–32.

respectable mouthpiece in the intellectual Simone Weil. An agnostic Jew with her *agrégé* in philosophy who identified herself closely with suffering humanity, Weil had mystical experiences of Christ in which she "felt, in the midst of suffering and through it, the presence of a love similar to that which one reads on the smile of a face well beloved."[12] In spite of some of the affinities in thought and experience to the Catholic church, she felt constrained to remain outside the church in order not to cut herself off from broader humanity. This influence is summed up in an article, "Sens et l'orientation du message de Simone Weil."[13]

> Men who had contact with this message underwent a strange change. They found themselves face to face with a new order of which they were most often ignorant. The thought of Simone Weil awakened them, and many were those who upon reading her perceived that they had been sleeping and passed suddenly from a mechanical experience to that of a conscious presence. A world wallowing in the mire recognized finally the sound of a pure and authentic voice. A world that was breaking up because of its prostitution of the sacred was hearing it proclaimed that the good is the only source of the sacred, and that it becomes a veritable ordeal to use such words as justice and love. A world that had forgotten God saw itself recalling that it had no other destiny, and that in going further and further away from him it was losing its own existence. The mystic was able to read the account of an inner experience, not in an old biography, but in the voice of a contemporary witness.

> This voice that made itself heard demanded an attention and a vigilance from all those who heard it. It forced the consciousness to reconsider some new dimensions. It was a woman's voice, not only that of a philosopher or an intellectual who had shared the strenuous labors of factory and field, but that of a spirit open to that which has the values of eternity, in all of the undertakings of the spirit, and in all the relations of the souls with the divinity. This genius knew no frontiers on the scientific level (from philology to mathematics), and it knew no limits on the religious level. It admired the Dialogues of Plato and the Upanishads and the Gita, but in this love is beauty.

---

[12] Simone Weil, *Attente de Dieu* (Paris: La Colombe, 1950), 38; my translation.

[13] M.-M. Davy, "Sens et Orientation du Message de Simone Weil," *Synthèses* 6, no. 69 (February 1952): 277; my translation.

Here was a genius that went even further—a sympathy for the Christ that demanded a conformity to his sufferings and to his death, an absolute emptying of the being. The soul, turned completely toward God, having become redemptive thanks to a new birth, was able henceforth to collaborate with creation on the level of the divine spirit. In this message men found a nourishment that satisfied their hunger. The echo of the work of Simone Weil has a fullness in direct proportion to the emphasis she gives to the sacred. Simone Weil is an answer; she fills a vacuum. There is no more timely message than hers. In pulling off all the masks, she places man before his own conscience—a naked conscience.

A final element that still plays a too-large role in contemporary dechristianized society is that of a group of people within the social and religious framework of the church who remain un-Christianized—those to whom the church has offered false hopes and superstition instead of a living Christ, and an institution instead of a throbbing, warm, and living body of Christ. To have, for example, the funeral procession pass by the church

> confers upon the deceased an appreciable dignity which extends to all of his family. This ceremony constitutes a sort of absolution for the existence which has just come to an end, a final seal authenticating it in good and proper form for eternal life—which idea is not absent from the popular consciousness. Those close to the deceased find in this ceremony a sort of consolation to be able to say that the loved one has not been buried in a hole like a dog.[14]

This note from the report of the religious life of a certain section of the city of Brussels, by a group of Benedictine monks, summarizes almost too well the cry of those who have asked for bread and have too often been given a serpent.

> I had a very Catholic aunt who had paid for over thirty years an insurance to a society for the souls of purgatory in order to have a funeral mass. So, of course we expected that she would have the rights to an eleven o'clock mass. But the priest asked

---

[14] Jean de Vincennes and Claude Olivier, *La Mèche qui Fume encore* ([Lodelinsart]: Éditions de Maredsous, 1949), 77–79.

seven hundred francs. We of course objected, and finally the priest consented to give the mass for three hundred francs.[15]

In giving this analysis of our society I have been at first quite general, and then have become more specific in going to some of the secondhand impressions of various aspects of this society, only to dramatize what James Stewart calls the "secret allies of God working in the hearts of those to whom one is sent"[16]—the sense of sin, the human heart's need of comfort, and what Julian Huxley calls "the God-shaped blank in the modern heart."

The final note to add to this varied description is this: that across this mixture of trends and thought patterns are being thrown the tentacles of propaganda of two conflicting politico-economic blocs, each offering itself as a savior—both of which in a certain sense stand already judged by history. This dechristianized society exists in a charged political atmosphere, so that even to have a particular religious point of view can potentially identify one with a particular economic-political bloc, or to have a particular social or economic view can immediately identify one with a special religious approach. Thus the potentialities of one who should be neutral are sharply limited. It is what François Mauriac means when he writes:

It is so obvious that it ought to dazzle us that these two great empires of the present, the U.S. and the USSR, resemble each other in the measure that they incarnate the same superstition and the same idolatry; scientific technology and economics. The two empires—for they are empires—do not at all understand the order of love where the individual Christian, if he knows how to hold himself to it, is assured of being invincible and of finality attracting all to himself—like a man who in a city that is besieged and doomed to destruction would have been the only one to have saved bread, and would have received the power to multiply it and would be the only one to know the source of living water, in such a way that none of his brothers in presenting themselves to him would be forced to leave him with hunger or thirst.[17]

---

[15] Ibid.

[16] James Stewart, *Heralds of God* (New York: Charles Scribner's Sons, 1946).

[17] François Mauriac, *La Pierre d'Achoppement* (Paris: Éditions du Rocher, 1951), 62; my translation.

With Mauriac we too are convinced that there must be a politically neutral, spiritually dynamic, and life-giving message in the midst of this dechristianized society. Let us look briefly at the nature of the message which must be brought to bear on the lives of individuals in that society.

The message

It is important to say at the outset that the message cannot be of the politico-economic order of Western Europe or its more intense form in the United States. These pseudo-democratic political entities with their socialistic-capitalistic economic systems do not determine our missionary message. In saying this, I am merely repeating what we all affirm, but I repeat it because in practice we perhaps do not affirm it as conspicuously as I am doing here. This political economic message is being preached, and there is the possibility that we too are preaching it more than we realize.

In a real sense, we cannot separate ourselves entirely from this system and its message, or at least we have not as yet done so. However much or little we ourselves are identified with this system, we must not fail to recognize that our message is not and cannot be identified with it but is rather its judge. And insofar as we are identified with our message, we too become the judges of this system in which we participate.

If our message is not the maintenance and propagation of this status quo—this so-called great achievement and end result of Western society—neither is it the historical manifestations of Christianity down through the ages in their Catholic, Protestant, Orthodox, or sectarian forms, whether of the first century, the sixteenth century, or our own day. Herbert Butterfield reinforces these sentiments when he writes:

> The supporters of what I should call the ecclesiastical interpretation of history tend to speak of toleration, political liberty, the democratic form of government, and the establishment of social justice as though these were due to the operation of the Christian spirit in society and even as though the credit for them should go to the churches. I have grave misgivings concerning that form of polemical history which seeks to promote the cause of Christianity by these mundane forms of justification and which really rather attempts to justify churchmen and ecclesiastical systems.

The genuine victory of toleration in Europe for example seems to me to have been due to the growing power in the world of secular interests and secular considerations. The churches seem to me to have refrained from persecution—or reconciled themselves to the abandonment of it—very much in proportion as churchmen lost the government of society, or lacked the power to behave as they wished. Indeed to me one of the terrible things in history—an issue which I cannot be satisfied to evade—is the fact that the Christian church began a cruel policy of persecution from the earliest moment when it was in a position (and had the power) to do so; while at the other end of the story both Catholic and Protestant churches fought to the last point of cruelty not merely to maintain their persecuting power— but fought a separate war for each separate weapon of persecution that was being taken from them. All this is not in any sense an argument against Christianity itself, but it is a serious comment on human nature even as it appears in ecclesiastical history.

Similarly, though I am aware of certain exceptions, I am not convinced that those advances in social justice which have taken place in modern times have taken place because of a Christian spirit which has widened the generosity of the more favored classes or even of the clergy (even those of a very high level sometimes) who seem to me to have bitterly resisted the changes. Some of the most signal improvements seem to have taken place because the working classes, organizing themselves as an interested party, had become a power too formidable to be ignored.

And if I am told how many programmes of social benefit go back to those of the sixteenth century Anabaptists or those of the Puritan sects in seventeenth century England, I cannot escape the fact that even in these cases the impulse to social change was an aspect of a rebellion against ecclesiastical authority. Sometimes, indeed, as in the case of freedom of conscience, the church has bitterly fought the world, and I am confronted by the anomaly that it was the world which stood for the cause now regarded as the right one even by the clergy themselves.[18]

---

[18] Butterfield, *Christianity and History*, 132–33.

This statement by Butterfield is another way of saying that the church has too often been the conservative force in a society that demanded radical changes, most often in the direction of the Christian ideal, and thus has itself justified the bitter denunciations it has received at the hands of the world. This only reaffirms the statement—which we do not always remember—that the Christian message, the gospel message, is other than the church, and becomes the judge of the church as well as society.

In saying all of this, however, we must recognize too that in our own contemporary culture and world, the message of the gospel may be seen from a perspective that adds to our comprehension of it because we know of its influence in society (with its culmination in the West) and church (with its social, political, and economic courses for more than 1900 years).

In its action across the centuries, we may see that the message of the gospel has resulted in movements and counter-movements that have released incalculable creative power within the human spirit and society. It is not necessary to insist on the creativity as seen in the art, literature, and music that are a direct result of that message, without even mentioning the indirect results of all this on non-Christian cultural expression. But consider the role of that message in destroying the dying paganism of a pre-Christian era. Consider the creative elements of the gospel in the development of Western Europe up to the period of the high Middle Ages—this transformation of a semi-primitive people into a civilized society. Consider the explosive power of that message in the sixteenth century. Consider the influence of that message for the creation of the new science. Consider the influence of that message indirectly for the development of a new India through the leadership of Mahatma Gandhi. Consider the influence of that message in the development of the new world. That message has demonstrated its creative forces.

At the same time we must recognize that the conservatism of the church across the ages has not always been the result of purely social and religious indolence and its hardening of religious life into lifeless forms. Rather we must recognize that there is implicit in the church, by virtue of its being a bearer of a basic message, in a real sense a given that does not change, which causes reaction to change and novelty, which produces finally a unity across the centuries, across the nations, and across the civilizations.

We must recognize our message to be a conservative force. God has revealed himself in his Son Jesus Christ in an absolute, once-for-all, historically concrete and personal manner. In the declaration of his birth, his life, his suffering and death, his resurrection, his ascension, his power, and his ultimate return in glory, there is that which pronounces humans sinners and the world a slave. This once-for-all revelation presents demands that create a desire internally and externally to realize these demands. That revelation was, is, and ever shall be a conservative force in the sense that all human effort is judged by its rapprochement to that revelation. But it is also conservative in the sense that each rapprochement to that revelation is an aid in the preservation of society. This is the salt in action.

But we must recognize this message to be also a powerful creative force, in the sense that this conservative revelation, which was a person, has now within that person and through his activity the redemptive power of love mediated through his continuing Spirit-presence. It is the power to effect in human beings, in society, and ultimately in history, what he demands—that is, that same redemptive love and ultimate redemption.

This creative redemptive power makes historical revelation relevant, contemporary, and timeless. Because the understanding of that revelation and the realization of its potential is always less than perfect, whether in the individual, the church, or in society, there is potentially a constant creativity. This is the leaven in action. This is also the validation of the revelation, from a human point of view. The church, insofar as it is the vehicle of this constant flow of creative power into individual lives—and only then, is a proof that the revelation was true.

The method

How then shall the church in a dechristianized society act as that vehicle? What is its missionary method? The church as the bearer of that message is required to remain sensitive to the currents of thought and attitude present in society and must freely adapt its methods to the conditions of that society. We have already examined these currents. Now let us see what they mean for the presentation of the message.

First of all, dechristianized society does not in general recognize "professional" missionaries, and a large part of it looks with suspicion and scorn at "agents" of the church. This creates first of all the problem of rapport. This society recognizes a pastor, because within this society there are still Christians to be pastored. But missionaries and evangelists as such, no! In a sense the churches and the missionaries must accommodate themselves to the demands of a highly materialistic society, which says that people may believe what they wish, but they have to prove themselves to be materially productive members of society before they have earned the right to speak about that which is spiritual or secondary. It is only as an integral part of formal society, as ones who are in the world—who have identified themselves with society in the modern sense of the word—that missionaries are qualified to bear the message.

Here is the explanation for the worker priests of Paris, of a Phillipe Vernier of the Belgian Borinage, of the rapid growth of a sect such as the Jehovah's Witnesses. The best missionaries are what Jacques Maritain has called "a new type of sainthood"—men and women "dedicated to God in their daily calling accepting their responsibility as citizens in devotion to Christ. Such men and women will not shrink from the world because of its sin. They will remember that the Master Himself touched the leper in order to heal him. They will take up again for the modern peoples a task analogous to that of the old Christian orders which ransomed captives and defended widows and the orphans."[19]

Listen to the testimony of this pastor in a dechristianized society: "I have had up until now almost thirty years of pastoral ministry with seventeen of them in the same place. I have colported scriptures in addition to my ministry from door to door for more than ten years. It is necessary to have the courage to say that all forms of evangelization no longer produce results, except for the 'soul to soul method.'"[20] This is one of many testimonies that could be offered by those who have worked in the field.

Second, if the individual in society, as an integral part of society, is the means of rapport between the message and the world, the missionary task is best fulfilled and accomplished through the training, education, and vitalization of a lay apostolate. The task is to train men and women to work and witness, to fill them with the glory of their Lord and the high sense of their calling as Christians. The most effective method of winning people is to keep before them a truly living evangel.

---

[19] Quoted from *Christianity and Democracy* (London: Geoffrey Bles, 1945), by E. L. Allen in his concise study of Maritain, *Christian Humanism: A Guide to the Thought of Jacques Maritain* (New York: Philosophical Library, 1951).

[20] A letter from Pasteur G. Parfait, Baudour-Douvrain, Belgium, pastor in the Belgian National Protestant Church; my translation.

Third, this lay apostolate must be formed and carried on through a live spiritual center—a center with a library, a study, a chapel, a lecture room. In this center, a twofold emphasis of study and worship would prevail.

This study would first of all include intensive biblical studies, not because of the current "biblical renewal," but for the same reasons that brought it about. Thus in a sense one would also capitalize on this renewal. Here is found the truth of revelation, and a solid biblical theology must be the foundation from which the "missionaries" present the gospel message.

In the second place, this study would involve analyses of current literary, theological, religious, philosophical, and social movements and trends. Lay missionaries must be conversant with their world. If they are grounded in the salt of biblical theology, they must also let that theology function actively as leaven in the thought of their contemporary world. The fruits of these studies would also become a means of presenting the Christian message to the world, in lecture and/or publication form.

The worship experience of such a center must be first of all one of corporate worship dominated by the word, through the Bible, through the devotional life and experience of the church universal, and through contemporary proclamation of it. This is the conservative note of the body, the unifying element across time, that which is not only an alternative to a particular social or cultural crystallization of the body but in a sense a deterrent to it.

The corporate worship experience must be one that is also spontaneous, Spirit led, almost charismatic, where in the freedom of the Spirit concerns and confessions are shared and the help of each of the worshipers is made available to all. "My brothers, whenever you meet let everyone be ready to contribute a psalm, a piece of teaching, a spiritual truth, or a 'tongue' with an interpreter. Everything should be done to make the church strong in the faith."[21] And, "confess therefore your sins one to another, and pray one for another, that ye may be healed."[22]

Here then again is the salt and the leaven at work in the vertical relationship of the body with its Lord and God.

---

[21] 1 Cor. 14:26 (J. B. Phillips, *The New Testament in Modern English* [New York: HarperCollins, 1962]).

[22] James 5:16 (ASV).

The Mennonites

This brings us naturally to an examination of the implications of such an approach for those of us who by tradition and confession are in the Mennonite wing of the Christian church. These next points I offer as suggestions, but as imperative suggestions.

1. The necessity to reemphasize and reaffirm the Bible-centeredness and Christ-centeredness of our message, with an avoidance of strict theological statement, and a reexamination of what biblicism means.

2. The necessity to reexamine our forms of worship with a view to universalizing our worship experience across time.

3. The necessity to intensify our consciousness and comprehension of the intellectual "world," first of all in terms of communication, and finally in terms of evangelization (too much of our "witness" has been to the church).

4. The necessity to make the full participation of all worshipers in the spontaneous witness and worship of the body not only normal but a requisite. This may demand a reexamination of our present practice of child baptism.

5. Finally, an examination of our relation to other churches.

I have tried in these reflections to be general enough so that what is offered would be applicable in any particular part of this dechristianized society. There would be particular applications of this program in a given locality, such as my own context in Belgium, which have not been treated here. But I trust that this shall have been stimulating enough to promote further discussion and suggestions that will be of value in our common calling as God's people "to know Christ, and to make him known."

9

Discovering the strategy of the Spirit

At work within the Roman Catholic society to which we were sent in 1950 was a small Protestant minority of less than one-half of one percent of the population of Belgium and bearing the marks of divided Protestantism all over the world. Among the some 50,000 Protestants were a national union of churches from Lutheran and Reformed background, a free Reformed synod (two varieties), Methodists, Plymouth Brethren (two varieties), Salvation Army, Baptists (three varieties), Pentecostals (three varieties), fundamentalist dispensationalists, Adventists, without counting the Jehovah's Witnesses and one of their divisions.

Belgian Catholicism, clearly of the pre–Vatican II variety, had among other things the best Catholic university in the world, and next to the United States, the world's strongest Catholic missionary force. Protestantism was of the pre-ecumenical variety, although the minority status forced cooperation at a number of points such as through the Belgian Bible Society. That the Belgian constitution recognized (and the state subsidized) Catholicism, Protestantism, and Judaism made for an officially liberal attitude, but within Protestantism tended to polarize the scene into national church (with official representation) and non-official churches (seen simply as nonprofit associations).

One thing there was *not*—in contrast to France, Germany, Holland, and Luxembourg—was a flesh and blood Mennonite community growing out of the Reformation period and to which we could relate. In the sixteenth century the Anabaptist wave, not considered to be Protestant by Lutherans and Calvinists, was widespread and paid the highest price in martyrs. All the larger and many smaller cities in Belgium had Mennonite congregations, but these were all wiped out by the middle of the seventeenth century.

Reprinted, with editorial changes, from *Being God's Missionary Community: Reflections on Mennonite Missions, 1945-1975* (Elkhart, IN: Mennonite Board of Missions, 1975), 23-30. Used by permission.

Foundations for mission

Why then did we come to this Maryland-sized country? On what grounds? To what would we relate? Our assignment, as we saw it, was triple:

1. To close out the existing Mennonite relief work initiated after World War II.

2. To build on the relief foundations of goodwill to "begin mission work" with the intention of establishing a Menno-denomination in the geographical place where it belonged because of its strong historical rooting in the sixteenth century.

3. To relate as possible to the Dutch Mennonites to the north (Flanders in the north being the most needy part of the country), and to the French Mennonites to the south (since the bilingual character of Belgium would automatically make us bilingual). This was the structure of our essential assignment of "presenting Jesus Christ" with total freedom in the Spirit to work it out.

Relief work was phased out by the end of 1951. This work had put us into contact with the uprooted postwar populations from Czechoslovakia, Hungary, Poland, Ukraine, Russia, Yugoslavia, as well as Belgians abandoned by their compatriots because of their attitude and relationship to the Nazis. We felt deeply the drama of the war in this way as we traveled into Germany, Austria, and Yugoslavia, visiting refugees. This contact with marginal peoples left on us a permanent impression, preoccupation, and gospel concern. Was Jesus' original proclamation at Nazareth and his ministry itself not oriented clearly to the marginal and the alienated?

In any case this intuition was not the sole inheritance of the relief period, for we have maintained permanent relations with the Slavic evangelical work now led by Vasil Magal, who in recent years has had an effective radio ministry to Russian peoples in working with Mennonite Broadcasts. Partial support is given to Sister Olga Grikman, active deaconess who continues the relating ministry with refugees she and her husband initiated after the war.

A second heritage from this period was the request to take over a struggling home of war orphans where Mennonite relief worker Esther Eby had served. Here again was a marginal context of need with a call in light of past services. Moving and resettling the home with new staff took the better part of a year. But it would hardly have been possible to find a better means of orientation to the Belgian scene than this forced contact with children, staff, social workers, welfare agencies, and unwed mothers. Certainly this year of orientation far surpassed the previous year's study of French literature, Belgian history, and philosophy at the University of Brussels, and the philosophy of Émile Boutroux at the new, struggling union faculty of Protestant theology.

The fact that we had not dismissed the administrative council of Home of Hope to replace it with Mennonite appointees left a deep impression on some folks. Through the work of one of the administrators, that way of working later related us to a new congregation at Bourgeois-Rixensart, twelve miles out of Brussels.

Further, when our experience proved that the Belgian Protestant community was not yet large enough to provide qualified professionals to maintain Home of Hope, we opted for the foster home solution for marginal children. We assumed responsibility for the children we had not placed by committing them to a recently converted family, who in collaboration with people from various churches maintained a foyer of their own until 1971. We cannot report success in winning the children to personal faith, but we can report good though imperfect results in social integration.

After Home of Hope was thus closed down, the property became the Mennonite center in which we held large children's camps during six summers and open house for groups desiring to use the facilities and our personal contributions during winter months.

The idea of a spiritual center out of which we would serve as doors were opened was a vision already clear in 1953—a vision that in some sense crowded out a denomination-building approach with a potential team of American paid evangelists working under French-speaking enlightened guidance and administration. Such an approach was not acceptable to our mission board.

Contacts with the French Mennonites during those early years led to responding to their call for a qualified couple to give leadership in their own children's ministry. Orley and Jane Swartzentruber served for a short time in Belgium, 1951–53, and then settled in the Paris area, hiring a young French evangelist to work in north Paris. Orley picked up contacts with scattered Mennonites while trying to relate to a peace group in the southeast suburbs. This was the foundation for the Mennonite congregation in Châtenay-Malabry, south of Paris, and the extensive work among handicapped children where Robert and Lois Witmer have exercised a strong social ministry in a congregational context.

Congregations and ministries in development

Although rejecting for a generation the idea of a group of American-supported evangelists, our mission board did support Belgian evangelist Jules Lambotte to work in one area of Brussels with our cooperation from 1953 to 1964. This ministry was simultaneous with a growing publishing effort, editorship of an independent evangelical monthly, and administration of a YMCA youth center. Since 1964 Lambotte has established independently a center in Flavion which he continues to operate as a publisher and promoter in the outlying villages where small groups are beginning to gather.

In 1966 Robert and Wilda Otto assumed pastoral responsibility for the Brussels congregation, composed mostly of older people and youth. In 1970 they moved that center closer to the edge of the city and among other things increased contact with African students. During these years they have also tried to maintain vital contacts with a wide range of service workers and missionaries en route to central Africa. Wilda eventually became secretary for the Protestant Missions Bureau, and Robert directed an international student foyer administered by Belgian Protestants.

The Rixensart congregation grew from a kitchen Bible study to a storefront building to the point where the members felt the need for a traditional church building to make a community impact. As a result, the building attracted a number of isolated Protestant families of various traditions in what gradually changed into an upper-middle-class suburban community. In addition to membership in the French Mennonite Conference, the Rixensart congregation affiliated also with the Belgian Reformed Church. Wilma and I were closest to this congregation, which we helped to establish and for which we provided part-time pastoral leadership for seven years.

Another chapter, important because of its concern for marginal populations, began with the work of Mauro Sbolgi, a communist youth baptized by Mennonites in Florence, Italy. He was brought to Belgium by Lewis Martin of Harrisonburg, Virginia, to work among the Italian migrant miners in Belgium. Along with preaching he helped with needs of housing, schooling, and employment. Two Spanish-speaking congregations grew out of this work; José Luis Suarez and José Gallardo were ordained for that ministry and related to an emerging witness in Spain. Meanwhile, Brother Sbolgi created a Social Service for Foreigners sponsored by the Federation of Protestant Churches with partial

Mennonite support. In 1974 Sbolgi received the Père Pire prize for outstanding work among migrants.

So today there are five small congregations where twenty years ago there was none; thousands of volumes of popular stories, historical documentation, and religious novels have been made available to French-speaking youth around the world; leaders from the five congregations get together for collective counsel; we have made a contribution to the Christian pacifist concern in the country; the gospel is broadcast into Russia as a result of our presence; but even then we must be humble about the total image that we have presented collectively.

This is what there is to report on the "successful" side of two decades. But how about all that failed? The meetings in Ruysbroeck, in La Hulpe, in Limal, in St. Nicholas-Liège, in Ohain, in Chapelle-lez-Herlaimont, that never continued; the relationship with the Baptist pastor in Brussels that broke down; the relationship to the struggling Flemish Baptist congregation in Ghent that never grew; the Portuguese Pentecostals who broke their relationship; the first baptized member of the Spanish congregation who is a Plymouth Brethren preacher in Spain today; the first baptized member of the Brussels congregation who was in prison for conscientious objection but joined the Reformed Church and there became a pastor, because he wanted to be in the church and not in a sect; the director of the children's home who broke off all contact with the church; the first leader of the Rixensart congregation who was never restored to fellowship; and the failure to build better bridges with the Dutch Mennonites.

Distillation of two decades

During my twenty years in Europe I was constantly torn between my roles as innovator and visionary within existing ecclesiastical structures, and missionary congregation builder—with calls coming from both directions. I was torn between the denominational concern—how to relate our congregations to the Mennonite family—and the more fundamental theological and ecclesiological concern of how to relate one congregation of God's people to other congregations of those who bear Christ's name in the immediate vicinity. I found it more and more impossible to be narrowly denominational, in spite of a clear ideological Anabaptist orientation.

Through the years I participated actively in (a) the Protestant Social Center where more than twenty various congregations created a strong service tool in the capital and a nationwide network of service and welfare organizations; (b) the Protestant Federation with its concern for immigrant workers; (c) the Protestant Association of Volunteers in Cooperation for the sending of volunteers to African countries in development projects and in lieu of military service; (d) the spiritual life of the congregations of the Free Reformed Church through leading congregational retreats, preaching occasional Sunday sermons, working in a commission for the future of the church, and serving on the editorial staff of their weekly paper; and (e) growing relationships with Catholic clergy in ecumenical dialogue.

This means that our development went from the vision of building a Mennonite denomination with an American-supported team, to that of a spiritual center from which we would be available as doors opened in many directions, to that finally of a congregation-based pastor relating to ecumenical Protestantism and post–Vatican II Catholicism with the concerns that grew out of my Anabaptist roots, my denominational relationships, and my Belgian congregation-planting experience.

Some of the paradoxes in my own stance have been:

- I was not an "ecumeniac" (as the president of the Belgian Protestant Church called himself), yet on a congregational level I found myself in continual ecumenical dialogue and ministry.

- I was not an advocate of church buildings, yet I found myself concerned much about a building for the church.

- I was not enthusiastic about episcopal reality, yet over the years I often found myself thoroughly involved as an administrative bishop minus the title.

- I have been inclined not to take ecclesiastical structures too seriously, yet I have found myself involved in them, and working with and through them when they appeared useful.

What missionary truth can be distilled from our two decades in Belgium?

1. Even if the goal is a mature people consciously living in the world as God's people, the Holy Spirit always starts working with people at the place where they are—culturally, ethically, spiritually.

2. The bridges of God (family, economic, class ties) must not be broken because of repentance and faith; they must only be desacralized and then used for gospel communication and a new community of faith.

3. The congregation is the fundamental key to mission—it is here that a new peoplehood can take on reality (as compared with the denomination, the mission organization, or even the leader).

4. Local congregations develop different styles of being and must have the liberty to do so, yet they must build relationships with others; a congregation, like a person, cannot live alone.

5. True maturity in a believer's life comes from exercise of responsibility early in the Christian experience.

6. Christian service cannot be used as a foundation for congregation building; yet one must respond to human needs, not caring who gets the credit, and then enter those doors that the Holy Spirit opens.

7. The basic strategy is that which grows out of obedience to calls that come into a context of personal availability; we moved nine times during twenty years, indicating our readiness for mobility.

8. The shift of personal identity can be seen as human compromise, but it is one of the Holy Spirit's effective ways of working.

9. The alienated, the marginal, the abandoned seem to reappear as the gospel target—with inherent dynamics for the future of God's people.

10. A denominational handle with worldwide dimensions can be a useful tool; it can also be a handicap. Like any good family name and its heritage, you use it with pragmatic wisdom and not as sacral authority.

The follow-through with persons, as the Spirit opens and leads, is clearly a person-centered strategy rather than the campaign, crusade, or total mobilization that plans a spiritual conquest. It is my conviction growing out of personal experience that a hard-sell approach is least effective in congregation building within a dechristianized society. For me, it is more important to discover the strategy of the Spirit as the Spirit leads through the persons given to the church, rather than to try to organize the church for the Spirit.

Section III Selected Essays

C Mission in the African context

David and Wilma Shank in Blokosso-Abidjan, Côte d'Ivoire
(1986)

The legacy of William Wadé Harris

In 1911 Monsignor Jules Moury, vicar apostolic in charge of the Roman
Catholic mission in the Ivory Coast, frankly despaired of the future of
the church in the neglected French colony. The priests of the Missions
Africaines de Lyon had arrived at the Gulf of Guinea in 1895, and after
more than fifteen years—with the help of brothers and sisters from two
orders—had expended a number of lives and much charity to build a
chain of eight major stations along the eastern coast of the Ivory Coast.
But they had yielded a slim harvest of only 2,000 baptized souls, and
the tribal peoples along the coast were clearly not turning to the light
of Christ.

By contrast, three years later in his annual report of 1914, Moury
was almost lyrical: "Space is lacking here for exposing the external
means which Divine Providence has used for the accomplishment of
His merciful designs. I must thus limit myself to exposing the effects.
These effects—it's a whole people who, having destroyed its fetishes,
invades our churches en masse, requesting Holy Baptism."[1]

The means that divine providence had used was the Glebo prophet
William Wadé Harris, who had left Cape Palmas, Liberia, on July 27,
1913, and headed east across the Cavally River, which separated Liberia
and the Ivory Coast, in obedience—as he maintained—to Christ's commission in Matthew 28:19. Accompanied by two women disciples—excellent singers playing calabash rattles—he visited village after village,
calling the coastal people to abandon and destroy their "fetishes," to
turn to the one true and living God, to be baptized and forgiven by
the Savior. He then taught them to follow the commandments of God,
to live in peace, and organized them for prayer and worship of God in
their own languages, music, and dance, to await the "white man with
the Book" and the new times that were to come.

Reprinted, with editorial changes, from *International Bulletin of Missionary Research* 10,
no. 4 (October 1986): 170–76. Used by permission.

[1] Archives of the Société des Missions Africaines (Rome), 12/804.07:28:761, 1914.

In 1926, when missionary methods and their effectiveness were discussed at the international conference at Le Zoute, Belgium, Dr. Edwin W. Smith, former missionary to Rhodesia, wryly remarked: "The man who should have talked at Le Zoute about preaching to Africans is the prophet Harris who flashed like a meteor through parts of West Africa a few years ago. Africa's most successful evangelist, he gathered in a few months a host of converts exceeding in number the total church membership of all the missions in Nyasaland now after fifty years of work. What was his method?"[2]

At the time of Smith's writing, the prophet's legacy was still a recent and almost unbelievable fact in Western missionary experience and literature: more than 100,000 tribal Africans baptized within eighteen months, with many of them ready to be taught by the "white man with the Book" ten years after the event. It is not altogether inappropriate today to take a new look at the prophet and his mission, described by one Catholic historian as "the most extraordinarily successful one man evangelical crusade that Africa has ever known."[3] In earlier years C. P. Groves[4] had pointed to "three notable missionary figures" during World War I in French Africa: Charles de Foucauld in the Sahara, Albert Schweitzer in the rain forests of Gabon, and the Prophet Harris evangelizing the pagan tribes of the Ivory Coast. The first two are well known through their writings, their work, and much that has been written about them by their interpreters. But for the African Harris, who left no writings except a half-dozen short dictated messages, the legacy is written only in the historical consequences of his work and ministry.

Who was William Wadé Harris?

In the immediate wake of his ministry of 1913–14, Harris's work was cursorily dismissed by the Catholic missionaries as that of an unscrupulous charlatan carrying out a "Protestant plot" against their mission. In the Gold Coast, Methodist missionaries and African pastors were divided in their appreciation of the man about whom they knew practically nothing, save that he had earlier related to the Methodist church in Liberia. The 1924 arrival in the Ivory Coast of the English Wesleyan

[2] Edwin W. Smith, *The Christian Mission in Africa* (London: International Missionary Council, 1926), 42.

[3] Adrian Hastings, *African Christianity* (London: Geoffrey Chapman, 1976), 10.

[4] C. P. Groves, *The Planting of Christianity in Africa*, vol. 4 (London: Lutterworth Press, 1958), 41.

Methodist missionaries and their assumption of Harris's succession made them the major source for knowledge of the man. Research in recent years has filled in many gaps of information and understanding, and we now have a fuller understanding of the man behind the prophet.[5]

Until the age of twelve years, Wadé (who was born around 1860) lived in a traditional Glebo village on the littoral east of Cape Palmas, Liberia. Son of a "heathen father," he claimed to be "born Methodist," indicating that it was at a time when conversion meant leaving the "heathen village" for the Christian village on the other side of the lagoon at Half-Graway. Wadé's mother quite exceptionally lived her life of faith in the midst of traditional family life with its sacrifices, divination, witchcraft, and the influences of the "country doctor." The other major exposure to Christianity during this traditional period was the common but ineffective evangelistic foray into the village by Episcopalian missioners.

A second period, with intense exposure to "civilization," came during his adolescence. This included six years with his maternal uncle, the Rev. John C. Lowrie, who took him as a pupil and apprentice into his Methodist pastor-schoolmaster's home in Sinoe, among the immigrant Liberians, outside Glebo territory and outside the influences of traditional life. Lowrie was a former slave, converted and educated at Freetown, and was a remarkable preacher as well as teacher. He baptized Wadé, no doubt gave him the name of William Harris, and taught him to read and write both Glebo and English. Though unconverted during this period, Harris was marked permanently by Lowrie's faith, piety, discipline, and biblical culture, as well as his role in society as a man of the Bible. This period concluded with four trips by Harris as a kroo-boy (a crew member, sometimes of Kroo ethnic background) on British and German merchant vessels going to Lagos and Gabon, and a stint as headman of kroo-boys working in the gold mines inland from Axim in the Gold Coast.

During a time of revival in Harper at Cape Palmas, when he was about twenty-one years of age, Harris was converted in the Methodist church under the summons from Revelation 2:5 ("Remember from whence thou art fallen and repent") by the Liberian preacher Rev. Mr. Thompson. "The Holy Ghost came upon me. The very year of my conversion I started preaching," he reported many years later. This new

[5] See David A. Shank, "A Prophet of Modern Times: The Thought of William Wadé Harris" (PhD diss., University of Aberdeen, Scotland, 1980).

Christian period was marked by his Christian marriage in 1885 to Rose Farr, the daughter of Episcopalian catechist John Farr, from the Christian village of Half-Graway. Harris, a stonemason, built their home in the village, and it bore all the marks of a "civilized Christian"—sheet-iron roof, second story, shuttered windows, fireplace, and so forth.

In 1888 he was confirmed in the Episcopal church by the first Liberian bishop, Samuel D. Ferguson. At the time, the Methodist church was weakening and was chiefly Liberian, while the Episcopal church was financially strong and worked especially among the Glebo. Indeed, Harris was later to condemn his action, taken "for money." But with additional schooling, and a breakthrough in 1892 when the tribe agreed to observe the Sabbath (the bishop called it "the sharp edge of our Gospel wedge"), Harris was appointed assistant teacher and catechist to his native village.

In a context of upward mobility within "civilization and Christianity," Harris was to be a regularly paid agent of the Episcopalian structures for more than fifteen years, until the end of 1908. First a simple catechist, then charged with a village Sunday school, he became a lay reader and eventually a junior warden in his church; in the school he moved from assistant teacher to teacher and thence to head of the small boarding school where his father-in-law and brother-in-law had preceded him. Outside the mission and church circles, he became official government interpreter in 1899 and enjoyed the prestige of go-between for local Liberian officials and the indigenous Glebo populations.

Tragically, this whole period was marked by intensive conflict between indigenous and immigrant Americanized blacks. If at the beginning Harris was committed to the "civilizing" pressures of the Episcopal church and the foreign patterns of the Liberian republic, it is also quite clear that halfway through the period a major shift in his loyalties was starting to take place. In 1903 he was temporarily suspended as head of the school and then reinstated in 1905, but his sympathies were clearly in favor of the Glebo people against the Liberian regime, which was fully supported by the bishop despite its unreadiness to assimilate fully the "Glebo dogs."

Two important patterns of thought were at work in Harris during this evolution. The highly influential Dr. Edward Blyden—born in the Virgin Islands and prominent in Liberia, the best-educated and most articulate Black of that period—constantly belabored the ineffectiveness and cultural imperialism of Western missions and firmly promoted an autonomous pan-African church; at the same time he was convinced that the political salvation of Liberia could come only by way of a British protectorate. And in Cape Palmas, Blyden's friend, the secessionist priest Samuel Seton, had created already in 1887 a separatist "Christ church" under the influence of the United States religious leader Charles T. Russell, founder of the group later to be known as Jehovah's Witnesses, whose apocalyptic writings were flooding the region despite the opposition of Bishop Samuel Ferguson.

During the last half of 1908, calling himself the "secretary of the Graway people," Harris engaged in threats and violence and the use of the occult in order to manipulate local Glebo chiefs against the republic, and in favor of the British. In February 1909, when a coup d'état involving Blyden failed in Monrovia, co-conspirator Harris—at the risk of his life—was flying the Union Jack at Cape Palmas in expectation of the immediate British takeover for which he had labored. His arrest, imprisonment at Harper, Liberia (Cape Palmas), trial, and condemnation for treason led to a $500 fine and a two-year prison term, for which he was paroled after making monetary payment for all the penalties against him. But he had lost his job with the Episcopal church and with the Liberian authorities for whom he had worked for nine years.

Defying the terms of his parole, William Harris preached vigorously against the Liberian regime, helping to stir up and arm the local population. When war broke out in January 1910, he was back in prison, no doubt for violating his parole. The war, won by Liberian troops supported by a United States warship, was a complete debacle for the Glebo—fleeing population, plundered villages, fines, forced resettlement—and the most expensive war the young republic had conducted. Harris was in prison, despondent over the turn of events, and it was there around June 1910 that his prophetic future was determined.

The vocation of the Prophet Harris

A trance visitation of the angel Gabriel was to William Wadé Harris like a second conversion. During three appearances, he was told that he was to be prophet of the last times; he was to abandon his civilized clothing, including his patent-leather shoes, and don a white robe; he was to destroy fetishes, beginning with his own; he was to preach Christian baptism. His wife would die after giving him six shillings to provide for his travel anywhere; and though he was not thereafter to have a church marriage, he believed God would give him others to help him in his mission. He then received in a great wave of light an anointing from

God: the Spirit came down like water on his head—three times. "It was like ice on my head and all my skin," he later reported.

The Gold Coast barrister Casely Hayford spoke with the prophet at great length in Axim, in July 1914, and was deeply impressed.

> Of his call he speaks with awe. It seems as if God made the soul of Harris a soul of fire. . . . He has learnt the lesson of those whose lips have been touched by live coal from the altar to sink himself in God. . . . When we are crossed in ordinary life we never forgive. When God crosses our path and twists our purposes unto his own, he can make a mere bamboo cross a power unto the reclaiming of souls. God has crossed the path of this humble Grebo man and he has had the sense to yield. He has suffered his will to be twisted out of shape and so he carries about the symbol of the cross.[6]

The man who in 1908 used whatever violent or occult means were at his disposal to try to achieve the political autonomy of his people was said to have reported six-and-a-half years later: "I am a prophet above all religions and freed from the control of men. I depend only upon God through the intermediary of the Angel Gabriel who initiated me to my mission of modern last times—of the era of peace about which St. John speaks in the 20th chapter of Revelation, peace of a thousand years whose arrival is at hand."[7]

The young man who had begun his "civilized" Christian faith and ministry together, at the age of twenty-one, had compromised it "for money," for a future that led him finally into the morass of political duplicity and manipulation and the way of occult violence for achieving the liberation of his people. Stopped suddenly by events he had helped to precipitate, he was turned back, as it were, to his original task of preaching, but turned forward in absolute confidence of the coming peaceful kingdom of Christ. "Christ must reign," he insisted. "I am his prophet." But this time it was also as a liberated African to fellow Africans rather than as a "civilized" person to the "barbarians."

Convinced through Russellite influences that Christ was soon to bring in the kingdom of peace, Harris predicted World War I as a judgment on the civilized world, and then announced a difficult period of

---

[6] Casely Hayford, *William Waddy Harris: The West African Reformer* (London: C. M. Phillips, 1915), 16–17.

[7] G. van Bulck, "Le prophète Harris vu par lui-même (Côte d'Ivoire 1914)," *Devant les sectes non-chrétiennes* (Louvain: XXXème Semaine de Missiologie, 1961), 120–24; my translation.

seven years, before everything was to be transformed in the reign of Christ. Seeing himself as the Elijah of Malachi 4, he felt he had appeared before the great and dreadful day of the Lord in order to prepare the people for the coming kingdom of peace, during which he was to be the judge responsible for West Africa. His mission was to prepare his constituency through preaching of repentance and baptism and peace, so the Lord would know his own. He had renounced political machination and violence but not a political vision; rather, he had reordered its character and its means and was committed to advance through preaching what would come through the Lord's own doing. He saw as his marching order Christ's Great Commission in Matthew 28:19–20.

Except for his identification with Elijah, the seven-year dating of the arrival of the kingdom and his own judgeship in it (none of which he imposed on others), Harris had been caught up in the very un-African eschatological dynamics of New Testament messianism and its spirit, with which he was mightily empowered. The politician Casely Hayford insisted: "You come to him with a heart full of bitterness, and when he is finished with you all the bitterness is gone out of your soul. . . . Why, he calls upon the living God. He calms, under God, the troubled soul. He casts out strife. He allays bitterness. He brings joy and lightness of soul to the despairing. This thing must be of God. He attaches no importance to himself. . . . He is the soul of humility."[8]

Fifty years later, when the historian Gordon Haliburton visited village after village in the Ivory Coast, seeking out the old men who could tell him about their memories of the Prophet Harris, more than once he was told, "He taught us to live in peace."

Harris's mission

After his liberation from prison in June 1910, Harris immediately began his prophetic ministry. Briefly reimprisoned, then released, he went up and down the Liberian coast preaching repentance and baptism with apparently only a limited success prior to his Ivory Coast and Gold Coast adventures. Dressed in a white cassock and turban with a cross-topped staff in one hand and a Bible and baptismal bowl in the other, he cut a striking and original figure as he attacked the local spiritual powers, disarming their practitioners, often in a contest where he proved to be the most powerful.

[8] Hayford, *William Waddy Harris*, 16–17.

In response, all the village people would bring their religious arti-facts to be burned. Then they would kneel for baptism while grasping the cross, and receive a tap of confirmation with the prophet's Bible. The prophet then taught the Ten Commandments, the Lord's Prayer, and on occasion the Apostles' Creed. Migrant Methodist clerks from Sierra Leone and the Gold Coast working in coastal commercial activ-ity were stirred up to follow through with the ministry. Elsewhere the prophet instructed each village to build a simple place of worship, and he would name twelve apostles to govern the new religious commu-nity. Where there was a Catholic mission, or the very rare congregation of foreign Methodists, he encouraged people to go there to be taught by men of God.

Harris's ministry was accompanied by remarkable healings and strange wonders—the burning of a ship when kroo-boy laborers were not discharged from Sunday work; the deaths in rapid succession of the administrator who chased him out of the French colony into the Gold Coast, and of his sergeant who had beaten the prophet; the falling of a church tower after a Catholic priest had dismissed him haughtily; the sudden deaths of those who were baptized but had only hidden, not destroyed, their fetishes. As the rumors of Harris's power and won-ders preceded him, masses of people were prepared for his coming and sought him out. In the western Gold Coast, the British administrator could scarcely believe the moral and sanitary transformation that had taken place in villages that he knew so well.

Despite his having been arrested and imprisoned three times in the Ivory Coast, the prophet returned there from the Gold Coast because he felt that God had commanded him to do so. The masses flocked to him in Grand Bassam and Bingerville, where again his baptizing was often accompanied by spectacular exorcism and healing. World War I had been declared in early August 1914, and in the French colony mis-sionary priests and colonial administrators answered the call to arms. A religiopolitical movement was under way that was controlled neither by the Catholic mission nor by the French administration. Harris and his three women followers were arrested, imprisoned, severely beaten, and a month later (January 1915) expelled by the same authorities who had earlier recognized their public utility. The prophet had, in fact, preached submission to authorities under God's law, had denounced alcohol abuse, and had clearly affected the moral climate of the popula-tions by his denunciation of adultery. Back in Liberia in early 1915, one of his singers, the young widow Helen Valentine, died as a result of the beatings she had received during her mission with the prophet.

Eight times Harris attempted to return to the Ivory Coast but was always stopped by the colonial authorities. But he went up and down the Liberian coast with his mission, often penetrating into the interior where missionaries had never gone. He went to Sierra Leone three times on foot, in 1917, 1919, and 1921. His ministry in Liberia, even if it gave problems to the Methodist missionary Walter B. Williams because of their differences over polygamous marriage, nevertheless provoked a mass revival movement in 1915 and the years following. Harris did not denounce polygamy but accepted it as a fact of African life, and this led to continuing problems with the Methodist groups and others.

In 1925 the prophet suffered a stroke, from which he only partially recovered; yet he continued his pilgrim ministry in the interior. When he was visited in 1926 by missionary Pierre Benoît from the Methodist mission, he had just returned from a mission where he had baptized more than 500 people. Benoît's contact grew out of the 1924 discovery by British Methodists of the fruits of Harris's labors in the Ivory Coast, which opened a new chapter in missionary history—admitting the facts, accepting responsibility for the legacy of the "Harrist Protestants," restructuring and absorbing them, teaching and disciplining them. Not all the baptized accepted the new Methodist government of their church life, and Benoît brought back from the aging prophet a Methodist-inspired "testament" to clinch the succession and urge the hesitant into the Methodist fold.

In 1927 the prophet received in his Spring Hill home a delegation of Adjukru leaders from the Ivory Coast for counsel about accepting Methodist control, and Harris supported the latter against the traditionalist "prophet" Aké. But in December 1928 Harris received another delegation from the Ivory Coast complaining of Methodist disciplines in family and finance. At this final meeting the prophet clearly indicated his disappointment with the Methodist controls and charged a young Ebrié chorister, Jonas Ahui, from the village congregation at Petit Bassam, to "begin again." Harris dictated a message to Ahui's father, the village chief who had been puzzled about how to respond to the missionary presence. To the village chief, the prophet asserted the validity of polygamy if God's law was followed, and denounced the taking of money for religious services performed. Harris was eager to return to the Ivory Coast but could not, for he was "about to go home." But he predicted a new war for France, warned about going to Europe, and referred again to Malachi 4. "If you say you are for God you have to suffer many tribulations. Never give up your God. . . . You must always have God before you. It is he who will guide you in all temptation: do not forsake or leave your God to save your life. . . . I am yours in Christ."

In April 1929 the prophet died. Almost seventy years of age, he was worn out and in total poverty. It is said that the simple Christian funeral in the village of Spring Hill was presided over by the local Episcopalian minister. Five of his six children and numerous grandchildren survived Harris. Today, an improvised but whitewashed cement tombstone in the Spring Hill village cemetery bears the crude hand-engraved epitaph: "In loving memory of Propha Wadé Harris born died in the year 1928 June 15 Erected by one Abraham Kwang in the year 1968." The local word is that there had been only a simple marker, but a man from Ghana had made the cement tomb marker out of respect and homage for the prophet who years earlier had raised up his mother three days after her death.

The legacy of Harris's ministry

It should be pointed out as a preface to a summary of the Harris legacy that when compared to other African prophets and their movements, his impact was exceptional—in its massive intertribal and intercolonial character; in its precedence to or major contribution to missionary Christianity; in Harris's initial positive attitude to both British and French colonial regimes, despite his pre-prophetic negative approach to the Black Liberian regime. These unique features condition the legacy in unusual ways.

Harris's work brought about a massive break with the external practices of traditional African religions all along the coast—disappearance of fetishes; disappearance of ritual sacrifices; disappearance of a variety of taboos about days and places; disappearance of lascivious dance; the "taming" of traditional festivals; disappearance of huts for isolating women during their menstrual periods; transformation of burial and funeral practices. Ten years after the passage of Harris, the English missionaries observed the great differences between the Ivory Coast and Dahomey or Togo, which they knew so well. It was described in 1922 by the colonial administrator Captain Paul Marty as a "religious fact, almost unbelievable, which has upset all the ideas we had about Black societies of the Coast—so primitive, so rustic—and which with our occupation and as a consequence of it will be the most important political and social event of ten centuries of history, past, present or future of the maritime Ivory Coast."[9]

There was created a new indigenous lay religious movement covering a dozen ethnic groups and involving new patterns of unity in the midst of diversity—one God, one theocentric law (the Ten Commandments), one day (Sunday) one book (the Bible), one symbol (the cross), one baptism (break with fetishes), one place of worship, one institution (church leadership by twelve apostles). Here prayer, including the Our Father, and transformed traditional song and dance replaced sacrifice and fetish worship. Although different from European Protestantism and Catholicism, the movement was fed by African lay Christians from neighboring colonies and constituted a reality so substantial that for Catholic missionaries in 1921 it "threatened" to make of the Ivory Coast a "Protestant nation."

The Catholic mission along the Guinea coast took off. By 1923 the Ivory Coast church counted 13,000 members and more than 10,000 catechumens. The official report of 1925 recognized Harris as the instrument given "to operate the salvation of the Ivory Coast—or at least to begin it." Father Bedel of Korhogo in the north lamented the fact that Harris had not got there to facilitate the evangelization of the Senufo. In Ghana, where there had been no baptized Catholics in Apollonia in 1914, there were in 1920 twenty-six principal stations and thirty-six secondary ones, with 5,200 members and 15,400 catechumens. Roman Catholic missionary George Fischer spoke of the "divine fire lit by the grace of the divine Master," but he made no mention of Harris. In Liberia where the Catholic mission had only reestablished itself in 1906, its prefect, Father Jean Ogé, wrote in 1920 that "the missions are going ahead by leaps and bounds . . . due to the former teaching of the famous prophet Harris. The pagans, deprived of their old gods, stream to our churches and ask for religious instruction."[10]

Protestant missions also experienced a major breakthrough. In Ghana the Methodist church was confronted with more than 8,000 people in the Axim area requesting church membership, with village after village requesting catechists and schools. In the Ivory Coast, the 1924 arrival of the British Wesleyans led within sixteen months to the reorganization of more than 160 chapels, and more than 32,000 names

[9] Paul Marty, *Études sur l'Islam en Côte d'Ivoire* (Paris: Éditions Ernest Leroux, 1922), 13; my translation.

[10] Quoted in E. M. Hogan, *Catholic Missionaries and Liberia* (Cork, Ireland: Cork University Press, 1981), 103.

on church registers. The "testament" brought back from Harris in 1926 increased that constituency. In 1927, in response to the Harris impact, the French Baptist Mission Biblique began its work in the southwest. In 1929 the Christian and Missionary Alliance arrived from the United States, eager to work with the fruit of Harris's labors, and began activities in the central Ivory Coast. These constitute three of the major Protestant churches today.

There came about a stimulation of a mass movement into the established Protestant churches in Liberia. The Methodist Episcopal church wrote officially in 1916 of

> the great revival movement among the natives with which God has blessed us. But for this our membership could not have made the advance it has. And yet we could not gather into the church all who professed conversion because we had not sufficient number of missionaries to instruct and train them. Many however went into other churches and were not lost to Christianity. Literally thousands, largely young people, have been swept into the Kingdom of God.[11]

Dr. Frederick A. Price described it as a "real tidal wave of religious enthusiasm which swept hundreds of people into the Christian church. . . . It was nothing else but Pentecost in Africa." But he also pointed out that because of their refusal to abandon polygamy, countless numbers were also refused by the churches, obviously in contradiction to Harris's understanding and preaching.

> Many of these people may be members of the invisible church of Christ even though we cannot admit them into full membership in the local assembly. . . . One remarkable feature about this great movement was the fact that tribes which seemed the most difficult to approach now became the most responsive to the preaching of the Gospel. . . . The revival fire soon spread from one end of the coastline to the other and certain sections of the interior shared the wonderful experience of getting in touch with Christ.[12]

There was also the creation of the Église Harriste (Harrist Church) in the Ivory Coast, in 1931, as a result of the 1928 visit of the Ebrié leader Jonas Ahui, who was consecrated by the prophet, given his cross and

---

[11] [Liberian Methodist Church,] *Liberian Conference Blue Book* (Monrovia: College of West Africa Press, 1916), 7–8.

[12] Frederick A. Price, *Liberian Odyssey* (New York: Pageant Press, 1954), 142–48.

Bible and the last written message from Harris. The church is today an important interethnic religious reality of perhaps 200,000 adherents, including communities in Ghana and Liberia. All seven weekly services (three on Sunday) are in the local languages and bear the distinct Harris stamp—strong anti-fetish accent on one God; prayer as a replacement for sacrifice; use of traditional music and dance; use of cross, Bible, calabash, and baptismal bowl as liturgical instruments; liturgical vestments following the model of Harris; traditional marriage practices, with preachers having only one wife; government by twelve apostles; self-supporting preachers chosen from within the local congregation. The elderly Ahui is still the active spiritual head of the church.[13]

There was a growth of "prophetism"—a kind of third way between traditional religion and the mission-planted churches. The phenomenon has occurred constantly since Harris's time in areas touched by his influence—in Dida country by Makwi, almost parallel with Harris; by Aké among the Adjukru and Abbey in the 1920s; by the prophetess Marie Lalou and the Deïma movement following the 1940s, along the northern edge of the areas influenced by Harris; Adaï among the Dida in the 1940s; Papa Nouveau among the Alladian in the 1950s; Josué Edjro among the Adjukru in the 1960s; Albert Atcho, from within the Harrist tradition, serving all the lagoon peoples. Although Harris is a partial inspiration for the phenomenon, none of these leaders had the authentic Christocentrism of the prototype. Though the movements maintain a certain continuity, there is also a constant movement from them into Christ-centered communities. In Ghana, the prophet-healing accents of the Church of the Twelve Apostles places it somewhat in the same lineage, dating back to two of Harris's disciples, Grace Thanni, who accompanied Harris from the Gold Coast, and John Nackabah.

A further result of the grassroots religious shift—coupled with the failures of the missions and churches to follow through (lack of staff, Western piety and disciplines, refusal to recognize polygamy with the élan of Harris)—is found among the many post-Harris autonomous "spiritual" churches of Ghana and Liberia in an evolving popular African Christianity.

An openness to modernity is striking. The opposition of the coastal peoples to the education of their children by the Western colonial schools was broken by Harris, who insisted: "Send your children to school." In September 1915, less than a year after Harris's arrest at the initiative of Lieutenant-Governor Angoulvant, the latter wrote:

---

[13] [Ahui died in 1992, a few years after the writing of this article.—Ed.]

At Jacqueville [on the Alladian coast where Harris ministered] the excellent upkeep of the village struck me again. But what I noticed most was the enthusiasm with which the children came to the school which I had just opened. And the great desire that they show for instruction once they have a trained and zealous master like the one I sent them. No school has ever had such success. And it was the chief of Jacqueville himself who furnished the building free of charge until the administration can furnish one.[14]

Those children and the many who followed in numerous other places were among the first cadres of an independent Ivory Coast in 1960—ministers of state, ambassadors, legislative deputies, directors of societies, and so forth.

There was a general climate of peace and cooperative submission, along with a deep inner rejection of colonialism with its brutal "pacification" prior to Harris, and its conscription and forced labor after Harris. This climate, nourished by the important new autonomous religious grass roots, constituted a particular kind of nationalism, which led to "independence with France" under President Félix Houphouët-Boigny, and made a significant contribution to the base of the modern-day so-called miracle of the Ivory Coast.[15] More than one well-informed observer has noted the relationship between the impact of Harris and the subsequent political climate in the Ivory Coast of the 1960s–1980s, characterized by the African accents of hospitality and dialogue, and by an absence of social and political violence. The president himself, in an early address to the national assembly, indicated his own awareness of the heritage from Harris that had preceded his own work.

Observations about the missionary strategy of the Prophet Harris

In the measure that Harris had a simple message, insisted on an African church, exploited indigenous values and structures, and respected traditional family structures, one could say that his strategy of African evangelization and church planting was very much that advocated by Blyden, the erstwhile Presbyterian minister who had given

---

[14] *L'Indépendant de la Côte d'Ivoire* [newspaper published at Grant Bassam, Ivory Coast] 137 (September 7, 1915); my translation.

[15] This is discussed in E. Amos-Djoro, "Les églises harristes et le nationalisme ivoirien," *Le mois en Afrique* 5 (1966), 26–47.

up his ministry and his hope for Western missions while retaining his faith in Christ and in the "God of Africa." At one point in his thought, Blyden felt that Christianity in its initial impact on "heathenism" should be quite similar to Islam in its simplicity of message, symbols, and ritual, and in its adaptability to Africa. After an initial implantation, faith could deepen through Christ into a fuller understanding of the African God, even as Islam itself could be such a stage forward to the fullness of the gospel. It was a strategy not unlike that of the Church Growth school of missiology, with its terminology of "discipling" and "perfecting."[16]

However, beyond Blyden the sophisticate, Harris understood that the issue was not just that of simplicity but rather that of power. Indeed, many have insisted on a break with the old powers as a crucial factor in evangelism in Africa. Islam has often effected that break, but has not yet fulfilled in any massive way Blyden's hope for it in Africa. Harris in a similar way with Christocentric hope and symbolism fulfilled the strategy from two points of view. First, Christianity in the lower Ivory Coast is rooted in African soil, and it is African Christianity despite heavy Wesleyan Methodist and Roman Catholic overlays. Second, as Captain Paul Marty observed in 1922, where Harris had left his mark, Islam would probably have no appeal. The important presence of Islam in the lower Ivory Coast is a result not of its influence among the coastal populations but of the massive immigrations to the prosperous south from upper Ivory Coast and the countries to the north, especially under the effects of French colonialism.

The new dimension in Harris's strategy was the administration of baptism immediately following the shift growing out of the power confrontation; this was a preventative measure to keep people from returning to the old powers. It was Trinitarian Christian baptism, even if the people did not grasp that meaning. Father Joseph Hartz at Grand Bassam wrote: "One day I asked him not to baptize. He therefore brought hundreds of people to me to baptize myself. Upon my request to wait until instruction could make of these people souls capable of grasping the character of Baptism, he answered me, 'God will do that.'"[17] If one

---

[16] The comparison of Church Growth theory and practice with the ministry of Harris has received attention in J. Stanley Friesen, "The Significance of Indigenous Movements for the Study of Church Growth," in *The Challenge of Church Growth*, ed. Wilbert R. Shenk (Elkhart, IN: Institute of Mennonite Studies, 1973).

[17] See van Bulck, "Le prophète Harris," 120–24.

were to subject the strategy to critique, positive or negative, it must be done at this point.

In the measure that Harris accented Sunday Sabbath-keeping as a continued sign of a break with the past, introduced prayer as a replacement for sacrifices, used the Bible in the chapel as a replacement for the collective fetish of the village, and introduced new festivals to replace the old, he was simply carrying out a standard Episcopalian pattern he had seen and practiced among his own people in the Cape Palmas area.[18]

The new dimension in the strategy was maintenance of traditional music with a transformation of the words, rather than the introduction of a new and foreign hymnody, though his own favorites included "Lo, he comes on clouds descending," "Guide me, O thou great Jehovah," and "What a friend we have in Jesus." The use of calabash and dance was a part of that strategy, despite the ambiguities implicit in their maintenance. But it was crucial for a people in a tradition of orality, and Harris did not see literacy as a prerequisite to faith.

Harris's strong awareness and expression of the power of the Holy Spirit and the Spirit's gifts—foresight, prediction, healing, exorcism, tongues, trance-visitations, empowerment of the word, wonders—was an appropriation of his own experience and of an important biblical and apostolic reality which had been nurtured by a deep biblical culture begun under the influence of the Methodist John C. Lowrie. But with Harris the expression of those powers had its own African color and shape, for which he had no other visual prototypes than the traditional "country doctors."

In the measure that he was driven by an eschatological urgency, confirmed by the Armageddon that was World War I, and had himself become the point of power confrontation in a major messianic breakthrough oriented to a kingdom of peace, Harris was involved in a quite un-African strategy influenced by the Russellite writings on the kingdom of God and the need for an Elijah people to proclaim and live it faithfully until the end, despite opposition from political or ecclesiastical powers. The Protestant missionary milieux he had known had giv-

---

[18] The differences among community conversion, individual conversions through the word, and individual conversions through the Holy Spirit power signs, in each of their social manifestations in the Ivory Coast, have been carefully studied by Charles-Daniel Maire, *Dynamique sociale des mutations religieuses: Expansions des protestantismes en Côte d'Ivoire* (unpublished thesis, Paris/Sorbonne, E.P.H.E., 1975).

en him an immunity from this New Testament virus, which he caught from the sectarians.

Indeed, the Harris strategy, like the legacy, was a synthesis of many strands. But the legacy, unlike the strategy, has unfortunately not maintained the central dynamic.

11

What Western Christians can learn from African-initiated churches

At the outset of the Christian movement's second millennium, the past hundred years are increasingly being seen as Christianity's "African century." Indeed, what has happened on the continent during this period of time is nothing short of phenomenal. From 1900, with something less than nine million members—including the centuries-old Coptic and Ethiopian churches—to a projected 343 million members in the year 2000, the African Christian population has grown beyond all human expectations.[1] Today, Africa holds, without rival, the distinction of being the place where the largest number of people have moved into the Christian stream of history in the shortest amount of time.

The emergence of African-initiated churches

Throughout the twentieth century, the Western missionary factor was extremely important in Africa for the growth of the Christian movement. But even more significant was the "African factor," set within a spirit world where mediation and sacrifices were dominant.[2] And central to that factor has been the emergence of African-initiated churches (AICs) by the thousands, found virtually everywhere throughout the sub-Saharan region of the continent.[3]

Reprinted, with editorial changes, from the *Mission Insight* series, no. 10, ed. James R. Krabill (Elkhart, IN: Mennonite Board of Missions, 2000). Used by permission.

[1] See David B. Barrett and Todd M. Johnson, "Annual Statistical Table on Global Mission: 1999" in *International Bulletin of Missionary Research* 32, no. 1 (January 1999): 24–25.

[2] See "Some Concluding Observations," in Lamin Sanneh's book, *West African Christianity: The Religious Impact* (London: C. Hurst and Co. 1983), 242–51.

[3] Various names have been used to describe these churches. See the website http://www.oaic.org/ of the continental, Nairobi-based "Organization of African Instituted Churches," first organized under Coptic initiative in 1978 as the "Organization of African Independent Churches."

Tens of millions of Africans are today living out their faith in these AIC communities, totally independent of the Roman Catholic, Protestant, Evangelical, or sectarian churches and denominations planted by Western missions. For this reason, these movements have often been referred to as African "independent" churches by Western Christians.

Other names, however, are also used by various groups around the continent. Thus, when breakaways from Western churches occurred in the latter part of the nineteenth century, some movements named themselves "Ethiopian" churches after the biblical term for Africa. Similarly, certain movements in West Africa, such as the "spiritual" churches of Ghana, emerged in response to specific spiritual needs felt by Africans—needs related to spirit powers, healing, trances, possession, witchcraft, dreams, visions, and prophecy. Among the Yoruba of western Nigeria, where much accent was placed on the healing power of God and where prayer largely replaced the traditional practices of sacrifice, new movements called themselves the aladura—"praying"— churches. Elsewhere, particularly in southern Africa, the new emerging churches preferred the name "Zionist," inspired by the imagery surrounding the biblical Zion—the place of God's abiding presence and eternal promise.

A full description of the many churches emerging from the dynamic encounter between Africa's traditional religions and various forms of Western Christianity goes far beyond the scope of our reflection here. The following well-known churches, however, are typical of what one can find more broadly across the continent—churches that came to life during the harsh years of European colonial rule (1885–1960), and that set the tone for the burst of indigenous energy Africa experienced in the decades to follow. Worthy of mention:

- The Church of the Nazirites led by Zulu Isaiah Shembe in 1911 near Durban, South Africa.

- The mission of the Liberian prophet William W. Harris in Ivory Coast and Gold Coast (Ghana), spawning a mass movement and eventually the Harrist Church.

- The Christ Army Church in the Niger Delta area, emerging in 1918 from the mass impact of the prophet-evangelist Garrick Braide.

- Yoruba prophets in the 1920s, including Orimolade, Babalola, and Oshitelu, and the young prophetess Abiodun in western Nigeria and Dahomey (Benin), who laid the groundwork for the Cherubim and Seraphim Church, the Apostolic Church, and the Church of the Lord (Aladura).

- The Church of Jesus Christ on the Earth by the Prophet Simon Kimbangu, estimated today to be more than five million strong, born as a movement in Nkamba in lower Belgian Congo (Zaire/Congo) by the ministry of Simon Kimbangu in 1921.

- Ethnic Luo spirituality around 1916 among Anglicans in Kenya, spawning splits in 1934 and 1958 and creating the Church of Christ in Africa, while a massive exodus from Luo Roman Catholicism in 1963 led to the Legion of Mary Church under the leadership of prophetess Audencio Aoko.

Since the 1960s, with the phasing out of the European colonial empire and its official recognition of Western mission efforts, this spontaneous African-initiated religious phenomenon has only increased as more and more Africans are reading the Bible for themselves in their own languages, and offering their own interpretations and applications.

In contrast to the "foreignness" of some of the Western-planted churches, many of these grassroots movements have been seen to be quite syncretistic in their adaptive use of local ethnic music, dance, ritual, and symbol, even as they continue to borrow selectively certain Western Christian practices and traditions of their own choosing. There are consequently—and not surprisingly—many differences among today's wide array of AICs in the ways they organize themselves and deal with issues such as polygamy, the ancestors, female circumcision, taboos, witchcraft, and exorcism.

All AICs, however, are necessarily caught up in the many tensions and crises of modernizing Africa, with the major shifts it is experiencing: from chiefdoms and kingdoms to Western colonies and modern nation-states with national leadership, from orality to literacy, from bush schools to universities, from barter systems to money and world economies, from ethnic solidarities to intraethnic nationalisms, from one-party regimes to multiparty democracies, and from hand tools to modern technology. And in addition to all these tensions, one cannot overemphasize the importance and significance of the dramatic shift taking place across the continent from a variety of traditional African religious worldviews to a biblical orientation where Jesus Christ's new covenant of grace and peace in the Spirit is daily taking on new meaning in the lives of so many.

It is this intention—God's intention for all nations—that has led North American Mennonites since 1959 to relate to a large number of AICs in ten of Africa's fifty nations.[4] And it is precisely this experience, as well, that has become for us an invaluable school of learning that we wish in turn to share with others.

Listening to and learning from the African church

We in the West are entering an era when we must learn to listen to what our brothers and sisters around the globe have to tell us. The nature of the world church requires it. Christ's new commandment to love one another calls for a reciprocity that goes beyond the motley band of twelve. At the outset of the twenty-first century since Christ's first coming to earth, that reciprocity reaches to the churches planted worldwide in both traditional village and secular contexts, in regional parochialisms, in structures of deceptive power, and in the explosive faith and hope of those who are weak and powerless. Here lies a whole dimension of our worldwide mission that remains essentially unfulfilled. These few gleanings from AICs by a Western observer and fellow faith-traveler should be seen as one step toward the fulfillment of that mission.

Learning 1: The faith of the powerful is irrelevant.
In their beginnings, many AICs grew out of a climate of protest against the power, pressures, and controls of Western Christian missions, often identified as instruments of the political, economic, and sociocultural forces put in place and held there by the colonial powers. This teaches us that in the West, where we have insisted on the separation of church and state, we have too easily assumed that our Christian mission was neatly separated from our Western and national ethos and ambitions.

In reality, they could easily become—though often unconsciously— a major dimension of our mission. Billy Graham is said to have been astonished to discover retrospectively how much American nationalism was injected into his foreign evangelistic crusades. More recently, some U.S. Christian leaders have made direct appeals to the government

---

[4] Starting in 1959 in Nigeria with Mennonite Board of Missions, then in Ghana, Ivory Coast, Benin, and Liberia; Mennonite Central Committee in Zaire in 1970 and later in southern Africa; Africa Inter-Mennonite Mission in Lesotho, Botswana, and South Africa's Transkei; Eastern Mennonite Missions in Swaziland.

to use military and economic power in ways that would "keep doors open" for the proclamation of the word . . . by American missionaries.

AICs have rejected domination by foreign Christians tied to foreign power and funding over which they, the AICs, have no control. The very existence of the AICs is a constant reminder that mission and domination—so tied together in Western Christianity and experienced by Africans as a failure in love—are a horrible distortion.

Biblical mission, in light of the Christ event, must be characterized by servanthood. And churches that reflect the ethos of America—the dominant world power, the richest nation on earth, and the economic leader of the world—must be taught that lesson over and over again. What we ourselves perceive as faith is perceived by others as power. People are understandably often attracted to that power, until they discover they do not have access to it. Then they must discover for themselves a relevant faith for people without power.

Learning 2: The gospel is the source of liberating power.

According to some observers, it was in the life and context of AICs scattered across the African continent that the gospel of Christ came into its own as a functional power of liberation. The Western missions, as honest reflections of their sending churches, had been generally powerless to make this dimension of the gospel effective. Many of their early converts lived out a rather superficial "cultural" Christianity— the new colonial religion—without a radical liberation from spiritual powers that kept them in bondage.

In AICs, however, Christ often penetrated more deeply into the African worldview and dealt with those powers that had for centuries been the guarantors of the traditional political and social structures. This caused a new sociopolitical reality to emerge from within the old society—the independent church as a community of faith living out its liberation. Thus, AICs were somewhat better prepared to engage in critique—often unselfconsciously—of the late twentieth-century forms of mammon—Caesar and Mars—while mission-planted churches were more likely to accept these idolatries almost uncritically and integrate them into their understanding of the new "modern" society emerging across the continent.

In churches of the West, where we have traditionally seen political and socioeconomic structures as God-given and good, the gospel has not always been perceived as a power of liberation from the spiritual powers and dynamics behind those structures. It has often, rather, been used as an instrument of inner freedom to move in tune with them, thus making our political and economic systems and social patterns quasi-sacred. These then become the carriers of history, replacing the community of faith liberated by Christ.

One may observe, unfortunately, that AICs too have often lost their capacity to critique in the time of postcolonial independence, and run the risk of sliding into a rapid sacralizing of the new independent African structures. But their movement into this new relationship with traditional life helps us understand the concept of the upside-down kingdom of the free-reigning Lord Jesus Christ, and the call of the gospel to create the new liberated community.

Learning 3: Faith is a spiritual combat.

One is impressed, in even superficial contacts with AICs, by how the climate of spiritual combat seems to predominate. One may hear prayers addressed to St. Michael, whom the book of Revelation presents as having won in the combat with the devil. People may come to the place of meeting as a place of refuge from the attacks of destructive powers. Prayer and fasting take center stage as offensive and defensive arms.

A permanent struggle is engaged against occult powers and witchcraft, sickness and death, fetishism and idolatry, oppression and repression. Since one must constantly be on the alert in order not to be overtaken or surprised by evil forces, perseverance in combat is the only solution to vulnerability. No point of arrival exists where striving is over. No plateau of peace is reached above the stress of struggle. These are reserved for the above and beyond; here below, we are fighting the good fight of faith. Maturity is not moving beyond the combat but knowing how to effectively carry on the spiritual warfare that is being waged.

Does this phenomenon simply reflect a religious culture with characteristics different from churches in the West because it does not reflect our modern, secularized worldview? Or is this a dimension of faith as perceived by Christ and the apostles that we in the West are incapable of demonstrating because we have already lost out in the fight? Alternately, perhaps we as Western Christians are carrying on our personal combat individually all alone, scarcely daring to suggest openly—or fearful of creating the embarrassing impression—that we are, in fact, spiritually deficient and immature.

Whatever might be the case, mission is a combat for the salvation of the world. Where this combat is not valorized, brought out into the open, carried and shared together, the mission of the people of God is dulled. And where there is no mission, the people perish.

Could it be that the church of the West is so hung up on money, management, and its programmed growth that it has forgotten a fundamental dimension of faith? Mammon, we must be reminded, cannot chase Satan, because it is his instrument in the combat against God.

We may, in our Western churches, have other ways of speaking about the life of faith, but if we eliminate the fundamental dimension of spiritual combat, this is surely more than just a cultural and language shift. AICs can teach us much about the nature and necessity of this combat in the life of God's people.

Learning 4: The Western interpretation of scriptures is not the final word.

One factor leading to the creation of AICs is said to be the translation and production of scriptures in the language of the people. When Africans started to read the scriptures for themselves, they discovered many things that had not been told them by the missionaries and their Western-trained leaders. At times, the Africans seemed to be more at home in reading the scriptures than in the interpretation and explanations that others had provided. We have already referred to the dimensions of liberation and combat, often overlooked or otherwise interpreted by Westerners, yet clearly present in scripture, and fully embraced by AICs in their life and worship.

Indeed, Western-trained African theologians in the mission-planted churches were themselves often impressed, as Africans, by what they called the "spontaneous theology" of AICs. The latter did not know that they were supposed to read the scriptures through a theological perspective coming from the West. They simply approached God's word from the perspective of their own grassroots needs and understandings—and their worship, practices, piety, and symbols all grew out of that reading.

Not surprisingly, AICs came out at a different place than did their Western-trained African colleagues. Because of their cultural proximity to the scriptures, they could vibrate with them in ways that modern Western Christians could not. All of this has had an effect on African Christian theologians who had been taught that the theological and biblical understandings of the West were universal—the way faith should be understood and interpreted by all people.

The AICs, and after them the African theologians of the mission-planted churches, are teaching us that our Western theology is *Western*, that our reading of the scriptures is a *Western* reading, and that our claims of universality with regard to our particular view of things are in reality a part of our own *Western* provincial arrogance.

This is a hard lesson to learn. When Westerners hear for the first time certain readings and interpretations given from an African perspective, an initial reaction is often, "How provincial!" "How particular!" "How naive!" "What a strange reaction!" "How unbiblical!" In reality, what is happening may be little more than a confrontation between two different readings, both provincial. Mutual listening and sharing are required, if we are to move from provincialism to a fuller, deeper understanding of God's word.

Walter Hollenweger writes about an AIC student in England who listened to his New Testament professor give an exposition of a Gospel passage that dealt with fasting. The student felt something was lacking and discovered that the expositor had never fasted. Such things must be lived and not just analyzed and talked about. For understanding, participation is just as important as analysis.

We seem to have a hard time understanding that African talk about a "white Christ" and his "foreign religion" is not an African idea but one that the West gave them. To discover one's own provincialism then, to name it and move beyond it, is never easy. The AICs can help us learn to do so.

Learning 5: God is experienced as an awe-inspiring divine mystery.

In our many contacts with Christians from AICs, we have repeatedly been impressed with the manner in which they experience and accept God and the ways of God as awesome, unsearchable, and deeply mysterious. The AIC journey of faith has within it—often from the beginning—the dimensions of the unexpected, the unpredictable, the overwhelming. The result is an exuberant, spontaneous response of awe, holy fear, and sacred joy—all finding full expression in a deep piety, a profound respect for the "house of God" (its servants, liturgies, symbols, and rituals), and an openness to signs and messages from God.

One may learn of a sudden change in plans for a spiritual leader because of an inspired warning given through a servant girl. Messages from God may come to the entire congregation through recognized women visionaries. A school director become preacher will explain how, when he was a practicing fetisher (manipulator of occult powers), God spoke directly to him (his wife in the same room did not hear it, and he still does not know why not), telling him to destroy his fetishes, then to destroy the three that he had secretly saved, and finally to destroy the last one (whose destruction he thought would kill him), to buy a Bible, to study it, and then to attach himself to a group of illiterate independent Christians in order to teach them the Bible. The schoolteacher will further explain how God proved his power to other fetish practitioners when, on receiving this word from the Lord, a pot of occult medicines burst before their very eyes.

One national leader of an AIC in Côte d'Ivoire, a former Catholic altar boy and catechist, left his church and joined the AIC because only in that church did he find a deep respect for what is holy. In this new church, people remove their shoes before entering the place of worship, and they present themselves before the presence of the Lord in congregational worship only when participants are dressed in white.

Another group knows of mysterious names for God revealed more than forty years before to the group's leader-founder through glossolalia. The possibility of knowing and using those mysterious names is seen to add to the holy character of the church's worship and life in community. God's mysterious messengers—the angels—intervene every so often to give direction in face of uncertainty and questioning. The life of faith in God is a life of mysterious wonder.

The first time one seeker attended an AIC meeting, he heard speaking in tongues and recognized his own situation in the interpretation, which revealed knowledge of two major personal questions he was facing. His was a mysterious, awe-inspiring beginning to a life of faith.

By contrast, much of Western Christianity can appear to be participation in a program rather than in worship, and with distrust of those mysterious dimensions that the AICs speak of as the spiritual—dreams, visions, revelations, direct messages from God, healing, casting out of spirits, and speaking in tongues with subsequent interpretations.

Our long history of theological tradition and philosophical reflection—through the Middle Ages; the Reformation; the Enlightenment; and the industrial, technological, media, and computer revolutions—has rationalized our thought, made our understandings doctrinaire, ferreted out the problems about God, and dulled our sense of mystery.

I myself was taught in a Mennonite seminary many years ago that one Western theologian thought of our Western religious situation as having "come of age," and tried to reflect how to understand a "religionless Christianity."

In stark contrast to this, another Western theologian has recently pointed out that the West today is experiencing a "boom in religion" such as it has never seen—a religion, however, that is not necessarily Christian or even Christian-oriented in nature or intent. Has this boom occurred, one might ask, because Western churches had made God over; domesticated God; Westernized and trivialized God; and reduced the mystery, the sacred, the otherness of God's free Spirit?

The AICs, among the last to appear on the stage of church history, may have much to teach us about their newfound Lord and God, even though we Western Christians were on the scene long before they were. Indeed, this may well be another illustration of one of Jesus' hard sayings: "The last shall be first." In any case, the Western churches, so bound to the rational and technological means of their culture, need to come to grips again with the holy mystery of God. "God is Spirit," said Jesus, "and they who worship him must worship him in spirit and in truth."

Learning 6: The power of the faith community is in the laity.

On the evening of November 12, 1984, following a lengthy period of inspired singing at their regular Monday night service, I preached for the brothers and sisters of the Universal Evangelical Association in Cotonou, Benin. The meeting was presided over by "Papa" Dossou, the spiritual father of this zealous Christian congregation in a populous part of the city. One of the local preachers served as my interpreter, and we were followed by Pierre, another preacher in the congregation.

During the daytime, Papa Dossou was an inspector in the city street-cleaning and garbage-disposal system. My translator was a plumber and owner of a small fleet of taxis, and Pierre was a shoe salesman. But on Sundays and four nights a week, they became congregational leaders, spiritual counselors, moral guides, preachers of the word of God. The Lord had called all of them to their active ministries in the church in addition to their full-time and demanding occupations. Outside the time required for their jobs, all their time and energy was spent in evangelism and the edification of the church.

These men had no formal Bible training in classes, but they had learned to read and interpret the Bible from one another, from tracts and pamphlets that had come their way, and from occasional books. But for them, *the* book is the Bible; they are thoroughgoing biblicists, reading and studying together, learning from one another, obeying what they know, and passing on what they have learned to the rest of the people in the congregation. As they do so, other spiritual gifts are given by the Holy Spirit to men and women, and are recognized and confirmed by the congregation, which is indeed a community of growing spiritual gifts. Pierre, the shoe salesman, told us, "All of us are very thirsty for the Word; we want to drink ever more deeply of its life and power. The whole congregation is always thirsty for more—all the time."

Such men and women are not religious professionals, an educated clergy who have studied how to lead worship, organize a congregation, administer the sacraments, conduct marriages and funerals, or choose appropriate music for a particular ceremony or church service. They know practically nothing of church history, historical theology, biblical exegesis and interpretation, sermon preparation, or pastoral counseling. They have been seized by the gospel of Christ, have experienced a new life of liberation, and have a powerful passion for God and his people and a compelling obedience to his word. Their congregation has grown because of that passion and compulsion, which they find sadly lacking in the pastors and congregations of the century-old Western missionary church in Cotonou. The Lord has taught them much through their many experiences, and they are growing and maturing in the word of God and their obedience to God.

This situation is typical of many AICs all over Africa. If in many contexts some AICs appear to be only one stage removed from African traditional religions, in many others their passion, obedience, and zeal have become a provocative challenge to the Western, mission-planted churches that have from the beginning been conscious of being the church. The latter, with their professionally trained clergy and theologians; their deep concern for social, economic, and political status; and their defensiveness about the institutional church and its tradition, may often appear to have lost their first love. At the same time, AICs, with their nonprofessional lay power, have an appeal for the grassroots masses, and they gather in the poor, bringing them the liberating power of Christ. No wonder one observer has called AICs the Anabaptists of Africa.

The power of AICs is in the authenticity of their laity, who operate and work freely as self-supported gifts of God to the people. Different gifts within the congregation may create an equilibrium of power rather than a hierarchy of power; many functions in the church are assigned so that each member may have a place and a task. Sometimes this distribution will take place in groups—members promoted to "pray-ers" or pray-ers promoted to "cross-bearers"—an open recognition of the need to grow, to mature, to move forward, to assume more responsibility, to enter another stage and exercise more gifts. But in this community of gifts, with all the discernment it requires, is to be found a power among the laity that is not usual in the typical mission congregation with its clergy and laity distinctions planted by the mission in bygone times.

The freedom of the Spirit to give and call forth gifts within the congregation that one discovers in the AICs comes as a challenge to our Western churches that have congregations to be served rather than congregations of servants who are God's ministers to the world.

The time has come for Western Christians to move from judgment to learning

Many Western Christians may be astonished to think of learning anything from African-initiated churches, since much of past reaction to them from Western missionaries and mission-planted churches has been negative. Blanket charges of sectarianism, syncretism, religious tribalism, unclear doctrine, misunderstanding of the Holy Spirit, exploitative leadership, weak Christology, and legalism have often been made against many of these churches. Indeed, some of those charges have been true for some of the movements. But many of the same things could also be said of some mission-related churches in Africa. To make such generalizations about either of these complex realities is not helpful. Both the mission-planted churches and the AICs have only recently emerged out of traditional African religious contexts; both are en route to the coming kingdom of God.

We have looked in these few pages at a number of characteristics of AICs from which Westerners can learn—the concept of the use and misuse of power, the themes of liberation and spiritual combat, contextualized interpretations of scripture, an awe of divine mystery, and the importance of laity in a community of spiritual gifts. Further study and mutual sharing would, no doubt, uncover other learnings.

The Holy Spirit of God is creating a new humanity in Africa. But we still have much to understand and learn about the patterns and dynamics of such religious change effected through the impact of the mixture of the gospel with Western culture, modernization, and the consequences of colonialism. While that is being more fully understood and interpreted, it is clear that AICs and mainline churches are learning from each other. The churches in the West owe it to the Lord of the church and to themselves not to shut themselves off from what the Spirit is saying to them through the African-initiated churches.

Section III Selected Essays

D Conversion

An ordinary Sunday meal after church in a Harrist community

12

Toward an understanding of Christian conversion

Ex-opera singer N. "came to Christ" out of suicidal despair; somehow she understood that there was hope for her in Christ. Teenager A., in conflict with his family, "came to Christ" in his search for personal identity and for an absolute to which he could commit himself. Middle-class "riser" L. "came to Christ" out of a deep need to replace a religious system that for him was neither adequate nor consistent.

Each of these persons in a different context perceived what it meant to be "outside of Christ." What they had in common was their conversion to Christ as known in the common life of the same congregation. Each had turned from a previous condition to what was a consciously different life in a new community. Yet the so-called Pauline experience of law and grace (Rom. 7), or the Lutheran experience of condemnation and justification by faith was not an obvious functional part of their conversions. How *do* we understand conversion?

Understanding conversion

The "Pauline"-Lutheran paradigm of conversion has colored traditional Protestant understanding. The style and message of evangelism and mission have consciously sought to effect conversion as defined by a particular mental and spiritual context. This is not, however, the paradigm that we find in the Gospels, where there is a call to follow and become a disciple. Neither is it the paradigm of the Old Testament, nor that of the Book of the Acts.

And yet in the Old Testament, Gospels, and Acts, as well as the rest of the non-Pauline authors, conversion is considered absolutely essential to salvation. Thus A. D. Nock in his classic study of conversion

---

Reprinted, with editorial changes, from *Mission Focus* 5, no. 2 (1976): 1–7. Used by permission.

in the first Christian centuries[1] points out that it is something found uniquely within the prophetic tradition of the Hebrew and Christian faiths. Other religions had adherents who "used" the religious thought, or system, or celebration, or priest without being wholly committed in faith to them, nor were they expected to be. Judaism and Christianity, however, "demanded a new life in a new people."

Judaism was oriented by the monotheistic, anti-idolatrous, and strongly ethical orientation, which contrasted with the contemporary religious climate. Hebrew youth knew when they were integrated into the covenant with God that a different community was their home. Christianity was centered in the lordship of a Savior Christ whose kingdom was based on his death, resurrection, and coming judgment. Nock points to the novelty in "the *motive* which it supplied for good conduct and the abhorrence of past bad conduct which it demanded. [It was] devotion to Jesus who had suffered so that sinlessness might be within man's reach and . . . love of the brethren, altogether more lively and far-reaching in Christianity." Further, "it claimed to give power to satisfy its requirements; . . . grace . . . and the special gift of the Spirit.[2]

Biblical illustrations of conversion— of turning from and turning to

The Jewish and Christian communities were constituted by conversion, which is essentially a turning from and turning to.

- With Abraham it was *from* country and kindred and father's house *to* "the land that I will show you" (Gen. 12:1);[3] he looked forward to the city which has foundations, whose builder and maker is God (Heb. 11:10).

- With Moses and Israel in Egypt, it was *from* sitting with the flesh pots and eating bread to the full . . . and dying in service to the Egyptians (Exod. 16:3), *to* going into the wilderness to serve Yahweh (Exod. 14:12).

---

[1] A. D. Nock, *Conversion: The Old and the New in Religion from Alexander the Great to Augustine of Hippo* (Oxford: Clarendon Press, 1933).

[2] Ibid., 218–20.

[3] Unless otherwise noted, scripture quotations are from the Revised Standard Version (RSV).

- With Caleb and Joshua it was to have been *from* dying in the wilderness *to* receiving from the Lord a land that flows with milk and honey (Num. 13:27). But conversion was refused, so they died. . . .

- With Samuel it was an appeal to convert *from* having a king to govern them like all the nations (1 Sam 8:20) *to* Yahweh's being king over them. But conversion was refused, so they were given a king.

- Jesus' own appeal was for the conversion *from* an evil and unbelieving generation (Matt. 17:17) *to* the kingdom of God that is at hand (Mark 1:15 et al). That conversion response was typified by Peter: "Lo, we have left everything and followed" (Mark 10:28).

- Peter's appeal, on the occasion of the coming of the Holy Spirit, was *from* this crooked generation (Acts 2:40) *to* forgiveness and the gift of the Holy Spirit in devotion to the apostles' teaching, and fellowship, breaking bread, and prayer—and no one claimed private ownership of any possessions (Acts 2:42; 4:32).

- Should we have mentioned Elijah on Mt. Carmel, and the appeals of Jeremiah (3:2; 32:40), Ezekiel (for example, 18:30), and Joel (2:12–13), where the prophetic thrust is on returning *to* God with whom the people are in covenant relation?

- And should we make more explicit the specific context of the exceptional kind of conversion of Saul of Tarsus in his turning *from* being a circumcised Benjamite Hebrew, a Pharisee zealous to the point of heretic hunting, and blameless in righteousness under the law (Acts 22) *to* knowing Christ Jesus as Lord, and being found in him with a righteousness of God through faith in Christ (Phil. 3:9)?

It is ever again the crucial response of "turning around" in repentance (most often *metanoia* in Greek), or "turning" or "re-turning" to covenant with God (*šûb*—a verb of motion—and its derivatives in Hebrew) that determines a future of salvation for Israel and the nations in the fulfillment of God's purposes. The shift from "away from God in judgment of death and destruction" to "with God and his righteousness in the salvation of life and peace, and fellowship in the kingdom" is at the heart of conversion reality. Here there is neither ambivalence nor ambiguity, only an either/or possibility.

Biblical versus contemporary understanding of conversion

The word *conversion* itself is used only once in the Revised Standard Version of the New Testament. When Paul and Barnabas passed through Phoenicia and Samaria en route to Jerusalem, they reported "the *conversion* of the Gentiles" (Acts 15:3), the main subject of the Jerusalem conference. There James spoke of that same reality as the "Gentiles who *turn to* God" (Acts 15:19). Where the 1611 King James Version translated "to convert," the RSV most often uses "to turn." The contemporary Western understanding of conversion often emphasizes the psychological and affective aspects of inner experience (emotion, release, feeling, self-consciousness) as over against the biblical accent on reversal of direction, transfer of loyalty, and change in commitment. It is this latter biblical emphasis on what Nock calls "a new life in a new people" that should orient our understanding of conversion.

Biblical conversion is typified in the story of Jonah's ministry at Nineveh. Jesus used it as a type of his own ministry. A whole population of the capital city of an empire was so wicked in its greatness that it was brought to the bar of the universal judge. God responded to the case with a call addressed to a prophet to "go and cry against it." When Jonah finally answered, the Lord sent him to "proclaim to it the message that I tell you," the overthrow of the city within forty days.

Scripture reports that the people believed God, proclaimed a fast, and put on sackcloth. Under the numinous impact of the word of judgment, they became as nothing. In reality this was a self-imposed "overthrow" in response to God's presence as experienced in the ministry of Jonah. Ultimately, the king himself in sackcloth and ashes proclaimed a dry fast for all living humans and beasts as total response to God: "'And they shall cry mightily to God. All shall turn from their evil ways and from the violence that is in their hands. Who knows? God may relent and change his mind; he may turn from his fierce anger, so that we do not perish.' When God saw what they did, how they turned from their evil ways, God changed his mind about the calamity that he had said he would bring upon them; and he did not do it" (Jonah 3:8–10, NRSV).

Faithfulness to the word of the Lord through Israel's unwilling prophet changes history, because it results in the temporal salvation of a city normally seen to be outside of God's covenant with Israel. Because a people turn collectively *from* wickedness and violence *to* God, the Lord in his holy freedom turns *from* anger and judgment *to* pity and mercy. God's turning is salvation; the people's is conversion—and salvation.

Here, then, is the type of Jesus' own ministry. Foreseeing the destruction of Jerusalem, he knows that it is possible to save it; Nineveh is the precedent. He proclaims the imminence of the kingdom of God (judgment and salvation) and the call to repent—a massive appeal to turn to God, to conversion, even to the extent of sending out seventy apostles to all the cities. If Jerusalem would not turn, the coming of the kingdom of God could only mean judgment and destruction. The Ninevite salvation only heightens Jesus' sense of outrage at his own people, who refuse his appeal. He sees the Jonah-converted Assyrians among the accusing witnesses of the judgment day who will condemn Israel for refusing to turn to God when invited by one "greater than Jonah" (Matt. 12:40–41).

As Peter so boldly pointed out at Pentecost, Jesus' death was a result of Israel's refusal of conversion. But the events between his death and Peter's sermon (resurrection, ascension, Pentecost) show God's turning in pity and mercy. Thus Peter appeals for repentance. As in the Jonah story in God's mercy a new Nineveh was created through a popular conversion, so in Jerusalem a new Israel is created through the conversion of the three thousand. It is that new people, the new community of faith, that becomes the evidence and vehicle of salvation in Christ for Judea, Samaria, and the nations. The old Jerusalem, which refused Jesus' strategy of overthrowing itself in conversion, was overthrown later in the Zealots' fight with Rome in AD 70.

The future belongs to the converted who respond to God's mercy in the prophetic word and ultimately in his Messiah who is seated at the right hand of God "until I make your enemies your footstool" (Acts 2:34–35, NRSV). From Abraham to Peter, as typified by Jonah and fulfilled by Jesus, conversion is seen to be essentially eschatological. It means a moving into and a participation in "the last days."

But it is not enough just to turn from the past to any future; rather it is from the past judged by God to that future offered by God in and through the Messiah. This Messiah Jesus, interpreted throughout all of the New Testament as the servant ('ebed, in Hebrew) Messiah, and even more as the suffering servant—Messiah of the Servant Songs in the Isaiah writings, who is "to establish justice in the earth" (42:4). It is the new and different posture of that servant as fulfilled by Jesus that makes him the "greater" one, greater than Jonah or even John the Baptist, the beginning and the ending of the last times.

The early Christians' awareness of the uniqueness of the servant stance was what made them out to be a new people in the new times. They saw themselves to be servants in the wake of "your holy servant Jesus" (Acts 4:29–30).[4] The same Spirit that was upon the servant in Isaiah 42:1—and 61:1, where he is seen as proclaimer of Jubilee—was also upon Jesus (Mark 1:9–12) and now upon the new believers (Acts 2–3). Justice and peace are being fulfilled in the new community. Peter calls it the "times of refreshing . . . from the presence of the Lord [until he] send the Christ appointed for you, Jesus, whom heaven must receive until the time for establishing all that God spoke by the holy prophets" (Acts 3:19–21). Conversion is to that fulfillment and expectation. Paul will understand that same Spirit coming upon the Gentiles as the new people being created in the major cities of the northern Mediterranean. This is the ultimate fulfilling in Jesus the Messiah of what was promised to Abraham in his blessing of all nations (see Gal. 3:14).

Henceforth, conversion is seen as a turning in total faith to the reigning and coming servant-Messiah, Jesus. This new life is fulfilled in the Spirit by baptism and is the ultimate movement in history. Conversion is eschatological but also total, in the sense of being for all peoples. The converted ones in turn model a pattern intended for all—a new shape for human life and community based on Jesus.

Personal conversion in the biblical context

This universal people's movement of conversion is nevertheless seen to be personal, for persons are the locus of the turning. Those who in Christ are integrated into his servant community can say, "The old has passed away; the new has come." The New Testament recognizes that personal context; indeed, it is a part of the uniqueness of that picture that so much recognition is given to individual persons as such (see, for example, Rom. 16).

Yet little accent is put on the description of the subjective—spiritual and psychological, affective and emotional—aspects, as Western peoples are wont to do. Western culture is preoccupied with the psychological and affective. Manipulation and control of these realities

---

[4] Henri Blocher, *Songs of the Servant: Isaiah's Good News* (London: InterVarsity Press, 1975), 21, underlines what is not often seen—"the need to recognize the pattern laid down in the songs *for our own service*. . . . Jesus Himself recalled the last Servant song when teaching the disciples the way to glory; and Peter quoted from it with the comment that 'you should follow in his steps' (Mark 10:41–45; 1 Pet. 2:21)"; my italics.

has become a multibillion dollar science and industry. It is studied in order to give market dynamic to an economy of abundance.

The personal character and context of conversion is underlined in John's Gospel—"born again" to Nicodemus, "drink the water I shall give" to the Samaritan woman, "eat my flesh" to the crowds filled with bread, "not walk in darkness but have the light of life" to the crowd on the last day of the feast, "enter by me—the door."

This same diversity in personal conversion contexts is evident in Paul's ministry as reported, for example, in Acts 16. There was Lydia, whose heart "the Lord opened." Then there was the slave girl with a spirit of divination which Paul charged "in the name of Jesus Christ to come out of her." In contrast to both, there is the jailer "about to kill himself. . . . Trembling with fear, he fell down before Paul and Silas. . . . He washed their wounds and was baptized at once." And finally, closely related and yet much different, there are the "households" of Lydia and the jailer.

But more important, Paul uses great variety in language in his epistles. Here the appeal, teaching, conceptual explanations, and interpretations will be somewhat different from his missionary message and call to repentance in the book of Acts. The latter will almost always have the thrust seen in the Jonah-Jesus type, while his epistles will speak of the real experiential diversity of the peoples who have turned to Christ from their personal (spiritual, social, ethical, religious, political) contexts outside of Christ. An examination of that language only emphasizes the fact that the existential and experiential reality of conversion seen as justification is one of many Pauline descriptions.

context of conversion	from	to	through Jesus
justification	sin	righteousness	the just
reconciliation	enemy	friend	mediator
resurrection	death	life	resurrection-life
regeneration	corruption	incorruption	life-Spirit
salvation	distress	deliverance	Savior
salvation	lost	found	Savior
communion	outside	access	head
election	nations	kingdom	Messiah
forgiveness	debt	cancelled	sufferer of loss
recapitulation	old creation	new creation	Lord
hope	despair	assurance	hope

redemption	slavery	freedom	Redeemer
adoption	foreigner	son	heir
victory	hell-Satan	heaven-god	conqueror
grace	guilt	pardon	grace
healing	sickness	health	healer-doctor
deliverance (exorcism)	possession	self-possession	more powerful one
sanctification	sin-profane	holiness	holy one

JUSTIFICATION

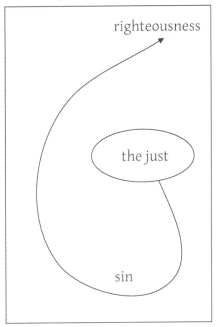

Each of these lines is a precise, personally experienced context, sometimes collectively—as with Jews in general, as typified by Paul. The personal conflict between sin and righteousness is resolved by Christ the just, and that conversion is known as justification. It is Christ through justification who frees Paul from his sin.

The different aspect of the word of Christ that becomes effectively functional within each box is variable. Here it is cross; there it is the resurrection; elsewhere it is both together. It may be Christ's obedience, or in another place his "in the flesh"–ness, or his reign, or his coming, or his anointing by the Spirit. Each aspect obviously is a part of the whole, yet the word comes into specific contexts in specific ways so that Christ is apprehended through the filters or grids of those who have turned to him.

It is of course much easier to see if we look through biblical language and words rather than contemporary missions and understandings of conversion. The writers of *The Lonely Crowd* make the enlightening observation that "tradition-directed" societies tend to express alienation in terms of shame; "inner-directed" societies with increasing accent on individuation tend to express relational alienation in terms of guilt; and "other-directed" modern mass societies tend to express such alienation in terms of anxiety.[5] This can be a fruitful understanding for those involved in the Christ-given mission of the servant community.

For example, F. B. Welbourn points out that the missionary brought to Africa the gospel of justification and grace, but the societies to which that message was taken were not guilt-oriented.[6] He asks what it would mean to preach the gospel to a shame-oriented people. Or again, Jacques Ellul demonstrates remarkably how Western—especially French—philosophy and thought have literally come to an impasse in anxiety-creating despair and hopelessness.[7] This is seen not as a theological concept or category but as an actual, existential state of humanity. Neither of these illustrations—the one from a context of pre-Christian religion and the other from Western secular thought—begins with the need for justification. Conversion is hardly functional in the context of that box.

Reading Riesman, Welbourn, and Ellul together could easily suggest that Western Christian missions to Africa, living out the anxiety of a mass-industrial society, tried to convert a shame-oriented people in premodern contexts, through a gospel appropriate to an individuated guilt-oriented society. Modern Western society needed freedom from guilt, and this shaped Western Protestant understandings of Paul. But this dynamic was not necessarily where the crunch came for Africans; in fact, Western mission structures often tended to increase shame as understood by Africans. Thus, we can understand partially how the

---

[5] David Riesman, Nathan Glazer and Reuel Denney, *The Lonely Crowd* (New Haven: Yale University Press, 1967), 9–26.

[6] F. B. Welbourn, "Some Problems of African Christianity: Guilt and Shame," in *Christianity in Tropical Africa*, ed. C. G. Baeta (Oxford: Oxford University Press, 1968), 131–38.

[7] Compare Jacques Ellul, *Hope in Time of Abandonment* (New York: Seabury Press, 1974), especially "Self-critical Interlude," 156–66.

separatist, independent, spiritual congregations in Africa—without excluding Christians in mission-created congregations—have sometimes heard a different gospel than that being preached, have been "converted" in terms of a different mental-spiritual-social box, and have sorted out biblical emphases other than those that were mission taught.[8]

Personal conversion
in the contemporary Western context

Just as there has been in the West a dominant theology of justification by faith, so there have understandably been other theologies for other contexts. Could we even suggest that the Lord-disciple theology—in contrast to Luther's—that functioned within some of the sixteenth-century left-wing Reformation movements, was also contextually defined by the strong hierarchical ordering of society?[9]

In this vision the direct relation to the new Lord practically eliminated the sociopolitical, hierarchical structures, yet functioned creatively in new holistic (social, political, religious, economic) communities that threatened the sacralism of the time. Given the biblical view, the crucial question about conversion is not the personal or collective contexts that give rise to modes of conversion in types of theologies, but the type of human community a particular theology of conversion creates.

Today we recognize the legitimacy—and even necessity, because of the nature of incarnation—of liberation theology, Black theology, and theologies of contestation. Theologies of hope, of humanization, of self-fulfillment, etc., all attempt to speak to experiential and existential realities. Following the New Testament, we can in fact make a list of boxes that define contemporary contexts of conversion.

context of conversion	from	to	through Jesus
acceptance	rejection	acceptance	love
direction	to err about	to aim at	call

---

[8] John V. Taylor, *The Growth of the Church in Buganda* (London: SCM Press, 1958), 253, illustrates how this happened in the Ugandan context. But it is also true that any minister or teacher of the word knows how many messages hearers have heard that he or she has never preached.

[9] I was impressed by and reported this aspect of the context of conversion in "Faith and Doubt in Menno Simons," an unpublished paper submitted to Fr. John Dunne, Notre Dame University, 1967.

festival	boredom	joy	feast-giver
meaning	the absurd	the reasonable	Word
liberation	oppression	liberation	liberator
becoming	nobody	somebody	invitation
fellowship	solitude	community	presence
creation	chaos	order	Creator
breakthrough	blocked	open	future (omega)
order	confusion	peace	structure
dialogue	I-it	I-you	you
conversation	monologue	dialogue	other
decision	indecision	choice	unique
fulfillment	nihilism	becoming	Being
solidarity	exploited	defended	leader
humanization	inhuman	human	human
growth	infantilism	maturity	adult
concientización	powerlessness fatalism	action hope	sustainer

Conversion and syncretism

It must be noticed that when we shift to contemporary human contexts of conversion, it is easier, in contrast to biblical language, to observe how the gospel can be turned into religions similar to the first-century rivals of Christianity. Using these modern boxes, we can see how easy it is to "bring Jesus into my box" to make him "mine," to "use him" for my purposes. Thus conversion can become a thing that happens strictly within the self, a personal experience with no particular relationship to God's purposes "for the establishment of all things"—the kingdom come and coming.

What we have not always seen is how this transformation is possible also with the use of the biblical categories. When justification—or any of the other boxes, biblical or modern—is seen to be the goal of the gospel and the intent of conversion (for example, turning to justification), the apostate character of syncretism becomes apparent (compare the box earlier in this chapter). Happily, it was the Lutheran theologian Dietrich Bonhoeffer who best helped the past generation to see this with his classic description—"justification of sin rather than that of the sinner."[10]

Not all justification is Christ-centered, if we review it in the community of the Spirit of the suffering servant who as Lord fulfills history with "the almighty meekness of the Lamb."[11] Nor is all election Christ-centered, in the servant ('ebed) sense. Nor is all redemption or healing or hope. And in the contemporary context we can say that all self-fulfillment is not Christ-centered, in the 'ebed sense of the word,[12] even if the word Christ is used. But neither is all solidarity, or liberation, or blackness, or openness.

The axis of conversion: The servant community of the servant-Messiah

Each of the contexts or boxes are potential syncretistic religious realities unless Christ is seen as the one who translates persons out of those specific personal or collective boxes into new community where justification, redemption, election, healing, hope, self-fulfillment, solidarity, liberation, blackness, openness become functional in the community as defined by Jesus the suffering servant–Messiah.[13]

---

[10] See Dietrich Bonhoeffer, *The Cost of Discipleship* (New York: Macmillan, 1946), chap. 1, for his discussion of cheap grace and costly grace.

[11] Norman Grubb used the fortuitous and significant phrase "Almighty Meekness" as title for chapter 7 in *As Touching the Invisible* (Lutterworth, UK: Lutterworth Press, 1966), 34–41.

[12] In fact it is probably the myth of self-fulfillment that has defined most totally the religious context of conversion in the contemporary West. See especially Jeremy Zwelling, "Religion in the Department of Religion," in *Functions of Faith in Academic Life*, ed. Myron B. Blow, *Religious Education*, 69, no. 3-S (May–June 1974): S94–S137. John Dunne has effectively pointed this out in his writings as well, where self-fulfillment is seen to be the contemporary Western myth, as definition of what life is, given the fact of death.

[13] This "religionizing" through emphasis, as compared to the major biblical thrust, is illustrated within the contemporary scene by Kenneth Kantzer's description of evangelical self-understanding: "[Evangelicals are] people who have received God's cure for the haunting and indelible guilt of sin and that corrosive emptiness of the heart for which Christ is alone the enduring solution. For this reason they have a message to share"; see *The Evangelicals: What They Believe, Who They Are, Where They Are Changing*, ed. David F. Wells and John D. Woodbridge (Nashville: Abingdon Press, 1975), 41. Such a tack can be one of the very real entries into kingdom reality which I have myself used in preaching, for example, in *Who Will Answer?* (Scottdale, PA: Herald Press, 1969), as conversion structure. But to define the gospel impact by a single emphasis or reduction is precisely the individualizing and existential spiritualism that ignores in its emphasis the fundamental biblical thrust. To the materialists of his time Jesus warned

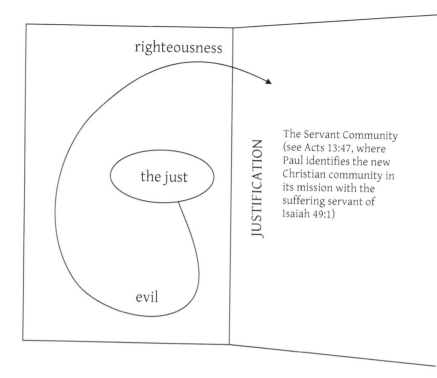

Of all these contexts it must be said, as Paul wrote of the expressions of the Spirit in the church at Corinth: "There are varieties of working, but it is the same God who inspires them all in everyone. To each is given the manifestation of the Spirit for the common good" (1 Cor. 12:6–7) "so that the church may be edified" (1 Cor. 14:3–5, 12, 26).

God. In terms of understanding God, conversion means a turn from the many gods, or from no god, or from belief in a distant, unknown, or inactive god to the living God.

Religious beliefs and practices. In an understanding of the religious, it means turning from myth to event and history (covenant, exodus, exile-return, Jesus-event, church in conflict with the powers). This includes turning from the periodic shift in sacred and profane (ritual, initiation, festival) to holistic sacred lifestyle (charism, forgiveness, service).

---

about "gaining the whole world and losing one's soul." Here the word might well be a warning about gaining one's soul, and losing the kingdom. For the biblical message has a different accent than that.

Time. In relation to time, it means turning from past to a new linear future and from the old age to the christological new age.

Spiritual power. In terms of spiritual power, it means turning from its use for primarily material orientation (fertility, success, prosperity) to primary ethical preoccupation on the one hand; it means turning from prayer as manipulation of power to prayer as discernment for decision and release of redemptive creativity.

Being human. To be human means turning from instrumentalism (that is, people are to be used) to personhood (that is, unique value of person in creation, redemption, gifts, development) and a turning from balance of powers and equilibrium in roles to mutuality (forgiveness, gifts, service, voluntary subordination).

Community. Conversion in specific regard to community means turning from ethnicity and tribalism to open covenant based on Jesus' lordship within the church, and from geographic and temporal parochialism and nationalisms to the universal present-and-coming kingdom.

All of this, it seems to me, is clear in Jesus' fulfillment of the Jonah type. Yet more basic than all of this is a foundational spiritual turning. This change is of the very essence of conversion, effected according to the biblical witness by God, the Holy Spirit. And it is at this level of ethos that it seems to me that all the other aspects of turning have to be ultimately discerned and judged.

Reality divides into either the "promethean" or "*'ebed*-ist" mentality. Roger Bastide suggests that all development today in the two-thirds world or anywhere requires a promethean mentality.[14] This signifies humanity's perpetual state of dissatisfaction, in spite of its increasing achievements in mastering and apparent control over its world and destiny, and its compelling ambition to push further and further into the unknown but presumably open future.

Today conversion is from such a promethean spirit. It is to a mentality that I have chosen to call *'ebed*-ist in order to follow Isaiah in accentuating the suffering-servant quality. The current concept of servanthood is distorted by modern notions of service growing out of

---

[14] See Roger Bastide, "Messianism and Social and Economic Development," in *Social Change: The Colonial Situation*, ed. John Wallerstein (Hoboken, NJ: John Wiley and Sons, 1966), 467–77. Bastide here expands an idea put forward by Georges Gurvitch. Prometheus, we recall, was the god of fire in Greek mythology, who stole fire from heaven in order to animate human life. He was punished by Zeus by being nailed to a mountain, where a vulture kept eating out his liver.

commerce and industry, on the one hand, and patronizing notions of charity, on the other. *'Ebed* defines that quality brought to us in Jesus the Messiah. The *'ebed*-ist spirit would be reflected in human renewal of covenant with God in his purpose for reconciling all humanity in justice and peace through Jesus Christ.

This quality is the basis for a covenant among men and women of solidarity in repentance and hope. It is expressed in Holy Spirit–endued service, in confident meekness, through the liberating proclamation and protest of his word, healing for wholeness, suffering for righteousness, total participation in freely restored community, as experienced in a local congregation of people where Jesus is confessed as Lord. It is that difference that can give Christian mission today its either/or quality and restore radical meaning to conversion.

Thus resurrection does not form the starting point of revolution from which anything becomes possible, and for which the future is completely open, as Roger Garaudy says. But God's incarnation in Jesus, his active obedience for justice and peace, his suffering unto death, his resurrection, his reign through the Spirit, his coming again in fulfillment of all things, all announce, on the contrary, that human community is possible under God in Christ, in the shape of Jesus of Nazareth. Because of him such community is at the very crux of history, as well as its end.

"The kingdom of God is at hand; be converted, and believe the gospel." Today this is still the essential cry of that community.

13

A religious itinerary
from African traditional religion
to New Testament faith

The *Alliance Witness* reported in the early 1980s an event not dissimilar to what has happened in many parts of Africa over the past 150 years.[1] Village Christians in Burkina Faso offered prayer for an aged man and his wife who were harassed by evil spirits. As a result, she slept well for the first time in many months, and the next day the man was praising God for answer to prayer. Since the couple wanted to "give themselves to the Lord," the missionary reported, Christians prayed with them and advised him to get rid of all his fetishes. The man, a seventy-year-old head of the blacksmith clan and a "leading sorcerer," was baptized the same day, while the Christians and the missionary took "all the idols and fetishes"—more of them than twenty-five Christians could carry in one trip—and burned them in a fire that lasted four hours. The other villagers were sullen, terrorized, or tried to obtain a few of the fetishes for themselves before the objects were destroyed.

Such an act of faith, with the radical, symbolic break from a religious past, marks the beginning of a new religious itinerary for this aged couple. But what is the nature of that religious itinerary? What is its direction and the content of the evolving religious experience within the new community of African Christians who prayed, baptized, and burned the symbolic past under the tutelage of the Western missionary? Since such events have occurred on countless occasions for a

---

Originally published as "African Christian Religious Itinerary: Toward an Understanding of the Religious Itinerary from the Faith of African Traditional Religion(s) to that of the New Testament." Reprinted, with editorial changes, from *Exploring New Religious Movements: Essays in Honour of Harold W. Turner*, ed. A. F. Walls and Wilbert R. Shenk (Elkhart, IN: Mission Focus, 1990), 143–62. Used by permission.

[1] The *Alliance Witness* was during this time the principal periodical of The Christian and Missionary Alliance. The story recounted here was found in *Alliance Witness* 118, no. 9 (April 27, 1983), 20.

century and a half, those experiences and their sequels—personal and collective—constitute the soul of African Christianity, conditioned and solicited by the message of the Bible filtered through the missionary or church communities.

Exploring the passage from traditional religion to New Testament faith

There is an inevitable passage from a community canon of oral tradition and experience of spiritual powers to a new religious community with a new approach to power, conditioned by the written canon of scripture fulfilled in the New Testament. Without questioning the "saving faith" involved in the initial radical break, it would appear important, if only for pastoral reasons,[2] to raise questions about the character of such a religious itinerary with its stages on life's way.[3]

Such stages are suggested by Dr. Harold W. Turner's comprehensive study of the phenomenon of new religious movements in primal societies, first of all in Africa, and then worldwide. His typological description of the whole gamut of movements growing out of the interaction between primal religions and Western Christianity in second-stage responses includes neo-primal movements, synthetist movements, Hebraist movements, independent churches, and autonomous indigenous churches directly related to missionary endeavor.[4]

In the first-stage response of Africans to Western Christian impact, this range of expression did not appear as such, because the religious reality embodied in these types was totally under missionary tutelage within the Christian villages, missionary compounds, or bush churches. Yet, different phases of religious understanding persisted within the new Christian communities, particularly as new Christians joined the

---

[2] As for reasons other than pastoral, one might profitably examine the dynamics and meaning of religious change, the African experience of Christianization, as well as insights into historical developments within Western Christianity itself.

[3] We recall Søren Kierkegaard's nineteenth-century religious analysis of Westerners as moving from the aesthetic to the ethical and on to the religious. The contemporary American theologian John Dunne has written in a similar way of the "immediate man," the "existential man," and the "historical man." More recently still, but in a different light, James Fowler has invited us to look at the "stages of faith" in the Western context.

[4] See Harold W. Turner, "Religious Movements in Primal (or Tribal) Societies," *Mission Focus* 9, no. 3 (1981): 49; and "A Further Frontier for Missions: A General Introduction to New Religious Movements in Primal Societies," *Missionalia* 11, no. 3 (1983): 103–12.

churches. That such phases would later appear as independent movements because of the arrangement between colony and mission is, of course, not surprising. What is surprising is that the mission-planted churches would fail to recognize the authenticity of those stages when not under their own tutelage. In any case, the itinerary of the African Christian is clarified by the phenomenological description.

My own reflections on this religious itinerary have grown out of relations with certain parts of the Harrist Church in Côte d'Ivoire, while I simultaneously maintained fraternal relationships and ministry within the larger Christian community. The Harrist Church is not accepted as an authentic Christian church by most of the rest of the Christian community—whether Roman Catholic, conciliar Protestant, or evangelical—even though it is given serious consideration by national authorities as one of the recognized religious realities, along with Christianity, Islam, and the traditional religions referred to officially as animism.

Yet, in my experiences I have discovered among Christians from the "authentic churches" religious understandings similar to those found among the Harrist people I know. These Christians are considered to be authentic because of their belonging to a "proper" church, while the Harrists with Christian understandings are not perceived to be authentic Christians, except perhaps at local, village levels. Late-arrival Western missionary that I was, I found it necessary to ponder these experiences and observations. The itinerary suggested by Dr. Turner's work was a good starting place for thought, and this article pulls together some of that reflection.

Two illustrations of faith journeys, from Togo and Côte d'Ivoire

In 1967, a Togolese theologian, Rev. Seth Nomenyo, wrote a little brochure to stimulate thought about the gospel, the church, and the Christian life in view of a churchwide effort of renewal. In it he projected a typical dialogue between an evangelist and a brother of the church. If one reads with Dr. Turner's description in mind, one discerns within the Evangelical Church planted by the Bremen Mission the personalizing of a religious itinerary not wholly unlike that model.

> *Evangelist:* My brother, all of the Evangelical Church of Togo is today searching, like you, for the true meaning of the Christian life. It cannot be content simply to follow a certain routine of worship, meetings, holiday festivals, sacraments, collections,

and funerals. It wishes to understand what the church is, what the Christian is in our world of today. The answer is in the word that God has given us and which enlightens by his Spirit. Shall we search together? But first of all, tell me what you believe you already know about the Christian life.

Brother: For myself, if I am a Christian, it is because I have chosen to serve the true God, the God of Jesus Christ, and have rejected the false gods that my ancestors worshiped. I believe and I worship the Great God; the pagans worship and serve Satan and his false gods. I belong to God, while the pagans belong to Satan—hence their name: Abossantowo (people of Satan). All the worshipers and servants of the Great God are kept, protected, and helped by him. It is to him that they cry in their distress. On the other hand, the pagans—servants and worshipers of Satan—trust in him and in his gods and their false priests.

I know that several of my Christian friends have divided hearts; several still believe in the protection of Satan and appeal to him in certain circumstances of their lives, while continuing to call on the true God! I think it is those that are called "[half] Christian, half-pagan."

But why do all people have need to believe in an all-powerful Being whom they can invoke and who delivers them? Because in our world the power of life and the power of death contend for people; these, in their fears, can only desperately seek a refuge in a being more powerful than death.

Evangelist: You do not speak of Jesus Christ; what place does he fill in your life?

Brother: I'm coming to that. The Christian, after having believed in a protector God, discovers a judge God—a God in the presence of whom humanity is sinful and merits punishment. This punishment is hell. To be Christian, therefore, is to flee the punishment of God and to prepare for oneself a place in paradise after death. If I cling so obstinately to the Christian religion, I confess that it is, above all, to make sure of paradise after death. And for that Jesus Christ is very useful. Is he not the Savior, the one who can wash away my sins, make me evade the punishment of God, and thereby even open for me the gates of paradise?

Evangelist: Thus you believe in the immortality of the human soul?

Brother: Surely! Everyone believes in that: the pagans, the Muslims, the Hindus, the Christians. All people are preparing for that great move that will transport their souls into the abode of the blessed (paradise), or on the contrary, into eternal fire (hell) according to the good pleasure of the gods (or of the Great God).

Evangelist: Are you preparing right now to enter into paradise? What are you doing in order to win heaven, and in order to get in the good graces of God?

Brother: I try to respect the law of God, and to live according to the Christian morals that the church has taught me since my childhood. Thus, I've often told myself that the Bible was a book of morals where one finds much counsel about the manner of living, with lists of virtues to practice and of vices to avoid. Then, too, I pay my dues.

Evangelist: Jesus Christ said one day to his disciples: "Blessed are they that are persecuted. . . . As I have been hated, you as well will also be hated." Are the Christians of your village also hated—persecuted by others?

Brother: No. On the contrary, with present-day evolution, Christianity is in style. A civilized person must be a Christian, and many confuse Western civilization with Christianity. If one wants to appear civilized, one must have a Christian name, have one's children baptized, participate in memorial services for deceased members of one's family, and act on each of these occasions in such a manner as to underline the importance of the family by a show of luxury. Therefore, Christianity in certain cases can be the occasion for a family to be shown off to advantage, to witness to its superiority over other families that are either non-Christians or "mixed."

Evangelist: You are an Eve Christian. I am an Akposso Christian; another is a Christian of Agou, or of Lama-Kara. Does your same faith unite you?

Brother: I must admit that it does not, apart from several exceptions. As for myself, I am Eve first, and then Christian. Perhaps our tribalism is even reinforced by Christianity. There is the church of Agu, the church of Daye, the church of Litime, that of Oblo . . ., each living separated from the others by tribal ties that are reinforced by Christian solidarity. For me, to be Christian is also, therefore, to seek to consolidate my tribe by consolidating my church.

Evangelist: My brother, I have heard you. I know that you have been frank, and that is indeed what you believe and what most of the Christians of our church believe. But the truth is not there. We have mixed the gospel with other beliefs, and in the mixture the salt has lost its savor. We have constructed a religion—a veritable scaffolding—in order for our immortal souls to arrive in paradise. . . . [However,] the Christian is a person recreated by God in Christ.[5]

Following Nomenyo, then, one finds a series of phases between the practitioners of traditional religion and the New Testament word: (1) the Christian of a divided heart; (2) the Christian worshiper of the great all-powerful protector God; (3) the Christian discovery of a God of judgment, and the sinful self as punishable; (4) the Christian who uses Christ to guarantee immortality, who practices morality and follows church rules in order to keep in the good graces of God, and evolves in Westernization, material status, and tribal reinforcement. The New Testament word itself calls for "the person recreated by God in Christ." And according to the theologian Nomenyo, most people in the church were in phase four, requiring an all-church program of renewal to bring the New Testament word to bear on the majority within that stage.

A second illustration is provided by Jean-Paul Eschlimann, Roman Catholic missionary in Côte d'Ivoire among the Agni, and a well-informed ethnologist of the Akan ethnic group. He writes of the 11,964 Christians and catechumens in his Mission of Tankesse with its population of 36,000 inhabitants.[6] Among them, he laments, are only some fifty "Christians" who have faith, that is, "who have the same trust in Jesus that their brothers give to the customs of the ancestors or to the Koran." The others, though "sacramentalized," continue to put their faith in the ancestral practices. The observer asks, "What then is the religious reality of those other 11,900 'Christians'?" Is it not essentially a synthesis of Roman sacrament and traditional religion? Indeed,

---

[5] This "typical dialogue" was created by Seth Nomenyo and appeared in *Tout l'Evangile à tout l'Homme* (Yaoundé: CLE, 1967), 12–15; my translation, used by permission of the publisher.

[6] Jean-Paul Eschlimann, in René Luneau, Lettre No. 10, *Afrique et Parole* (November 1984).

Eschlimann himself complains honestly that as the administrator of the sacraments, he ends up—even though he is a Christian evangelist at heart—by presenting God as immutable, repetitious, legalistic, and particularly concerned about ritual and sacraments, in sum, "a God without a future."

Understanding the stages of faith development

With the use of Turner's model, one might say that a form of Hebraism (a religious reality similar to that of Israel before Christ) is being injected into a synthetist reality, out of which have emerged less than a hundred whose faith in Christ is inscribed in their daily life conduct. Here again are several religious stages between the Western Catholic filter of the Bible with its impact, and that of traditional religion. One may, of course, ask whether there was, in the beginning, the same kind of break in power confrontation as that described in the first pages of this text.

But even if it had taken place, experience often proves that after such a break, the pull of the old powers creates a time of intensive tension, testing, and threat of apostasy, as witnessed by a Roman Catholic catechist from among the Senufo people of northern Ivory Coast:

> Say that the fetishes don't have power? No! They do have, and whoever keeps them and wants to reject them immediately because the Father said so, I can assure you that he will not be able to do without them; he is going to return to them.

> I had [about two years after my baptism] nevertheless some real times of fear: I'd think, I've thrown my fetishes away; I don't go to the charlatan anymore; what is going to happen to me? I said, "Good! I know God is strong, Jesus is powerful." And if I would feel fearful, immediately I would pray. As for that—I say it many times when talking with people—prayer is truly the arm of the Christian. Without prayer, I wonder if I could have resisted and remained Christian like I have.

> When I had surmounted that step—for me it was the most difficult—to my surprise there was still another struggle, a struggle with my character. When I hear the word of God, I leave most

saddened because I want to change and I can't succeed. Things like meanness; I was born hard.[7]

Indeed, many do not surmount that step, but it is significant that the Senufo catechist perceived it clearly as a new stage in his faith.

Another illustration of such an itinerary under missionary tutelage is given by John V. Taylor in his study of the church in Buganda. He reports the moving experience of evangelical missionaries discovering that their

> Christians were not hearing and preaching their clear evangelical emphases as much as they were the news about the transcendent God. "Katonda," the unknown and scarcely heeded creator, was proclaimed as the focus of all life, who yet lay beyond and above the closed unity of all existence. This in itself was so catastrophic a concept that, for the majority of hearers, it appeared to be the sum of the new teaching. . . . Later on, as the same [evangelical] preaching was reiterated, a certain number in the church heard more of it. It is this that accounts for the successive revivals.[8]

R. H. Leakey, quoted by Taylor, wrote of the "mission" of 1893: "Many who had long been looked upon as leading Christians realized a new force and power in their Christian life. Some said to us, 'Why have you been here so long and never told us this glad news before?' All we could say was, 'You have been told, but have not believed it.'"

Taylor's comments on this are worth rereading, for they speak to the question of progressive revelation as well as to the problem of religious communication from one cultural platform into another cultural auditorium. Indeed, it is at this point that we part company with Turner's phenomenological description of stages provoked by the impact of Western Christianity. What if the New Testament fulfillment of the Old Testament, rather than Western Christianity, were seen as the effective pole? This would exclude the too-facile identification of Western Christianity—in whatever national, cultural, or denominational wrappings—with the description of New Testament life, experience, and thought whose accents and emphases are often filtered out by Western Christianity's selectivity. How does this New Testament religious faith

---

[7] As reported by Raymond Deniel in *Chemins de chrétiens africains* (Abidjan: INADES, 1981), 14–15. This booklet is one of ten small brochures in a series offering unusual insight into the religious experience of Catholic Christians at the grass roots.

[8] John V. Taylor, *The Go-Between God* (London: SCM, 1972), 252–53.

compare with traditional African religion? If it functions effectively as a conditioning and critiquing canon, what are the stages that it stimulates, solicits, and provokes?

Three major shifts taking place

From magic to prayer

Before attempting an answer to that question, let us look at a situation that was not under missionary tutelage. The event with which we began—an initial break in a context of power confrontation—was given massive expression in 1913–14 when the Glebo prophet from Liberia, W. W. Harris, provoked the baptisms of some 100,000 people after they destroyed the external signs of their traditional religions and turned to the one true and living God as their only recourse. When "discovered" ten years later, they deeply impressed the British Methodist missionaries, because all fetish practice had disappeared. Nevertheless, even though the missionaries observed that the masses had "replaced heathen superstitions with Christian prayer,"[9] the missionaries constantly raised serious questions about the nature of their religious reality, because of the masses' ignorance of Christ and their biblical illiteracy. Nevertheless, it was a major religious shift. Monica Wilson has written that "a shift from magic to prayer is the great leap in shift from outward forms to inner religion."[10]

When Western Christians were asking about the authentic Christian nature of the Kimbanguist Church in Central Africa, the Zairian scholar Martial Sinda insisted, as criticism, that there was not just a simple formal analogy between Kimbanguist and Protestant/Catholic models but that

> the break with the traditional religious structures is conscious and significant. The essential religious act has become that of prayer. By simplifying to the extreme, we can say that prayer has replaced sacrifice.
>
> What is represented in this passing over? Sacrifice in traditional Black religion is an efficacious technique; its daily or periodic use is the guarantee of the maintenance of a certain order. The role of individual initiative—that of the gods or that of men—is,

---

[9] This description was offered by missionary Pierre Benoît at the time of his 1926 meeting with the Prophet Harris at Cape Palmas, Liberia.

[10] Reported by Monica Wilson, in *Religion and Transformation of Society* (Cambridge: Cambridge University Press, 1971), 43.

if not insignificant, at least always controllable. Thus, the strict observance of ritual rules brings about the effective realization of a sought-after result. . . .

In such a perspective, religious anxiety does not exist. Prayer on the contrary, if it remains a religious technique, does not possess the efficaciousness of sacrifice—at least not an immediate efficaciousness. The initiative remains with God; upon God alone depends the final result of the religious act. This is why religious theory opens out to miracle, and it is also why anxiety sets in at the heart of believers. That this passing over from sacrifice to prayer is accompanied in the believer by a progressive awareness of his responsibility for himself—in a word, of his solitude—illustrates, if it were necessary, the deep gap between Christian religion and the so-called primitive religions.[11]

This major shift dominates the first major stage in the itinerary. It is essential to hear how important it is to an African.

From anthropocentric to theocentric ethics

A second major shift, with all its ramifications, is related to what Charles-Daniel Maire calls a change from anthropocentrism to theocentric ethics. The difference between traditional and biblical spiritualities is such that in the latter, the theocentricity of its vision of the world modifies completely the meaning of fault as being that which is against God.[12] The historian Gordon Haliburton, searching for oral tradition about the Prophet Harris fifty years after his impact, was told by five old men in the village of Petit Bassam, where the mother church of the Harrist Church is located: "When Harris came, the Bible taught us good and evil—sins. [After that] we knew that to kill somebody was a sin. Previously, we knew that it wasn't right, but not the sin aspect."[13]

This also means a major shift in an understanding and internalization of personal responsibility. This is so much so that one French anthropologist has severely judged the contemporary Harrist healer Atcho, whose discourse and technique is seen to effect such a displacement. For Marc Augé, the problem of evil—no longer a result of the externally attacking spiritual powers—is still external to the individual in

---

[11] Martial Sinda, *Messianisme congolais* (Paris: Payot, 1972), 90–91.

[12] Charles-Daniel Maire, "Dynamique sociale des mutations religieuses" (diss., Sorbonne/E.P.H.E., 1975), 138–39.

[13] From personal notes shared with author.

new economic and political structures, and not within the individual in society as in certain Christian understandings of original sin.[14] It would be overstating the facts to suggest that the forces of modernization and urbanization were just, or played no role whatsoever in the process of individualization taking place in Côte d'Ivoire. But what these do not do, in their secularizing impact, is produce personal—and internal—responsibility to and before the Creator.

In the context of this stage, the Western Christian observer is traditionally overwhelmed by the legalism, both ethical and ritual, despite all efforts to reduce it. However, it would appear rather that Torah was creating a new path out of traditional taboos and prohibitions through the maze of rapid social, economic, cultural, and religious change. In that stage en route, the sacred "house of God," where one can act "before God,"[15] as well as the mediating priest, pastor, or missionary, are often also seen as an integral part of that educational process. And that new way, despite the Westerners' contrary understanding, is perceived by the participants as a gift from God.

From legalistic to free obedient response to God's grace

A further major stage is where the grace and the Spirit of God are known as presence of Christ-in-community, a free obedient expression of the coming kingdom of God, demonstrated in the personalized gifts and potential in the service of the peace, justice, healing, and reconciliation of the new creation. This stage of eschatological faith drove the Prophet Harris beyond the bounds of the Western missionary model and enabled the breakthrough into a new itinerary for thousands. He did not communicate that religious phase to those people in the countless villages, but he had himself undergone an itinerary of more than thirty years before entering it. Many of his disciples today might well be seen as Hebraist.

One may be struck with certain parallels between such an itinerary and that of Israel, led in covenant to the "fullness of times." One recalls how the apostle Paul saw the faith of Abraham, David, and Habakkuk—and his own faith—as part of a common itinerary of saving faith (Rom. 1–4), yet all were expressed within different contexts of religious perception and understandings in which God had revealed himself and

[14] Marc Augé, *Théorie des pouvoirs et idéologie* (Paris: Hermann, 1975), 237–307.

[15] Here also Dr. Harold W. Turner has done pioneering work in phenomenology of religious architecture; see *From Temple to Meeting House* (The Hague: Mouton, 1979), chap. 2, 3.

solicited faith. The illustration from Uganda above suggests that the gospel, the preaching of Christ, the word of grace, and the good news of the kingdom tend to be perceived differently at each stage as new response is made to that word.

It is thus not surprising that African evangelical theologians write openly of how the gospel of Christ is capable of "meeting the primal man at the points of his greatest need" in a "process or processes of 'power encounter' between the Christian and the primal worldviews."[16] In an approach that they have outlined, there is a "gradual unfolding of Christian truth," where Christian understandings of sin, deliverance, humans gone astray, belief and trust in God as revealed in Christ "begin to open up," "begin to be appreciated," "begin to be apprehended"; the primal person "begins to see," "begins to realize." This is the language of itinerary that is not native to the typical Western evangelical.[17]

The African Christian religious itinerary in summary form

Were we to set up a cursory description of African traditional religions on the one hand, and a parallel description of New Testament religion on the other, we might suggest a typical itinerary following the pattern shown in the diagram on pages 262–63.

Remaining questions and observations

In such a perspective, one would discover in Catholic, Protestant, and evangelical as well as in independent milieux many people in different stages—on the way. The manner in which the New Testament canon is screened through preaching, worship, institutions, charisms, traditions, ritual, and doctrine conditions its effectiveness in soliciting and provoking to a further stage on the way. Some movements, as well as individual persons within them, will be blocked in a phase because of the way canonical reality is ignored, excluded, distorted, or disobeyed.

At the same time, such a typical itinerary indicates nothing about the length of time that a person or a group may spend within a given

---

[16] "Thailand Report," *Christian Witness to People of African Traditional Religion,* No. 18 (Wheaton: Lausanne Committee on World Evangelization, 1980), 15–18.

[17] One of the African participants in the Thailand encounter explained how a Western theologian present at the discussion could not conciliate this African perception with his own evangelical doctrine of regeneration, and tried to have this particular section deleted from the final draft of the findings.

stage. Illumination with commitment may happen repeatedly in rapid succession, or it may happen rapidly at one stage and be delayed at others. Neither does the suggested itinerary indicate a natural religious evolution; implicit at each stage is the input from the biblical canon, new understandings, and illumination based on previous experience followed by commitment. Each time a new religious reality is produced, a new spirituality is born. Appropriate here is the description of John V. Taylor's "three aspects of the creative activity of the Holy Spirit, the Lord, the Giver of Life."

> From within the depths of its being he urges every creature again and again to take one more tiny step in the direction of higher consciousness and personhood; again and again he creates for every creature the occasion for spontaneity and the necessity for choice, and at every turn he opposes self-interest with a contrary principle of sacrifice, or existence for the other. And, in the fullness of time, this was perfectly disclosed in Jesus Christ who was conceived by the Holy Spirit and to whom the Holy Spirit has been directing [human] attention ever since.[18]

This itinerary does not answer the question of whether it is possible to skip a stage en route. Godfrey Phillips, following the analogy of the progressive revelation of God in Israel's history, insists that no stage can be skipped.[19] Indeed, the African Evangelical theologians in their suggested process imply that the legalistic stage could be skipped, since it is the result of missionary failure: starting "with a moral code from a 'God' whom they [Africans] hardly understood or trusted, thus producing 'Christians' who spent the rest of their lives trying to obey God and be good by pleasing the missionaries or pastors, only to fail at every turn."[20] Phillips had turned the equation around by writing of the church "whose teachers give it the Gospel without first giving it the law, and are surprised to find that it interprets the Gospel as if it were law, misses the whole point of divine redemption, and produces an essentially legalistic Christianity."[21]

---

[18] Taylor, *Go-Between God,* 36.

[19] Godfrey Phillips, *The Old Testament in the World Church* (London and Redhill: Lutterworth, 1942), 95–97.

[20] "Thailand Report," 17.

[21] Phillips, *The Old Testament in the World Church,* 95–96.

1. African traditional religions

a. Reign of the ancestors (traditions, the elders, orality)
b. Creator God, distant and unknown (believed in without experience)
c. Tribe, clan, family (birth and initiation)
d. "Life" means power, prosperity, fertility, success (maintained through harmony and equilibrium via repression, submission, compensation)
e. Totem, taboos (fear, submission)
f. Good spirits: divinities, genies, "living dead" (sacrifices and ritual for blessing and prosperity)
g. Evil-doing spirits: divinities, genies, "living dead" (sacrifices and ritual for protection)
h. Diviners, "fetishers," religious specialists (divination, possession, mediation, revelation in dreams, visions, trances)
i. Witchcraft and magic (expose and destroy the guilty; protection through sacrifice, ritual, fetish)
j. Festival, ritual (necessary, efficacious celebration)
k. Reincarnation (discerned after birth)
l. After-life: village of the dead, spiritual counterpart to here and now
m. Present life: duty, roles, past traditions, cyclical
n. Myth dominant: preexistent story of life and existence
o. Shame a dominant undercurrent, in response to sociocultural pressures

2. Process of gradual appropriation of Christian truth:

Conversion to all-powerful God (compared to less-powerful entities)	Struggle to abandon old sources of power and protection	Law of God and Bible and cross replace fetishes and taboos
* *	* *	* *
Present and active	Constant threat to apostasize	God *requires* WORSHIP in sacred place
* *	* *	* *
Known through his acts of power and protection for health, prosperity, fertility, success in this life	One true God is tested over and over and over again	Religious specialist is necessary for mediation of God's power concerning law of church, discipline, forgiveness
* *	* *	* *

Deep concern for after-life
Deep appreciation for old covenant
Power signs are very significant
Prayer replaces sacrifices
(a major shift . . . with anxiety)
Shame dominates
Spirit as punctual intervention

3. New testament faith

new apprehensions, new applications

Discovery of personal responsibil-ity before God and fellow humans **	Discovery of grace of God revealed in Christ **	Discovery of life in the Spirit ** Gifts and fruits of the Spirit ** Freedom **	Discovery of the church as com-munity of the Spirit and sign in the world of the coming kingdom

Disquiet and anguish because of sinfulness within, in-capacity to avoid sin or to do good **

Deep concern for new creation/mission in the world
Deepening appreciation of the new covenant
Ministry of the word and teaching very significant
Liberation from legalism and formalism

Guilt increasingly important
Spirit of Christ-presence

a. Kingdom of God, present and coming (Bible, church, Holy Spirit)
b. Redeemer God, revealed in Christ (faith/commitment to purpose; communal worship)
c. The church, the people of God (new birth, baptism, Lord's Supper, based on personal deci-sion)
d. "Life" means service, justice, peace, holiness, freedom (life in Christ, life in the Spirit via repentance, forgiveness, accep-tance)
e. Christ and his teaching, the fulfillment of God's law (love-obedience, discipleship, partici-pation)
f. Angels; fellowship of the saints (thanksgiving, rejoicing)
g. Satan vanquished, with demons and evil spirits (faith, prayer, exorcism, fellowship)
h. The church, a community of gifts (charisms) (fellowship, sharing, intercession, dis-cernment of dreams, visions, trances)
i. Providence, intervention of God, mutual aid of the congre-gation (forgiveness for guilty; and trust, hope, prayer, heal-ing)
j. Festival, ritual (voluntary cel-ebration for edification)
k. Resurrection (hope, expecta-tion after death)
l. After-life: fulfillment of God's purposes for peace, justice, unity
m. Present life: anticipatory ex-pression of future hope; linear
n. History dominant: story of God's redeeming acts and promises in fulfillment
o. Guilt a dominant undercurrent, in response to internal pressure

One is tempted to conclude that any stage that is skipped over will ultimately be experienced at a later time. In that sense, the stages as suggested may not always be the exact order of experience. When I suggested elsewhere[22] that the "legalism" experienced by Westerners in much of African Christianity is such a "stage" in a divine pedagogy of salvation, this was helpfully contested in the name of the apostle Paul who denounced the "backward" legalistic movement of the Galatians who had been bewitched.[23] Yet from the perspective of missionary experience and history, one might ask whether the Galatians initially understood and experienced Paul's preaching of Christ's grace, the Spirit, and gospel freedom in the same way that he, the apostle, did, when they first believed. In fact, Paul was doing his missionary task by bringing the New Testament gospel and canon to bear on a stage that he himself had experienced and transcended.

From the perspective of this suggested itinerary, when in the initial power confrontation Christ is fully trusted, at each succeeding stage he will be experienced differently: the more powerful, the faithful protector, the new lawgiver, the holy one, the giver of grace and life, the ever-present, the Creator of a new humanity. Is this indeed the answer to the questions I raised about the religious itinerary of the seventy-year-old fetisher–head of the blacksmith clan in a village of Burkina Faso? If so, at every stage Christ is good news, and at every new stage Christ brings renewed freedom.

But this is a description by a Westerner. An African Christian, minister of state in his country, put the African religious itinerary somewhat differently: "The way that leads to God is his own Word. This way is long, very long, and is set like a ladder that is visible from any point, but whose bottom and top rungs are invisible. Nevertheless, when one steps on a rung—at whatever level—and willingly hangs on, the Spirit of God Himself progressively unveils to the climber the different rungs behind and before, which permit him to advance and to reach Him at the Kingdom of Light and Life where He awaits us."[24]

Here is a vertical ladder, rung after rung, instead of a forward itinerary, stage after stage. Both images catch the essential note of new response to new illumination. But the direction is not a secondary ques-

---

[22] David A. Shank, "Une response imprévue à l'action missionnaire," *Perspectives Missionnaires* 6 (1983): 55–66.

[23] See Thomas Béarth, "Pédagogie divine et cheminement humain: un piège missiologique? *Perspectives Missionnaires* 6 (1983): 78-80.

[24] Mathieu Ekra, *L'échelle sans fin* (Abidjan: INADES, 1977), 16.

tion; the Western church was itself sidetracked for many years on "a ladder reaching to a God without a future."

Section III Selected Essays
E Anabaptism and mission

David and Wilma Shank in Harrist worship

14

Anabaptists and mission

These reflections grow out of my missionary commitment and ministry in Belgium from 1950 to 1973 in what has been called a post-Christian culture. Significantly, Anabaptists had been particularly active in that area four hundred years earlier. A post-Christian culture contrasts sharply with pre-Christian areas of missionary endeavor, as it does also with a so-called Christian culture in which the Anabaptists flourished, or with a similar phenomenon in North America throughout much of the twentieth century. My own reflection on this subject is done from within a religious tradition that has emerged from the Anabaptist breakthrough of the sixteenth century. Further, I recognize the influence that Anabaptist studies have had on my own thinking; yet I am not an Anabaptist scholar and must necessarily do much of my reflection with the aid of secondary sources.

At the outset, I must readily admit the importance for me of hearing Franklin Littell's chapter on the missionary motif within Anabaptism, when he presented it to Mennonite Central Committee staff and workers in the spring of 1946,[1] six years prior to its publication in what was to become the classic *The Origins of Sectarian Protestantism.*[2] At that moment in my personal pilgrimage, a clear statement of the missionary roots of my tradition—with which I was not then certain I could identify—indeed helped me make the decision to remain with the Mennonite Church.

Reprinted, with editorial changes, from *Anabaptists and Mission,* ed. Wilbert R. Shenk (Scottdale, PA: Herald Press, 1984), 202–28. Used by permission.

[1] Published as "The Anabaptist Theology of Mission" in *Mennonite Quarterly Review* 21, no. 1 (1947): 5–17. Reprinted in *Anabaptism and Mission,* ed. Wilbert R. Shenk (Scottdale, PA: Herald Press, 1984), chap. 1.

[2] Franklin Hamlin Littell, *The Origins of Sectarian Protestantism: A Study of the Anabaptist View of the Church,* rev. ed. (New York: Macmillan, 1964). Originally published as *The Anabaptist View of the Church: An Introduction to Sectarian Protestantism* (Hartford: American Society of Church History, 1952).

My use of the word *Anabaptist* in this chapter is not limited to what have sometimes been called the evangelical Anabaptists. Instead, I tend to include the whole pluralistic gamut within the early movement of the radical left wing of the sixteenth-century Reformation and observe it evolving toward a consensus into evangelical Anabaptism around 1550. The great diversity in the earlier years is significant, as George Williams[3] and J. M. Stayer[4] have indicated. But even Littell's presentation, particularly concerning mission, appears also to take that much broader and diverse expression of Anabaptism as the source of his study.

My use of *Anabaptism* here refers to an evolving Christian movement of spiritual breakthrough. It will be seen first as a historical phenomenon, second as a typical stance within Christian history and ecclesiology, and finally as a source for defining the contemporary task in the last quarter-century of the twentieth century. But before looking at those three relationships of Anabaptism to mission, we must first provide an understanding of the latter.

How shall we understand mission?

Historical approaches

In English-speaking Christian circles, the word *mission* usually refers to the organized, institutionalized sending out of spiritually and professionally qualified workers. These workers go from a Christian church, community, and people to a non-Christian religious context such as Buddhism, Hinduism, Shintoism, Confucianism, Islam, or the so-called animism of primal societies. On the European continent in Christian circles, mission most often denotes much more the idea of the essential task of a person or group, or church. These differences in usage have sometimes resulted in a lack of clear communication.

R. Pierce Beaver, the dean of American missiologists, sees mission as an apostolate beyond the congregation and home locality, involving commissioning and sending representatives to witness on behalf of the sending church and its disciples.[5] This he contrasts to the local apostolate of the church, which is called evangelism. Mennonite theologian John H. Yoder has indicated that when stripped to its root, mis-

[3] George H. Williams, *The Radical Reformation* (Philadelphia: Westminster Press, 1962).

[4] J. M. Stayer, *Anabaptists and the Sword* (Lawrence, KS: Coronado Press, 1972).

[5] See R. Pierce Beaver, "The Apostolate of the Church," in *The Theology of the Christian Mission*, ed. Gerald H. Anderson (Nashville: Abingdon Press, 1961), 263–64.

sion does refer to someone being sent from a geographical or cultural home with a mandate to testify in some other home.[6] Ray Gingerich, an interpreter of Anabaptist missionary understandings, suggests that mission must extend beyond the etymological meaning to include the witness of the church outside its social perimeters, and to include the forming of new communities.[7]

These are all helpful guides to understanding mission, yet none of these definitions picks up the full implication of what might also be called mission consciousness or the sense of mission. This consciousness was particularly evident among Anabaptists of the sixteenth century; the historian C. J. Dyck has described their particular pattern of zeal growing out of a sense of "sent-ness" as *Sendungsbewusstsein*.[8] This was clearly distinct from the simple witness of piety and life.

In a different direction, mission as an obedient fulfillment of Christ's Great Commission has been a major missionary dynamic for the past two centuries, at least since the time of William Carey. This was also, according to Littell, a major part of the Anabaptist thrust of the sixteenth century; it was indeed my own understanding of mission in 1946 as crystallized by Littell's presentation.

In another direction, the Roman Catholicism of pre–Vatican II times understood mission as planting the (Roman) Church in every region where it was not fully established.[9] But the post–Vatican II stance sees *mission* rather as the "duty to spread the faith and the saving work of Christ *in virtue of the express command* [of Christ] . . . and in virtue of that life which flows from Christ into his members. . . . The mission of the Church is therefore fulfilled by that activity which makes her fully present to all men and nations," as compared to *missions,* which "is the term usually given to those particular understandings by which heralds of the gospel are sent out by the church and go forth into the whole world to carry out the task of preaching the gospel and planting

[6] See John H. Yoder, "Reformation and Missions: A Literature Review," *Occasional Bulletin from the Missionary Research Library* 22, no. 6 (June 1971): 1–9. Reprinted in *Anabaptism and Mission,* ed. Wilbert R. Shenk (Scottdale, PA: Herald Press, 1984), 40–50.

[7] "Proposal for an Anabaptist Theology of Mission," manuscript dated January 14, 1974.

[8] C. J. Dyck, "Early Anabaptist *Sendungsbewusstsein,*" unpublished paper for a church history course at University of Chicago, 1957.

[9] André Seumois, "The Evolution of Mission Theology among Roman Catholics," in *The Theology of the Christian Mission,* ed. Anderson, 126.

the church among peoples or groups who do not believe in Christ."[10] The importance of the mandate of Christ can clearly be perceived in both mission and missions as understood by present-day Roman Catholicism.

Lesslie Newbigin concluded more simply that mission is the crossing of a frontier of strangeness between faith in Christ as Lord and unbelief in order "to make Christ known and obeyed as Lord among those who do not know and obey him."[11] Here the crossing of the frontier is accentuated, not Christ's mandate or the missioner's obedience to it; the resulting church-as-community is implicit only in the expression "obeyed as Lord."

Mission of the Church: The "Great Commission"

This diversity of understanding of mission calls for clarification. I will use the word *mission* in the sense of fulfilling the Great Commission of Christ (in Matthew 28 and Mark 16). This understanding of mission gives the other definitions and understandings their proper perspective. But in so doing, I have come full circle in my thinking. My own decision and commitment included a clear sense of obedient response to Christ's commission. I had a clear awareness that this obedience was not an option but was, on the contrary, central to an understanding of the gospel, and indeed was central to my own tradition's roots in its earliest and most dynamic years.

Over the years, however, the use of the expression "obedience to the Great Commission" seemed to me to evoke and conjure up a wooden literalism on the one hand, and an unbiblical romanticism on the other hand. The Great Commission seemed to deal more with mission activity—mission boards, fund-raising, going abroad, foreign fields—than with the real mission to which the Great Commission calls. William R. Hogg has pointed out how this happened within Protestant missions in general.[12] Since the Bible was seen as the word of God, and the scripture text said "Go!" missionary obedience meant going. So people went to be obedient, and missionary activism has often been the result.

[10] See "Decree on the Missionary Activity of the Church" (*Ad Gentes*), in *The Documents of Vatican II*, ed. Walter M. Abbot (New York: Guild Press, 1966), 589; my italics.

[11] See Lesslie Newbigin, *One Body, One Gospel, One World: The Christian Mission Today* (London: International Missionary Council, 1958), 29.

[12] See William Richey Hogg, "The Rise of Protestant Missionary Concern, 1517–1914," in *The Theology of the Christian Mission*, ed. Anderson, 101, 109.

Much of the literalistic obedience, superficial activism, and unwise enthusiasm of the past two centuries merited the critique of Harry Boer, who has written that the Great Commission's "meaning for and place in the life of the missionary community must . . . be differently construed than is customarily done [since it] derives its meaning and power wholly and exclusively from the Pentecost event."[13] I, too, have experienced and insisted on the importance of the Holy Spirit in the fulfillment of Christ's mission and the whole missionary enterprise.[14] Yet the work of the Holy Spirit in suspending obedience to the letter, superficialism, and the carnality of missionary activism does not remove the fact that that commission is fundamental and central for the existence of the church. In reality, as one reads the account of Luke, it becomes apparent that the command and the promise of the Great Commission came fully alive when the Jerusalem community received the Holy Spirit. It is so reported by Peter in his much later meeting with Cornelius: "He commanded us to preach unto the people, and to testify that it is he which was ordained of God to be the Judge of quick and dead" (Acts 10:42, AV). Christ's prior command gave clear structure and order to the experienced power of the Holy Spirit.

The significance of this prior order of Christ has been effectively pointed out in an exegesis of Matthew 28:16–20 by Karl Barth:

The kingly ministry of the Messiah is here entrusted to the first disciples constituting the king's troops. . . .

As recapitulation and anticipation revealing the hidden reality of the eschatological community, the Great Commission is truly the most genuine utterance of Jesus. . . .

The command to baptize is . . . the transferral of the messianic power of Jesus, the priest of all [people] . . . [and] as baptism constitutes the existence and the nature of all discipleship, teaching constitutes the ways and works of the disciples. . . .

They are to live within the earthly confines of the kingdom of God and to submit to the order of life established there. . . . All baptized become *eo ipso* subservient to this order of service, the very foundation of the Christian community . . . [that] exists only where the things commanded by Jesus are "observed." . . .

Because of Jesus' presence the Great Commission of the risen

[13] See Harry R. Boer, *Pentecost and Missions* (Grand Rapids, MI: Eerdmans, 1964), 47.
[14] See my pamphlet, *His Spirit First* (Scottdale, PA: Herald Press, 1972).

Lord to baptize and evangelize is valid throughout the days of this "last age."[15]

The importance of the Great Commission is also indicated by *Lumen Gentium,* Vatican II's "Dogmatic Constitution on the Church," which begins by citing Mark 16:15: "Go ye into all the world and preach the Gospel to every creature." This important Roman Catholic declaration reaffirms that the Great Commission is central to the definition and existence of the church.

The personal and corporate experience of the power of the Holy Spirit must mark the ongoing life and history of the church. That will intensify the social and communal character of the church, making its presence an effective witness to God's purposes. However, both the Spirit and the community can tend—for a moment—to eclipse the Great Commission. But such an eclipse does not remove the all-encompassing mandate-with-promise of the resurrected Lord of heaven and earth; it is indeed operative until the close of the age. The mission of the church is not only defined and created by that commission but response to it must be a major criterion of the church's fidelity. The effectiveness of the church in giving continuity to the carrying out of that mandate—itself an essential part of "all I have commanded you"—becomes a major determinant of the future of the church. The present study of Anabaptists and mission is done with that understanding of mission.

Anabaptism and mission as a historical phenomenon

As a movement evolving from 1520 to the middle of the century, Anabaptism had its genesis in a context of rapid cultural, social, and political change. The return to the scriptures that had begun before the turn of the century meant that new spiritual and ethical understandings were being fed into that rapidly changing human scene. The development of those understandings was taking place in a situation where the authority of scripture was set alongside other authorities, both ecclesiastical and political. Differing patterns of reformation developed in Germany, Switzerland, and France; yet out of a great diversity of experiences, affirmations, hesitancies, and oscillations a Protestant consensus emerged. Lutherans and Zwinglians never came to complete unity. Later developments in England and Scotland underscore the pluralism within that growing consensus. But this diversity within Protestantism

---

[15] Karl Barth, "An Exegetical Study of Matthew 28:16–20," in *The Theology of the Christian Mission,* ed. Anderson, 63, 67–69.

makes the diversity within Anabaptism all the more understandable. Stayer's examination of the early diverse positions on the use of the sword among Anabaptists justifies his rejection of the facile categorizing by the first generation of American Mennonite historians of Anabaptism.[16]

Indeed, early Anabaptism included the revolutionary and the moderate, the chiliast and the ethicist, the charismatic and the weird, libertinism and legalism. Such divergences within the movement did lead to mutual nonrecognition and mutual rejection even among adherents who were then closer to each other than they were to the Protestant consensus or the magisterial Reformation. The major difference between the latter and the Anabaptist movement is to be seen in the relationship of each to the society at large. Where the Protestant Reformers consciously and intentionally assumed responsibility for the mainstream of society, the Anabaptists were a marginal movement. This distinction between mainstream and marginal soon became the difference between legality and illegality. At the same time, the marginal and illegal character of the movement must not give the impression that the impact of the movement was unimportant. On the contrary, the whole society felt that impact.

In that period of rapid change, all society was caught up in an eschatological excitement. When Michelangelo's *Last Judgment* was unveiled in the Sistine Chapel on October 13, 1541, all Rome is said to have flocked to gape at the spectacle, the most urgent in advertising the perpetual imminence of the last day. The city shuddered in awe and stupefied admiration."[17] Martin Luther's own expectation of the imminent return of Jesus Christ was such that from today's perspective he would appear to be like the *Schwärmer,* a term he reserved for those he judged to be irresponsible enthusiasts. Against that backdrop, the intense eschatological expectation that lay behind the Anabaptists' sense of mission is not surprising. But it was not the eschatological intensity that marginalized them; it was rather the ethical, social, and political content of their hope that created their marginality and their impact on society.

Thomas Müntzer's social radicalism, related also to his belief that God's kingdom was coming soon, directly influenced Anabaptism, particularly through one of its greatest evangelists, Hans Hut. The impact

---

[16] See Stayer, *Anabaptists and the Sword.*

[17] From Leo Steinberg, "Michelangelo's 'Last Judgement' as Merciful Heresy," *Art in America* 63, no. 6 (1975): 49.

of the chiliast Melchior Hofmann on the pre-Mennist covenanters in the Netherlands, and the outbreak of the Münsterite kingdom in Westphalia have left a permanent mark on the Anabaptist stream, even when—following Menno Simons—it was in reaction. The later Hutterian eschatology and the sense of mission it engendered is also a part of a greater stream. None of these tendencies began a new movement of eschatological anticipation; they responded differently to the eschatological urgency characteristic of their times.

Obedience to the command of Christ

Here we must note that one of the major differences between Anabaptists and the magisterial Reformers was the centrality of the Great Commission. This was true of all the tendencies.

> No texts appear more frequently [than Matthew 28, Mark 16, Psalm 24] in the confessions of faith and court testimonies of the Anabaptists and none show more clearly the degree to which Anabaptism was different in conviction and type from the intact and stable ways of Magisterial Protestantism. . . . No words of the Master were given more serious attention by his Anabaptist followers than the Great Commission. . . . The form of the Commission seemed to sum up His whole teaching in a glorious program comprehending the whole world. . . . It was fundamental to individual witness and to the ordered community of believers as well. . . . [It was] not only obeyed most seriously, but it was given sweeping application. It applied to all Christians at all times. . . . The Anabaptists were among the first to make the Commission binding upon all members.[18]

These words from Littell are confirmed by the research of Wolfgang Schäufele, with the exception that baptism was carried out only by "Anabaptist office-bearers" since "apart from the very beginning of the movement, no ordinary member was authorized to baptize."[19] "The missionary activity of the ordinary members of the brotherhood was limited to oral proclamation of the Anabaptist message of repentance and salvation which they themselves had accepted, and to which they conformed their own lives."[20]

---

[18] See Littell, *The Origins of Sectarian Protestantism*, 109–13.

[19] Wolfgang Schäufele, "The Missionary Vision and Activity of the Anabaptist Laity," *Mennonite Quarterly Review* 36, no. 2 (1962), 101. Reprinted in *Anabaptism and Mission*, ed. Wilbert R. Shenk (Scottdale, PA: Herald Press, 1984), 70–87.

[20] Ibid., 208.

This was true not only for the working man who testified to his fellow laborers, according to Schäufele, but also for a remarkable number of women. "The woman in Anabaptism emerges as a fully emancipated person in religious matters, and as the independent bearer of Christian convictions. The gospel was carried aggressively and emphatically into everyday life. The 'sacred area inside the church buildings' disappeared as the only place where salvation is mediated."[21]

Karl Barth has written in his exegetical study of Matthew 28: "The existence of the new community consists not only in the apostles' preaching of the Gospel and of their fellow men's listening. It is constantly renewed as the listeners themselves become 'apostolic' and as new disciples begin to proclaim the good news."[22] There is no doubt about this being the exegesis of the Anabaptists; this was indeed the dynamic produced among them in a time of opposition and persecution.

The content of discipleship—"observe all things that I have commanded you"—that was to grow out of obedience to the Great Commission was observable within a month after a community formed in Zollikon near Zurich. In his February 18, 1525, letter to the Zurich council, Felix Manz wrote with clear reference to Matthew 28:

> [God] has sent his Son with all power in heaven and on earth so that whoever calls upon him and trusts him would have eternal life. In like manner, Christ sent his disciples commanding them that they should go to all peoples to teach, giving them such power from God his Father and through his death, so that all who would call upon his name might have forgiveness of sins and to baptize with the outer sign. So as he was teaching in this way, certain came to him with tears asking that he baptize them—and he didn't refuse them, but *first taught them love, and unity, and communion of all things, as the apostles also in Acts 2,* and to think on the death of Christ and not to forget his shed blood, finally the meaning of the breaking of the bread, and the drinking of the wine, *how we are all saved by one body and all washed with one blood and are become a union the ones of the others,* brothers and sisters in Christ our Lord.[23]

---

[21] Ibid., 113.

[22] Karl Barth, "An Exegetical Study of Matthew 28:16–20," 63.

[23] See No. 42a, in *Zürich, Quellen zur Geschichte der Taufer in der Schweiz* I:, ed. Leonhard von Muralt and Walter Schmid (Zürich: Theologischer Verlag, 1952), 49; my italics.

A month earlier, Manz had written his Protestation to the Zürich council. On two occasions before the council he clearly stated the centrality of the Great Commission in the preaching, baptizing, and teaching ministries. In the first week after the Zollikon congregation was formed, George Blaurock went into the parish church there and asked the priest what he was planning to do. "Preach God's word," was the answer. But Blaurock spoke out: "Not you, but *I am sent* to preach."[24] Here is indeed the *Sendungsbewusstsein* that Dyck has underscored. This same Blaurock, along with Stumpf, "pressed Zwingli most consistently to gather a purified 'community of all things as also the apostles [had it] in Acts 2.'"[25] The community intention of both Manz and Blaurock was an expression of more than "simply Christian charity."[26] Indeed the appeal to Acts 2 is found over and over again.

The other elements of the "all things" that Christ commanded, as reported by Manz, were love and unity. These had been carefully defined by the Zurich brethren in the months that preceded the January 21, 1525, founding of the congregation. An intense study of the scriptures was the basis for those understandings. The faith commitment those understandings had engendered involved a stance like "sheep in the midst of wolves" where violent coercion in matters of faith was excluded. War and violence as method and stance in the word were also excluded on the basis of the Lamb of God himself and his overcoming strategy. Grebel's letters to Müntzer in the fall of 1524 and to Andreas Castelberger in May 1525 are good expositions of that understanding.

Finally, Fritz Blanke's *Brüder in Christo*[27] describes the way baptism gave coherence to a revival in Zollikon; conviction of sin, repentance, and faith were all elements that took on congregational shape through baptismal commitments. It was on the day following the founding of the congregation in Zürich; the pattern was the same.

All the elements of the Great Commission were clearly present in those early days—an awareness of being sent; preaching the gospel; faith, repentance, forgiveness of sins; baptizing into the body; teaching what Christ commanded, that is, love, unity, community, and the Great

---

[24] Ibid., no. 29, 39; my italics.

[25] Cited by Littell, *The Origins of Sectarian Protestantism,* 1964, 121n60.

[26] It is thus characterized strangely by Ekkehard Krajewski in "The Theology of Felix Manz," *Mennonite Quarterly Review* 36, no. 1 (1962): 85.

[27] Fritz Blanke, *Brothers in Christ: The History of the Oldest Anabaptist Congregation, Zollikon, near Zurich, Switzerland,* trans. Joseph Nordenhaug (Scottdale, PA: Herald Press, 1961).

Commission itself. The final command of Christ became the ordinance of life; it offered a mandate and an explicit strategy that became the center and organizing principle of a whole movement.

Emerging mission strategy

A large gathering—later called the Martyrs' Synod—was held in August 1527 at Augsburg to work out a clear missionary strategy. One of the major missioners at this synod was Hans Hut, who had been responsible for baptizing hundreds of Anabaptists. We learn something of how Anabaptists saw mission work from what he taught those whom he sent out. One of them, a Georg Nespitzer from Passau, described the baptismal covenant thus—"to abstain from sins and where one sees his brother sin, shall he punish him; also where there is need, to help so far as body and life reaches; but whosoever wishes not to do this, he should abstain from baptism and zealously stick to that decision."[28]

Another of Hut's converts, Leonard Schiemer—a former Franciscan friar—was sent to Bavaria, Salzburg, and the Tyrol. He described the "fellowship of the saints" in his own articles of faith, where he used the term from the Apostles' Creed. Citing Acts 2, 4, and 5, he wrote that the baptized "must keep love and fellowship with the congregation." This was further defined as "holding with his congregation all the gifts received from God, whether teaching, skill, goods, money, or other. . . . [These] he must invest in the congregation's needs."[29]

According to Christian Hege and H. S. Bender, more than sixty leaders and representatives from South Germany, Switzerland, and Austria were present at this important missionary synod. Hans Hut's presence in this assembly was crucial, since as the leading evangelist he had won and baptized more people in the previous two years than all the other leaders combined. But his chiliasm with its clear prediction of events prior to the return of Christ—expected in 1528—did not have the approval of everyone present. In fact, his views apparently were at the center of the discussions in council, along with the issues of the use of violence and the community of goods.

All the questions were resolved, even if in ways unacceptable to Hubmaier in later discussions. An apparent consensus was obtained, for "in spite of the cruel persecution, no Anabaptist took recourse to

---

[28] See W. Wiswedel, *Bilder und Fuhrergestalten aus dem Täufertum II* (Kassel: Oncken, 1930).

[29] See Lydia Müller, *Glaubenszeugnisse oberdeutscher Taufgesinnter I* (Leipzig: Heinsius Nachfolger, 1938), 67, 56.

violent resistance nor was there evidence of a planned attack against the government in all the cross-examinations even on the rack."[30] There were indeed variations on the theme of the use of violence: Hubmaier accepted the notion of a regenerate magistracy; Hut felt that violence should be put aside until the return of Christ; Müntzerite ideas were revived in Esslingen yet in 1527; and in the north, the Münster debacle was still to come.

But these can be seen as variant fringes of a central thrust that put an accent on a community of brotherhood, peace, and unity in discipleship. This inner consensus was to be spelled out again at Schlatten in 1527, in what is known as the Schleitheim confession; the need for the definition was again the existence of the fringe tendencies. The central thrust has always needed to struggle with a pull in the direction of a spiritualism on the one hand and the magisterial tendencies toward theocracy on the other hand. Each has had its own forms of deviation from what was perceived by many to be the consensus. For that, the major pull appears to be the coming kingdom of Christ and its manifestation in the life of Jesus.

Thus in a climate of strong eschatological hope, Anabaptist end-time obedience to the Great Commission carried a universality that became particular as baptism created local communities of committed disciples. The forms of economic sharing differed, but the exigency was there; the same was true for the rejection of coercion in faith and social relationships. These dimensions seemed to be essential to the gospel that was preached, to the teaching of what Christ commanded, to the covenant of baptism. The communities developed a three-pronged protest: ecclesiastical, social and economic, and political.[31] The amazing thing is not that fringe deviations were present, but that the central thrust remained functional in spite of the strong pulls.

One major deviation can be linked to Melchior Hofmann with his distorted dualism, his deformed Christology, and his belief that he was the promised Elijah preparing the final advent of Jesus. He apparently built on earlier sacramentarian influences in the Netherlands and stimulated the movement that at one pole ended in the Münsterite the-

---

[30] Christian Hege, quoted by H. S. Bender in *The Mennonite Encyclopedia* (Scottdale, PA: Herald Press, 1957), 3:531.

[31] See Walter Klaassen, "The Nature of the Anabaptist Protest," *Mennonite Quarterly Review* 45, no. 4 (1971): 291–311. For Klaassen, the Anabaptists "raised questions about basic assumptions of European religion and culture."

ocracy with its tragic end.[32] But his ministry also provided the groundwork for an emerging consensus in the north as it was later formulated by Menno Simons and Dirk Philips, both in constant dialogue with deviant fringes.

It is important to understand the place of the Great Commission in Hoffmann's thought. In his *Ordonnantie* of 1530 he makes it clear that the Great Commission is the ordinance of the Lord which orders all else. This thrust deeply influenced Menno Simons, whose use of the Great Commission often appears to be a simple defense of the practice of "faith first, baptism second."

But a closer reading of Menno's writings makes it clear that it is Christ the king who has given his great command, order, or ordinance, which now orders life in new spiritual, social, and political relationships. That his understanding was strongly flavored by what C. J. Dyck calls a flesh-spirit ontological dualism[33] justifies to some extent Ernst Bloch's critique of Menno as favoring social and political withdrawal, when compared to the earlier thrust of Thomas Müntzer.[34] But Müntzer as a "spiritualist" revolutionary, if indeed pulled by an eschatological hope, was not structured by the Great Commission; baptism, construed to be inner, was in the spirit, and spiritual leading superseded the written word. This constituted a major pull away from the central Anabaptist core; the real question is not how Menno compares with Müntzer—the Marxist philosopher's hero—but whether there is another norm for both: the fulfillment of the mission made explicit by the Great Commission of Christ.

The specific Hutterite community model was another derivative of the basic pattern of a missionary community of mutual and total commitment to the leader Christ, carrying out his Great Commission in a confrontation with a *getäufte Heidentum*.

The "Christ as leader" motif appears to be a major one among the Anabaptists; it needs much more careful study than it has yet received. Erasmus' *Enchiridion* had set a model for the Christian as the "knight under orders" which could understandably lead to relativizing all earthly authorities. For example, nine days after the Zurich baptismal fellow-

---

[32] The coins minted by the Münsterite kingdom had struck around their diameter the first letters of the Latin words in the text of the Great Commission.

[33] C. J. Dyck, "Anabaptism and the Social Order," in *The Impact of the Church upon its Culture*, ed. Jerald C. Brauer (Chicago: University of Chicago Press, 1968).

[34] Ernst Bloch, *Thomas Münzer als Theologe der Revolution* (Munich: Kurt Wolff Verlag, 1921).

ship of January 21, 1525, which Williams calls the birthday of Anabaptism, twenty-five members of the Zollikon congregation—including Manz and Blaurock—were arrested; one of their number declared that he "had enrolled under the Dux Jesus Christ and would go with Him to death."[35] The image of the knight in service to his lord was used later by Menno Simons as well. A reading of Anabaptist texts, with that relationship in mind, can give the impression that the use of the pair "disciple-Lord"—or the milder "disciple-Master"—to describe the Anabaptist understanding is probably a weak expression of the sixteenth-century ethos in which Christ was seen to be the new Lord and king in contrast to the contemporary dukes, lords, and kings. The Anabaptists saw themselves much more as subjects of Christ than as disciples. As Christ's subjects they obeyed the first ordinance—the Great Commission—of the ruler of the realm.

The existence of a mobile community of commitment subject to a universally commanding Lord of the realm created a whole new sociopolitical configuration. It was not, indeed, dissimilar to A. D. Nock's description of the primitive Christian church: "a holistic reality—a new life in a new people."[36] Indeed the binding character of the Great Commission for all members meant a new exploitation of all the gifts within the community for the sake of the gospel. Early in the movement, in what would today be called charismatic outbursts, the formerly nonvocal and passively receptive people, both men and women, became a responding and responsible people of God. J. Lawrence Burkholder has gone so far as to suggest that the outstanding feature of their discipleship was their obedient response to the Great Commission.[37]

The way that new sociopolitical reality related to the states and magistracies has only been suggested in passing. Stayer has indicated several tendencies, and even an overlapping of tendencies in adaptation to varying circumstances. My suggestion is that these divergent emerging patterns may be more clearly seen and understood in the light of a model of a typical messianic movement. The phenomenon of messianism and its dynamics may perhaps be effectively employed for a better understanding of the movement than we have had.

[35] Cited in Williams, *The Radical Reformation,* 125.

[36] See A. D. Nock, *Conversion: The Old and the New in Religion from Alexander the Great to Augustine of Hippo* (Oxford: Clarendon Press, 1933).

[37] J. Lawrence Burkholder, "The Anabaptist Vision of Discipleship," in *The Recovery of the Anabaptist Vision,* ed. Guy Hershberger (Scottdale, PA: Herald Press, 1957), 138.

Anabaptism, as a type: Messianic resurgence

Three types of mission understandings in the sixteenth century can be observed. The first is that expressed by the Roman Catholic and magisterial Protestant dictum, *cuius regio, eius religio.* In Protestant countries everyone was Protestant, and in Catholic countries everyone was to be Catholic. The population was Christianized, people believed the gospel, and mission was fulfilled. Particularly among the Protestant Reformers, the Great Commission was regarded as binding only for the early apostles; the apostles had fulfilled the mandate, and the contemporary Protestant state was the beneficiary.

Within Catholicism, this type carried on mission by colonial expansion; the *corpus Christianum* extended itself by annexing foreign territories and claiming them for the church as well as the monarch. Christopher Columbus saw himself as explorer and missionary, and his royal backers shared his perception. Here the Great Commission was binding, but understood as involving the exportation of a total religious, social, cultural, and political complex. It was a new sacral reality imposed on the inhabitants of territories which were to be incorporated.

A second type was that illustrated by the Jesuit order in the 1540s; it is the foreign missionary sent by the missionary order into lands that—if they were not politically annexed through colonial ties—were, nevertheless, often under the impact of, for example, Portuguese commerce. Francis Xavier, active in the Far East, typified the approach that often involved hasty instruction followed by baptism of the masses. A large population was integrated into the church via baptism rather than through strict political expropriation. The missionary specialist was sent by a specialized order to gather in the masses. In Latin America—Mexico and Peru—a missionary in 1536 estimated the baptized at between four and nine million; in reality the missionary was often in the forefront of later political annexation. But the work of a Matteo Ricci in China at the end of the sixteenth century indicates how attempts were made to introduce Christianity within a cultural pattern and a sociopolitical structure without annexation. It was a work accomplished by remarkable experts sent by a highly expert missionary order.

The third type, as we have seen, was that which made the Great Commission binding on all church members; the mission was to those who were of the Christian religion by simple acculturation within a so-called Christian civilization. There, as we have seen, it was a call to become freely subject to the Lord Christ within a disciplined congregation practicing fraternal community and peace, and whose essential nature was to be for the world.[38] It was a rejection of the ecclesiasticism that blessed the existing political, social, economic, and cultural patterns. It called for a congregation of those voluntarily responding to Christ's call, and who then confronted the violence, greed, and domination of that society; the congregation was created by a free response of obedience to Christ.

Free-church tradition

The implications of this type for missionary history are significant for the period starting in the eighteenth century and going well into the nineteenth century, the period Latourette called "the age of the most extensive geographic spread of Christianity." A majority of the missionaries spreading the gospel in other lands in this period were influenced by this free-church type. Because of that influence, parallels between sixteenth-century Anabaptism and nineteenth-century missions are noticeable. Quite often a critique of the colonial regimes was inherent in the missionary presence; active assistance by governments in the nineteenth century was minimal; the missionary movement was a people's movement; women played an important part in this century of expansion. Missionaries set high standards for admission into the congregations which constituted the newly forming "younger church."

According to Latourette,[39] in the thousand years prior to this period, mission work involved group movements and mass baptisms. In nineteenth-century missionary practice, entrance into the church came by individual decision rather than by collective movement. The result: at the end of the century in the areas of missionary effort, Christians were a small, disciplined minority with an extraordinary effect on the non-Christian populations.

However, important differences exist between the free-church type of mission in the nineteenth century and the earlier phenomenon of Anabaptism in the sixteenth century. In the latter case, the missioners were full participants in the history and culture of the people whom they addressed; in the nineteenth century, the missioners were foreigners working in new languages in exotic cultures among peoples whose history was unknown. Missionaries went from a literate, so-called in-

---

[38] See John H. Yoder, "Die Sendung als Wesen der Gemeinde," *Täufertum und Reformation in der Schweiz* (Weierhof: Mennonitischer Geschichtsverein, 1962), 178–82.

[39] See Kenneth S. Latourette, *A History of the Expansion of Christianity: The Great Century in Europe and the United States of America A.D. 1800–A.D. 1914*, vol. 4 (Grand Rapids, MI: Zondervan, 1941), particularly "The Process by which Christianity Spread," 47–52.

dustrial society to preindustrial societies conditioned by orality. The sixteenth-century Anabaptist mission was within a common religious heritage and tradition; the nineteenth-century missionary went from one religious tradition—Christianity—to another, and serious confrontation with a new religious system and tradition took place for the first time. In the sixteenth century, generally the underprivileged people protested in faith against the ecclesiastical and sociopolitical domination to which they were submitted.[40]

The nineteenth-century missionary impact was parallel with colonial developments, and the missionaries were identified with those developments even if they opposed certain colonial policies. In the sixteenth century, leadership appeared to emerge spontaneously and charismatically with the development of the movement; this pattern indeed served as a critique of the established church leadership patterns which were not geared to the Great Commission but to established parishes. In contrast to the free-church type of leadership, the nineteenth-century missionary carefully supervised newly planted churches, and leadership models were provided according to established Western patterns. These differences are important.

What can we say about these various types in our contemporary missionary context? First of all, the free-church type has now become the majority position of contemporary Western Christianity. Littell has pointed out how, within the American understanding of separation between political and religious covenants, all American churches have become the first modern manifestations of so-called younger churches, religious communities gathered out of a context of unfaith.[41] From this perspective, most modern Western missions have, for all practical purposes, planted free churches.

Even the Roman Church since Vatican II declares itself to be a free church in this sense; in a striking manner, *Dignitatis Humanae* early refers to the carrying out of the Great Commission as the way to establish

---

[40] Even H. S. Bender seemed to recognize the validity of this judgment which he felt was overplayed by the Marxist-socialist theoreticians. "Perhaps H. Richard Niebuhr is right in asserting in his book *The Social Sources of Denominationalism* that the Anabaptist movement was a movement of the socially and economically oppressed lower classes, but it is difficult to apply this theory to the founder of the movement." See "Conrad Grebel," *Mennonite Encyclopedia* (Scottdale, PA: Herald Press, 1956), 2:567. Most of the class-theory protagonists recognize, of course, that usually the leadership for the lower classes does not come from those classes.

[41] See Franklin Hamlin Littell, *From State Church to Pluralism: A Protestant Interpretation of Religion in American History* (Garden City, NY: Anchor Books, 1962).

religious liberty. *Ad Gentes* begins with the Isaiah messianic text about the "light to the nations" and then immediately quotes the Markan Great Commission. Further, in *Lumen Gentium* the dominating notion of "people of God" (as compared with "body of Christ") situates the church in a stance not unlike the Anabaptists' missionary stance in the sixteenth century.

Much of the sixteenth-century uniqueness of the free-church type has now been dissipated with the breakup of Constantinian patterns. We can rejoice that the old state-church patterns have broken up; but the increasing universality of free-church patterns is not as such a subject for rejoicing when we discover free churches, both in the West and in what were formerly seen as mission fields, functioning in unconscious or voluntary liaisons with governments, in societies and cultures, as uncritical supporters of socioeconomic and political patterns. This is not the same phenomenon as the oppressive state church of the Constantinian synthesis, but the fact that it is freely accepted dare not hide the fact that it is also a far cry from the Anabaptist fulfillment of mission. A modern free church is not necessarily a continuity of the Anabaptist vision.

Believers church tradition

The language of free church to describe the Anabaptist-type mission and church has thus shifted in recent years to that of "believers church." A conscious effort to develop the concept of a believers church as a church type, perhaps best illustrated by the sixteenth-century Anabaptists, was made in 1967 at the Conference on the Concept of the Believers' Church (Louisville, Kentucky).[42] Since then, the typology has become better known through Donald F. Durnbaugh's history that appeared the following year.[43] The conference of 1967 recognized both the limitations of the free-church type and the fact that believers church as type has not been commonly used in the expanding ecclesiological vocabulary of twentieth-century Christians.[44] Nevertheless, since that time the use of the typology has become—at least in Mennonite circles—commonplace. It is an attempt to accentuate, even in a free democratic society, the difference between a mass church—a cul-

---

[42] James Leo Garrett, Jr., ed., *The Concept of the Believers' Church* (Scottdale, PA: Herald Press, 1969).

[43] Donald F. Durnbaugh, *The Believers' Church* (New York: Macmillan, 1968).

[44] Garrett, *The Concept of the Believers' Church*, 5.

ture religion, a popular church of popular religious acculturation—and congregations of committed believers.

Within the conference itself, the new language—not yet thoroughly defined—was not always helpful to all participants. Dr. Pope A. Duncan suggested that people from believers church traditions should function more ecumenically, "if for no other reason than to discover whether there is any longer any distinction between believers churches and others."[45] Yet in the same conference, after process, such distinctions were clearly affirmed. Reflecting the Anabaptist experience, the believers church type was thus defined in relation to mission: "The congregation is called out of the wider society for a communal existence within and for, yet distinct from, the structures and values of the rest of the world. This distinctness from the world is the presupposition of a missionary and servant ministry to the world. At times it demands costly opposition to the world."[46]

Elsewhere, as a part of that definition, the missionary stance is perceived as working out "the church's being as a covenant community in the midst of the world."[47] Indeed, the Anabaptists did this latter in fulfillment of the Great Commission; we have seen how the economic, social, and political protest was indeed an inherent consequence of the obedience to the "all things" of the effective sovereign over the community—the Christ. One senses that in the shift from history to type, it is possible that the centrality of the Great Commission of the sovereign may subtly be shifted to the self-realization of the community. Part of the shift is a result of the nature of the typology itself. As with the free-church type, it is comparing types of ecclesiastical communities, and by definition in Western experience it is in contrast to the fallen church, the state church, the official national church, or the acculturated church. It is a type still based on the Troeltschian church/sect distinction of Constantinian times.

The fact that the believers church type is, as such, a Western type, growing out of Western developments, could indeed alert us to the problems of its potential irrelevance to the context of world mission, where many situations are clearly similar to pre-Constantinian times in the West. At the same time, in its attempt to recover a pre-Constantinian Christian community, Anabaptism as perceived in the believers church type cannot be wholly irrelevant, even in pre-Constantinian

---

[45] Ibid., 242.

[46] Ibid., 318.

[47] Ibid., 320.

situations. Yet I have heard Mennonite missionaries speak of the irrelevance of the Anabaptist vision to their particular missionary assignments. That vision, the church/sect typology, the free church, and the believers church are all models that help an American church understand itself and refocus its calling in the midst of freedoms and pressures peculiar to its life. The implications of those typologies, however, extend much beyond a denomination or even Western Christianity, even if the typologies do not apply universally.

At the same time, sociologist of religion Allen W. Eister has indicated how the Troeltschian model was "valid for the setting of *cuius regio, eius religio*" but that there was no valid reason for "transporting it across the Atlantic."[48] Thus Eister finds it not always helpful in understanding the dynamics of numerous American sects that have developed in a context of separation of church and state. But he finds it even less helpful for understanding the millenarian, messianic, and nativistic movements of the two-thirds world with its cargo cults and separatist churches. Indeed some of these movements may be seen developing in contexts where the free-church type of Western Christianity was involved in missionary endeavor.

Messianic community

For those who believe that the Anabaptist historical manifestation was indeed one that has Spirit-given lessons for the whole church of Christ—"all that in every place call upon the name of Jesus Christ our Lord, both theirs and ours" (1 Cor. 1:2, AV)—I should like to suggest that there is indeed in it a manifestation of another type, more universal and more in line with the missionary mandate. It is the messianic community type.

The French sociologist of religion Henri Desroche, in a lengthy introduction to his dictionary of messianisms gives a helpful and suggestive typology which he calls the messianic cycle. This typology has grown out of his study with a team of collaborators from several continents; it covers the manifestations of messianism within the Christian era.[49] According to Desroche, following the impact of a messiah on

---

[48] See Allen W. Eister, "Toward a Radical Criticism of Church-Sect Typologizing," *Journal for the Scientific Study of Religion* 6, no. 2 (1967): 85–90.

[49] Henri Desroche, *Dieux d'hommes: Dictionnaire des messianismes et millénarismes de l'ère chrétienne* (Paris: Éditions Mouton, 1969), 1–32; this was later expanded into his *Sociologie de l'Espérance* (Paris: Calmann-Lévy, 1973). Desroche defines messianism following Hans Kohn as "essentially the religious belief in the coming of a redeemer who will put an end to the present order of things either universally or for a particular group

a socially, politically, economically, and religiously oppressive human context, a three-directional explosive movement tends to appear as followers believe and follow in the promise of a new holistic humanity, or a new kingdom. The first direction points to that promised coming reality and works already at its creation. But from that direction two major deviations generally appear, resulting from a loss of faith in the coming kingdom, because of its nonappearance.

Both directions tend to justify the previous movement, but in different ways. One deviation emphasizes the religious aspect of the message and of the kingdom that has not appeared; it then reinterprets the messiah in religious terms, forgetting the social, economic, and political dimensions of the hope that person had created. On the other hand, a second deviation emphasizes the sociopolitical aspects of the message, and reinterprets the messiah in political terms. This deviation minimizes the whole dimension of inner life and faith and authenticity which appears to be religious and alien to structural aspects of society that make social and economic changes possible.

Significantly, Desroche points out how from the perspective of the deviations, a messianic resurgence becomes possible as the over-religious again reorients to the holistic messianic community of the original vision. Similarly, the resurgence can come from the political deviation as it again reorients to a holistic religio-socio-politico-economic intention, reflecting the messianic promise.

For Desroche, this is a pattern of hundreds of messianic movements, each with its own variation of the typology which he develops in detail. In this sense, he is not describing Christianity as such, but a universal phenomenon that recurs when conditions in a society appear to engender a messiah. I would differ from Desroche in my use of his typology in affirming, on other grounds, the universal and crucial character of the messianic movement that has grown out of the impact of Jesus of Nazareth whom we confess as *the* Messiah, and whose birth, life, death, resurrection, and return constitute a context of history within which other movements occur, whether in relation to him or in apparent indifference to him and his impact.

But within this typology, Anabaptism itself is seen as a messianic resurgence, a part of a greater resurgence created by the rediscovery of the word of scripture in a context of rapid change. That resurgence

and will install a new order made of justice and happiness;" see "Messianism," *Encyclopedia of Social Sciences*, vol. 9 (New York: Macmillan, 1933). (See figure 1. *Processes and stages of the messianic dynamic,* in chapter 6 of the present volume.)

290 | Selected Essays: Anabaptism and Mission

deviated in the revolutionary spiritualism of a Müntzer as well as in the magisterial Protestantism of Luther and Calvin, all of which were seen as a revolt against the sacral *corpus Christianum,* so far afield from the commands and intent of Jesus of Nazareth. The spiritualizing of Schwenckfeld and the theocracy of Münster are further deviations from the central consensus of the Anabaptists, apparently shared by Luther and Zwingli, before their realism led them to deviate from the community of faith, love, unity, brotherhood, and peace which the coming kingdom of Christ announced.

In this typology, the sacral oppressive society of Judaism under Rome is simply replaced by the sacral oppressive society of Constantinianism. This latter has been effectively described by Leonard Verduin,[50] who points out the parallels between the Donatists of the time of Augustine and the Anabaptists of the sixteenth century. Both, indeed, were forms of messianic resurgence from out of that sacralism.

John H. Yoder, in his paper at the 1967 Believers' Church Conference, gave a description much fuller than the Troeltsch polarization, in delineating—following a suggestion from the latter—four specific ecclesiological and religious models at the time of the breakup of the Constantinian sacral reality in the sixteenth century.[51] These four models were those of the *corpus Christianum,* the *theocratic* type, the *spiritualist* type, and the *believers' church* type. Yoder, in his description of what he calls the classical options seen in the sixteenth-century Reformation, writes: "The same demonstration could be derived elsewhere as well; it seems that the same possibilities spring forth in every age."[52] Indeed, following the Desroche typology, within Christianity they spring forth from within a context of the universal messianism fulfilled in Jesus Christ and the kingdom of God. The messianic typology situates the believers church in an eschatological tension and indicates how it can move away from its intended vision, how indeed resurgences can spring forth in every time. Elsewhere Yoder has written effectively of a *messianic* ethic and a *messianic* community.[53] They are much better perceived in the typology of a messianic cycle, their inherent context.

[50] Leonard Verduin, *The Reformers and Their Stepchildren* (Grand Rapids, MI: Eerdmans, 1964).

[51] See John H. Yoder, "A People in the World: A Theological Interpretation," in *The Concept of the Believers' Church,* ed. Garrett, 250–51.

[52] Ibid., 254.

[53] John H. Yoder, *The Politics of Jesus* (Grand Rapids: Eerdmans, 1972).

From the perspective of our concern here, as illustrated by the Anabaptists, the Great Commission appears as the vanguard thrust of a universal messianic movement. To understand the history of Christianity as a messianic movement places ecclesiastical realities in much better perspective. But it also suggests a canonical direction for the critique of movements, and not simply four ecclesiastical options, equally valid in inner consistency; indeed it illustrates the New Testament language of apostasy. Most of all it best illustrates the world-kingdom opposition inherent in the biblical data and which is said by Littell to be a basic element in the concept of the believers church,[54] as illustrated by Anabaptism. Further, the messianic model helps to understand better and interpret the challenge presented by non-Christian messianic movements in the world today, themselves a critique of established Christianity.[55]

Anabaptism and missions today

We have already observed how the Anabaptist missionary thrust within sixteenth-century Christendom differed from the free church–inspired missionary thrust of the nineteenth century in a non-European context. We may appropriately ask what that historical movement can contribute to our modern understanding of the missionary task, even though the context in the last two decades of the twentieth century is again different from both of those periods. The idea of the irrelevance of the Anabaptists' experience for today is based on the assumption that theirs was a response to an unfaithful church in sixteenth-century Europe that in no way parallels the task of missions in a context where the church has emerged from a non-Christian past. This is, of course, true. But when one has understood the dynamics of Christian messianism and its expression in Anabaptism, one can find important parallels and analogies for today's missionary task.

The way the life of the community was ordered by the worldwide missionary task in obedience to the coming Messiah is exemplary. Since the Lord is bringing in his kingdom, it is incumbent on his disciples already to prepare others for the unity, love, brotherhood, peace, and justice of that kingdom in a community of faith where those fruits of his presence are operative in the power of the Spirit of the Lord.

---

[54] Garrett, *The Concept of the Believers' Church,* 29.

[55] Gottfried Oosterwal, *Modern Messianic Movements as a Theological and Missionary Challenge* (Elkhart, IN: Institute of Mennonite Studies, 1973).

The sacralism out of which such a breakthrough occurs may no longer be the *corpus Christianum*; it may rather be that of some primal society, or of a techtronic society of the West. In many places of the two-thirds world, one may in fact find layers of each of these super-imposed. In each context, in any case, an essential part of the mission-ary task is to discern those oppressive, destructive, life-denying human patterns that religion tends to sacralize and which the Spirit of Christ denounces as in the biblical world of 1 John 2. This reminds us that the contexts of mission differ greatly, even if the messianic thrust remains the same. It also means that the spin-offs of a messianic thrust may not always be identical in different contexts, but they are recognizable; they should be recognized for what they are—deviations—and not just as pluralism in missionary expression.

The fact that Anabaptism emerged as a messianic resurgence re-minds us of the latent possibilities within nonmessianic and establish-ment forms of Christian religiosity. These indeed are within the his-torical context of the Christian messianic cycle which contains its own potential, given the right conditions, for a resurgence oriented by the coming kingdom of Christ.

The Anabaptists with their simple grasp of the universal nature and call of the Great Commission never allowed that to hinder them from local, specific commitments as expressions of their obedience which others often interpreted as legalism. The hesitancy arising from sophisticated knowledge of inevitable sect cycles must not interfere with the freedom that sees messianic resurgency as God's own strategy for giving continuity to his purposes in the world. The "weight of sin that so easily besets us" must not receive the bias of favor; that rather must go to the newly created cells of enthusiastic obedience to the sov-ereign Lord of the coming kingdom.

The Anabaptist identification with the human suffering of Christ, the rejection of the then-current triumphalism of Christendom, and the awareness that espousal of violence was a refusal of Christ—all point to the specific messianism oriented by the suffering servant of Isaiah 53 as fulfilled in Jesus' life. This model of discernment in answer-ing "Who is the Lord?" remains absolutely urgent in our time. M. M. Thomas has written:

> The call to . . . three-fold liberation leading to freedom as mas-tery over nature, as search for self-identity and justice in so-ciety, and as creativity with openness to the future, clearly has arisen within the cultural and spiritual climate created by

what has been called "messianic" religions with their historical consciousness, though it has risen in protest against them;
and this messianism has been maintained even in the secular
ideologies of the modern period. In fact, with the forces of modernity making inroads into all cultures and societies, they
are all absorbing the messianic consciousness. . . . Therefore,
the spiritual question modernity poses for [humankind] is the
question of discerning the character of the messiah and the
messianic community and the nature of the hope of eschatological unity which will make freedom a promise of mature
humanity to men and women universally, and that of distinguishing them from messianisms which betray that promise
and dehumanize men and women.[56]

Finally, the eschatological kingdom orientation of the Anabaptists
remains the essential mainspring of mission—of Christian messianism.
Neither sixteenth-century deviations nor twentieth-century spiritu-
alisms, Mormon or Moonie, dare function to reduce the driving hope
that the history of all nations shall be fulfilled in a "new heaven and
a new earth" when "every knee shall bow and confess that Jesus the
Messiah is Lord."

Until that time the classic Anabaptist consensus remains perhaps
the most important missionary mentor that God has given the church
of Christ, except for their servant Lord and the first church that grew
out of the obedience of those whom he sent, when he said, "All power
is given me in heaven and on earth. Go, therefore, and make disciples of

---

[56] M. M. Thomas, "Two kinds of messianism," *Ecumenical Review* 26, no. 4 (1974):
558–59. The statement is all the more remarkable because of the author's own roots
in the sacral culture of India. In this connection, his concluding word should also be
heeded. In writing of the spirituality of the conquering messiah, the superman who
repudiates the suffering Messiah, which leads inevitably to aggressiveness, misuse of
earth's natural resources, abuse of power, etc., Thomas concludes: "Modern history,
with the inhumanities of Imperialism, Racism, Fascism and Stalinism, and Vietnam,
provides sufficient proof of this. Many moderns are therefore beginning to view
the messianic spiritual consciousness itself as the source of dehumanization in the
modern world and to advocate a return of [humankind] to the spiritual tranquility of
some form of nature-religion, or the unitive spiritual vision of the primal, monistic
and gnostic religions. This however would mean the repudiation of the whole experiment of modern history, of the search of men and women for adulthood and maturity
in freedom; it would even halt the self-awakening of the peoples of the two-thirds
world of Africa and Asia and the significant renaissance of their cultures and religions
taking place through the impact of modernity. [Humankind] can avoid these two
alternatives—self-destruction in freedom and survival through a return to the womb
of unfreedom—only through the messianism of the Suffering Servant" (ibid., 560).

all nations, baptizing them, . . . teaching them to observe all that I have commanded you; and lo, I am with you always, to the close of the age."

15

Reflections on relating long term to messianic communities

In 1967, when I was engaged in pastoral ministry in francophone Belgium,[1] my pacifist friend Jean van Lierde[2] telephoned to ask whether I was interested in meeting with two Kimbanguist leaders who were stopping off in Brussels, en route to Kinshasa from Copenhagen. "They wish to contact Belgian pastors, but I can't find anyone interested, because they are from an African sect, but it strikes me that this might be your kind of thing." I had never heard of Kimbanguism, so it was my first awareness of two-thirds world messianic movements.[3]

That call led to dinner in our home with "Citoyen" Lucien Luntadi-la, who was general secretary of the Church of Jesus Christ on the Earth by the Prophet Simon Kimbangu, and was accompanied by the personal secretary of Joseph Diangienda, the supreme head of the so-called Kimbanguist Church and son of the prophet Simon Kimbangu. To me, their story sounded strikingly similar to that of sixteenth-century Anabaptists. That meeting eventually led to the placement of volunteers from the Mennonite Central Committee and Eirene[4] at a Kimbanguist

---

Reprinted, with editorial changes, from *Evangelical, Ecumenical, and Anabaptist Missiologies in Conversation,* ed. James R. Krabill, Walter Sawatsky, and Charles E. Van Engen (Maryknoll, NY: Orbis Books, 2006), 149–57. Used by permission.

[1] The story of our ministry there is told in chapters 4, 8, and 9 of the present volume.

[2] Well known as a Catholic socialist and labor unionist, Jean van Lierde worked laboriously and successfully, with our wholehearted cooperation, for a legal statute for Belgian conscientious objectors. As president of the Belgian chapter of the Mouvement International de la Réconciliation he had returned from Copenhagen with the Kimbanguists, as pacifists invited by francophone secretary Jean Lasserre, who had earlier connected with them in Zaire.

[3] See, for example, Vittorio Lanternari, *The Religions of the Oppressed: A Study of Modern Messianic Cults* (London: McGibbon and Kee, 1963). The first edition in Italian was published in 1960.

[4] Eirene is a European service agency initiated by André Trocmé and others, together with the historic peace churches, to provide service outlets for conscientious objec-

experimental farm and several Kimbanguist schools, and ultimately in 1971 to an invitation to visit Diangienda in Kinshasa and his church in Nkamba on the occasion of the celebration of the fiftieth anniversary of its beginnings.[5]

Marked for life by encounters with messianic communities

I was marked for life by those contacts and the time spent with Diangienda. It was my first meeting with a head of such a community. At a time of transition in Belgium, those encounters contributed to our being open to an inquiry from Wilbert Shenk, then our mission agency's overseas secretary: Would Wilma and I consider my serving as a teacher of scripture in francophone West Africa, among so-called African Independent Churches (AICs)[6] that were emerging openly in the postcolonial "independence" of the 1960s. It was a major shift for me to move from the dechristianizing ethos of western Europe into the christianizing context of sub-Saharan Africa. Since then, we have had contacts with other such leaders including Ivorian John Ahui, supreme head of the Harrist Church; Dahomean Joseph Oschaffa, founder-head of the Church of Celestial Christianity; Nigerian primate Adejobi of the Church of the Lord (Aladura); Kenyan bishop Ngala, head of the Brotherhood Church, and the son of Zulu Isiah Shembe, who founded the Nazaretha Church of South Africa.

From 1979 to 1989[7] we were led to serve out of the Ebrié village of Blokosso-Abidjan, Côte d'Ivoire, at the invitation of several leaders of AICs in Cotonou (Dahomey) and of Ahui of the Ivorian Harrist Church, who was aware of my in-depth study of that church's founder, prophet William Wadé Harris (ca. 1860-1929).[8] For increased exposure to the

---

tors to military service from countries where such objection was not then legally recognized.

[5] I reported on this event in "An Indigenous African Church Comes of Age: Kimbanguism," *Mennonite Life* 27, no. 2 (1972): 53–55.

[6] The terminology was created by H. W. Turner as phenomenological language but rejected by the churches themselves. It later shifted to other forms, "African Indigenous Churches" (which was confused with mission-planted churches under African leadership), and then to "African-initiated churches," the more current usage.

[7] See my article, "A Decade with God's Mission among African-Initiated Churches in West Africa," *Mission Focus: Annual Review* 11 (2003): 85–104.

[8] See "A Prophet of Modern Times: The Thought of William Wadé Harris, West African Precursor of the Reign of Christ" (PhD diss., University of Aberdeen, Scotland,

Harrist reality, we drew deeply during this period from the learnings of our colleagues James and Jeanette Krabill living in the Dida Harrist village of Yocoboué.[9]

In addition to these contacts, I was invited to research the Bassa AICs in Liberia and ministered to leaders of AICs in Monrovia, to Ghanaian AIC leaders in Côte d'Ivoire, and to others in Cotonou, Benin. I also did related research in Kenya and South Africa for our Abidjan-based Documentation and Research Center managed by Wilma Shank for our Group for Religious and Biblical Studies. During two teaching terms at the Faculté de Théologie Evangélique de Bangui (FATEB) I connected with several AICs in the capital of the Central African Republic.

During those years we also related to the whole gamut of local Ivorian Christian expression.[10] In 1986 Wilma and I organized in Abidjan the first pan-African conference[11] of Westerners serving within a dozen such AICs, and in 1989, together with Dr. Marie-Louise Martin, we planned and hosted a second pan-African conference[12] that included a dozen leaders of AICs and Westerners who were serving among them.

Contacts with key African expressions of two-thirds-world messianism

Both the Kimbanguist Church and the Harrist churches have been major classic African embodiments of two-thirds-world messianism.[13] The Harrist Church began in 1913 as a mass movement of more than 100,000 people baptized within a year's time under Harris's impact, with village congregations in Ivory Coast and Gold Coast. It breathed

---

1980), 3 vols. Africanist Dr. Jocelyn Murray abridged it as *Prophet Harris, the "Black Elijah" of West Africa* (Leiden: E. J. Brill, 1994).

[9] Some of those experiences are reflected in James R. Krabill, *The Hymnody of the Harrist Church among the Dida of South Central Ivory Coast, 1913-1949* (Frankfurt am Main: Peter Lang, 1995).

[10] In *L'Afrique en crise: Quelles perspectives?* (Abidjan: Presses Bibliques Africaines, 1999), I addressed the larger African Christian scene.

[11] See David A. Shank, ed., *Ministry of Missions to African Independent Churches* (Elkhart, IN: Mennonite Board of Missions, 1987).

[12] See David A. Shank, ed., *Ministry in Partnership with African Independent Churches* (Elkhart, IN: Mennonite Board of Missions, 1991). The consultation called for the creation of a journal, the *Review of AICs*, as an instrument of communication.

[13] On this term, see H. Kohn, "Messianism," in *Encyclopedia of Social Sciences,* (New York: Macmillan, 1933), 10:358, where Kohn defines *messianism* as "primarily a religious belief in the coming of a redeemer who will end the present order of things, either universally or for a single group, and institute a new order of justice and happiness."

life into an impotent Catholic mission, became the source of an Ivorian Methodist church a decade later, and opened the populations to other Western missions. Only since 1998 is it a member of the World Council of Churches (WCC), and it reports members in Liberia, Côte d'Ivoire, Ghana, Burkina Faso, and Benin.

The Kimbanguist movement began in 1921 in the Lower Congo with the ministry of Simon Kimbangu. Despite severe Belgian colonial persecution that pushed it underground, it has since reportedly grown to well over five million members in the countries of central Africa. It is a member of the WCC. Both Harris and Kimbangu saw themselves as Christian prophets within the larger movement of Christ's work and coming kingdom. But the impact of each was such that they were often misinterpreted by their followers and others[14] as an "African Christ" (Harris), or as "the promised Holy Spirit" (Kimbangu). Dr. Marie-Louise Martin became a member of the Kimbanguist Church and taught for two decades in their theological training center. Her odyssey within that messianic movement was during its amazing rapid growth in the postcolonial context, and a major dimension of her ministry was seeking to correct misperceptions. My relationship with the Harrist Church (1979–89) as an invited outsider happened more than sixty-five years after the powerful movement that initiated it, during a time of its seeking status as a national religious institution.

Simultaneously, many and diverse AICs of Benin[15] shared a developing Christology, a strong Holy Spirit dynamic, and an eschatology of imminence. It was a grassroots messianic movement emerging out of traditional African religion, under a failing Marxist regime. Through the sponsorship of the regime-recognized Interconfessional Protestant Council of Benin and its president, Pastor Harry Henry,[16] I was invited to lead annual five-day Bible seminars specifically oriented to AIC leaders (1983–89). Despite the amazing diversity of the Beninese AIC leaders, I witnessed annually their deeply shared, dynamic sense of the

---

[14] For example, Christopher Wondji, *Le Prophète Harris: Le Christ Noir des Lagunes* (Paris: ABC; Dakar et Abidjan: Nouvelles Éditions Africaines, 1977).

[15] Benin became the Marxist regime's name for the former French colonial Dahomey. We served more than thirty churches there, described in some detail in James R. Krabill, ed., *Nos racines racontées* (Abidjan: Presses Bibliques Africaines, 1996), 42–70.

[16] Pastor Henry, as president of the Benin Methodist Church, and Bishop Ed Weaver met providentially and shared concerns about AICs at the All-African Council of Christian Churches meeting in Abidjan in 1968. By 1983, Henry had also become the executive officer of the AACCC.

("already") presence of the ("not yet") coming messianic kingdom of God.[17]

Three questions worth asking about our ministry with AICs

I can scarcely believe how much significant learning we appropriated from African peoples, history, culture, traditional religion, and Christianity, affected by such forces as Islam, "new world" slave traffic, European colonialism, Western modernity, and the Western missionary enterprise. We learned experientially[18] that there are indeed substantial cultural and spiritual differences between Western Christianity and African Christianity. The life, spontaneity, color, dynamism, creativity, and spread of African Christianity amid the traditional spirit world transformed me. My reflections here are really answers to questions that come to me more or less spontaneously fifteen years after our African ministry.

Was the missiological strategy worth the investment of funds, time and energy?

As missiologist and administrator for Mennonite Board of Missions, Wilbert Shenk never questioned, to our knowledge, the cost of our involvement in this unique ministry. Although for Shenk the ministry of the word of Christ was essential, and strategy for investment of personnel and funds was important, his questions seemed to us rather to be: Where is the Spirit calling us to serve? What does it mean to be obedient to the Spirit? What is the Spirit teaching us through our experiences of obedience? How does what the Spirit teaches us inform our decisions and commitments?[19]

In addition to whatever Spirit-led good may have been accomplished on the terrain, there were also especially the exceptional learnings shared with the larger worldwide missiological community.

---

[17] For more details on these Bible-teaching experiences, see Rodney Hollinger-Janzen, "A Biblical Teaching Program by the Interconfessional Protestant Council of Benin with Mennonite Cooperation," in Ministry in Partnership, ed. Shank, 161–70.

[18] Our beloved mentor Andrew Walls at Aberdeen so taught us, but we learned it in Africa. Walls saw the African theologians becoming the African church fathers, similar to the Greek and Latin church fathers.

[19] In late 1970, I returned from Belgium to the United States to lecture in Mennonite circles on the Holy Spirit and mission. See David A. Shank, His Spirit First (Scottdale, PA: Herald Press, 1971).

It would seem retrospectively that the investment was fully justified. But it was not evident a priori.

What informed the stance we took as workers in ministry with AICs?

We went as teachers of scripture in response to specific invitations from AICs at a time when full-time missionaries were leaving Africa en masse, to the cry of "Missionary, go home!" Should we, like Dr. Martin with the Kimbanguists, have sought to become members of the Harrist Church? Identified openly as Mennonites, but as a study group rather than a mission, we took the stance of participant-observers. When not invited elsewhere on a Sunday morning, Wilma and I attended Ebrié Harrist services quite regularly in the villages of Anono, Cocody, or Petit Bassam—the Harrist "mother" church. And we were often invited out to Attié, Alladian, Adjukru, Agni, or Dida congregations and celebrations. Like Harrists, we always dressed in white for worship, and often integrated with the *koya* (choir) in the dancing to the home of the head preacher for closing prayers. At festive meals, we were always seated with the preachers. But we were not Harrists, or seen as Harrists.

There were always those who mistrusted our motives, since the well-established tradition was that Western missionaries always took charge and determined the "foreign" religious patterns. After all—some Harrists wondered—were the Mennonites not really interested in recuperating Harrist church members for their mission, in the way the Catholics and the Methodists had done?[20]

During those years I was never invited to speak, teach, or preach inside a Harrist church, in the area behind the pulpit—the exclusive domain of Harrist preachers, apostles, and elders. As a "specialist," an "invited guest," or a "good friend," I would be invited to "speak" or "lecture" or "share," often under an outdoor *apatam*[21] prepared for the occasion beside or near the church building. There, other villagers—Catholics, Methodists, Muslims, or *païens* ("pagans," the local term)—were often invited along with Harrists to hear publicly the story of their prophet hero as told with understanding and appreciation by this

---

[20] Even a trusted Ebrié consultant such as (Methodist) ambassador Ernest Amos-Djoro suspected this, as reported in his doctoral thesis at the Sorbonne, on post-Harris developments in Côte d'Ivoire.

[21] A temporary framework of branches covered with palm branches, constructed as a shelter from the equatorial sun.

rare "white" who had done a lot of research about Harris and strongly affirmed his ministry. Indeed, other local Christian traditions looked down on and derided the prophet as just another untrained, illiterate, "spirit-power" worker, one of the many impostors and charlatans that emerged during the successive crises subsequent to the imposition of French colonial rule during the early twentieth century.[22] Even if we as Mennonites had wished to identify fully with the Harrist Church, it became clear during the presidency of the youthful rising star Tchotche-Mel Felix that it would have been unthinkable because of the constant internal political chatter about the church being a strictly African achievement untainted by *les blancs* ("white people").

For our mission among the Benin AIC leaders, it was absolutely necessary that we be outsiders and not members of any of the local churches, or of a denominational church-planting mission. Indeed, in the early years, the intense competition between the local AICs, in part because of the acknowledged practice of mutual "sheep-stealing" between them, made it inevitable that if we started to plant churches we would be seen as one more competitor, further advantaged by the teaching role we had been invited to assume. The necessary trust in this outsider role had to be earned, session after session, day after day, year after year.

Over a period of seven years, the annual seminar which first began with only a dozen heads of churches developed into a gathering of about 140 participants from nearly forty denominations. It was that trust in the outsiders'—in this case, the Mennonites'—biblical theology that permitted the grassroots movement, particularly after the demise of the Marxist regime, to become a multichurch cooperation in the development of a clinic/hospital, a Bible institute, a multi-city program of garbage collection hiring seven hundred workers, and programs of cooperative village development, mostly among AIC people, as monitored by Mennonite Service of Benin. Yet how often during this period Western Mennonite workers wished that they had a local "Mennonite" church on location . . . just for show-and-tell!

How important was it to work from a historical perspective?

A significant initial tool for our ministry was a set of principles for work among AICs that had been developed under the initiative of Wilbert

---

[22] See, for example, Bohumil Holas, *Le séparatisme religieux en Afrique noire: L'exemple de la Côte d'Ivoire* (Paris: Presses Universitaires de France, 1965); and more recently, Jean-Pierre Dozon, *La cause des prophètes* (Paris: Éditions du Seuil, 1995).

Shenk, on the basis of Edwin and Irene Weaver's work in Uyo, Nigeria. These principles called for a relationship that would take seriously a given AIC's history.[23] We took such an approach among the Harrists, since Bible teaching was difficult to implement despite our formal invitation from the church's supreme head, John Ahui, to teach the Bible. Although leading preachers, such as Staff-Carrier Akpé Léon of Anono, openly desired it, the Bible-teaching pattern never developed among the Ebrié and Attié around greater Abidjan, because certain of their influential preachers and leaders mistrusted any such initiative.

Bible-teaching initiatives by colleague James Krabill did however emerge among the Dida to the west, under the initiative of Apostle Beugré Lévry Modeste of Mené, and Head Preacher N'Guessan Légré Benoît of Yocoboué, with the full approval and blessing of Supreme Head Ahui. But my formal ministry at a national level and among the Ebrié and Attié was limited largely to a role of historian-specialist and documentalist of the Prophet Harris. Many of the prophet's own important biblical and Christian understandings and convictions were not a functional part of the Harrist tradition, so when I lectured I would seek to communicate some of those elements, relating them to Harrist symbolism that he had determined.

I interpreted Harris in the context of one of their own oral traditions, stronger among the Dida than among Harrists closer to Abidjan, that saw Harris as fulfilling Christ's ministry in Africa, "since Jesus never got to Africa because the whites killed him." It challenged the important Ebrié and Attié oral tradition that placed Harris in a special prophetic role for Africans parallel to those of Jesus for whites and Muhammad for Arabs.[24] I sought to communicate the good news of the grace and peace of the biblical messianic worldview fulfilled in

---

[23] "Respecting history. . . . We must be prepared to travel with a people into their past if we are to understand their present and future." See "Ministry among African Independent Churches," *Mission Focus* 9, no. 3 (September 1981): 44.

[24] This view was articulated as early as 1956 in the first published Harrist catechism, *Premier livret de l'éducation à l'usage de l'Épiscopat* (Petit Bassam: Programme de l'Épiscopat, 1956). It is not clear to what extent "helpful outsiders," seeing the largely illiterate movement at that time as an asset in the movement for political independence, gave their own explicit interpretations in a context of confusion, rather than the personal thought of the illiterate John Ahui, the head of the church. Ever since our first meeting with Ahui in 1973, his talk to us was always Christ oriented. In any case, as Harrist youth became literate starting in the 1960s, they tended to rely on the interpretation provided in the *Livret*. The Christ-oriented Prophet Harris that I presented was often, indeed, a revelation.

Christ through the story of their prophet whose thought I had learned through careful historical research.[25]

The Harrists' own catechism had accented Harris's exemplary non-violence, but not in relation to Christ. By taking the fuller story of Harris seriously in this way, I sought to strengthen the larger movement's christological orientation. This was particularly well understood by the schooled younger generation,[26] which ultimately took over the national leadership and guided the church's admission into the World Council of Churches in 1998, less than a decade after our departure. The fact that I was in some ways clearer about the prophet's thought than they were was probably seen by some as a threat, since it could challenge established leaders and provoke unwanted change.

Three key lessons learned along the way

Understanding the nexus between traditional African spirituality and Christian faith

The many parallels between socioreligious expressions of primal religion[27] in the Old Testament scriptures and within the living religious reality of traditional Africa are so striking as to impose a recognition of God at work long before the advent of Western missions. How that becomes fulfilled through the grace and peace of Jesus Christ is "messianism," a major concern of the *missio Dei.* Here the tools of Dr. Turner's analyses became for us an important point of departure. As Turner pointed out, the diverse primal religions of Africanity, shaken by the Western colonial project and the highly Westernized Christian missionary project, gave rise to a whole gamut of religious movements.[28]

---

[25] Already in 1983 I had published "Bref résumé de la pensée du prophete William Wadé Harris," *Perspectives Missionnaires* 5 (1983): 34–54. Several thousand copies of the sixteen-page offprint found their way into the hands of Harrist youth.

[26] This was clear already during our mission, as evidenced in Paul William Ahui, *Le Prophéte William Wadé Harris: Son message d'humilité et de progrès* (Abidjan: Les Nouvelles Éditions Africaines, 1988). Its bibliography included my doctoral thesis and my comprehensive bibliographical analysis with its conclusions.

[27] We were deeply indebted to our mentor, Dr. Harold W. Turner, for his expositions, analyses, and appreciation of what he called "primal" (not primary or primitive, but rather prior and foundational) religious phenomena, as inspired by the concept of the numinous in Rudolf Otto's *The Idea of the Holy* (1917).

[28] See Harold W. Turner, "Classification and Nomenclature of Modern African Religious Groups (Chart)," in *African Independent Church Movements,* ed. Victor E. Hayward (London: Edinburgh House Press, 1963), 13.

Such movements ranged from neotraditional and synthesist to Hebraist and independent churches, as African-created realties, each with their own hymnody, structures, spiritual dynamic, and vital preoccupations. Most of these latter movements intend to be Christ-oriented-but were yet independent from the Western, mainline mission-planted churches, and then were often not accepted by them as authentic churches.

As we became acquainted with many individual Christians from different mission-founded and African-initiated churches, this schema suggested what was to become an important learning: Africans tend to "convert" from African traditional religion to New Testament understandings of faith through an itinerary of successive stages of faith[29] in which spirit(s) and the Holy Spirit confront and interact variously to effect transformations, not wholly unlike in scripture the fulfillment of God's covenants in Israel amid the Baals. In such a perspective, the Harrist Church could be seen as a significant religious achievement in movement, even though largely "blocked" at a Hebraist-like stage (God, clergy, law, ritual, holy place)[30] in its itinerary in which the new covenant messianic pull forward of the love of Christ and his Spirit was not a vital part of its living tradition. At the same time, one discovered many individual Harrists for whom the latter was a vital reality, even as one learned that in Western mission-initiated churches there could be many Christians who, like the Harrist movement, were really novices en route to a full-orbed Christian faith.[31] But the emerging itinerary, when solicited by the good news of Christ, his teaching and his Spirit, was indeed messianic.

This became our understanding of the dynamics happening within African Christianity as a whole, and oriented our ministry among the Harrists and with the AICs in Benin. One senses retrospectively that as cultural foreigners to religious life and practice in sub-Saharan Africa, it was an important dimension of our learning, fully recognized and confirmed over and over again by Africans themselves.[32]

[29] More detail is provided on this matter in chapter 13 of the present volume.

[30] In 1973, a highly qualified Ivorian informant with Harrist parents told us that the pressures of Islam, descending from the north, "will simply absorb the Harrists into Islam; they have no other option."

[31] See particularly the account of Catholic missionary Jean-Paul Eschlimann in chapter 13 of the present volume.

[32] When I shared these ideas with theology students at a Kenyan theological seminary, they spontaneously stood and applauded at some length, only to hear their Dutch theology professor insist that they should attach no importance to it whatsoever.

Understanding the dynamics of messianism

Working with a messianic movement called for an appreciation of the ways such movements typically develop. Both the Harrist Church and the diverse grassroots AICs of Benin were such movements. However, at the time of our involvements, each was at a quite different place in the typical dynamics of such a movement. But what are those dynamics, and how does one do such discernment? It was the work of Henri Desroche, then France's doyen of sociologists of religion, whose work was to provide an inestimably important key for our understanding.

Desroche explained to me how as a former Dominican worker priest he was obliged to deal at the grass roots with the way the French working class was literally obsessed with Marx's dictum that religion is the opium of the people. It sent him back to the study of history. There he discovered that the early church missionary endeavors, and many so-called sectarian movements, had often been moving at the forefront of transformative sociopolitical change. As he systematically studied their histories, he observed that with only a couple of exceptions in traditional societies, they have been largely inspired by the Hebrew-Christian messianic, eschatological hope.

A too-brief summary of the typical dynamics of Desroche's "messianic circle" is as follows. In a context of oppression or alienation, a "messiah" (God-sent deliverer) is either expected (Judaism), or come (Christ), and (possibly) will return (Christ, as believed by Harris and Kimbangu) in order to establish a new religio-socio-political order of justice, peace, and prosperity/well-being. The serious followers break with the old order and (1) emerge in (already) holistic religio-socio-political communities, which become both a serious critique of the old and a foreshadowing of the (not yet) coming fully new. In the face of opposition, loss of nerve, disbelief, disappointment, or nonappearance, the new holistic community may well seek to persevere but is typically (2) either sidetracked into a largely religious orientation, or (3) into a largely political one, both of which tend to reinterpret partial accents of the original holistic direction of the movement. The movement ultimately either abandons its original vision and (4) returns to the previous state, makes peace with the old religious order, or seeks power to change the old status quo by revolution or political evolution. With time and in new conditions, the original holistic religio-socio-political élan may be recovered by either of the sidetracked itineraries, with a messianic resurgence redirected as in the original thrust of the movement.[33]

In this perspective, the Harrist Church in 1979, originally seen by French colonial authorities as an autonomous religiopolitical threat, and in the 1940s and 1950s as an important grassroots movement for political independence, had become a largely religious sidetrack that simply confirmed and supported the Ivorian political status quo, yet was still receiving members out of traditional *fétichisme.*

Benin's AIC communities, on the other hand, were in the midst of their initial enthusiastic élan with significant social dynamic through changed lives at the grass roots,[34] including, with Mennonite accompaniment, their Bible institute, clinic/hospital, multi-city service of garbage collection, and village development. My ministry among these churches (1983–89) was necessarily different from that among the Harrists; it was quite particular for each, since each was at a different place within the typical dynamics of messianism.

Seen in this way, it was essential for the Harrists to reconnect their movement to a christological dynamic where the coming reign of Messiah Jesus and his Spirit would become once again the forefront of the institutionalized movement, as it had been for Prophet Harris, the founder of their church.[35] On the other hand, it was essential for the Benin AICs to understand that their communities were not a religious sidetrack absorbed through Western evangelicalism for how to get to heaven and not be left behind, but as transformed signs of the vast reign of God that in turn were called to transform society as leaven and salt. More importantly, Desroche's messianic circle led me to understand and relate in a new way to all Christian churches and movements.

When the genius and dynamic of Christianity with its many diverse ecclesial expressions is understood as a messianic movement, then the

---

[33] I had come to understand these dynamics as a shaper of mission in August 1978, prior to our mission in West Africa (1979–89). See "The Shape of Mission," in *Mission Focus* 8, no. 4 (December 1980): 69–74, where I portray a variation of Desroche's "messianic circle." (See figure 1. *Processes and stages of the messianic dynamic,* in chapter 6 of the present volume.)

[34] Dr. Daniel Goldschmidt-Nussbaumer, the French Mennonite physician who was the originator/overseer of the African-staffed clinic-become-hospital, explained: "I need the whole gamut of [non-Roman] Christianity for it to work: the Methodists for their sociopoliticial status and connections, the 'evangelicals' for their expertise in crossing a 't' and dotting an 'i,' the AICs for absolute integrity at the cash register and the medicine supply, and the white-robed, barefooted women of the prophet movements for preparing food for the crowd waiting in the courtyard."

[35] So my argument in "Bref résumé."

direction of movement becomes the preoccupation of dialogue and so-called interchurch relations. Congregations and denominations as well as individual Christians tend to move in four basic directions:

1. **forward as disciplined messianic communities,** oriented by Jesus' coming kingdom of God, working to recreate holistic religious, social, economic life under the authority of Jesus Christ, in costly interaction of service to and challenge from the surrounding religio-socio-political culture;

2. **religious sidetracking** as doctrinal institutions working at dealing strictly religiously with the unavoidable spiritual problems of human existence and destiny;

3. **sociopolitical sidetracking** as activist institutions working essentially at shifting political, social, and economic disparities, whether by revolution or reform;

4. **backward as established societal institutions** providing religious affirmation for the dominant, oppressive, unjust sociocultural status quo.

Within that framework, a given congregation or denomination may be seen as more or less oriented in one of those directions, but not all directions are of equal significance in the messianic intention. The messianic community may often be described as sectarian by the three other general tendencies, but is not troubled by the onus placed on it. Rather, it anticipates both individual resurgents and collective resurgences out of the other directions, in virtue of the reality of Messiah and the coming kingdom. And it will recognize the strong pulls of the other directions with their attractions and gains.

My growing awareness of these realities within Christianity made it more and more evident that my own Mennonite denomination had emerged, in fact, from a crucial dimension of messianic resurgence among the sixteenth century's types of reformation.[36] As a somewhat "hardened" socioreligious entity, it had experienced its own messianic resurgence by seeking to fulfill under Orie O. Miller, J. D. Graber, and Wilbert Shenk the apostolic mission inherent in its Anabaptist roots, as reformulated by Harold S. Bender and his students, such as the initial

---

[36] Types could include: Catholic/Anglican, Lutheran/Spiritualist, Calvinist/Reformed, Anabaptist.

Concern Group,[37] even as the Roman Catholic Church sought to do in Vatican II.[38]

My perspectives on mission thus have been shaped by my answers to these important questions: in this particular ecclesial context, where do I discern its place and direction to be within the messianic circle, and how can I best encourage and help to orient, reorient, and reshape that context as a messianic community and a sign of the kingdom of God? Retrospectively, for me, the convergence of biblical theology, the Anabaptist/Mennonite story,[39] and Desroche's messianic circle illuminated[40] our African experience.

---

[37] I refer to the influence and published works of Irvin Horst, John W. Miller, Paul Peachey, Calvin Redekop, John Howard Yoder, and myself; this group gathered in Amsterdam, Easter 1952, and began publishing Concern (1954–72). Without any reference to Desroche's messianic circle, historian Paul Toews underlines the significance for Mennonites of the messianic community as clarified in Yoder's *Politics of Jesus* (Grand Rapids, MI: Eerdmans, 1972); see Toews's *Mennonites in American Society, 1930-1970* (Scottdale, PA: Herald Press, 1996), 234–37, 334–42. Yoder, working earlier for Mennonite Board of Missions, saw some parallels with AICs in his efforts to understand and interpret the Weavers' work at Uyo, Nigeria. Of that Concern Group, I alone was privileged to work extensively among Christian believers emerging from what Turner called "primal religions" and could thus formally relate the messianic resurgence of Anabaptism and two-thirds-world messianic movements through the Desroche typology.

[38] The newly created expression *populus messianicus* is found twice in *Lumen Gentium*, no. 9. Fr. Yves Congar, who later published *Un peuple messianique* (Paris: Éditions du Cerf, 1975), had tried during Vatican II to enter the same expression into a passage of *Ad Gentes,* no. 5, but it was erased during corrections and revisions. The insertions were inspired by Msgr. Marty, archbishop of Rheims, who had been alerted to the significance of two-thirds world messianic movements by Fr. M.-D. Chenu, who had followed these as a personal interest. The expression is not a description of the Roman Church but of God's intention that the church of Christ be a messianic people, living out in the world the life and virtues of the Messiah, who has come and is coming.

[39] John H. Yoder's studies in the sixteenth-century Swiss Reformation had led him to discern independently the outworking of a four-directional pattern in the break-up of medieval Christianity. See his "A People in the World: A Theological Interpretation," in *The Concept of the Believers' Church,* ed. James Leo Garrett, Jr. (Scottdale, PA: Herald Press, 1969), 250–83.

[40] Indeed, the 1989 seminar at Cotonou, gathering 140 leaders of churches predominantly in the greater Cotonou area, providentially treated the "Sermon on the Mount and the Kingdom of God" at a time when the collapse of the Marxist regime was imminent and active party members were in attendance. That week of intense teaching, taken back into the many local churches *à l'africaine,* made its own grassroots contribution to the nonviolent "velvet revolution" via a popular Cotonou assembly presided over by the nonviolent Msgr. Isidore de Souza, former rector of the Catholic institute in Abidjan.

Understanding the important contribution of African Christian theology

Was our work just one more illustration of Western Christianity imposing Western (in this case, Mennonite) interpretations and understandings on an emerging African Christianity?[41]

In fact, my doctoral research on the Prophet Harris had exposed a significant African Christian theology, and it was messianic.[42] African Christian theology must by definition be an African creation out of Africans' appropriation of scripture and its interaction with their own worldview, history, spirituality, and vital concerns. I saw my task as teacher of scripture not as an attempt to create or to teach African theology but to expose the scriptures, as best I knew, in their eschatological and messianic perspective as fulfilled in the Messiah Jesus with his empowering Spirit and his promises and work of fulfillment in and through his messianic community. The Africans' appropriation of that teaching[43] and its experiential practice and transmission can then become African Christian theology.

As I reflect back on the richness of our years in Africa, I carry an immense debt of thankfulness to African neighbors, friends, sisters, and brothers in Christ the Messiah, and wish to extend to them sincere apologies for all my Western, American, and missionary faux pas. But I am indeed grateful for being enabled to teach, at their request, our common scriptures and their own Christian history, to provide tools for them to do their own African Christian theologizing. What a blessing, indeed, as an outsider, to have been personally enriched by such deep involvement during a decade in which more than 55 million Africans reportedly entered into the stream of the Spirit, faith, life, and hope opened up by the Messiah of the new covenant of the wholly other God.

---

[41] In the editor's preface to my book, *Prophet Harris, the "Black Elijah" of West Africa,* Adrian Hastings writes that "Dr. Shank has given us not just a rewriting of history but also the sensitive reconstruction of a complex theology: an African theology, most certainly, but no less a genuinely biblical theology; the personal theology of Harris but, no less, a popular theology whose appeal was convincing for thousands" (ix).

[42] Indeed, the three most influential African Christian prophets, who ministered "outside" missionary circles—Harris, Kimbangu, and Ntsikana (in South Africa)—were all empowered by a messianic dynamic.

[43] In AIC seminars in Benin, for example, a third of each half-day session was committed in small group discussion to the process of contextualization by the participants themselves.

16

John Howard Yoder, strategist for mission with African-initiated churches

Theologian John Howard Yoder's role in developing a strategy for Mennonite ministries with African independent—or indigenous, initiated—churches (AICs) is scarcely known or appreciated. The recent volume by Yoder biographer and specialist Mark Thiessen Nation[1] makes no allusion to it; the index does not include the words "Africa," "Independent churches," "Nigeria," "Uyo," or "Weaver." *The Uyo Story,*[2] Edwin and Irene Weaver's seminal volume on pioneering Mennonite ministries to AICs in southeastern Nigeria, traces those frustrating beginnings in 1959 under Mennonite Board of Missions (MBM). But no mention is made of Weavers' crucial correspondence and partnership in dialogue with John Howard Yoder, the young administrative assistant to MBM's executive secretary, J. D. Graber.

Yoder's service at MBM from 1959 to 1967[3] fully coincided with the Weavers' pioneering ministry in eastern Nigeria. Indeed, the challenges of their novel situation were one of the first things on Yoder's agenda when he started with MBM at Elkhart in 1959. Similarly, Yoder is but briefly referenced in James Krabill's recent, excellent summary

---

Reprinted, with editorial changes, from *Mission Focus: Annual Review* 15 (2007): 195–217. Used by permission.

[1] Mark Thiessen Nation, *John Howard Yoder: Mennonite Patience, Evangelical Witness, Catholic Convictions* (Grand Rapids, MI: Eerdmans, 2006).

[2] Edwin and Irene Weaver, *The Uyo Story* (Elkhart: Mennonite Board of Missions, 1970).

[3] Yoder's mandates at MBM were as follows: 1959–65, full-time as administrative assistant for overseas missions; and 1965–70, associate consultant. During this same period, Yoder served as part-time instructor at Associated Mennonite Biblical Seminaries, 1960–65, and from 1965 onward, full-time professor at AMBS, with occasional courses at the University of Notre Dame beginning in 1967.

of such Mennonite ministries in West Africa.[4] And I made no allusion to him in the summaries of our ministries in West Africa.[5] Indeed, I have consistently spoken or written of the "Weaver strategy" of ministry with AICs.

The Weavers' further work in Ghana[6] involved the creation of The Good News Bible Training Institute in Accra, and Ed's West African study trips led to ministries with AICs in Benin, Côte d'Ivoire, and Liberia. The Weavers pioneered further in opening up such ministries in southern Africa: for Africa Inter-Mennonite Mission in Botswana, Lesotho, and Transkei; for Eastern Mennonite Board of Missions in Swaziland; for Mennonite Central Committee (MCC) there as well as in Lesotho,[7] and most recently, for Mennonite Mission Network in South Africa.

Only by 1980—two decades after the Uyo beginnings—had MBM finally approved a policy statement for such ministries, as summarized and drawn up by MBM Overseas Secretary Wilbert Shenk, Graber's and Yoder's successor in 1967. It is he who has recently credited Yoder for this significant missiological contribution: "Yoder's gifts of penetrating analysis, theological acuity, wide acquaintance with both ecumenical and evangelical missions, and awareness of the literature of the day were crucial to the process."[8] Missiologist Joon-Sik Park more recently quoted Shenk and added: "Particularly [Yoder's] understanding of ecumenism was highly relevant to the very conflicting, confusing and fragmentary church situation in that region. In that environment, he

---

[4]   James R. Krabill, "Evangelical and Ecumenical Dimensions of Walking with AICs," in *Evangelical, Ecumenical, and Anabaptist Missiologies in Conversation*, ed. James R. Krabill, Walter Sawatsky, and Charles E. Van Engen (Maryknoll, NY: Orbis Books, 2006), 240–47.

[5]   "A Decade with God's Mission among African-Initiated Churches in West Africa," *Mission Focus Annual Review* 11, no. 23 (2004): 85–104; and my more recent "Reflections on Relating Long-Term to Messianic Communities," in Evangelical, Ecumenical, ed. Krabill et al., 149–57. The latter piece is reprinted as chapter 15 in the present volume.

[6]   Edwin and Irene Weaver, *From Kuku Hill: Among Indigenous Churches in West Africa*, Missionary Studies Series, no. 3 (Elkhart, IN: Institute of Mennonite Studies, 1975).

[7]   See their *Letters from Southern Africa* (Elkhart, IN: Council of [Mennonite] Mission Board Secretaries/S. African Task Force, 1974).

[8]   Wilbert R. Shenk, "'Go Slow Through Uyo': Dialogue as Missionary Method," in *Fullness of Life for All: Challenges for Mission in the Early 21st Century*, ed. Inus Daneel, Charles Van Engen, and Hendrik Vroom (New York: Editions Rodopi, 2003), 334. The article has a dozen or so footnotes with references to Yoder's correspondence relative to the AIC phenomenon.

argued for Christian unity as a biblical call and imperative."[9] Unfortunately, however, Park does not there give the reader a clear understanding that Shenk and he are both referring to a strategy for the relations of Western missions and their mission-planted churches to the more than 225 AICs within a five-mile radius of Uyo. Park's text simply refers to Yoder as a "mission strategist" who "developed a new kind of postcolonial mission strategy for southeastern Nigeria."[10]

Yoder did indeed develop such a strategy, but—as noted above—his approach would reach well beyond that parochial Nigerian situation. Several dozen Mennonite missionaries would become involved with long-term assignments in eight other countries in West and southern Africa. Several graduate theses and dissertations were to emerge from those relationships, as did several all-Africa conferences grouping other denominations with Mennonites working at such ministries across Africa, along with some of the AIC leaders. A *Review of AICs* for networking and dialogue among those involved in such ministry was published regularly for fifteen years. And Yoder's strategizing enabled a remarkable development in Benin which emerged out of a series of annual Bible seminars starting with a dozen AIC leaders: the Benin Bible Institute, the Bethesda clinic, a small-investment lending program for village women, and a garbage collection processing industry—starting with Cotonou and now involving several other important cities.

The best way to spell out Yoder's crucial contribution is to illustrate Wilbert Shenk's summary of his contribution by letting Yoder speak for himself through a selection of half a dozen documents from the decade of the 1960s. The first of these is dated November 21, 1961, and was sent to Robert Nelson, General Secretary of the United Christian Missionary Society of the Disciples Church.[11] It was written from Boucq, France, where Yoder was then living with his young family while serving with Mennonite Board of Missions.

---

[9] See Joon-Sik Park, "John Howard Yoder as a Mission Theologian," *International Bulletin of Missionary Research* 30, no. 1 (January 2006): 14.

[10] An earlier publication of Park's article (*Mennonite Quarterly Review* 78, no 3 [July 2004]: 363–84) did quote Alan Kreider (365n9) concerning the effect of this ministry of Yoder, that is, "a Mennonite involvement for the first time among Western missionaries in the life of African Independent Churches (whom Yoder saw as having parallels with the Anabaptists) without seeking to build Mennonite churches or add to Mennonite global numbers" (personal correspondence, March 13, 2004).

[11] Mennonite Church USA Archives: Hist. Mss. 1-48; 85/37, John H. Yoder (1927–1997): African Independents 1965–69.

Your letter of the 9th followed me to France, where I am spending a year in a mixture of furlough, ecumenical brainstorming, missions administration[12] and writing. I'll try to answer only the second section, since whatever damage was done by the way the IMC/WCC merger procedings [sic] were handled is by now irrevocable.

I think my letter to you acknowledged Donald McGavran as the man who directed me to you; I rather expected that meanwhile he would also have shared with you the vision that seemed already more than half-hatched when he visited us some months ago.

The entire dream hangs on the presupposition of a specifically free-church vision of what church unity means, a vision which for historical purposes may be qualified as "anabaptist" but whose most prominent American incarnation has been the Disciples' tradition.

Current gobbledygook about the "organic" nature of the unity we seek only confuses the discussion as to whether it does or does not mean hierarchical polity. Nor does fundamentalist counter-gobbledygook about "spiritual unity" and the virtues of the competitive economy help.

Granted the specificity of the Free Church vision of the Church's unity and mission, we who by heritage represent that tradition must admit that much of our missionary machinery and much of our *recent* [Yoder's italics] ecumenical organizing ignores our tradition if it does not in fact betray it. The McGavran vision presupposes that repentance and renewal are possible at this point.

We now know about what is wrong with the host of autonomous indigenous churches in West Africa; Calabar, where we [MBM] are working with the blessing of the older missions in groups they formerly ignored [AICs], is the home of some of the most flagrant rackets. Yet what we forget is the extent to which this phenomenon was provoked by the unbiblical, unwise, unanthropological, and un-free-church approach of the

[12] Yoder was administering MBM's program in Europe—including our ministry in Belgium—and Algerian ministries amid the war for Algerian independence. See Marian Hostetler, *Algeria: Where Mennonites and Muslims Met, 1958-1978* (Elkhart, IN: Marian Hostetler Edition, 2003).

dominant missions. Administering from the top down because the local congregational life was thought either not to exist, or not to be trustworthy, disciplined by the rule book without regard for the inadequacy of (e.g.) European marriage patterns, led in worship in post-reformation concentration on the sermon and elimination of the aesthetic, ministered to by paid mission trainees to the exclusions of the multiplicity of native gifts given by God in the local fellowship, these mission churches were asking for what finally came. And we should be the first to understand the "independents" without approving of their methods.

The dreams of the major missions and Christian councils, dominated as they are by churches of the pedobaptist and state-church traditions, call for these independents to be brought back into a structurally "united church." They are willing to be a little more tactful with the discipline, a little more patient with the babes in faith, and a little more permissive with drums and hand-clapping, but basically the pattern has not changed.

I submit that there is another approach, just as honest and responsible as that of the Christian Councils, but more biblical, and incomparably more likely to be helpful. It will take some doing to work out a clear grasp of how it differs from the mine-run ecumenists on the one side and the free-competition freelancers on the other, but it can be done. The key is a fundamental respect for the reality and the reliability of the work of the Spirit of Christ in the local congregation, whatever the educational level of the minister or the moral achievements of its members. Serving this reality, and not getting all the churches of a given area into one synod, would be our first concern. This *leitmotif* would permit a coordinated program of service to the independent churches, with no effort to line them up as Mennonite, Disciples, or Baptist, and a subsequent economy of the effort usually spent in organizing them, being sure they're worthy of our dole, and all the rest.

I just might be in Nigeria sometime in February; do you know anything of the when and where of your trip?

Fraternally yours, John H. Yoder

The second document is a letter also from Boucq, France, on March 2 of the following year (1962), to The Rev. Harold W. Turner in Oxford, United Kingdom.

Dear Mr. Turner,

I was delighted to receive from Edwin Weaver of Ikot Inyang and Uyo a copy of your essay or article on "The Significance of African Prophet Movements." It represents a viewpoint which was needed and which I hope can get a full hearing as the WCC Division of Mission and Evangelism studies the same topic.

This particular article refrains from drawing further conclusions which I think might logically follow from it and which you have perhaps discussed elsewhere. The renewal perspective you advocate encourages me to ask what you would think of such a prolongation along the lines you have laid down.

There is the question of normative evaluation. The anthropological sciences can judge whether these independent churches are integrated in their culture or not, whether they make people happy or not, whether they can survive changes in leadership or not, but not whether they are right or wrong. Theological and spiritual analysis such as you call for on the other hand, while seeking to be fair and objective in finding the facts, is not neutral when it comes to evaluating them. Is there then a sense in which one can claim that the independent movements are right? At least as right as Luther, or Knox, or Campbell in their times and places? If you say "the independent movements are to be understood doctrinally and not only politically or anthropologically" without drawing this radical conclusion, then the folks who in the first place pushed the prophets out will agree; this is what they always thought: schism, heresy, spiritual pride . . .

What would it mean to say that in the basic issues which were at stake the independents were more right than the missions (not then called churches or operating as such) they seceded from? Here I have only hypotheses for your examination: hypotheses growing out of my study of the spiritual breakdown of the West and not invented to fit Africa.

A. *As to the church and social structure.* Since before Constantine, but especially since his time, belonging to the Church has been taken for granted: pedobaptism is only the symbol of this. By controlling a whole society, the Church guaranteed her future membership; her moral claims on an individual were not based on her message and his response, but . . . on her social power as the official religious institution of her society. This is still not essentially different in the more pluralistic pattern of the Anglo-Saxon free churches.

In missions the Western churches sought to follow this same pattern. Whether by mass movements, by negotiating with the chief, or by writing off the old society and building a new one around the compound, they sought a position in which the church would be secure in her own society, with a proprietary claim on everyone's allegiance. *Against this "constantinian" attitude protest was needed.*

B. *As to the spiritual reality of the Church. The fundamental Christian reality is the charismatic presence of Christ in the gathered fellowship of his disciples.* Doctrinal forms, polity patterns, ethical standards, liturgy are both the normal expressions and the necessary safeguards of this reality; but they are not the reality. Missions, reproducing faithfully the spiritual weakness of the West, have passed on the expressions and the safeguards, whether or not the kernel was still there. *Against this, protest was called for.*

There is the general question of "missionary" methods in dealing now with these groups; this is Edwin Weaver's task. If the independents are wrong, then the only change possible is to replace belligerent methods of combat with wiser, more patient and permissive ways of bringing them back into the fold, reuniting them on the level of expressions and safeguards with the mission-true churches. If, on the other hand, the independents are "right"—not all of them, and not in every way, but at the critical points which led to their expulsion or secesstion [sic] and which have made them socially viable in their independent existence, then not only our methods, but also our goal will be different. We then need to help them to be more orderly, better educated, more responsible. . . . But we need just as much to bring the older "churches" (many of which are still not socially viable if they had to run on their own resources) to recognize the legitimacy of the independents' existence.

This is enough to testify to the importance I attach to the problems you are working with. I should be happy for the chance to meet you should you get to the continent in the coming months; I just got back from Britain and don't know when I can get their [sic] again.

Sincerely yours, John H. Yoder

cc: E. Weaver; J. Graber, Elkhart

A third document is a September 21, 1965, memorandum to Wilbert Shenk, with a copy to J. D. Graber, whom Wilbert Shenk replaced as overseas secretary, as he had earlier replaced Yoder as assistant. It is entitled "Edwin Weaver Papers: Independent Churches."

This is an effort to begin conversation on the evaluation on the pack of papers which you received from Edwin Weaver regarding the independent churches in East Nigeria.

In much of Edwin Weaver's writing on the subject, I am bothered by a continuing ambiguity in the background. It is hard to be sure of oneself or accurate in describing this problem, which is the reason I am sharing this only in an internal memorandum, rather than continuing to share correspondence with the field.

The two significantly different perspectives which seem to me to be mingled in Edwin's mind may not make an enormous difference in the immediate present interpretation and implementation of our concerns; but in the long run they are nevertheless fundamentally opposed, and I am not sure on which "side" Ed will be found.

The same ambiguity lies behind the relationship of the World Council of Churches and the Theological Education Fund in their attitudes toward these churches. On the one hand there is the position which might be labeled as "traditional but tolerant." This is the perspective taken by the most understanding of the senior missionaries in the older churches. These people would hold with regard to church unity that what is ultimately necessary is one great united church, and with regard to ministry they would hold that the ideal and the ultimately necessary form of ministry was that which was brought by the mission. But then they would look with tolerance and understanding on the inadequacies of the independent churches, being quite ready to admit that the churches growing out of the missionary work are also deficient, and therefore being ready for great patience and fraternal understanding.

Yet behind this patience and fraternal understanding, the ultimate goal would still be to lead the independent churches back into an organized unity, and the pattern of ministry which would be respectable according to traditional standards of the older missions. The purpose of efforts related to them such as education would therefore be to make the independent churches more like the older churches, or at least more like what the older churches have been trying to achieve.

On the other hand there would be the perspective which one might call the "Radical Free Church" perspective. From this point of view one would say that there is no reason to assume that the goals of the traditional missionary agencies are the best goals. There is no reason to assume that the creation of one national unified church organization is the best expression of Christian Unity, and no reason to assume that the pattern of ministries and worship life imported from Europe is, even as a goal, the best.

We would rather begin by recognizing the legitimacy in principle of the independent churches as being just as valid as the claims of the mission-related churches. The point of our contributing to their work would not be to make them come closer to the idea of ecumenical or missionary agencies, but to help them to find a pattern of greater faithfulness in their own context.

One of these positions, in some way, would find the independent churches to be basically deficient, and would explain the willingness to work with them as the best strategy to make them respectable. The other would accept their position as fundamentally valid, and would work with them to help them be more genuinely themselves.

The first few years of picking up contacts and operating a rudimentary Bible School have been able to go without distinguishing clearly between these two approaches. It is also quite possible that in the future there would continue to be types of activity which could fit in both frameworks. But increasingly, as the effort is interpreted and publicized, as various kinds of support are found and increasing investment of personnel is possible, there will be points where we will need to decide between them.

My impression is that Harold Turner of Nsukka, and I on the basis of doctrinal prejudices, would tend to take the "free church" position, whereas Edwin Weaver is closer to the "traditional" position. Over against the intolerant attitude of some traditional missionaries, Edwin represents the cause of tolerance, which is a great difference; but he would still seem to be interpreting this tolerance as the most effective way to help the independent churches become respectable. He represents symbolically therefore a greater degree of openness to change than he actually would be likely to carry through in detail.

One place where this difference shows through is the language and practice regarding "leaders." By "fully trained," Edwin assumes the adequacy of the traditional western patterns of ministry as a yardstick, rather than some other pattern of education whose standards would grow more directly out of the independent churches themselves. As a result of this standard of education and support for the recognition of a minister, all of the missions in Africa, including our own, have been [sic] created sub-ministerial categories. Some call them catechists; Edwin calls them "leaders." These people have the full responsibility of local congregational coordination, but are not given recognition as Christian ministers. The difference shows in that the white "bishop" must come around to give authority to baptism and to make communion be valid. I was quite surprised to observe the extent to which the communion service, partly by being reserved to the foreign "full minister" and partly because of the use of western patterns of administration, was a completely foreign element instead of being the central fellowship experience of the African congregation when it meets in its own right.

Another side of this vision of the ministry is that the idea that ministers might be self-supporting is looked at as a concession or a passing adjustment, rather than a possibility which might be permanently valid for the entire life span of the generation we are now helping to educate. As long as self-support is thought of as a lesser evil we have not freed ourselves after all from the western alliance of the ministry with economic abundance and have not fully absorbed the lessons of the "tent-making" studies.

There would be other points in the Weaver papers where this question of perspective shows through perhaps less clearly. This should be enough to get the matter on the agenda for some talk before you leave.

More than three years later, Shenk was still appealing to Yoder—then also part-time professor at Associated Mennonite Biblical Seminaries—for help in determining strategies for the Bible teaching program of Edwin Weaver, who proposed to start with the Old Testament. Shenk's request followed discussions with B. Charles Hostetter, then directing a Bible school for the Church of the Lord (Aladura) in Lagos, and Paul M. Miller who had spent time in East Africa and had written on the question.[13] The latter insisted on starting with the New Testament. The memo referred to Harold W. Turner's recent *Profiles through Preaching*, which had examined texts used by Aladura preachers, and discovered the dominance of Old Testament texts. On February 10, 1969, John Howard responded to Wilbert Shenk with a memorandum entitled "Teaching Approach in Aladura Bible School."

> This responds to your note of February 6, with which you passed on to me Ed Weaver's letter of January 24. There are two questions which I should try to respond to, but cannot do very much this first time around.
>
> The first topic has to do with the Old Testament and has two phases. One is whether the place of the Old Testament has a special significance because of the place of tribal religion in the background of the independent churches. Here it suggests that there is a difference between Sundkler and Turner. To this I cannot try to speak because Ed does not explain what that difference is or what its implications are.
>
> The other aspect of the question is whether the teaching emphasis should begin with the Old Testament or not. My own first leaning would be to feel that this is not a question with a yes-no answer. There is much about the cultural forms within which the Old Testament story is told which are understandable in any other primitive culture; but what really matters about the Old Testament is not the cultural form within which

---

[13] Paul M. Miller, *Equipping for Ministry in East Africa* (Scottdale, PA: Herald Press; and Soni, Tanzania: The Vega Press, 1969).

322 | Selected essays: Anabaptism and mission

the story happened, but what the message is. Abraham is understandable because he had the conception of the importance of having a large posterity, as does the tribal African, but one must be sure that the story of Abraham is told in such a way as to make it clear that he trusted God and jeopardized his posterity by his migration, by his faithfulness to God at other points, and even by the willingness to give up his Son [sic]. So what matters is not only where you get the source material but what you use it to teach. According to Hebrews, Abraham is a type of faith.

But it is certainly not only the Old Testament that fits within the cultural context of a simple society. This is also true of the gospel story, though perhaps not of the Pauline epistles or Hebrews. I would certainly think that the teaching concentration would be upon the gospel stories and Acts and the general epistles to begin with more than on the more "doctrinal" writings of Paul and Hebrews.

The other subject is stated by Ed as "difference between mainline reformers and the Anabaptists on their views of faith and works." Ed is correct in looking for such a distinction. The reformers were strongly in favor of a high level of moral performance for the Christian, especially in the case of Calvin. But they were committed to two other values which had the effect practically of undercutting this concern. One was that they were committed to maintaining within the church the bulk of the population and especially all of the major respectable leaders of their society. This meant that there could be no process of congregational admonition which would come to the point of jeopardizing the prestige of the major powerful persons within a society or which would call into question the membership of any large segment of the population.

The other concern was the strong desire to be protected against self-righteousness and any concept of justification through one's works. They made no distinction between "good works" in the sense of Christian obedience and "works of the law" in the sense of meeting ritual requirements, so they taught against the real importance of Christian behavior as an essential portion of the Christian life.

I do not feel at all confident in carrying this discussion over from the 16th century to Africa. My impression has been strong that the Africa churches have often fallen into a kind of legalism which is not of the gospel, whether because of their cultural level of some predisposition of their tribal religion, or because of the way the missionaries taught them. I would thus not feel personally right about simply playing this into the hands of this legalistic tendency or about considering it an advantage that Mennonites also have been legalistic.

But the alternative is not to pay no attention to moral standards, nor to set a lower level of moral performance as a target. The alternative is rather to find ways of dealing with Christian obedience in the context not of rules to be learned but of grace to be reflected. What is valuable about the epistles of James and Peter is then that they teach morality in the context of the missionary minority rather than concentrating on the development of rules by which it will be possible to manage a whole society. They also concentrate less on the sins of poverty and puberty and passion, which are the sins Pharisaism concentrates on, and more on the temptations of pride and prosperity and power.

These first comments are all that I find rising to the surface without having more extended correspondence with Ed or without going back to the tape of the December meeting. I am sure there is more to be said on the question of the Old Testament, but without refreshing my memory I would not be sure to be speaking to the right issue.

cc: Ed Weaver; B. Charles Hostetter.

A quite lengthy document appears to be Yoder's functional last word on the subject, since the administrative ball was by then fully in Wilbert Shenk's court, with John Howard Yoder now the president of Goshen Biblical Seminary.[14] It is a memo from that office to Wilbert Shenk, dated February 14, 1970, and entitled "Policy of Mennonite Mission and Service Agencies Toward African Independent Churches."[15] It

---

[14] Yoder was president of Goshen Biblical Seminary, and Erland Waltner, president of Mennonite Biblical Seminary. The two worked jointly with one dean in what was then known as Associated Mennonite Biblical Seminaries.

[15] Mennonite Church USA Archives: Hist. Mss. 1–48; 85/35. John H. Yoder (1927–1997); West African Policy Study, 1970–1972.

appears to be at Yoder's initiative, both according to the text, and in the light of other correspondence.

> We have already exchanged some thoughts about the need for a statement of what Elkhart [MBM] and MCC [Mennonite Central Committee] are doing with independent churches in West Africa and Congo.[16] This is needed partly to explain to ourselves the decisions we might make about the relative priority of such contacts, partly to guide what we actually do, and partly to explain ourselves to other denominations, to traditional mission agencies and to such people as our friends in the World Council.

> The following draft is just an indication of the kind of material we might be wanting to gather. I would assume that you and those who receive carbons of this would have some items to add in the first section, and especially that there would be more items to add in the second section dealing with policy directions. This is being circulated only to get thinking started.

> I do not assume that all of the same considerations would apply in the same way in East Africa where the Mennonite mission is much older, a Mennonite denomination is well established, and where the particular form of the independent church movements is somewhat different. The best examples for the application of the text which follows here would be a [sic] sizable, second generation independent movements of Kimbangu and Aladura.

Policy of Mennonite mission and service agencies toward African independent churches

Along several relatively independent lines of development, Mennonite mission and service agencies have come into contact with some of the major independent church movements in West Africa and Congo. Out of these contacts have arisen requests for specific types of relationship and assistance, re-

---

[16] MCC, at my initiative, had placed people from the Pax program and from the Teachers Abroad Program in Kimbanguist schools and an agricultural project. That is why I received a copy of this correspondence at that time. I later visited and consulted with the Kimbanguists in 1971, when I was invited by the head of the Kimbanguist church for the celebration of the fiftieth anniversary of the church's founding.

quests [that] if taken seriously would mean directing to these needs resources in funds and personnel and administrative attention which otherwise would be expended in other ways. There therefore needs to be careful thought about the reasons for and the policy governing such a special investment of Mennonite resources in relation to these independent churches. Is this relationship an arbitrary or chance occurrence? Or is there some intrinsic appropriateness to Mennonite agencies developing such a relationship, as over against leaving [it] to any other particular denominations or to inter-denominational agencies?

This question could be dealt with partly in the form of historical narration, on the assumption that the set of developments which have brought Mennonites into such relationships in more than one place might have some purposive providential meaning, or might be evidence of some pervasive identity, but the present outline seeks only to speak to the question of theological appropriateness.

For our purposes it might be fruitful to distinguish among several ways in which it is possible to relate the institutional identity of a missionary agency to theology. One, which we might label as "sectarian" (seeking to use this term only in a descriptive way), is that which considers the missionary agency as but one arm of a church institution, whose theology and identity are so closely linked that it can perceive of genuine missionary activity only in the form of bringing into being and relating to churches which meet its own description, or in other words as extension of its own identity. This would be the approach of some kinds of fundamentalism, of Seventh Day Adventist missions, and of Catholic missions.

To some extent, perhaps more completely in practice than their theology would tend to justify, this may be the approach of the Southern Baptists and other conservative protestant groups. Then any serious relationship to independent churches would be a contradiction, except to the minor extent to which (as sometimes has happened in West Africa) a given independent church might be willing to join that denomination in return for the institutional support of the mission.

As second style might be termed that of the "denomination," taking this term in the technical sociological sense of a church body which recognizes that it has many sister groups. A "denominational" missionary agency, whether working alone or in cooperation with others of its kind, is not free to have, nor desirous of having a very specific theological identity. It tolerates diversity of theological opinions within its midst. If there be any particular norms concerning theological faithfulness, they are pointed in the direction of moderation and tolerance and mediating positions. From such a perspective it is possible to recognize the validity of the existence of independent churches, if they live up to certain standards of age, size, sobriety, and good manners. Their distinctive existence is recognized and approved of, but it will be [the] nature and intent of the cooperative relationship to tend to lead or move the independent group toward the middle of the spectrum, toward conformity and cooperation. This is the attitude of most protestant groups in WCC and TEF [Theological Education Fund].

It is a peculiarity of Mennonite mission agencies in the last third of this century that they can fit in neither of the above categories. They are without apology committed to a particular theological orientation. They do not seek to enclose within their staff and membership every possible view on theology or church practice, and they feel responsible to steward their very limited resources with a view to a maximum contribution to certain causes which are not carried by other denominations. In this sense, a Mennonite mission agency is "sectarian." Yet it differs from other agencies given as examples under this heading in a number of significant ways:

1. The normative theology to which a Mennonite mission agency is committed is not identified with the institutional existence of a Mennonite constituency. This is the case because the theology which a Mennonite mission agency considers itself to be mandated to propagate is the result of renewal within recent Mennonite experience, rather than being the deposit or the distillate of a recent history or a constituency creed. Mennonite relief and service agencies are committed to a theology of the church's mission which they may designate by the type label "Anabaptist," in the honest awareness that the Mennonite constituent churches which support the effort not only do not

fully realize this vision in their own life, but are not even really committed to it in every way.

2. From the fact that the Mennonite constituency is not a fundamentally adequate vehicle of the "Anabaptist Vision," it follows as well that the outcome of the missionary effort of Mennonites need not necessarily be the creation of churches belonging to the Mennonite denomination. There is a strong concern to propagate the essentials of the Anabaptist vision (such as meaningful membership expressed in baptism of believers and congregational discipline, or personal discipleship expressed in servant-hood and nonresistance), but there is no solid insistence that Christians or churches holding these convictions must necessarily express them by membership in Mennonite polity agencies.

3. It is not enough to say that in point of fact the Anabaptist Vision and the Mennonite institution are distinguishable. There is an empirical, formal, or structural observation, and it might have been otherwise. It must however further be said that the substance of Anabaptist conviction about the mission and nature of the church includes further considerations (which shall be spelled out below) which would further militate in favor of a plurality of possible structures and against the "sectarian" model of commitment to one's own agencies.

A. Why Mennonites ought to work actively with independent churches

1. Anabaptist understandings of the church and her relation to society intrinsically *reject colonialism as a model* for the propagation of the church. This comes partly from our insistence on an indigenous congregation as the normal form of the church, partly from the rejection of the support given to the church by the other powers of society, notably the state, partly from the concern for the authenticity of the decisions of faith which underlies the rejection of infant baptism and mass conversions.

Today all intelligent missionary thought rejects colonialist patterns of church planting, on the ground of results and other kinds of considerations both pragmatic and theological. But this rejection does not flow intrinsically from the theological options of the founders of the several denominations as it does from the radical reformation position.

There is a sense in which at least some of the phenomenon of independent churches in Africa can be understood as a valid protest against the colonial patterns of missionary work and structure. They may be rejecting that structure for the wrong reasons, or they may be using questionable forms and methods to dramatize that rejection, but it could be hoped that the sister churches most [sic] be able to help them in formulating this rejection theologically and the appropriate alternative to a colonial church would be those with the most basic theological commitment to the same critique.

There is in independentism a danger of the wrong kind of over-compensation. In reacting against the way the white man's religion was brought to them as a part of white culture, there is a serious danger of replacing it with a black man's religion too uncritically rooted in black culture.[17] Again it would be hoped that a theological position committed to the critical questioning of the links between faith and culture would be more ready to be critically helpful at this point, than churches who were traditionally, out of theological conviction, less critical of their own acculturation back home.

2. In correlation with this consideration, as a sub-heading which makes it more pointed and visible, *the Anabaptist tradition rejects coercion and war.* War was not the heart of the benevolent intentions of colonialism, but certainly was its confidence in its right to coerce at the center of its effectiveness.

Some of the African independent groups are pacifist. The commitment of Kinbanguist tradition is most clear at this point, both because of its linkage with the fate of the prophet [Simon Kimbangu] and because of the testing the church has undergone in the last five decades. The Church of the Lord (Aladura) is much less self aware at this point, but its international character, its transcending of tribal boundaries, and its vision of social wholeness move in this same direction.

The dimension of simple biblical literalism which is widespread in the independent churches tends to a kind of naive pacifism. It is thus fitting that Christian pacifists from the Fellowship of

---

[17] We, the Shanks, found this tendency to be present in Côte d'Ivoire (1979–89) among the "*vieux*" Ebrié Harrists and somewhat absorbed by the rising literate generation of "*jeunes.*"

Reconciliation or the Historic Peace Churches should be the most appropriate visiting teaching resources, whereas the advocates of the non-pacifist majority Western tradition might, if serving as teachers, feel obligated to try to win the Africans away from the naivete of their pacifist commitment. There will be occasion enough in continuing ecumenical encounter, and in struggling with the real problems of political existence, to call that naive commitment into question; proper fraternal etiquette would ask that those who accept invitations to serve as guest teachers would respect that position.

3. One of the tragic dimensions of the Western-managed missionary enterprise has been the extent to which it has exported to Latin America and Africa the *polarization of American Protestantism* between "ecumenical" and "evangelical" forces. Western initiative in setting up councils and anti-councils is no less aggressive now, when we are aware that it is ethically and ecclesiastically questionable, than it was ten years ago when people on both sides were less aware that it could be challenged. Mennonites are among those who believe that this polarization not only is regrettable but was not necessary and still can be rejected and worked against. In point of fact, Mennonites have avoided taking sides in many places.

A number of the distinctive characteristics of Mennonites, partly as a theological position and partly as a cultural experience, which would be congenial to a supportive relationship to independent churches would be:

(a) An affirmative attitude to moral bindingness as expressed in personal and group discipline. Numerous Protestant groups find their dealing with ethical imperatives to be somewhat undercut by a Lutheran concern for dialectic of Law and Gospel, or by a modern relativism about ethical norms, or by embarrassment about naivete or the authoritarianism with which earlier moral judgment and teaching has proceeded. This makes them less able to cooperate constructively in some modern pluralistic situations; it might also make them less embarrassed about coping with the moralistic tendencies which are rather typical of independent churches.

(b) While not advocating any rejection of leadership structures, Mennonites have generally been the advocates of a less rigidly structured definition of ministerial qualifications than many other denominational bodies. Sometimes this meaning has expressed itself in a preference for an economically self-supporting [ministry], sometimes in suspicion of academic meaning of ordination, sometimes in debate about the sacramental meaning of ordination, sometimes in the call for a plurality of ministerial leaders rather than one clergyman. This orientation should liberate Mennonites to deal with the variety of educational and economic patterns of leadership in the independent churches rather than feeling concerned to impose upon them some particular theologically normative leadership pattern imported from the West.

(c) Mennonites have by and large survived and maintained some kind of theological identity without focusing this on any normative teaching institution. When there have been schools, these have been primarily the expression of a position already defined elsewhere, rather than being, as in the more magisterial traditions, the agencies for the definition of proper theology.

The alternative to the normative school, for both Mennonites and African independents, is not to have no theological identity at all, but rather to have it defined and propagated by other patterns. Specifically: (i) by the itineration of specifically charismatic figures and, (ii) by informal lay socialization processes in the life of the local congregation, its liturgy and its neighborhood relations.

Resulting from some of the above-mentioned particularities and in a sense summing them up, the Mennonite style of theological communication is what might be called *lay evangelicalism*. This is not the result of any particular theological insight or wisdom although perhaps a theological case might be made for the advantages of such a position; it is rather a result of culture lags in North American Protestant experience. It is not the same as the militant evangelicalism of some Protestant denominations and independent churches. *But its alternative to fundamentalisms is not liberalism but rather a particular simplicity and lack of sophistication in the articulation of biblical faith. Much the same thing would have to be said (for the present generation) of the theological articulations which are at home in the African independent churches.*

B. Policy concerning Mennonite work with African independent churches

1. *We affirm the theological legitimacy of the distinct existence of church bodies which do not stand in any direct juridical relationship to a specific "mother church" in Europe or North America.* An organizationally structured unity with an older church is a desirable thing but not essential for the recognition of the legitimate existence of a church body. This is not to say that the criteria of formal continuity are to be disregarded; but they must be applied in ways which take account of the failures of the churches and missions, past and present. Among the necessary criteria are the following:

(a) The affirmation of the saving uniqueness of the work of Jesus Christ;

(b) The recognition of canonical scripture as a criterion of Christian conviction superior to the confessions, prophecies and practices of later leaders;

(c) Some recognition of the existence of other Christian bodies and traditions and a desire to learn from them and share with them;

(d) An awareness that loyalty to Jesus Christ demands choices and sacrifices in daily life, thereby standing in judgment on one's own culture.

These criteria are met by the Kimbanguist and Aladura groups.

2. *We affirm the propriety of a certain tendency to legalism in the African church.* In recent years missionary statesmen have been very concerned about the tendency of national churches to reduce the meaning of Christian faith to a way of life which one attempts to commend to an entire society with all kinds of motivations. Missionaries have been correct in wanting to undo the effects of the imposition of certain ethical patterns by the authority of the missionary, especially where these patterns were culturally foreign. The missionaries have likewise been concerned, as good Protestants, for the safeguarding of the basic Protestant message of justification by faith. To this is added a substantial element of modern western personalism, with its tendency to discredit any behavior that is not a matter of personal conviction. As valid as are all these concerns, the critique which they exercise must be expressed within

rather than against an acceptance of the tendency of an African culture to deal with morality as a matter of the life style of the community rather than focusing only upon the integrity of personal faith obedience. We cannot begin by asking of the African a style of individualism in religious experience which would be fitting for a Luther or a Wesley, and which even the Western traditions of individualized religious experience have great difficulty in linking with morality.

It is appropriate that the preoccupations of the independent church should be especially with concerns which the traditional churches did not deal with (healing, prophecy and indigenous forms of worship) and with issues arising out of end of colonialism (nation building, nonviolence, education and institutional development).

Western missionaries will at some points feel good reasons to chide for provincialism or "over correction" or imbalance. It will however not be the responsibility of the visiting churchmen or teachers to concentrate on restoring "balance" except as such maturation is the normal result of deepening insight. The very considerations which call forth the imbalance incapacitate the westerner to correct it.

3. *We affirm the legitimacy of patterns of leadership growing out of congregational life and continuing to be rooted within the congregation.* Theological education must be structured in such a way as to retain this rootage of leadership in local experience or community.

4. *We affirm the necessity of projecting visions of a Christian life style in which inward piety and the expression of community witness, inviting men to faith and building them up in the faith cannot be dealt with as alternatives.*

The above concern for a pattern of leadership and this concern for a pattern of life should [sic] be fitting the Gospel will result in the unembarrassed acceptance of catechisms and patterns of fraternal discipline which lack in theological articulateness and which may in fact need to be propagated by rote learning with no expression at all in a formal ordered polity which would be recognized by Europeans as such.

JHY sab

cc. David Shank,[18] Marlin Miller, Paul M. Miller

This text tells us, of course, much more about Yoder's thought in 1970 than just his approach to African-initiated churches. It also reports on his appreciation—as new president of AMBS—of the Mennonite Church, its mission agency, and its stance within the Western world of missions, as well as the sine qua non of an "independent church" that for him would qualify as "church."

The final document of this selection is a letter[19] dated and dictated on October 6, 1970, from Buenos Aires, Argentina, where Yoder was on a teaching and lecturing mission; it is addressed to Edwin I. Weaver, then in Accra, Ghana.

Dear Ed,

Wilbert passed on to me a copy of your circular of September 8 with a suggestion that I might comment on it.

I am not acquainted with the book by Mbiti, and you do not actually say much about its contents, so my response will only be to your own thoughts.

One such item is your way of putting the West and Africa in equal or parallel positions. You say that the church in the West has followed the culture of the West and that the newer African movements are following the African prophets, as if that was somehow parallel. But the West that the churches in the West have been listening to is to a great extent the product of centuries of Christian influence. Does conformity to the West, whose patterns are the result of those centuries, stand on the same level either as a value or as a threat, with conformity to African patterns which have no such history? I am clear in criticizing western forms of Christianity, but I am not sure that it is not an oversimplification to picture the two kinds of cultural identification as if they were somehow of the same magnitude just in opposite directions. The difference is more complicated than

---

[18] See n10 above.

[19] Mennonite Church Archives: Hist. Mss. 1–696, 5/1. Edwin & Irene Weaver Collection: Yoder, John Howard, 1965–72.

that in that one has centuries of Christian history behind and the other does not.

You notice, I think correctly, that the westerner is often the most zealous to Africanize the church. I do not understand your rapid conclusion that this shows that he is not informed. What the African really wants is often a great degree of westernization, for obvious material reasons. The reasons [sic] that *some* westerners are more zealous about Africanization than *some* Africans is that this particular selected group of westerners has been provided by history and education with a particular kind of cultural perspective which by its very definition cannot be a part of the African culture, because it too is a western product. Precisely because the (western) techniques of anthropological understanding are needed in this kind of concern, there is a particular contribution to Africanization which only such qualified outsiders can make. I think this observation speaks as well to your last paragraph.

The place where your outline leaves me waiting for more is on the level of concrete detail. The three requirements which you state—biblical theology, listening to each other, working within the life of the church—are the prerequisites for valid theology in any culture. They apply to Africa because they apply to Elkhart. But what are the specific issues around which this approach will come up with something that is God's leading for a faithful African church?

The concrete example you give at the beginning of the paper is the reference to the church as community. Perhaps experience with Africa helps some of us to see that, but it is not a truth discovered in Africa. Harold Bender and Robert Friedmann were writing this on the basis of historical studies before any Mennonite missionaries started appreciating African culture. Will studying in an African context actually help us to see truths that were not seen before, or will it simply help us to take sides on issues which were already present within the varieties of Christianity in the West?

Another aspect of the same question is to ask also whether there are negative points in African culture which should be challenged by the Bible in a way in which the same challenge is not needed in the West. The concept of the closely knit social group results for instance in scholarship frauds and in nepotism which is bad both for efficiency and for the brotherhood church. Will your approach strengthen our capacity to deal with the judgmental impact of the Bible as well as with the places where it reaffirms pre-Christian cultural values?

One other item of agenda which is hard to handle from this perspective of balancing western and African orientations is the fact that Africa will be westernized whether we like it or not by technology and urbanization, which have their own materialistic motivations and mechanisms. While we are in the bush trying to record African music and anthropological ideas before they get lost, the population of Africa is moving to the cities where financial and housing considerations will increasingly break the family down to the nuclear unit, weaken tribal identifications, and create a culture of television watchers. Just at the time we have become very concerned about Africanization in missionary policy, westernization in urban sociology is getting out of hand. Is it possible for the church to find African patterns of community which will create a different kind of cities or a different kind of television watchers than have made western urban man what he is?

The fact that I see questions in your outline does not speak to [and] does not indicate any lack of respect for the effort you are undertaking. I just hope to hear more about how this vision will take on flesh.

Fraternally yours, John H. Yoder

cc: Wilbert R. Shenk, David A. Shank, Marlin E. Miller.

John Howard Yoder is known largely as a Western theologian, working out the implications of the distinctive "free church" type as over against the "Constantinian church" type. He is scarcely known as one who related to realities of the global South. What is interesting here is the way his typology tends to associate the 'traditional' missionary churches of the colonial period with Constantinianism and the independent churches with the free church, thus recognizing their right to be and to critique the traditional mission-planted church, and thus to be taken seriously. Second, since the task of the free church is to be the faithful church, the role of external teachers working with AICs is to help them grow in faithfulness in their context. Third, and quite significant, is his accent on ecumenicity from the point of view of the local congregation, and the role of the Spirit of Christ—not mission-ary clergy—in working out its life and the calling out of leaders. These three Yoderian motifs have been in the forefront of broader Western Mennonite involvement with the African AICs.

17

Qualities that enable Mennonites to relate to African-initiated churches

- We have a believers church stance that does not require institutional identity with American Mennonitism as a precondition for work within and/or for a movement, or as a necessary consequence of missionary endeavor.
- We are latecomers to the scene in West Africa and do not have to overcome a stigmatizing history of colonial involvement; the believers church stance is one of nonidentification with the powers that be, colonial or otherwise.
- Our history of rejection—and sometimes oppression—by mainline Christianity gives us a measure of credibility to movements that have the same experience.
- Our history of being a "third way" as compared to the Catholic or Protestant options in the sixteenth century, to the liberal or fundamentalist options, and the service or evangelism polarizations of this century, helps us understand those who do not fit the usual— even Western—ecclesiastical categories.
- We have a tradition of biblicism as compared to philosophical theology.
- Our tradition of distance from and critique of Western culture from within makes us open to others who from their own tradition maintain distance and critique from without.
- Our tradition of ethical guidelines—often perceived as legalism and moralism—gives us understanding of movements that lay down ex-

Reprinted, with editorial changes, from a report to the Overseas Committee of the Mennonite Board of Missions, 1974. Used by permission. This summary, a handout for a 2003 anthropology and missions class at Eastern Mennonite University (Harrisonburg, VA) was prepared by Calvin Shenk, who taught the class. He had extracted the list from a 1974 report by David A. Shank to the Overseas Committee of Mennonite Board of Missions (of which Calvin was a member).

plicit life patterns in an attempt to give guidance through the maze of cultural confusion.

- Our tradition of congregational consensus and discipline gives us an openness to collective patterns of life that are often far removed from the individualistic faith and spiritual life patterns of much of Western Christianity.

- Our history and tradition of lay leadership and evangelism make us open to leadership patterns that are less acceptable to hierarchically or institutionally controlled ecclesiologies.

- Our nonresistant tradition differs from most missions that have been tied to the Western powers. Some independent movements— the Kimbanguists in Zaire and the Harrists in Côte d'Ivoire—share this stance.

- The small size of our church keeps us from being a threat to others.

- Our struggle to be a confessing church under the pressures of ethnicity gives us understanding and insight into ethnic movements working toward mature faith.

Section IV Bibliography of the writings of David A. Shank

David Shank at work in Blokosso-Abidjan office, Côte d'Ivoire
(1987)

Bibliography of the writings
of David A. Shank

Crissie Judith Buckwalter, compiler

1942
"And That's How It Was." *Goshen College Record,* September 8, 1942, 1.

1943
"What a Social!" *Goshen College Record,* January 19, 1943, 3.

1944
[Feature editor.] *The Vanguard* [Denison, IA, CPS camp publication] 18, no. 1 (1944), 1–2.

1945
"Joy in Service." *Gospel Herald,* February 2, 1945, 877.

"Race Criminals." *The Vanguard* [Denison, IA, CPS camp publication] 19 (1945).

1946
[Editor.] *CPS Bulletin.* Akron, PA: MCC, March 28–June 20, 1946.

[Editor.] *CPS Bulletin Supplement,* May 16, 1946, and June 20, 1946.

"Christian Witness and Conscription." *CPS Supplement.* MCC Akron, PA, May 16, 1946: 9.

[Editor.] *Goshen College Record,* Fall Semester 1946–47.

"Growth to What End?" [editorial]. *Goshen College Record*, October 8, 1946, 2.

"It's All Greek to Me" [editorial]. *Goshen College Record,* October 22, 1946, 2.

"Why Are We All Here?" [editorial]. *Goshen College Record,* September 24, 1946, 2.

1947
"Adequate Defenses?" *Goshen College Record,* January 21, 1947.

"Disgusting Discussion" [editorial]. *Goshen College Record,* January 21, 1947, 2.

1948
"The Mennonite Family in Transition: 1945–46. A Questionnaire Study of the Mennonite Family Which Was Formed during the Last Year of the War." November 20, 1948. Sociology senior seminar paper; in Mennonite Historical Library.

1949
"Jesus Perceived Their Thoughts." *Worship. A Booklet of Ten Selected Chapel Addresses Given at Goshen College 1948-1949.* Goshen, IN: Goshen College, 1949, 8–11.

"A Religious Life Analysis." Goshen College. Unpublished manuscript.

1950
"Jesus Perceived Their Thoughts." *Youth's Christian Companion,* March 5, 1950, 75, 80.

1951
"Three Who Represent Thousands." *Gospel Herald,* February 13, 1951, 158.

1952
"Between East and West." *Gospel Herald,* February 26, 1952, 207.

"Perspective . . . and then Perseverance." *Gospel Herald,* February 5, 1952, 128.

1953
"Our Witness in Belgium." *Gospel Herald,* December 29, 1953, 1246–47.

1954
"A Missionary Approach to a Dechristianized Society." *Mennonite Quarterly Review* 28, no. 1 (1954): 39–55.

"Our Witness in Belgium." *Gospel Herald,* January 5, 1954, 14–15.

"Our Witness in Belgium." *Gospel Herald,* March 23, 1954, 278–79.

"Our Witness in Belgium." *Gospel Herald,* May 18, 1954, 473, 476.

1955
[and John Howard Yoder.] "Biblicism and the Church." Concern No. 2, 26–69. [Goshen, IN]: [Sponsoring Group], 1955.

1956
"A Mission Program versus Mission-Mindedness." *Gospel Herald,* September 25, 1956, 926–27.

Response to Horst Gerlach of April 3. *Gospel Herald,* May 15, 1956, 464.

Review of *Principes et doctrines mennonites,* edited by Pierre Widmer and John H. Yoder. *Mennonite Quarterly Review* 30, no. 3 (July 1956): 229–30.

1957
"Evangelizing in Belgium." In *Ye Are Witnesses,* 39–41. Elkhart, IN: Mennonite Board of Missions, 1957.

1958
[Van Gille, Ernest (penname).] "That Same Tune in a Different Key." Unpublished manuscript.

1961
"God or Caesar's?" In *The Historical Context.* MCC: Pax Europe, 1961.

1965
"On Misunderstanding Patience." In *From the Mennonite Pulpit,* edited by Paul Erb, 31–40. Scottdale, PA: Herald Press, 1965.

"Le divorce, faillite du marriage." In *Le chrétien et la vie conjugale, 30–33.* Brussels: A.P.R.T.,

1966
Report on Berlin World Congress on Evangelism, October 26–November 4, 1966. Genval: Belgium. Unpublished manuscript.

1967
"Biblisches Friedenszeugnis im Öffentlichen Leben." In *Der Weg des Friedens.* Karlsruhe: Deutsches Mennonitisches Friedenskomitee, 1967.

1968
"The American Mennonite Witness in Latin Europe." *Gospel Herald,* January 23, 1968, 74–75.

"Erosion." *Mennonite Brethren Herald,* September-December 1968, 4–6.

"Faith and Doubt in Menno Simons." Unpublished manuscript submitted for class on faith and doubt, taught by John Dunne, University of Notre Dame, South Bend, IN.

"God's Love Builds in His Church." *Gospel Herald,* December 10, 1968, 1078–80.

"The Implication for His Ecclesiology of Menno Simons' Doctrine of the Incarnation." Unpublished manuscript submitted for class on free church history, taught by John Howard Yoder, University of Notre Dame, South Bend, IN.

1969
"Mennonites—Pasteur David Shank [interview]: Les coeurs sont un petit peu plus touchés." *TV Panorama* 52 (Antwerp), December 27, 1969, 13.

"Pour ceux qui ne partent pas." *Publications de la Radio-Télévision Protestante* 31, no. 69. Brussels: A.P.R.T. Bruxelles. Transcript of the program of August 4, 1969.

Who Will Answer? Scottdale, PA: Herald Press, 1969.

1970
"Discerning the Spirit in Belgium." *Gospel Herald,* July 21, 1970, 614–15.

1971
"Good News that Fits" [messages 166 and 375]. Harrisonburg, VA: The Mennonite Hour. Reprinted in *Gospel Herald,* June 15, 1971, 538–39.

His Spirit First. Scottdale, PA: Herald Press, 1971.

"The Time of the Spirit" [message 165]. Harrisonburg, VA: The Mennonite Hour.

1972
"La contestation dans l'église." *Paix et Liberté* (Brussels), September 22, 1972, 4–5.

"An Indigenous African Church Comes of Age: Kimbanguism." *Mennonite Life* 27, no. 2 (1972): 53–55.

1973
"The Shape of Mission Strategy." *Mission Focus* 1, no. 3 (1973): 1–7. Reprinted in *Mission Focus: Current Issues,* edited by Wilbert R. Shenk (Scottdale, PA: Herald Press, 1980), pp. 118–28.

"The Spirit Leading in Discerning the Spirit of the Times," "Led by the Spirit in Personal Life-Style," and "Led by the Spirit in Witness." *Goshen College Bulletin,* August 1973, 2–4.

1974

"King Jesus' Call to Mission." *Gospel Herald,* March 5, 1974, 793–95.

"What Is a Person?" In *Discovery of the Person,* 1–6. Goshen, IN: Goshen College. Messages for Perspectives Week, September 23–27, 1974.

"Who is Jesus?" Goshen College Campus Ministries, February 28, 1974. Unpublished manuscript.

1975

"The Call," "One-Anothering," and "Questions . . . before Advent" [Messages Nos. 344–82]. Harrisonburg, VA: The Mennonite Hour, 1975.

"Discipleship" [Messages Nos. 344–55]; "The New Community" [Messages Nos. 356–69]; and 13 other messages [Messages Nos. 370–82]. Harrisonburg, VA: The Mennonite Hour, 1975.

"Discovering the Strategy of the Spirit." In *Being God's Missionary Community: Reflections on Mennonite Missions, 1945-1975.* Elkhart, IN: Mennonite Board of Missions, 1975, 23–30.

"Non-Violent Revolution." In "Talk Free." *Engage/Social Action* 15–16, no. 3 (March 1975): 15–16.

1976

"Four Models of Jubilee." *Gospel Herald* 69, May 25, 1976, 446–49.

"Man's Inhumanity to God." *Gospel Herald,* December 14, 1976, 947–49. Reprint of The Mennonite Hour presentation.

"The Spirit of Incarnation." *Gospel Herald,* December 7, 1976, 926–27. Reprint of The Mennonite Hour presentation.

"Toward an Understanding of Christian Conversion." *Mission Focus* 5, no. 2 (1976): 1–7.

"Who Has Rights over My Body?" *Gospel Herald,* August 10, 1976, 608–9.

1977

"Eglise et état." *Paix et Liberté* 77, no. 3 (February 1977): 4–5.

Review of *Kindgom, Cross and Community,* edited by John Richard Burkholder and Calvin Redekop. *Mission News Notes* 77, no. 17, Mennonite Board of Missions, 1977.

"A Time of Loss and a Time for Repentance." *Mission Focus* 6, no. 1 (1977): 9–12.

1978

"Comment on Vietnam Appraisal." *Mission Focus* 6, no. 5 (1978): 13–15.

"Is There More than One Way to Do Theology?" *Gospel in Context* 1, no. 1 (1978): 35–36.

"The Meaning of the Church. *Builder,* June 1978, 18–21.

1979

Compte-rendu de la Conférence Mennonite "Racines Mennonites." MCC, Kinshasa-Ngombé. Unpublished manuscript.

"The Problem of Cross-Cultural Communication Illustrated: Research Notes on 'The Finding of the Prophet Harris by M. Benoît, September 1926.'" *Missiology* 7, no. 2 (1979): 211–31.

1980

"And a Man from Africa Says to the Churches." *Journal of Religion in Africa* 11, no. 3 (1980): 225–31.

"A Prophet of Modern Times: The Thought of William Wadé Harris." 3 vols. PhD diss., University of Aberdeen, Scotland, 1980.

Review of *Readings on Missionary Anthropology II,* edited by William A. Smalley. *The Bible Translator* 3, no. 3 (1980): 343.

Review of *Spirituality and Mission: Historical, Theological, and Cultural Factors for a Present-Day Missionary Spirituality,* by Michael Collins Reilly. *International Review of Mission* 69, no. 274 (April 1980): 231–33.

Review of *Théorie des pouvoirs et idéologie. Etude des cas en Côte d'Ivoire,* by Marc Augé. *Journal of Religion in Africa* 11, no. 1 (1980): 74–75.

"The Shape of Mission." *Mission Focus* 8, no. 4 (1980): 69–74.

1981

"An Open Window into the Harrist Church." *Mission Focus* 9, no. 3 (1981): 69–74.

"Readers Say." *Gospel Herald,* June 16, 1981, 493.

Review of *African Christianity. Patterns of Religious Continuity,* edited by George Bond, Walton Johnson, and Sheila S. Walker. *Journal of Religion in Africa* 12, no. 1 (1981): 68–70.

1982

"An Approach to Understanding 'Mission' to Independent Christianity among the Bassa People in Liberia, W[est] A[frica]." March 4, 1982. Unpublished manuscript.

"La culture américaine via Paris vers le tiers monde." In "Courier," *Le Nouvel Observateur* 932 (September 30, 1982): 19.

1983

"Bref résumé de la pensée du prophète William Wadé Harris." *Perspectives Missionnaires* 5 (1983): 34–54. Reprinted as independent "extract" publication.

"The Prophet Harris: A Historiographical and Bibliographical Survey." *Journal of Religion in Africa* 14, no. 2 (1983): 130–60.

"Une réponse imprévue à l'action missionnaire." *Perspectives Missionnaires* 5 (1983): 55–66.

1984

"Anabaptists and Mission." In *Anabaptists and Mission,* edited by Wilbert R. Shenk, 202–28. Scottdale, PA: Herald Press, 1984.

"Introduction à la théologie chrétienne africaine." Faculté de Théologie Evangélique de Bangui, Central African Republic. Unpublished manuscript.

"Répertoire non-inclusif de mouvements religieux en Côte d'Ivoire." *Africa* 157 (January 1984): 32–34.

Review of *West African Christianity: The Religious Impact,* by Lamin Sanneh. *Missionalia* 12, no. 2 (August 1984): 96–97.

1985

"African Independent Churches." In *Christianity in Today's World. An Eerdmans Handbook,* 144–55. Grand Rapids, MI: Eerdmans, 1985.

"Évangile et culture." *Connexe Bruxelles,* September 14, 1985, 6–7.

"The Harrist Church in the Ivory Coast." Literature review article in *Journal of Religion in Africa* 15, no. 1 (1985): 67–75.

"Mission Relations with the Independent Churches in Africa." *Missiology* 13, no. 1 (January 1985): 23–44.

Review of *The Religious Revolution in the Ivory Coast: The Prophet Harris and the Harrist Church,* by Sheila S. Walker. *International Bulletin of Missionary Research* 9 (July 1985): 140–41.

"A Survey of American Mennonite Ministries to African Independent Churches." *Mission Focus* 13, no. 1 (1985): 1–5.

"Wat de Afrikaanse Inheemse kerken de Westerse kerken kunnen leren." *Algemeen Doopsgezind Weekblad,* June 1, 1985, 4–5.

"What African Indigenous Churches Can Teach Western Churches." Elkhart, IN: Mennonite Board of Missions, 1985.

1986

"David A. Shank's View: Celebrating Leadership Training in Ivory Coast." *Sent.* Elkhart, IN: Mennonite Board of Missions, September 1986, 8.

"The Legacy of William Wadé Harris." *International Bulletin of Missionary Research* 10, no. 4 (October 1986): 170–76.

Review of *No Other Name? A Critical Survey of Christian Attitudes toward World Religions,* by Paul F. Knitter. *Mission Focus* 14, no. 4 (December 1986): 57–59.

Review of *The Priestly Kingdom: Social Ethics as Gospel,* by John H. Yoder. *Mennonite Quarterly Review* 60, no. 2 (April 1986): 215–16.

1987

[Editor.] *Ministry of Missions to Independent Churches.* Elkhart, IN: Mennonite Board of Missions, 1987.

"Readers Say." *Gospel Herald,* July 14, 1987.

"The Work of the Group for Religious and Biblical Studies in West Africa." In *Ministry of Missions to Independent Churches,* edited by David A. Shank, 13–32. Elkhart, IN: Mennonite Board of Missions, 1987.

1988

Review of *Jesus Christ our Lord,* by C. Norman Kraus. *Mennonite Quarterly Review* 62, no. 4 (October 1988). Reprinted in Richard A. Kauffman, ed., "A Disciple's Christology: Appraisals of Kraus's *Jesus Christ Is Lord,* 104–16. Elkhart, IN: Institute of Mennonite Studies, 1989.

Review of *Mennonites and Reformed in Dialogue,* edited by Hans Georg vom Berg et al. *Mennonite Quarterly Review* 62, no. 2 (April 1988): 178–80.

Review of *Religion Alive: Studies in the New Movements and Indigenous Churches in Southern Africa,* edited by G. C. Oosthuizen; and *Speaking for Ourselves,* edited by Archbishop N. H. Ngada [Braamfontein, South Africa: Institute for Contextual Theology, 1985]. *Mission Focus* 15, no. 4 (December 1988): 101–2.

1989

"La religion africaine traditionnelle." Paper presented to the Groupes Bibliques Universitaires d'Afrique Francophone/Congrès de Jacqueville (August 1989). Unpublished manuscript.

"A Response to Howard Charles' 'Homosexuality: Toward Understanding the Relevant Biblical Texts.'" Goshen, IN (April 23). Mimeo-copy.

"Salut et perdition dans la société africaine." Paper presented to the Groupes Bibliques Universitaires d'Afrique Francophone/Congrès de Jacqueville (August 1989). Unpublished manuscript.

1990

"African Christian Religious Itinerary: Toward an Understanding of the Religious Itinerary from the Faith of African Traditional Religion(s) to that of the New Testament." In *Exploring New Religious Movements. Essays in Honour of Harold W. Turner,* edited by A. F. Walls and Wilbert R. Shenk. Elkhart, IN: Mission Focus, 1990.

"Concern Reflections: David A. Shank." *Conrad Grebel Review* 8, no. 2 (Spring 1990): 177–91.

1991

"Africa and Our Future." *The Witmarsum* 77, no. 16 (February 15, 1991): 3, 7.

[Editor.] *Ministry in Partnership with African Independent Churches.* Elkhart, IN: Mennonite Board of Missions, 1991.

"African Independent Churches, African Theology, and Western Workers in the *missio Dei.*" In *Ministry in Partnership with African Independent Churches,* edited by David A. Shank. Elkhart, IN: Mennonite Board of Missions, 1991.

1992

"Readers Say." *Gospel Herald,* October 20, 1992, 4. (See also "Correction" in GH of November 2, 1992).

Review of *Through No Fault of Their Own? The Fate of Those Who Have Never Heard,* edited by William V. Crockett and James G. Sigountos. *Mission Focus* 20, no. 2 (June 1992): 38.

1993

"Consummation of Messiah's Mission." In *The Transfiguration of Mission: Biblical, Theological and Historical Foundations,* edited by Wilbert R. Shenk, 220–41. Scottdale, PA: Herald Press, 1993.

"David Shank on Christology." *Review of AICs* 4, no. 2 (May 1993): 18.

"Jesus the Messiah: Messianic Foundation of Mission." In *The Transfiguration of Mission: Biblical, Theological and Historical Foundations,* edited by Wilbert R. Shenk, 37–82. Scottdale, PA: Herald Press, 1993.

"Letter to the Conference on Partnership with African Indigenous Churches from David Shank." *Review of AICs* 4, no. 2 (May 1993): 4.

Review of *Jésus Christ aux marges de la réforme,* by Neal Blough. *Mennonite Quarterly Review* 67, no. 3 (July 1993): 356–58.

1994

Prophet Harris, the "Black Elijah" of West Africa. Leiden: E.J. Brill, 1994. Abridged by Jocelyn Murray. No. 10 in *Studies of Religion in Africa* series, supplements to the *Journal of Religion in Africa.*

"Readers Say." "For in the Peace of the City You Will Have Peace." *Gospel Herald,* November 8, 1994, 6–7.

"Readers Say." "Missionary Hugging." *Gospel Herald,* September 6, 1994: 5.

Review of *Pennsylvania Dutch Spirituality,* edited by Richard E. Wentz. *Mennonite Quarterly Review* 68, no. 4 (October 1994): 562–63.

"William Wadé Harris, ca. 1860–1929. God Made His Soul a Soul of Fire." In *Mission Legacies: Biographical Studies of Leaders of the Modern Missionary Movement,* edited by Gerald H. Anderson et al., 155–65. Maryknoll, NY: Orbis Books, 1995.

1995

"Let Us Get to the Shore . . ." *Gospel Herald,* December 10, 1995, 5.

"My Understanding of the Christian Perspective on Same-Sex Tendencies and Practice." In *Resources for Congregational Discernment.* Elkhart, IN: Mennonite Board of Congregational Ministries, 1995.

"Readers Say." "Now is the Time for Men . . ." *Gospel Herald,* January 31, 1995, 6.

Review of *Two Kingdoms: Church and Culture through the Centuries,* edited by Robert G. Clouse et al. *Mennonite Quarterly Review* 69, no. 3 (July 1995): 408–10.

1996

"Bref résumé de l'histoire de l'église en Afrique jusqu'en 1895." In *Nos racines racontées,* edited by James R. Krabill, 11–26. Abidjan: Presses Bibliques Africaines, 1996.

"Change Is Possible." *Mennonite Weekly Review,* February 29, 1996, 4.

"Correction Accepted." *Mennonite Weekly Review,* April 25,1996, 4.

"Evolving Harrist Views of the Prophet Harris." In *African Independent Churches Today,* edited by M. C. Kitshoff, 51–74. *African Studies* series, vol. 44. Lewiston/Queenston/Lampeter: The Edwin Mellen Press, 1996.

"The Exegesis of an Ethos." Unpublished manuscript.

"Itinéraire religieux d'un chrétien africain." *Perspectives Missionnaires* 31 (1996): 30–52.

1997

"Deus Absconditus." *Gospel Herald,* August 26, 1997, 5.

Review of *AD 2000 and After: The Future of God's Mission in Africa,* by John S. Pobee. *Review of AICs,* May-August, 1997, 24–27.

"The Taming of the Prophet Harris." *Journal of Religion in Africa* 27 (1997): 59–95.

1998

". . . As the Yeast Leavens the Lump." *Mission Focus Annual Review* 6 (1998): 113–18.

"From a Long-time Friend and Mission Colleague." In *Tributes to John Howard Yoder (1927-1997). Conrad Grebel Review* 6, no. 2 (Spring 1998): 103–5.

"Histoire de l'institut de formation (biblique) du service Mennonite au Bénin. Unpublished manuscript.

"Readers Say." "The French Connection." *The Mennonite Weekly Review,* December 8, 1998, 4.

Review of *Images of the Church of Mission,* by John Driver. *Mennonite Quarterly Review* 72, no. 3 (July 1998): 455.

1999

"John (or Jonas) Ahui," "William Wadé Harris," and "W(illiam) J(ames) Platt." In *Biographical Dictionary of Christian Missions,* edited by Gerald H. Anderson, 8, 281–82, and 549. New York: Simon and Schuster; Grand Rapids, MI: Eerdmans, 1999.

"Le Pentecôtisme du Prophète William Wadé Harris." *Archives des Sciences Sociales des Religions* 105 (January-March 1999): 51–70.

2000

"Elfenbeinküste (Côte d'Ivoire)," and "Harris, William Wade." In the revision of *Religion in Geschichte und Gegenwart (RGG),* vol. 3 (2000).

Litany for "Mother's Day," "Valentine's Sunday," and Easter Sunday—'Christ Is Risen.'" In *A Worship Anthology.* Nurture Commission of the Indiana-Michigan Mennonite Conference, 2000.

"Locust Grove Recognizes Ministry of Interim Pastor." *Gospel Evangel,* October 2000, 2.

"Mennonite Post-War Relief in Belgium, 1945–50." Text prepared for the 50th anniversary of Mennonite ministries in Belgium (October 2000).

Review of *CIM/AIMM: A Story of Vision, Commitment, and Grace,* by Jim Bertsche. *Mennonite Quarterly Review* 74, no. 1 (January 2000): 125–28.

Review of *Theological Education on Five Continents: Anabaptist Perspectives,* by Nancy Heisey and Daniel S. Schipani. *Mennonite Quarterly Review* 74, no. 2 (April 2000): 346–47.

"Le triomphe de l'Agneau." *Texte des Interventions: Culte de Reconnaissance pour les 20 ans du Centre Mennonite Bruxelles et les 50 ans du Retour des Mennonites en Belgique (October 10, 2000),* 11–18. Brussels: The Brussels Mennonite Center, 2000.

What Western Christians Can Learn from African-Initiated Churches. In the *Mission Insight* series, no. 10, edited by James R. Krabill. Elkhart, IN: Mennonite Board of Missions, 2000.

2001

"Accompanying the Larger Church." *Missions Now.* Elkhart, IN: Mennonite Board of Missions, 2001, 6.

"Cultural Desert." *The Mennonite Weekly Review* 4, no. 12 (March 27, 2001), 3.

"The Fourth Dimension of the Anabaptist Vision." *The Mennonite Weekly Review* June 5, 2001 23.

"Locust Grove Welcomes John Troyer as Pastor." *Gospel Evangel,* March-April, 2001, 6.

2002

[and Wilma Shank.] "American Power." Viewpoint. *Mennonite Weekly Review,* March 4, 2002, 4.

"How Do They Do It?" *Gospel Evangel,* January/February, 2002, 4

"Milestone No. 4—Accompanying the Larger Church: A Declaration for Independents that Extends beyond Ourselves." In *Handing on the Legacy: MBM Celebrates 12 Milestones from 120 Years of Ministry, 1882–2002,* edited by Tom Price. *Mission Insight* series, no. 24, edited by James R. Krabill. Elkhart, IN: Mennonite Board of Missions, 2002.

Review of *Eschatologie et vie quotidienne,* edited by Neal Blough. *Mennonite Quarterly Review* 76, no. 4 (October): 503–5.

"What in the World Is Going On? The *Missio Dei* in World History; the *Missio Dei* and the Church." Unpublished presentation given at Bluffton College, February 5–7, 2002.

2003

"American Anabaptists, the Pax Americana, and the New Constantine." Unpublished manuscript.

"The Story of Locust Grove Mennonite Church's 'Mary: A Mother's Story.'" Sturgis MI: Locust Grove Mennonite Church, 2003.

"Warring Arguments." *Christian Century,* April 19, 2003, 44.

"With the Suffering." *Mennonite Weekly Review,* April 14, 2003, 4.

2004

"A Decade with God's Mission among African-Initiated Churches in West Africa." *Mission Focus: Annual Review* 11 (2004): 85–104.

Review of *Vivre Pleinement,* by Pierre Widmer. *Mennonite Quarterly Review* 78, no. 1 (January 2004): 150–52.

2005

"Karel van Mander's Mennonite Roots in Flanders." *Mennonite Quarterly Review* 79, no. 2 (April 2005): 231–49.

"Mission Essential." Viewpoint. *Mennonite Weekly Review,* October 24, 2005, 4–5.

"More about Mary." Letters. *Christian Century,* February 25, 2005, 65.

"Shank Not Shenk." Letters from Readers. *The Mennonite,* April 5, 2005, 5.

"Wrong Way." In *Letters: Books and Culture—A Christian Review.* March-April, 2005, 4.

2006

"A Dutch 'Anabaptist' among the 'Powers.'" *Mennonite Quarterly Review* 80, no. 3 (2006): 415–33.

"In Which Direction Are We Moving?" *The Mennonite,* September 5, 2006, 18–19.

"Jesus' Teaching." Viewpoint. *Mennonite Weekly Review,* January 2, 2006, 4.

"Reflections on Relating Long Term to Messianic Communities." In *Evangelical, Ecumenical, and Anabaptist Missiologies in Conversation,* edited by James R. Krabill, Walter Sawatsky, and Charles E. Van Engen. Maryknoll, NY: Orbis Books, 2006.

2007

"John Howard Yoder, Strategist for Mission with African-Initiated Churches." *Mission Focus: Annual Review* 15 (2007): 195–217.

"... and the Medicines." *The Mennonite,* August 7, 2007, 14–16.

"A Parochial Western Mennonite Conversation." In *Stumbling Toward a Genuine Conversation on Homosexuality,* ed. Michael A. King, 103–9. Telford, PA: Cascadia Publishing House, 2007.

"Scripture and Homosexuality." Letters. *Christian Century,* July 10, 2007, 44.

2008

"Election Year Musings: Preferring One Fox Over Another." *The Mennonite,* July 22, 2008, 8–10.

"Marinating in the Culture." *Purpose,* September 2008, 14–15.

"Not (Yet) Tuned In." In *Crossing the Frontier: Stories and Poems by Senior Writers, Elkhart and St. Joseph Counties, Indiana,* ed. John Bender. Goshen, IN: Greencroft Communities.

"Someone Wise Enough to Judge." *The Mennonite,* April 21, 2008, 16–17.

2009

"Biblical context." Viewpoint. *Mennonite Weekly Review,* May 18, 2009, 4.

[with John Howard Yoder.] "Biblicism and the Church." In *The Roots of Concern: Writings on Anabaptist Renewal, 1952-1957,* ed. Virgil Vogt, 67–101. Eugene, OR: Cascade Books, 2009.

"Histoire de l'Église Protestante de Rixensart." In *Courants* [Newsletter of the Protestant Church of Rixensart, Belgium], January-February, 2009, 10–13.

"Histoire de l'Église Protestante de Rixensart (II)" In *Courants* [Newsletter of the Protestant Church of Rixensart, Belgium], April-May, 2009, 10–13.

2010

[James R. Krabill, ed.] *Mission from the Margins : Selected Writings from the Life and Ministry of David A. Shank.* Elkhart IN: Institute of Mennonite Studies, 2010.

"W. W. Harris, prophète de Christ et artisan de la paix par excellence." Presentation prepared for an international colloquium on the Prophet Harris convened by The Harrist Church, Paris, France.